P9-BYE-171

LIBRARY IN A BOOK

WEAPONS OF MASS DESTRUCTION

Mary Byrd Davis
Arthur H. Purcell

An imprint of Infobase Publishing

CABARRUS COUNTY PUBLIC LIBRARY
CONCORD LIBRARY
CONCORD, NORTH CAROLINA 28025

3 3083 00546 1600

Weapons of Mass Destruction

Copyright © 2006 by Mary Byrd Davis and Arthur H. Purcell
Maps and graphs copyright © 2006 by Infobase Publishing

All rights reserved. No part of this book may be reproduced or utilized in any form or by any means, electronic or mechanical, including photocopying, recording, or by any information storage or retrieval systems, without permission in writing from the publisher. For information contact:

Facts On File, Inc.
An imprint of Infobase Publishing
132 West 31st Street
New York NY 10001

Library of Congress Cataloging-in-Publication Data
Davis, Mary Byrd.
Weapons of mass destruction / Mary Byrd Davis and Arthur H. Purcell.
p. cm.—(Library in a book)
Includes bibliographical references and index.
ISBN 0-8160-6082-7
1. Weapons of mass destruction. I. Purcell, Arthur H. II. Title. III. Series.
U973.D38 2006
358′.3—dc22 2005018168

Facts On File books are available at special discounts when purchased in bulk quantities for businesses, associations, institutions, or sales promotions. Please call our Special Sales Department in New York at (212) 967-8800 or (800) 322-8755.

You can find Facts On File on the World Wide Web at http://www.factsonfile.com

Text design by Ron Monteleone
Maps and graphs by Jeremy Eagle

Printed in the United States of America

MP Hermitage 10 9 8 7 6 5 4 3 2 1

This book is printed on acid-free paper.

CONTENTS

DELOACHE 30.00 5-08 CON

PART III
APPENDICES

PART I

OVERVIEW OF THE TOPIC

CHAPTER 1

INTRODUCTION TO WEAPONS OF MASS DESTRUCTION

The term *weapons of mass destruction* was first used in a communiqué dated November 15, 1945, that was drafted by Vannevar Bush, director of the U.S. Office of Scientific Research and Development. Bush wrote of atomic weapons and weapons that could be adapted for the purposes of mass destruction. By the latter, he later specified, he had meant biological weapons. In August 1948 the United Nations Commission for Conventional Armaments defined "weapons of mass destruction" as including "atomic explosive weapons, radioactive material weapons, lethal chemical and biological weapons, and any weapons developed in the future which have characteristics comparable in destructive effect to those of the atomic bomb or other weapons mentioned."[1]

The web site of the Nuclear Threat Initiative (http://www.nti.org) states that most U.S. documents define weapons of mass destruction as nuclear, biological, and chemical weapons. It adds, however, that some recent U.S. documents include radiological or conventional weapons that can cause massive casualties in their definitions of weapons of mass destruction and that these documents tend to focus on response to possible use of weapons of mass destruction within the United States.

This book uses the UN Commission's broad definition and covers nuclear, biological, chemical, and radioactive material weapons, now known as radiological weapons. For purposes of completeness, in the discussion of radiological weapons, this book also looks briefly at other types of weapons, such as industrial chemicals that are capable of causing major damage and that are sometimes characterized as weapons of mass destruction.

It should be noted at the outset that weapons of mass destruction under any definition of the term are not equal in destructiveness. Mass destruction is a relative concept. A single nuclear weapon can in seconds destroy a city, kill thousands of people, and contaminate a vast area with long-lived radioactivity. Neither chemical nor biological weapons can wreak such harm. Furthermore, protective measures are available against chemical agents and some biological agents but not against nuclear weapons.

Emphasis on the term *weapons of mass destruction* can have a negative effect. Equating nuclear, chemical, and biological weapons may make decision-makers and the public forget the scope of the destruction that a nuclear explosion could cause. On the other hand, grouping the weapons may lead people to overlook the particular problems that need to be faced in regard to biological and chemical weapons.

NUCLEAR WEAPONS

Nuclear weapons are devices in which most or all of the explosive energy is derived from fission, fusion, or a combination of the two. Nuclear fission is the splitting of an atom into two or more parts. Nuclear fusion is the joining or fusing of two atoms to form a single heavier atom. The simplest nuclear weapons are fission weapons (often referred to as "atomic bombs"). Boosted weapons and thermonuclear weapons (hydrogen bombs) incorporate fusion to increase their yield. Tests of nuclear devices have ranged in yield from less than one kiloton up to 50 megatons. (A kiloton is the equivalent of 1,000 tons of TNT, and a megaton is the equivalent of 1 million tons of TNT.)

Two distinct characteristics distinguish nuclear weapons from other weapons and make them particularly deadly: the amount of energy unleashed by their detonation and the radioactivity dispersed through their detonation. The explosive energy of an atomic weapon means that a given size weapon can exact more thorough physical damage over a wider area than any nonnuclear weapon of its size. Similarly, the tremendous heat energy released by an atomic weapon can cause thermal damage on an unprecedented scale compared to nonnuclear weapons. And while the energy from an atomic weapon produces vast immediate killing power, the radioactivity released from a blast causes long-term fatal illness in affected populations and poisons affected land for very long periods.

MATERIALS IN NUCLEAR WEAPONS

Within nuclear weapons, plutonium or highly enriched uranium—which can sustain a chain reaction—is generally used as the source of fission energy. Deuterium and tritium (or compounds that produce tritium) are generally used as the source of fusion energy.

To understand the preparation of materials for nuclear weapons, some understanding of atoms is necessary. Each atom consists of a central core, or nucleus, surrounded by electrons, or negatively charged particles. The nucleus for each element except hydrogen contains both protons and neutrons (hydrogen has only one proton). The protons are positively charged and equal the electrons in number. Neutrons have no charge and are close in mass to protons. The number of protons in each atom of a given element remains constant; the number of neutrons varies. A given element may exist in various forms or isotopes. The isotopes are identical to one another chemically but differ in their physical properties because each has a different number of neutrons in its nucleus and thus a different weight. An atom of uranium 238, for example, contains more neutrons and is heavier than an atom of uranium 235.

Uranium

Uranium is widely distributed in nature, always in combination with other elements. Sixteen isotopes of uranium exist, but only three are found in natural uranium. Uranium 238 is by far the most abundant, constituting 99.28 percent of natural uranium. Uranium 235 makes up 0.71 percent of natural uranium. Uranium 234 constitutes only 0.0058 percent.

Uranium 235 is fissionable and fissile—that is, it can be split by slow (zero energy) neutrons as well as by fast (highly energetic) neutrons. Many heavy elements are fissionable, but only fissile materials, those that can be split by slow neutrons, can sustain what is known as a chain reaction. A chain reaction is a self-sustaining series of fission reactions—neutrons produced by fission cause more fission. Both nuclear weapons and nuclear reactors are based on chain reactions. When a nuclear weapon is detonated, the chain reaction suddenly liberates an enormous quantity of energy; in a nuclear reactor the reaction is controlled, and the energy is released little by little.

The minimum mass of fissile material that can sustain a chain reaction is known as the critical mass. For a given material, the quantity that comprises a critical mass varies according to such factors as the shape of the mass, its density, and the presence of substances to moderate (slow) or reflect neutrons.

A nuclear weapon is triggered by suddenly creating a supercritical mass of fissile material (a mass greater than the critical amount). The two basic means of doing this are the gun assembly technique and implosion. In the gun assembly technique, two (or more) subcritical masses of fissile material are brought together to form a supercritical mass. This may be achieved by propelling one mass down a tube, as through a gun barrel, toward the other. In implosion a chemical high explosive surrounds a mass of fissile material that is not sufficiently dense to comprise a critical mass. The explosive is uniformly detonated in such a way as to compress the fissile material into a supercritical conformation. The gun assembly technique is simpler and easier to engineer than the implosion technique, but it can be used only with uranium 235. The implosion technique can be used with either uranium or plutonium.

Uranium 233 is also fissionable and fissile, but it is an artificial isotope produced by exposing thorium 232 to radiation that is capable of breaking apart atoms (ionizing radiation). For various reasons, uranium 233 is little used in nuclear weapons, and it is not used in the reactors that generate electricity today.

Uranium 238 is fissionable and fertile (i.e., it can create fissile material). An atom of uranium 238 that absorbs a neutron becomes, by means of intermediate stages, an atom of plutonium 239. The transformation of uranium 238 into plutonium 239 normally takes place in a reactor where uranium 238 is the main constituent of the fuel or in targets or covers placed near the core of a reactor.

Military reactors are engineered and operated to produce a maximum of plutonium, but civilian power reactors create plutonium as a by-product of their production of energy.

Uranium-bearing ore generally contains 1 percent or less of uranium mixed with metals, sulfurs, isotopes of various elements resulting from the gradual decay of uranium (i.e., the disintegration of atoms of uranium over time), and other materials. The uranium initially has to be separated from the rock ore and concentrated. After further processing, it may be transformed into a metal for fashioning into nuclear weapons components or into fuel or targets for production reactors; or it may be made into uranium hexafluoride (UF_6), a feed material for enrichment plants. Enrichment changes the proportion of isotopes in uranium to produce a relatively small quantity of uranium with more than 0.71 percent of uranium 235 (enriched uranium) and a large quantity of uranium with more than 99.28 percent of uranium 238 (depleted uranium).

Gaseous diffusion and centrifuges are the two main uranium enrichment technologies. Both use UF_6 in gaseous form and rely on the fact that atoms of uranium 238 are heavier than those of uranium 235. In gaseous diffusion plants, UF_6 is forced through a series of membranes, through which atoms of uranium 235 pass slightly faster than atoms of uranium 238. In centrifuge plants, UF_6 is spun at high speed in a series of vessels or centrifuges. The rotation tends to force the uranium 238 toward the outer wall of each centrifuge and to allow the uranium 235 to concentrate toward the center.

Very highly enriched uranium (uranium composed of more than 90 percent uranium 235) is the choice for weapons designers. However, nuclear devices can be made of uranium that is only "highly enriched," that is, uranium containing more than 20 percent but no more than 90 percent uranium 235. Low-enriched uranium is used as fuel for U.S. commercial power plants.

Depleted uranium and sometimes natural uranium are used as components of nuclear weapons. Uranium 238 can be split by the fast neutrons emitted by the reaction in the center of the bomb. When split, it releases neutrons. Therefore, a cover of depleted or natural uranium around the core of a bomb increases the power of the bomb.

Depleted uranium and natural uranium are used in nonnuclear weapons for their high density. The military deploys tank armor and kinetic projectiles from depleted uranium.

Plutonium

Plutonium exists in the natural world only in traces. Virtually all the plutonium that exists today is the result of human activity in the 20th and 21st centuries.

Fifteen isotopes of plutonium are known, although only plutonium 239 and 241 are fissile. For various reasons plutonium 239, rather than plutonium 241, is generally used for the production of electricity and nuclear weapons. Plutonium 240 and 242 are both neutronic poisons, meaning they absorb neutrons without splitting. Therefore, they are undesirable in nuclear weapons although they are found in weapons because it is not possible to separate them completely from the plutonium 239.

As previously noted, the irradiation of uranium 238 in a reactor generates plutonium. After fuel and any targets and covers have been removed from a reactor, they may be chemically treated to separate the uranium and the plutonium. The treatment is known as chemical separation or reprocessing. Generally a wet process known as the Purex process is used for such treatment. This process is considered to be "wet" because it involves dissolving the fuel or other materials in a bath of nitric acid to produce a solution containing plutonium and uranium along with other substances. After the separation of the plutonium and uranium from the solution, a highly radioactive liquid waste remains.

Plutonium is classed according to the percentage of plutonium 240 that it contains. Weapons-grade plutonium has less than 7 percent plutonium 240; reactor-grade plutonium has more than 18 percent plutonium 240. However, this classification is misleading, as even reactor-grade plutonium can be used to fabricate a nuclear device.

Deuterium

Deuterium is a stable isotope of hydrogen. Hydrogen normally contains one proton but no neutrons, whereas deuterium has one proton and one neutron. In its natural state deuterium is found in all sources of hydrogen, including ordinary water, where it represents 0.014 percent of the hydrogen. Water in which most of the hydrogen has been replaced by deuterium is called heavy water or simply deuterium. Ordinary water can be treated by distillation, electrolysis, or isotopic exchange to produce heavy water.

Deuterium is a thermonuclear material. Two atoms of deuterium or one atom of deuterium and one of tritium (a hydrogen atom with two neutrons) can fuse at very elevated temperatures to produce a heavy atom, helium, and release energy. The reaction of deuterium-tritium occurs faster at realizable temperatures than other fusion reactions.

Weapons designers use fusion in boosted weapons and in thermonuclear weapons. In boosted weapons the fusion reaction does not directly increase the yield of the weapons. The reaction is simply used to produce neutrons, which increase the effectiveness of the fission reaction, and the fusion material is located in or near the core. Thermonuclear weapons are composed of at least two stages, with the primary stage based on fission and the secondary on fusion. At normal temperatures the fusion reaction proceeds very slowly. Therefore, in thermonuclear weapons a fission stage triggers a fusion stage by bringing the fusion materials to the temperature and density required for fusion to take place. The fusion reaction then directly liberates an enormous quantity of energy.

Tritium

Tritium, like deuterium, is an isotope of hydrogen. It has one proton and two neutrons and is unstable. It exists naturally, as it is continually made in the atmosphere by the interaction of cosmic rays with the nuclei of nitrogen, oxygen, and argon present in the upper atmosphere. Incorporated in rain, it comes down to Earth.

Tritium is produced artificially by the irradiation of targets of lithium 6 in a reactor. Tritium is also a by-product of nuclear testing and of the operation of nuclear reactors, which generate tritium in their fuel when nuclei split into three products.

Lithium

Lithium is a light, nonradioactive metal that is essential to the artificial production of tritium. Natural lithium is composed of 7.5 percent lithium 6 and 92.5 percent of lithium 7. Before natural lithium can be used in targets for making tritium, it must be enriched in the isotope lithium 6. One of the methods for doing so, used by the United States in the past, is the Colex process. To separate lithium 6 and lithium 7, an amalgam, or solution, of lithium and mercury is prepared by electrolysis. An exchange then takes place between the amalgam and a water-based solution of lithium hydroxide. Lithium 7 concentrates in the amalgam.

EFFECTS OF UNCONTROLLED CHAIN REACTIONS

The effects of detonating a nuclear weapon can be grouped under the categories "immediate" and "delayed." Actual consequences vary with the design and yield of the device, the height at which it is exploded, and the weather. The immediate consequences consist of blast (shock wave), thermal radiation or heat, prompt ionizing radiation, and electromagnetic effects.

Blast refers to the shock wave created by a nuclear explosion that causes a massive increase in air pressure (called overpressure) and generates high winds. The overpressure collapses buildings, and the winds hurl objects through the air.

When a weapon is detonated on or near the surface of the ground, the blast leaves a crater. Much of the dirt that the blast removes from the area of the crater rises. The particles are quickly irradiated and return to the ground as radioactive fallout.

Thermal radiation refers to the fireball produced by the explosion of a nuclear weapon that gives off intense light and heat that lasts from about one-tenth of a second to several seconds. The heat is experienced before the blast because of the speed with which thermal radiation travels. The heat can be greater than 1,000 watts per square centimeter, "similar to direct exposure to the flame of an acetylene torch." A 20-megaton bomb can cause third-degree burns, likely to result in death, as far as 40 kilometers from the epicenter. The intense light that accompanies the heat may cause "flashblindness," temporary blindness, or damage to the retina.

The thermal radiation also starts fires, particularly in conjunction with the blast. A firestorm can develop if scattered fires join to become one huge blaze.

In a firestorm, a column of hot air rapidly rises above an intense fire, causing winds to blow into the fire area, fanning the flames. The firestorm continues until all combustible material in the area has burned.

Prompt ionizing radiation refers to how the explosion itself, whether fission, fusion, or a combination of the two, emits gamma rays and neutrons, which can result in intense irradiation of people and other ecological species near the epicenter. Exposure in this area may also come from fallout that occurs within a few hours after the explosion. Such prompt irradiation and fallout are not, however, a cause of death in explosions with a yield of hundreds of kilotons or more because people who would experience this radiation would already be dead from the blast and heat.

Electromagnetic pulse refers to how the absorption of gamma radiation by the air and ground may result in production of an electromagnetic wave similar to radio waves but with a much stronger electric field and consisting only of a single pulse lasting a fraction of a second. An electromagnetic pulse (EMP), as the phenomenon is known, can damage electrical or electronic equipment temporarily or permanently and block short wavelength radar and radio signals. A significant EMP occurs only if a weapon is detonated at below 4,000 meters or, with greatest effect, over 30,000 meters.

The major delayed consequences of chain reactions include radioactive fallout, damage to the ozone layer, and nuclear winter. Radioactive fallout refers to the long-lived radioactive material created by the explosion that gradually falls to the earth. It is largely composed of the debris from fission reactions or fission products. This material is also created by the capture of neutrons by nonradioactive materials inside the bomb and in the environment. After radioactive decay of some isotopes, the fission products may include some 300 isotopes of 36 elements.

The larger the yield of a device, the higher and faster the fission products will be raised above the earth. From the stratosphere, the products descend over a period of months or years after a large portion of them have decayed to stable, nonradioactive isotopes. Products that do not rise above the troposphere descend in days or months, as the result of rain and other weather phenomena, while they are still radioactive.

The fission products that are of particular concern to human health are cesium 137, iodine 131, and strontium 89 and 90 because they are relatively abundant in fallout and can have significant effects on the body. Cesium 137, a beta and gamma emitter, acts like potassium and is absorbed by the body as a whole; iodine, a beta and gamma emitter, concentrates in the thyroid; strontium 89 and 90, beta emitters, are stored in the bones. Other isotopes of concern, though not direct fission products, are tritium and carbon 14.

An increase in the risk of cancer as a result of exposure to radiation fallout has been widely documented. A federal study of radioactive fallout from weapons tests worldwide showed that the fallout from atmospheric tests likely caused 15,000 or more residents of the United States to die of cancer and caused at least 20,000 others to suffer from nonfatal cancers.[2] Radiation may also cause genetic damage, resulting in birth defects in the offspring of victims of nuclear explosions.

Plants and animals gradually concentrate radioactivity in their bodies. Therefore, people eating them receive a greater dose than they would have received directly from the fallout at the time it reached the ground.[3]

Ending nuclear testing in the atmosphere did not end the threat posed by nuclear fallout. The federal government said in 1979 that more than 35 of the approximately 330 underground nuclear tests that it admitted conducting at the Nevada Test Site during the 1960s and early 1970s released radioactivity that went beyond the boundaries of the test site.[4] A study published in 2004 states that "the major source of HT [tritium] to the atmosphere between 1962 and the early 1990s was the underground testing of nuclear weapons."[5]

For each megaton yield of a nuclear explosion, some 5,000 tons of nitrogen oxides will be produced from the oxygen and nitrogen in the air. A series of big nuclear explosions could be expected to cause serious damage to the ozone layer from these oxides. Presumably the large atmospheric tests of the 1950s and 1960s seriously depleted the ozone layer, but the ozone measurements made at the time were unable to distinguish between the results of testing and other causes of depletion.

Nuclear winter refers to a theory published by five scientists in 1983.[6] Dust raised by low-level nuclear explosions and, more significantly, soot resulting from the burning of cities and petroleum supplies would drastically decrease the amount of sunlight reaching the ground. The lack of light and the reduction in temperature would cause crops to fail and would result in widespread starvation, possibly even endangering the existence of the human race. The report was strongly criticized at the time, but a number of later studies have confirmed the scientists' basic conclusions. Detonation of 100 megatons over 100 cities would cause Earth's temperature to drop between five and 15 degrees centigrade.[7] A smaller attack would result in a smaller drop in temperature, but most of the world's crops would suffer severely from a decrease of only one degree centigrade during the growing season.

PROTECTION FROM NUCLEAR DETONATIONS

Private citizens can do little to protect themselves against a nuclear bomb, although some prophylactic medications exist. Medicines to protect against radioactivity are discussed later on in this chapter in the section on radiological weapons, since they might be more useful in connection with a "dirty bomb" than with an actual nuclear weapon.

In the early years of the cold war, building bomb shelters to protect against nuclear attack became a lucrative industry. Research has shown, however, that shelters—provided they withstand the initial blast—would be of limited effectiveness. A bomb shelter would offer assurance of protection against a nuclear bomb only if supplied with the means of preventing a firestorm from sucking the oxygen out of the shelter and providing long-term protection from fallout.

With the possible exception of shelter complexes built for high government officials, few shelters could sustain conditions needed for survival.

HISTORY OF NUCLEAR WEAPONS

Nuclear weapons have their origin in research in physics and chemistry in the early 20th century, mostly in Europe. The first atomic device was exploded in New Mexico in July 1945. Less than a month later, the United States bombed the cities of Hiroshima and Nagasaki in Japan. Nuclear weapons have not since been used against an enemy. Nevertheless, the threat of the use of nuclear weapons still exists. The future of nuclear weapons and of civilization depends on the nuclear-weapon states and the would-be nuclear-weapon states reaching a workable agreement on controlling their production and use.

First Development of Nuclear Weaponry

In 1939 at the Kaiser Wilhelm Institute in Berlin, chemists Otto Hahn and Fritz Strassman discovered evidence of nuclear fission. The discovery followed more than 30 years of study of the structure of the nucleus, radioactivity, and radioactive elements by chemists and physicists, mostly in Europe. The rise of Adolf Hitler to power and the advent of World War II drove many European scientists to the United States, where they collaborated on research with Americans. They feared that the Germans would develop an atomic bomb, a fear reinforced by Hitler's banning the export of uranium from Czechoslovakia after the Nazis occupied it.

One of the refugees from Europe, Leo Szilard, drafted a letter to President Franklin Roosevelt on the German atomic threat and persuaded Albert Einstein to sign it. As a result, Roosevelt, in October 1939, established an ad hoc uranium committee, which recommended that the United States attempt to build an atomic bomb and that physicist Enrico Fermi be supplied with uranium and graphite to create an initial reactor or "pile." Fermi and colleagues constructed a secret reactor in a squash court under the stands of the University of Chicago's football stadium. There in December 1942, they initiated the world's first self-sustaining chain reaction. It lasted only 4.5 minutes, but it produced a little heat. The potential of the atom for energy production as well as for weapons had been made evident.

Meanwhile, President Roosevelt had transferred control of the nation's atomic program from scientists to the U.S. Army. Within the army he established in the summer of 1942 a new office to carry out the task, the Manhattan Engineer District, later called the Manhattan Project. Because the project would entail major construction projects, General Leslie Groves, an engineer who had supervised the building of the Pentagon, was given command of the project.

Groves constructed the Hanford Engineer Works near Richland, Washington, to produce plutonium, and the Clinton Engineer Works at Oak Ridge, Tennessee, to enrich uranium. The design and assemblage of atomic weapons took place at a laboratory at Los Alamos, New Mexico, directed by physicist

Robert J. Oppenheimer. The first experimental atomic bomb, code-named "Trinity," was detonated on July 16, 1945, at the Alamogordo Air Base, 210 miles south of Los Alamos. The fissile material was plutonium from Hanford.

First Testing and Use of Nuclear Weapons in the World

By November 1944 U.S. officials knew that Germany could not create an atomic bomb. Nevertheless, the Manhattan Project had assumed a momentum of its own. In April 1945 President Roosevelt died and Harry S. Truman assumed the presidency. Roosevelt had told Truman nothing about the Manhattan Project. Some scientists, led by Leo Szilard and another refugee from Europe, James Franck, opposed the use of the atomic bomb against Japan, at least without forewarning. However, the top people connected to the Manhattan Project assumed that the bomb would be used, and Truman, accepting their position, authorized the dropping of two bombs on Japan. On August 6, 1945, the B-29 *Enola Gay* released a single gun-type uranium bomb, nicknamed "Little Boy," over Hiroshima. On August 9 an implosion-type plutonium bomb, code-named "Fat Man" was dropped on Nagasaki. The yield of the weapons was approximately 15 kilotons and 20 kilotons, respectively. The population of the two cities totaled less than 500,000, but the bomb caused the deaths of 200,000 residents.[8]

During the war the United States and the United Kingdom exchanged atomic information. However, the United States did not notify its then ally the Soviet Union about its atomic program until July 1945. By that time Stalin knew of U.S. atomic efforts through spies within the Manhattan Project, and the Soviet Union had begun the development of its own atomic weapons. Nevertheless, President Truman decided not to share atomic secrets with the Soviet Union. In a press conference on October 8, 1945, Truman stated that the Soviets would have to build an atomic bomb "on their own hook." Asked by a reporter if that meant that an arms race was under way, he agreed but added that the United States "would stay ahead."[9]

Staying ahead was not as easy as Truman then believed that it would be. The Soviet Union tested its first fission bomb, a 22-kiloton device, on August 29, 1949, some four years earlier than U.S. officials expected. The British, who were able to capitalize on cooperation with the United States, exploded an initial fission device on October 3, 1952. The French tested a fission bomb in 1960, and China exploded its first fission device on October 16, 1964.

The Arms Race between the United States and the Soviet Union

In 1947 David Lilienthal, chairman of the Atomic Energy Commission, informed Truman that the United States possessed seven atomic bombs, only one of which was "probably operable."[10] A major reason for the low number was the scarcity of plutonium and uranium. This problem was lessened when the United Kingdom agreed to supply uranium to the United States, and the United States built additional plutonium production reactors. By June 1950 the United States had a stockpile of almost 300 atomic bombs. Gradually it developed domestic sources of uranium.

The United States exploded a 46-kiloton fission bomb boosted by fusion in May 1951, in its first test of this type of weapon. By that time Truman had given the go-ahead for work on the thermonuclear (hydrogen) bomb. Edward Teller, a Hungarian refugee who had worked as a physicist on the Manhattan Project and who was obsessed with the hydrogen bomb, was a major influence on the president's decision, but the final factor was a warning from the Pentagon that the Soviets might have several atomic bombs and a hydrogen bomb. The United States conducted its first test of a thermonuclear weapon in October 1952. The Soviet Union tested its first fission device boosted by fusion in August 1953 and its first two-stage thermonuclear device in November 1955.

In the late 1940s the United States had decided to defend itself against the Soviet Union with atomic bombs carried by long-range bombers. Air force bombers remained the only means of delivery for the nation's atomic weapons until the 1950s. In 1954 the United States successfully tested lightweight nuclear warheads. The Eisenhower administration consequently decided to develop missiles. The liquid-fueled Atlas, which could carry a one-megaton warhead, was the nation's first intercontinental ballistic missile (ICBM). It became operational in 1959. During the Eisenhower administration, Thor, the nation's first intermediate-range ballistic missile (IRBM), and the Minuteman, a solid-fueled ICBM, were also approved for development. The Minuteman replaced the manned bomber as the main component of the nation's strategic nuclear force when it went into service in 1962.

The U.S. Army and the U.S. Navy did not want the U.S. Air Force to have a monopoly on missiles. Lobbying for its share of the new technology, the navy obtained permission to develop the Polaris submarine-launched ballistic missile (SLBM). Low-yield tactical nuclear weapons to equip the army's and the navy's nonstrategic arsenals were also developed.

In the mid-1960s the Johnson administration initiated a further major change in warhead delivery. It ordered the equipping of the Polaris A-3 SLBM with multiple reentry vehicles (MRVs) and the Minuteman III ICBM and the Poseidon SLBM with multiple independently targetable reentry vehicles (MIRVs). A missile with MRVs can send multiple warheads in a close pattern to a given target. A missile with MIRVs can send multiple warheads, each of which is guided internally, to several different targets. The Minuteman III had three warheads; the Poseidon had 10. Equipping a single missile with numerous warheads allowed the United States to increase rapidly the number of warheads in its strategic arsenal.

The Soviet Union also developed missiles to carry nuclear warheads, but it did not deploy them as early as many in the United States assumed that it had. The Soviets' launching of the Earth-orbiting satellite *Sputnik* in 1957 aroused fears of a "missile gap," the belief that the Soviets had operational ICBMs although the United States had none. Not until early 1961 was the United States able to determine that the Soviets actually had deployed a small number of

ICBMs. The Soviet Union tested its first MIRVed missile in 1973 and deployed the MIRVed SS-18 Satan and SS-19 Stiletto in 1974 and 1975, respectively.

The United States reached its peak number of warheads, 32,500, in 1967. The peak for the USSR came in 1986 and was considerably larger, 45,000 warheads.[11] The warheads were of many types (the United States had 24 types in its stockpile in 1983, for example) and were to be delivered by a variety of means, including cruise missiles and artillery.

The two nations justified their stockpiles in terms of ensuring world peace. Both used the word "deterrence" as a reason for building stockpiles. Each claimed that its ownership of thousands of nuclear weapons deterred the other nation from ever using its stockpiles. Neither would launch a nuclear attack against the other for fear of being destroyed by a retaliatory assault. The situation was spoken of as Mutual Assured Destruction (MAD).

Though nuclear weapons were brandished during the nuclear arms race, they were not used. In fact, history's only examples of the detonation of nuclear weapons against an enemy remain to this writing the U.S. bombings of Hiroshima and Nagasaki, both in Japan, in 1945.

The closest that the world has come to the detonation of another nuclear weapon against an enemy may have been the Cuban Missile Crisis in October 1962. The United States discovered that the Soviet Union was installing missiles in Cuba. After President John F. Kennedy confronted Soviet premier Nikita Khrushchev with the evidence and a U.S. naval blockade was placed around Cuba, Khrushchev withdrew the missiles; part of the conditions of withdrawal was a pledge by the United States not to attempt to invade Cuba. The United States also offered to remove obsolete missiles from Turkey.

Other Developers of Nuclear War Materials

The Nuclear Non-Proliferation Treaty (NPT), the key treaty designed to control the spread of nuclear weapons, was signed by 62 nations in 1968 and went into force in 1970. It divides the parties to the treaty into two groups: the nuclear-weapon states (each nation that exploded a nuclear device before January 1, 1967) and the nonnuclear-weapon states (the remaining nations). Under the terms of the treaty, three nations in addition to the United States and Russia are nuclear-weapon states: the United Kingdom, France, and China, all of whom exploded a nuclear device before January 1, 1967. Each had, and still has, a relatively small stockpile, but each believed in a variant of MAD. Although they had fewer nuclear weapons than did the United States and Soviet Union, they theorized that they had enough to inflict unacceptable damage on a nuclear attacker. Thus, they thought, the weapons put them into a position of equality vis-à-vis the major powers.

Since January 1, 1967, India and Pakistan have tested nuclear weapons. A third nation, Israel, is widely believed to possess a nuclear arsenal but is not known to have conducted a full-scale nuclear weapons test and has never declared that it owns weapons. None of the three is a member of the Nuclear Non-Proliferation Treaty, and each had, and has, its own reasons for obtaining and retaining a nuclear capability. Various other nations have embarked on nuclear weapons programs but have abandoned them. Iran and North Korea are suspected or known to be actively seeking nuclear weapons as of mid-2005. Because they pose particularly acute problems for efforts to prevent nuclear proliferation, they are discussed in the section of this chapter on the future of nuclear weapons.

During World War II British scientists helped the Americans to develop the bomb. After the war the United States had no interest in sharing military atomic secrets. Therefore, to counter the Soviets should they obtain nuclear weapons and to bolster its position in the world, Britain developed its own bomb. Its first nuclear weapon to become operational was the plutonium bomb Blue Danube, which went into service with the Royal Air Force in 1953. In 1962 Britain put into service its first thermonuclear gravity bomb (a bomb dropped from an airplane) and thermonuclear air-launched cruise missiles.

Britain put its nuclear forces at the disposal of the North Atlantic Treaty Organization (NATO), formed in 1949 by the United States and the nations of Western Europe to defend Western Europe in the face of the growing Soviet power in Eastern Europe. It made and owned its own warheads for its strategic delivery systems but obtained other warheads from the United States under arrangements among NATO members for sharing warheads. The peak number of warheads owned is 410, reached in 1969.

France embarked on a secret nuclear weapons program in 1954 and 10 years later delivered nuclear gravity bombs to its strategic air force. Its first two-stage thermonuclear test was detonated in 1968, and a thermonuclear warhead entered into service in 1977. Unlike the United Kingdom, France developed ICBMs, which became operational in 1971. It armed nuclear submarines with long-range missiles and produced gravity bombs and air-launched missiles. Its number of warheads peaked at 540 in 1993. France was always reluctant to integrate its military forces with NATO's forces and in 1966 withdrew from the military structure of NATO entirely.

China, the last of the NPT weapons states to test a fission device, embarked on a nuclear weapons program in 1955. Eventually it developed an arsenal composed of fission and thermonuclear weapons to be delivered by nuclear armed bombers, land-based missiles, and submarine-based missiles. By 1993 it had 450 nuclear warheads, its peak number.

A desire to be able to stand up to the United States was its main motive in acquiring nuclear weapons. China's nuclear program received an immense amount of assistance from the Soviet Union. However, the two nations severed their relationship in the mid-1960s and eventually fought each other along their common border. As a result China switched the target of its nuclear forces from the United States to the Soviet Union. China reportedly assisted Pakistan in developing nuclear weapons by supplying Pakistan with technical information and fissile material.

Israel, believing that the Holocaust justified all means deemed necessary to defend the Jewish people, began searching for uranium in the Negev Desert in 1949 and created an Atomic Energy Commission in 1952. By 1953 Israel had learned how to recover uranium from phosphate deposits in the desert and had developed a method of producing heavy water. In 1956 France agreed to build a reactor and a reprocessing plant in Israel. The facilities were secretly constructed at Dimona in the Negev Desert.

The United States learned in 1958 through overflights of the U-2 spy plane that Dimona existed but did not realize for two years that it was a nuclear facility. In December 1960 Israeli prime minister David Ben-Gurion announced that the Dimona complex was a center for civilian nuclear research. By the mid-1960s U.S. officials knew that Israel had a nuclear weapons program but did little to try to stop it. The first concrete evidence of the program available to the public was photographs and a description furnished to the *London Sunday Times* in 1986 by Mordechai Vanunu, a former Israeli nuclear technician. After the publication of the material, the Israelis captured, tried, and imprisoned Vanunu.

India took advantage of the atmosphere of trust that prevailed in the early years of a U.S. Atoms for Peace initiative, launched in 1953, to obtain from Canada a research reactor suited to the production of plutonium and from the United States a portion of the heavy water needed to operate the reactor. It declared that its intentions were peaceful. In 1964 India commissioned a facility for separating plutonium from the fuel removed from the research reactor. Ten years later, using plutonium made in the reactor and extracted by the reprocessing plant, India exploded a fission device. It again conducted tests in 1998, and in a 1999–2000 report stated for the first time that it was actually developing and deploying weapons. The major impetus for India's embarking on a nuclear weapons program appears to have been fear of China, with which it had a border clash in 1962. Later, rivalry with Pakistan became a major motive.

Pakistan secretly established a military nuclear program in 1972. In contrast to India, Pakistan obtained fissile material by enriching uranium. To do so it smuggled uranium enrichment technology and equipment into the country from Europe. Abdul Qadeer Khan, who had worked at a centrifuge enrichment plant in the Netherlands, oversaw the building of Pakistan's enrichment facility. By 1985 it was producing weapons-grade uranium, and in 1998, shortly after India had detonated five nuclear tests, Pakistan conducted tests and stated that it was a nuclear-weapon state. Khan has admitted secretly exporting nuclear technology to Iran, Libya, and North Korea.

India and Pakistan have engaged in numerous conflicts within the past 50 years, notably in regard to Kashmir. The international community therefore feared that the two nations' possession of nuclear weapons could result in a nuclear war. However, India and Pakistan have negotiated a variety of confidence-building measures aimed at reducing this possibility. Among them is a bilateral testing moratorium, a nuclear hotline between their respective foreign ministries, and an annual exchange of lists of their respective nuclear facilities.

According to the Institute for Science and International Security (ISIS), four nations started and ended a nuclear weapons program before 1970, when the NPT went into force, and signed the NPT. The four are Australia, Egypt, Sweden, and Canada. Also according to ISIS, nine nations began or are suspected of having begun a nuclear weapons program but ended the program, if they had one, after 1970. They are Argentina, Brazil, Romania, South Africa, South Korea, Spain, Switzerland, Taiwan, and Yugoslavia. Algeria and Syria have been suspected of intending to produce nuclear weapons, but no program has been identified in those countries.

The only nation that has actually produced nuclear weapons and then destroyed its nuclear weapons program is South Africa. South Africa established an Atomic Energy Commission to assess uranium reserves in southern Africa in 1948. It then acquired a nuclear research reactor from the United States under the Atoms for Peace program and in 1969 began to build a pilot enrichment plant. According to President Frederik Willem de Klerk, the government decided in 1974 to develop nuclear weapons. In 1979 Israel and South Africa may have conducted a joint test over the Indian Ocean, as a U.S. satellite perceived a flash that could have been such a test. No other tests by South Africa are known or suspected. By 1992, when the newly elected de Klerk ordered the nuclear weapons program and nuclear weapons destroyed, South Africa had built six nuclear devices. Destruction was completed that year. South Africa has joined the NPT, and its remaining stock of highly enriched uranium is safeguarded.

Nuclear Weapons Tests

As of 2005 the five major nuclear powers, India, and Pakistan are known to have conducted 2,051 nuclear tests. The United States 1,030 tests; the Soviet Union 715 tests. After them is France, with 210 tests; the United Kingdom and China, with 45 tests each; India, with four; and Pakistan, with two. Approximately one-fourth of the total tests conducted worldwide, or 528 tests, were detonated in the atmosphere. The remainder are classified as underground tests.

The bombs detonated by the Soviet Union had a greater average yield than those detonated by the United States. The Soviet Union detonated tests equaling 285 megatons, while the United States tests equaled only 179 megatons.

The United States tested in the Pacific, at Enewetak and Bikini (both in the Marshall Islands), and in the vicinity of Christmas Island and Johnston Island. Within the United States, tests were conducted not only at the Nevada Test Site where the majority of the U.S. tests have taken place but also in such diverse places as Hattiesburg, Mississippi, and Amchitka, Alaska.

The Soviet Union conducted all its tests within its own territory— in Kazakhstan (mainly at Semipalatinsk), Russia (mainly at Novaya Zemlya), the Ukraine, Uzbekistan, and Turkmenistan. France tested in Algeria and, after January 1996, in the South Pacific at Fangataufa Atoll and Mururoa Atoll. The United Kingdom detonated bombs at Christmas Island and Malden Island in the Pacific, at three locations in Australia, and, in cooperation with the United States, at the Nevada Test Site. China tested within its borders at Lop Nur. India and Pakistan also test within their own countries.

The world's last known nuclear tests were conducted by France (January 27, 1996), China (July 29, 1996), India (May 13, 1998), and Pakistan (May 30, 1998). The Soviet Union stopped testing in 1990, the United Kingdom in 1991, and the United States in 1992.

The effects of nuclear explosions on organisms in general are discussed in the next section. It should be noted here, however, that the various national testing programs have not only caused harm to humans but also wreaked massive environmental damage. To mention only one example, blasts from U.S. testing in the Pacific dug huge craters in reefs, vaporized entire islands, and spread radioactive debris over wide areas. Topsoil has had to be removed from islands in efforts to decontaminate them, and even today some areas are too radioactive for evacuated residents to return to them. None of the nations that tested have fully assumed the burden of restoration and compensation, although the United States has done more in this direction than most.

Some nuclear weapons tests were in part experiments on human subjects, as military personnel were stationed relatively near detonations in order to determine their effects. The United States and presumably other countries also carried out scientific experiments on individuals. Secretary of Energy Hazel O'Leary announced in December 1993 that the United States had experimented on humans since the 1940s. A House committee headed by Congressman Edward Markey had attempted to call attention to this fact in 1986, but neither the public nor officials paid attention to the subject at that time. Many of the tests were reportedly performed without the formal consent of subjects, or the subjects were not fully informed of the risks to which they were being exposed. The release of O'Leary's report caused a public outcry.

Although in 2005 no country may be conducting nuclear weapons tests, nations are still from time to time conducting subcritical experiments. These involve chemical high explosives and stand-ins for fissile material or fissile material itself in configurations and quantities that do not produce a self-sustaining chain reaction. Plutonium 238 and plutonium 242 are frequently used in current U.S. subcritical experiments. The United States has been conducting such experiments underground at the Nevada Test Site to gain information on the hydrodynamic properties of plutonium.

Since the mid-1990s the United States and France have been developing sophisticated programs to simulate nuclear explosions. Computer simulations are to replace actual nuclear tests in demonstrating weapons' performance. The U.S. Advanced Simulation and Computing Initiative began in fiscal year 1996. France began its program at about the same time.

The U.S. Department of Energy's budget request for fiscal year 2005 included funding to reduce the length of time needed to restart full-scale underground nuclear tests at the Nevada Test Site from between two and three years to 18 months. Congress specified that the lead time be reduced to 24 rather than 18 months.

NUCLEAR WEAPONS TODAY AND ATTEMPTS TO RESTRICT THEM

Seven nations have confirmed nuclear arsenals (China, France, India, Pakistan, Russia, United Kingdom, United States); one additional nation (Israel) is generally believed to have an arsenal, and a ninth (North Korea) has produced nuclear weapons material and claims to have produced weapons. At least one other nation appears to be interested in developing weapons. Various means of controlling nuclear weapons, ranging from treaties to cooperative programs to secure nuclear materials, are in effect. Nevertheless, at this writing the pro-weapons forces across the world seem to be gaining on the voices of restraint, particularly following the unsatisfactory close of the 2005 review conference on the Nuclear Non-Proliferation Treaty.

Arsenals in Existence Today

Today the five major nuclear-weapon states are the United States, Russia, France, the United Kingdom, and China. Their stockpiles of warheads and the deployment of their warheads are as follows:

United States As of early 2005 the United States possessed approximately 5,000 active warheads (4,530 strategic and 780 nonstrategic). Almost 5,000 additional warheads were in the "responsive reserve force" or inactive (without their tritium). The active and inactive warheads together numbered approximately 10,350.

U.S. strategic forces are composed of land-based and submarine-based intercontinental ballistic missiles and of bombers. After the withdrawal of 10 remaining MX/Peacekeeper missiles by October 2005, the only land-based missiles will be 500 Minuteman III missiles deployed in silos at three air force bases: Malstrom, in Montana; Minot, in North Dakota; and Warren, in Wyoming. Each carries a single warhead or two or three multiple independently targetable reentry vehicles. On 14 nuclear-powered submarines, 336 Trident missiles (the Trident I C4 and the Trident II D5) are deployed. The submarines together carry 2,016 warheads, about 48 percent of U.S. operational strategic weapons. Two types of long-range bombers, the B-2A Spirit and the B-52H Stratofortress, can carry out nuclear missions. They are not maintained on continual alert, and they have other missions. The B-52 can deliver gravity bombs and cruise missiles; the B-2, only gravity bombs. As of 2003 the B-2As were deployed at Whiteman Air Force Base in Missouri; a total of 94 B-52s were at Barksdale Air Force Base in Louisiana and Minot Air Force Base in North Dakota.

The United States has about 780 operational nonstrategic nuclear weapons: 200 Tomahawk land-attack cruise missiles (TLAM/Ns) and 580 B61 gravity bombs of three types. Various U.S. and NATO planes would deliver the B61s. In the United States the bombs are assigned to squadrons based at Seymour Johnson Air Force Base in North Carolina and Cannon Air Force Base in New Mexico. In Europe a total of 480 B61 bombs are deployed in six countries: Belgium, Germany, Italy, the Netherlands, Turkey, and the United Kingdom. The United States is the only nation in the world that deploys land-based nuclear weapons in foreign countries.

Russia As of early 2005 Russia had an estimated 7,200 active warheads (3,800 strategic and 3,400 nonstrategic) and about 8,800 warheads in reserve or waiting to be dismantled. This gives a total of approximately 16,000 warheads.

As with the United States, Russia's strategic forces are composed of intercontinental ballistic missiles based on land and on submarines and of long-range bombers. Russia deploys 130 SS-19s; some 100 SS-18s divided among three sites: Dombarovski, Kartaly, and Uzhur; probably 15 rail-based SS-24s at Kostroma; and 300 SS-25s divided among nine sites. Twelve nuclear-powered ballistic missile submarines are operational. They conduct deterrent patrols but not nearly as many as the more than 60 a year conducted by the United States. A force of 78 aircraft of three types (Tu-160 Blackjacks, Tu-95 MS6 Bear-H6s, and Tu-95 MS16 Bear-H16s) are assigned approximately 872 cruise missiles and bombs.

An estimated 3,400 nonstrategic warheads are operational. They are used by tactical aircraft, naval vessels, and air and ballistic missile-based defense systems. Thousands of additional nonstrategic warheads may be held in reserve or stored in retired status.

China China possesses some 400 warheads. At the end of 2003 China had about 120 operational ballistic missiles of four types (the DF-3A, DF-4, DF-5/5A, and DF-21A), each with a single warhead. The ranges vary between 1,800 and 13,000 kilometers. The 13,000-kilometer missiles are approximately 20 liquid-fueled F-5s, deployed in 1981.

Two ballistic missiles are currently under development, the DF-31 and the DF-31A. The DF-31 is a three-stage, solid-fueled missile, with an estimated range of 8,000 kilometers. The DF-31A, which is also solid-fueled, is expected to have a range of up to 12,000 kilometers and could be deployed by 2010.

China has one submarine capable of carrying ballistic missiles, the Xia. At the end of 2003 it was not fully operational. China is expected to deploy single-warhead Julang 1 missiles, with an estimated range of 1,700 kilometers, on the submarine. However, China has experienced difficulties with its submarine program, and the Pentagon and the CIA consider the Julang 1 to be experimental.

China is not known to have tactical nuclear warheads. According to the Pentagon's report *Chinese Military Power*, China deploys conventional warheads on its short-range ballistic missiles.[12]

France France possesses 348 warheads. Three missile-launching nuclear submarines were operable as of August 15, 2004. Each carried 16 M-45 missiles for a total of 48 missiles, with a total of 288 TN-75 warheads. The missiles have a range of 6,000 kilometers. Their home base is at Ile Longue. Three squadrons of Mirage 2000N are assigned 50 TN 81 ASMP (air-land-medium range) missiles. Two flotilla of Super-Etendard are assigned 10 TN 81 ASMP.

United Kingdom The United Kingdom owns 200 warheads. It operates four Vanguard nuclear submarines, each with 16 Trident II D-5 missiles. The missiles, which were obtained from the United States, could carry up to 12 warheads each for a total of 192 warheads per submarine. However, the stockpile totals only 200 warheads. The missiles have a range of at least 6,000 kilometers. They are based at Faslane on the Clyde in Scotland.

Other Nations The two other states with confirmed stocks of nuclear weapons are India and Pakistan. India is believed to possess 40–90 nuclear warheads; Pakistan, 30–50 warheads.

India's army, navy, and air force are equipped with short-range, nuclear-capable Prithvi ballistic missiles. India has tested and is reported to be producing the two-stage, solid-fueled Agni II missile, with a range of 2,000–2,500 kilometers and a payload of 1,000 kilograms. Indian scientists are working to increase its range to 5,000 kilometers, with a 1000-kilogram payload. India also has various nuclear-capable aircraft. A variant of the Russian TU-95 can carry nuclear weapons 5,000–6,000 kilometers.

Pakistan deploys nuclear-capable short-range and medium-range ballistic missiles. The medium-range Ghauri III is based on North Korea's Nodong. It also operates F-16 combat aircraft that are capable of carrying nuclear weapons.[13]

Israel, which has never admitted that it has a nuclear weapons program, is believed to possess 100–200 warheads. Israel deploys the short-range Jericho I and the medium-range Jericho II. Both can carry nuclear warheads. It is working to develop the Jericho III, variously reported to be an intermediate-range or a long-range missile.

North Korea, which has withdrawn from the NPT, announced publicly for the first time in February 2005 that it has nuclear weapons. Whether it actually does is not known.

As of 2001 a total of 35 nations possessed ballistic missiles. Twenty-four of those nations owned only short-range missiles (with a range of less than 1,000 kilometers), most with ranges of 300 or fewer kilometers. The other 11 nations with longer-range missiles are the eight discussed previously and Iran, North Korea, and Saudi Arabia. The last has medium-range missiles acquired from China in 1987. Iran and North Korea are cited by the 2001 National Intelligence Estimate as being the states most likely to develop intercontinental ballistic missiles by 2015.

Iran already has the medium-range Shahab 3, based on North Korea's Nodong. North Korea announced in August 2004 that it had developed a new ballistic missile in both a mobile land-based and a sea-based version. The land-based missile has an estimated range of 2,500–4,000 kilometers and the sea-based version, 2,500 or more kilometers. The missile could thus strike the continental United States if deployed.[14]

Missile Defense

The United States is the only nation that spends a substantial part of its defense budget on missile defense.[15] U.S. missile defense systems are less than half a century old. Work on the first operational system, the Nike-Zeus, was not begun until 1957. Five years later work started on the Nike X system, designed to eliminate an array of technical flaws in Nike-Zeus. In 1967 President Lyndon

Johnson announced plans for the Sentinel, a follow-up to Nike-X. The Sentinel system was intended to protect the United States against light missile attacks. President Nixon changed the name of the system to Safeguard and ordered it to protect only U.S. deterrent forces. In 1974 installation of Safeguard, which consisted of Sprint and Spartan missiles, was completed at Grand Forks, North Dakota, where it was to protect the site's missiles. Safeguard was terminated in 1976 because of the high cost of maintenance and fears that it was not reliable.

In 1983 President Ronald Reagan announced the Strategic Defense Initiative (SDI), or "Star Wars," as opponents dubbed it. The SDI was envisioned as an advanced technology missile-intercepting system. The Phase I Architecture included a space-based interceptor, two space-based sensors, and a ground-based interceptor and sensor. The Strategic Defense Initiative Organization (SDIO), charged with developing SDI, was chartered in 1984. President George H. W. Bush continued research work on SDI but focused on the development of "Brilliant Pebbles," a space-based interceptor technology relying on approximately 4,000 orbiting satellites intended to launch projectiles at incoming ballistic missiles.

In 1991, during the Persian Gulf War, the first actual application of interceptor missile technology proved to be disappointing. A study by the General Accounting Office determined that only 9 percent of intercept attempts made by Patriot missiles were fully successful.

President Bill Clinton renamed SDIO the Ballistic Missile Defense Organization (BMDO). He signed the National Missile Defense Act of 1999 but listed four criteria he would use to make a deployment decision: threat, cost, technological status of National Missile Defense (NMD), and adherence to a renegotiated Anti-Ballistic Missile (ABM) treaty. In September 2000, Clinton decided not to proceed with NMD system deployment, citing the status of technology, concerns among U.S. allies, and opposition from Russia and China.

One of President George W. Bush's first pronouncements on his accession to the White House was support for a strong NMD system. The administration advocates a program designed to be effective against short-, medium-, and long-range missiles. In 2002 it renamed the BMDO the Missile Defense Agency (MDA), a step that increased the agency's independence. The MDA groups its systems under the categories boost phase defense, midcourse defense, and terminal phase defense.

The principle system under development to destroy long-range ballistic missiles is the Ground-Based Midcourse Missile Defense system, designed to intercept the missiles outside the atmosphere. Heat-seeking sensors on satellites and radar on Navy Aegis ships are to detect an enemy's launch, and radar in Alaska is to track the incoming missile. If all goes well, an interceptor missile, guided by radar on the ground and its own sensors, will strike the incoming missile with an impact that will destroy the missile and itself.

At the end of 2004 two interceptor missiles had been installed in silos at Vandenberg Air Force Base in California and six at Fort Greely, Alaska. Ten additional missiles are to be installed at Fort Greely in 2005. As of early 2005 the system was largely untested, and parts, such as a sea-based X-band radar, were still missing.

Another midcourse system, the sea-based Aegis Ballistic Missile Defense system, is under development. It will build on technologies in the existing Aegis Weapons System aboard U.S. Navy ships. Short- and medium-range missiles would be intercepted in the ascent and descent phases of midcourse flight.

Terminal phase systems are directed against short- and medium-range missiles. The Patriot Advanced Capability-3 (PAC-3) is the most mature missile in the Ballistic Missile Defense program and was deployed in 2003 as part of the war against Iraq. It is designed to intercept Scud-type missiles.

The Terminal High Altitude Area Defense (THAAD) system is intended to shoot down short- and medium range missiles as they reenter the atmosphere high above the Earth. It has four major components: truck-mounted launchers, interceptors, radars, and a command, control, and battle management system (C2BM). All components fit inside a C-130 aircraft for rapid shipment around the world.

Also in the terminal phase group is the Arrow system, developed jointly by the United States and Israel to allow Israel to defend its borders and U.S. troops in the region. The Medium Extended Air Defense System (MEADS) is a cooperative effort between the United States, Germany, and Italy to develop a mobile and transportable missile defense system. MEADS is based on the PAC-3 and can be used against planes, as well as against missiles.

For boost phase defense, the most mature element is the Airborne Laser (ABL). It is designed to destroy short-, medium-, and long-range weapons immediately after they are launched and is carried by a plane equipped with infrared sensors and a modular Chemical Oxygen Iodine Laser (COIL). When fired at a missile, the laser is intended to heat up the missile's metal skin and cause it to burst. In November 2004 the laser was tested for the first time, and in December 2004 the plane made its first flight since installation of a beam control system.

The Possibility of Accidental Firing

A weapon can be constructed and stored in such a way as to virtually prevent unintentional firing or firing by an unauthorized person or group of people. However, a weapon might be deliberately fired by authorized personnel because of a false warning of an incoming missile.

Protection Nuclear weapons are protected from malicious or accidental detonation by measures built into them that vary with their age, the manner of deployment, and the nation that manufactures them.

One measure is an exclusion zone with strong and weak links. Surrounding the detonation system, the zone prevents electrical energy from reaching the detonation equipment unless an arming system closes a strong link such as a motorized switch. Should the integrity of the exclusion zone or strong link be compromised by an accident such as an explosion or a lightning strike, the resulting abnormal stress will cause weak links within the exclusion zone to fail and prevent detonation.

A Permissive Action Link (PAL) is a coded switch or lock designed to prevent unauthorized activation. Today PALs are usually electronic; in the past they were usually manual. Following the "two-man rule," which requires that at least two authorized people be present when there is human contact with weapons or code material, each of two people must insert a code into the device to arm the weapon. PALs vary in the sophistication of the code system. If an incorrect code is repeatedly inserted, the weapon may lock and can only be reset at the assembly plant. This feature is known as "limited try." After the PAL has been activated, a unique and complex electrical signal from a generator outside the weapon or digital communications and codes is required to arm and fire the weapon.

An Environmental Sensing Device (ESD) may be attached to the weapon. The device must experience certain external effects such as free falling, pressure changes, and temperature changes in the proper sequence and within preset parameters or it prevents detonation.

Modern weapons may have additional safety features. Some have nonviolent (without explosion) disablement systems that can be triggered by remote control. Some use insensitive high explosives that resist being set off by fire or mechanical shocks and mechanisms that break bomb components if an excessive number of attempts at arming the weapon are detected.[16]

Launch on Warning The United States and Russia still have launch-on-warning policies that they adopted during the cold war. These policies mean that either would launch a retaliatory strike after early warning radar and/or satellites indicate that one or more opposing missiles has been launched. Each country would have about 20 minutes to reach a decision. Presumably an electronic alert would lead to a "threat conference" among operators and commanders and then, if the warning appears to be valid, contact with the president. In the past numerous near-launches have occurred. Early warning technologies are clearly imperfect, and as time goes by the risk of their providing false information likely increases. Antiquated technologies in the Russian system may pose a particular risk.

De-alerting has been proposed as an answer. What de-alerting generally means is that a physical change could be made in weapon systems that would prevent an immediate launch. One possible change would be separating payloads from missiles. Such a radical step would presumably necessitate negotiations and would take time. An alternative that could be put in place more quickly, possibly while de-alerting is being worked out, would be a policy of "no launch on warning" or RLOAD (Retaliatory Launch Only after Detonation). To ensure that a retaliatory attack would be launched after a detonation, positive signals from existing explosion detectors could be routed to launch silos, which could be set to release a counterattack once a bomb has been detected.[17]

U.S. Nuclear Weapons Plants

At the end of World War II the U.S. nuclear weapons production network was largely made up of scattered, privately owned facilities. Gradually, large government-owned production plants replaced them. The government-owned plants were and still are operated by private companies under contract.

Over the years the government agency in charge of the network of weapons production plants (often called the weapons production complex) has changed. The Manhattan Engineering District (1942–46) was succeeded by the Atomic Energy Commission (AEC; 1946–74). As set forth in the Atomic Energy Act of 1946, the AEC owned the nation's nuclear plants and all fissionable materials. Following a speech by President Dwight Eisenhower extolling the peaceful use of the atom, Congress passed the Atomic Energy Act of 1954 to encourage the use of nuclear power to generate electricity. It made possible the private ownership of fissionable materials and reactors and gave the AEC the roles of promoter and regulator of civilian nuclear power plants, as well as manager of nuclear weapons production.

The AEC's dual role in regard to nuclear power embodied a conflict of interest. To end the conflict of interest, Congress in 1975 abolished the AEC and created from it the Energy Research and Development Administration (ERDA; 1975–77), charged with reactor development, military applications, and research, and the Nuclear Regulatory Commission (1975–), responsible for licensing and regulatory functions. In 1977 Congress created the Department of Energy (DOE), which absorbed ERDA along with other entities. The DOE conducts research on energy and develops and produces nuclear weapons. In 1999 the National Nuclear Security Administration (NNSA) was created as a semiautonomous agency within DOE to manage the weapons plants.

Production of nuclear weapons in the United States came to an end in 1992. Several of DOE's weapons plants have shut down or no longer play a military role. Among them are the Feed Materials Center in Fernald, Ohio (production of uranium metal); Hanford Plant in Richland, Washington (production of plutonium); K-25 Gaseous Diffusion Plant at Oak Ridge, Tennessee; Mound Laboratory, Miamisburg, Ohio (tasks relating to tritium); Paducah Gaseous Diffusion Plant in Paducah, Kentucky; Pinellas Plant, near St. Petersburg, Florida (production of neutron generators); Portsmouth Gaseous Diffusion Plant in Piketon, Ohio; and Rocky Flats Plant, near Denver, Colorado (production of plutonium pits). Below are listed, under key functions, the major plants still in operation.

Plants That Design Nuclear Weapons The nuclear portion of weapons design is carried out at Los Alamos National Laboratory and at Lawrence Livermore National Laboratory near San Francisco. Sandia National Laboratories next to Livermore and at Kirtland Air Force Base in Albuquerque, New Mexico, develop nonnuclear components and integrate them with the nuclear components.

Plants That Produce Nuclear Materials The United States has more than enough plutonium and enriched uranium on hand to meet the needs of its military programs. Presumably it also has sufficient deuterium and lithium 6, as the only special nuclear material that it is known to be producing is tritium.

In autumn 2003 DOE began irradiating lithium targets to produce tritium for nuclear weapons in the Watts Bar electricity-generating reactor in Tennessee owned by the Tennessee Valley Authority (TVA). TVA's Sequoyah I and II reactors are also licensed to produce tritium. This is the first time that the United States has produced weapons material in civilian reactors.

Plants That Produce Warhead Components The Kansas City Plant in Kansas City, Missouri, manufactures a variety of mechanical and electrical components. The Y-12 plant at Oak Ridge, Tennessee, is concerned with lithium deuteride components for secondaries of thermonuclear weapons and uranium components. Los Alamos National Laboratory produces plutonium pits on a very limited scale. Pantex in Amarillo, Texas, produces high-explosive components from explosives that it manufactures or obtains from commercial suppliers.

Plants That Maintain or Modify Warheads The Pantex site in Amarillo, Texas, is responsible for routine maintenance of warheads. Repairing damage usually involves replacing components. For this purpose, the weapons are partially dismantled in bays and cells. Nuclear material may, in some cases, need to be added.

The tritium in weapons must be replenished periodically. Because tritium has a relatively short half-life, only 12.3 years, 5.5 percent of the tritium in a weapon disappears each year. Pantex sends depleted tritium reservoirs to the Savannah River Site for withdrawal of the remaining tritium. The reservoirs are replenished at the Savannah River Site and returned to Pantex.

Pantex is also responsible for the modification of warheads. It disassembles and reassembles the warheads, but other sites are involved in refashioning and making components for them.

Plants That Destroy Warheads The only facility in the United States that disassembles nuclear weapons today is the Pantex Plant. After a weapon has been broken up, various nonnuclear components are returned to the facilities that produced them. The chemical high explosive is burned at Pantex. Tritium is sent to the Savannah River Site for reuse in active warheads. Uranium and subassemblies containing fusion material go to the Y-12 plant at Oak Ridge for storage or processing. Plutonium pits are packaged and stored at Pantex. As of January 2004, Pantex stored more than 12,000 plutonium pits. (When the United States was manufacturing new weapons, much of the plutonium and uranium that was removed from warheads was reused in new warheads.)[18]

Plants That Dispose of Nuclear Waste The U.S. weapons production complex has generated and still generates massive amounts of radioactive and toxic waste. The plants released much of this waste into the air, water, and soil, particularly during their early years of operation when dilution was considered to be an effective disposal technique. Programs designed to alleviate environmental contamination have had to be undertaken at every site that handled or still handles nuclear materials. Particularly threatening is the contamination of surface and groundwater. Major rivers at risk include the Columbia River in Washington, the Clinch River in Tennessee, and the Savannah River in South Carolina. Among the aquifers (underground water that permeates rock, sand, or gravel) in which pollutants have been detected are the Snake River Aquifer in Idaho, the Ogallala Aquifer in Texas, and the Great Miami Aquifer in Ohio.

Numerous wastes have also accumulated in storage facilities at the plants. Wastes from weapons production represent the four categories of waste as defined in the United States: high-level waste (irradiated fuel and the highly radioactive liquid resulting from reprocessing this fuel), transuranic waste (waste containing more than 100 nanocuries of transuranic nuclides per gram of material), waste (or tailings) from uranium mills, and low-level waste (everything not included in the prior categories).

As sites are cleaned up, low-level wastes are incinerated or shipped to the Nevada Test Site and to commercial low-level radioactive waste sites such as Envirocare in Utah. Uranium mill tailings are largely remediated where they were produced. (At uranium mines and mills, no distinction was made between uranium that would end up in nuclear weapons and uranium that would end up in nuclear reactors.) Transuranic waste goes to the Waste Isolation Pilot Project (WIPP) in New Mexico for burial deep underground in a salt formation. The acidic, highly radioactive liquid waste that has resulted from reprocessing is for the most part still stored in tanks at the sites where it was created. If a high-level waste repository is created at Yucca Mountain, Nevada, any liquid waste that has been solidified in blocks of glass will be shipped to that repository.

The Future of the Plants The United States is currently rejuvenating its nuclear weapons complex. Existing facilities are being upgraded and assigned new tasks, and new facilities are planned or already under construction.

The Stockpile Stewardship Program, initiated by President Bill Clinton by presidential directive in 1993 and confirmed by Congress in the National Defense Authorization Act of 1994, is intended to assure the "safety and reliability" of the nation's stockpile in the absence of nuclear testing. To simulate testing, DOE is

- installing nuclear weapons advanced simulation and computing (ASCI) centers at each of the three weapons laboratories: Los Alamos, Livermore, and Sandia
- constructing a National Ignition Facility (NIF) at Lawrence Livermore. A 196-beam laser facility, the NIF is intended to ignite fusion in a droplet of deuterium and hydrogen. The fusion would illustrate what occurs in the thermonuclear stage of a nuclear weapon. As of 2004, the NIF was scheduled for completion in 2008, but actually achieving ignition is expected to take longer
- constructing the Dual Axis Radiographic Hydrotest Facility (DARHT) at Los Alamos. This facility will make three-dimensional X-ray images of imploding surrogate primaries (i.e., the fission stage of a weapon). The material used in

DARHT will imitate weapons-grade plutonium but will not involve a chain reaction. DARHT is scheduled to become fully operational in 2007

Meanwhile, the Stockpile Life Extension Program, which was established in 1996 by the Office of Defense Programs as an extension of the Stockpile Stewardship Program, is increasingly occupying the nuclear complex. Refurbishment of the W-87 strategic warheads for the land-based Peacekeeper missile was completed in 2004. The W-80 warhead, carried by a B-52 bomber or a cruise missile launched from an attack submarine; the B-61 bomb, carried by a B-52 or B-2 bomber; and the W-76 warhead, carried on a Trident II missile, will be refurbished in the near future.[19]

The Alliance for Nuclear Accountability (ANA) fears that the Life Extension programs are gradually moving beyond the original goal of stockpile stewardship and are increasingly intended to enhance the performance and capabilities of warheads. Much of the information about the programs, however, is classified.

Meanwhile, DOE is rejuvenating the weapons complex not only to assist in carrying out the Stockpile Life Extension Program but also to achieve the capability to resume mass production of warheads, if necessary, and to develop new weapons or adapt existing weapons for use against nations and terrorist organizations that threaten to use weapons of mass destruction. In the 2005 Omnibus appropriations bill, Congress cut off funding for the Robust Nuclear Earth Penetrator (RNEP) and for the Advanced Concepts Initiative, which included research on low-yield nuclear weapons. The ultimate fate of these programs, on which DOE had already begun work, is uncertain, however.

At the Savannah River Plant, DOE is constructing a tritium extraction facility to remove tritium from rods irradiated in the Watts Bar and Sequoyah reactors. At Savannah River or elsewhere, DOE intends to construct a modern pit facility to fabricate fission cores for nuclear weapons. In 2005 a final environmental impact statement for the facility is being compiled even though a specific site has not been chosen. DOE is also enlarging the facilities at Pantex and at Oak Ridge's Y-12 plant and is resurrecting the ability of Los Alamos National Laboratory to fabricate and certify the performance of plutonium pits. Furthermore, the agency is making changes at the Nevada Test Site to shorten the length of time required before testing could be resumed.

Needless to say the many changes are generating controversy. Whether the United States should rejuvenate its nuclear weapons production complex is a subject that is widely debated.

Controlling Nuclear Weapons Production and Use

Even before an atomic bomb was dropped on Hiroshima, opponents of the bomb were speaking out. The public had no knowledge of the bomb prior to the attack, but certain scientists who had worked on the Manhattan Project urged the administration not to use the bomb against Japan without adequate forewarning. Later, additional scientists from the Manhattan Project worked against nuclear testing and the buildup of nuclear arsenals. The public first became heavily involved in nuclear issues in relation to nuclear testing, an understandable issue that arguably affected the health of individuals and of the general population. Under pressure from the public, governments have undertaken measures to try to control nuclear weapons. Their attempts have taken a variety of forms: treaties and agreements, dismantling of warheads, disposing of nuclear materials, and cooperative threat-reduction initiatives.

Treaties and Agreements The multilateral Treaty Banning Nuclear Weapon Tests in the Atmosphere, in Outer Space, and Under Water, known as the Partial or Limited Test Ban Treaty and signed in 1963, was the first major nuclear treaty. It resulted from massive pressure by members of the public, who feared the health effects of the fallout from atmospheric testing. In 1967, two treaties banning weapons in certain locations were signed. One, known as the Outer Space Treaty, prohibits the placement of nuclear weapons or other weapons of mass destruction in orbit around the Earth; the other is the Treaty for the Prohibition of Nuclear Weapons in Latin America and the Caribbean. Several other treaties setting up regional nuclear-free zones have been enacted.

The Nuclear Non-Proliferation Treaty (NPT) was signed by 62 states in 1968 and came into force in 1970. It is still the strongest international agreement in place to limit the development and spread of nuclear weapons but, as of 2005, is in danger of disintegration. The world had to wait more than 20 years after the negotiation of the NPT for the signing of another major multilateral nuclear treaty, the Comprehensive Test Ban Treaty (CTBT). Although the CTBT was first signed in 1996, as of June 2005 the treaty has not gone into effect because it has not been ratified by all the states that according to the terms of the treaty need to do so. The United States is among the missing.

Meanwhile, starting in the 1970s the United States and the Soviet Union/Russia negotiated a number of treaties aimed at preventing nuclear war between them. The Strategic Arms Limitation Talks (SALT I) extended over two and a half years and ended in May 1972, with President Richard Nixon and Soviet general secretary Leonid Brezhnev signing the Anti-Ballistic Missile (ABM) Treaty and the Interim Agreement on strategic offensive arms.

The SALT II agreement, signed in 1979 by President Jimmy Carter and Brezhnev, was to replace the Interim Agreement with a long-term treaty that would limit strategic offensive weapons systems. Because of subsequent conflicts between the United States and the Soviet Union, the U.S. Senate never ratified it, but the agreement was observed.

The Intermediate-Range Nuclear Forces (INF) Treaty, signed by President Ronald Reagan and Soviet general secretary Mikhail Gorbachev in 1987, was ratified. As a result of the treaty the Soviet Union and the United States eliminated all nuclear-armed ground-launched cruise and ballistic missiles with ranges between 500 and 5,500 kilometers (approximately 300 to 3,400 miles) by May 1991.

The Strategic Arms Reduction Treaty (START) signed by President George H. W. Bush and President Boris Yeltsin in 1991 also resulted in actual reductions of nuclear forces; START II, signed in 1993 by the same two leaders, was to eliminate heavy or multiple-warhead intercontinental ballistic missiles (ICBMs) and to reduce the strategic weapons deployed by each country to two-thirds of pre-START levels. However, Russia withdrew from the treaty when the United States withdrew from the ABM Treaty.

In 2002 President George W. Bush and President Vladimir Putin signed the Strategic Offensive Reduction Treaty (SORT), which limits deployed strategic warheads but has no schedule for implementation other than the expiration date of the treaty and does not require that the warheads that are withdrawn be destroyed. Arms control advocates regard it as embodying a loss of momentum toward control of strategic nuclear weapons. It should be noted that neither SORT nor any other bilateral treaty deals with tactical (essentially shorter-range) nuclear weapons.

Various informal international coalitions and arrangements, implemented in some cases by national legislation, help to restrain exports in the areas of nuclear weapons and missiles. The first to be created, the Non-Proliferation Treaty Exporters Committee, or the Zangger Committee, was formed in 1971 to establish guidelines for implementing the Nuclear Non-Proliferation Treaty. The second, the Nuclear Suppliers Group (NSG), was formed in 1975.

Two arrangements to curb missile proliferation have been set up. The G-7 governments announced in 1987 the Missile Technology Control Regime (MTCR), a policy and the means to implement the policy. In 2002 an international code of conduct against ballistic missile proliferation was promulgated. The code is designed to supplement the MTCR, but membership in it is not limited.

The Wassenaar Arrangement was established in 1996 as a means of coordinating national controls on exports of conventional arms and dual-use technologies. The dual-use items relate to a great extent to weapons of mass destruction, including nuclear weapons.

The Proliferation Security Initiative is an informal, voluntary partnership of states that are together developing a range of measures to stop shipments of weapons of mass destruction, missiles, and related technologies by air, land, and sea. It was announced by President George W. Bush in May 2003 and, as of September 2004, had 15 core member states. The core states hold meetings, conduct training exercises, and have released a statement of interdiction principles. Legal restrictions on boarding planes and ships and inspecting cargo govern their activities.

Dismantling of Warheads Between 1945 and 1992 the United States built approximately 70,000 nuclear warheads of some 70 types for use in more than 120 weapon systems. Approximately 60,000 of those warheads have been dismantled, leaving about 10,350 in the stockpile as of December 2004. As of January 2004 "only a few hundred more"[20] were to be dismantled. However, in June 2004 DOE announced that it will withdraw "almost half"[21] of the warheads in the U.S. stockpile by 2012 and eventually dismantle them.

The Soviet Union produced up to 55,000 nuclear warheads between 1949 and 2003, and their stockpile as of July 2004 contained an estimated 17,000 intact nuclear warheads. Some 38,000 warheads have presumably been dismantled, but the pace of dismantling is not known. The United Kingdom produced 1,200 nuclear warheads between 1952 and 2001 but has only 200 in its stockpile. France manufactured 1,260 warheads between 1960 and 2003 and, as of August 2004, had 348 in its stockpile. China's estimated production between 1964 and 2003 was 750 warheads. An estimated 400 warheads are in its stockpile. The nuclear-weapon nations destroyed many of the nuclear weapons because they were obsolete, not for reasons of arms control.

Disposing of Fissile Materials World stocks of plutonium and highly enriched uranium, totaling more than 3,700 metric tons and located in some 60 countries, would furnish material for hundreds of thousands of additional nuclear weapons. The bulk of the plutonium, 1,700 metric tons, results from the irradiation of uranium fuel in electricity-generating reactors and is categorized as civilian. Military plutonium stocks total 155 tons. Most of the highly enriched uranium comes from dismantled nuclear weapons. Therefore, the bulk of world stocks, 1,725 metric tons, is categorized as military. Civilian stocks of highly enriched uranium total 175 tons.

Three nations have declared a portion of their military plutonium stock to be in excess of military needs: Russia has declared 50 tons; the United States, 52.5 tons; and Britain, 4.4 tons.[22] Russia and the United States each plan to dispose of 34 tons of their excess weapons-grade plutonium by incorporating it in mixed oxide fuel (MOX; uranium oxide and plutonium oxide) and using the MOX in electricity-generating reactors. Irradiation will change the isotopic content of the plutonium, making it difficult though not impossible to use in weapons.

Russia and the United States have also declared a portion of their highly enriched uranium to be in excess of military needs: Russia has 500 metric tons of excess, and the United States has 174.4 metric tons. Both are in the process of disposing of their official excess by downblending it (mixing the highly enriched uranium with low enriched uranium to make a large quantity of low-enriched uranium for use in uranium fuel for electricity-generating reactors).

The disposal programs have their critics: Many people think that, given the urgency of disposing of fissile materials, the programs are too limited in scope and moving too slowly. Others generally support disposal plans but criticize the methods to be used. The latter fear that the fabrication and use of MOX fuel presents a health and environmental hazard and establishes a dangerous precedent for the use of plutonium in civilian reactors. The mixing of plutonium with nuclear waste and the transformation of the product into glass has been proposed as an alternative method. Some find it ironic that highly enriched uranium (HEU) is made into fuel for nuclear reactors, which generate plutonium.

Cooperative Threat Reduction Under a series of cooperative threat-reduction programs, the United States has given assistance to the nations of the former Soviet Union in order to help them secure special nuclear materials and weapons.

The United States assisted Belarus, Kazakhstan, and the Ukraine to transfer all of the nuclear warheads on their territories to Russia by 1996. It also helped these countries eliminate their strategic nuclear-delivery systems. Ongoing programs include helping Russia to secure its nuclear weapons against theft and to construct a storage center for fissile materials that were formerly in warheads. With U.S. assistance, border security guards and customs officials are trained to detect and stop any attempts to smuggle nuclear material out of Russia.

Iraq

Iraq illustrates what can and cannot be done in regard to controlling nuclear weapons. The recent history of this nation shows the difficulty in uncovering a clandestine program and shows that attacks from the air may not destroy such a program. On the positive side this history demonstrates that inspections, accompanied by sanctions, can work.

Iraq began small-scale efforts relating to nuclear energy in the late 1960s. In the early 1970s then vice president Saddam Hussein ordered the creation of a nuclear weapons program. Iraq planned to develop an ostensibly civilian fuel cycle and to use it as the basis of efforts to acquire weapons material. In 1975 it obtained the Osiraq research reactor, fueled by highly enriched uranium, from France. Israel bombed and destroyed this reactor in 1981. The reactor fuel would have yielded plutonium when reprocessed. After the reactor was destroyed, Iraq experimented with various processes for enriching uranium.

By the start of the Gulf War in 1991, the United States and other countries suspected that Iraq had a nuclear program, but they had no idea of its magnitude. After the war they learned that Iraq had a many-faceted nuclear program and that, following its invasion of Kuwait in August 1990, it had embarked on a crash program to produce a single nuclear weapon by April 1991.

The coalition air attack in early 1991 destroyed two research reactors and some of the other nuclear facilities that Iraq was then operating. After the war inspectors from the United Nations and the International Atomic Energy Agency (IAEA) sought out and destroyed remaining facilities and related equipment. In late 1998 Saddam Hussein refused to allow inspectors to work freely inside Iraq unless all sanctions imposed by the United Nations were lifted. Unable to work, the inspectors left Iraq in December 1998.

Renewed United Nations and IAEA inspections took place in the months preceding the U.S. attack on Iraq in 2003, and the United States and its coalition partners searched for nuclear weapons as well as for biological and chemical weapons during the war. David Kay, head of the Iraq Survey Group (ISG) responsible for the search, reported in September 2004 that the ISG found that Saddam Hussein had not attempted to rebuild Iraq's nuclear program after the Gulf War. The group said that it had, however, found evidence that Saddam Hussein intended to re-create his nuclear, biological, and chemical weapons programs after sanctions had ended. The United States abandoned the search for weapons of mass destruction in Iraq in late 2004.

NUCLEAR WEAPONS IN THE FUTURE

Three issues will largely determine the future of nuclear weapons and possibly the future of civilization as we know it. One is whether the United States and other nuclear-weapon states expand or reduce their arsenals. A second is whether nations not known to have nuclear weapons abandon their ambitions to acquire them. A third is whether nuclear weapons can be kept out of the hands of terrorists.

United States and Other Nuclear Powers

The United States is the key player among the nuclear nations. Since the disintegration of the Soviet Union, it is recognized as the world's only superpower, and the Bush administration has been outspoken about its position in regard to nuclear weapons. The United States is reducing the size of its arsenal, but it is shifting its position on the role of nuclear weapons in a way that appears to make them more likely rather than less likely to be used.

For decades the United States maintained a "firm line between the use of conventional weapons and nuclear bombs." According to official U.S. policy, nuclear weapons would "be used only against countries that possess nuclear weapons or ally themselves with a nuclear power."[23] A Nuclear Posture Review (NPR) completed by the U.S. Department of Defense in 1994 during the first Clinton administration confirmed the policy of deterrence. It also confirmed the existing nuclear triad, composed of bombers, land-based missiles, and submarine-based missiles and restated its support of multinational and bilateral arms control agreements.

Three years later President Bill Clinton, in Presidential Decision Directive 60 (PDD-60), broke with long-standing U.S. policy by permitting nuclear war planners to target so-called rogue nations—those perceived as not honoring international agreements or principles of legal conduct—whether or not they possess nuclear weapons themselves. The succeeding Bush administration's NPR picked up this change and went beyond it. The document, which was completed at the end of 2001 and delivered to Congress in January 2002, is classified, but journalists have learned much about its content. In part as a result of the attack on the World Trade Center on September 11, 2001, the old concept of deterrence as the justification for a nuclear force has been replaced by a much more proactive approach to the use of nuclear weapons.

The Bush administration's NPR calls for the development of contingency plans to use nuclear weapons against at least seven nations: Russia, China, Iran, Iraq, Libya, North Korea, and Syria. (Libya has since abandoned its weapons of mass destruction programs, and the status of Iraq has changed since its recent occupation by U.S. and allied forces.) Occasions in which nuclear weapons might be used in the future include an Arab-Israeli conflict; an attack by North Korea against South Korea; the need to destroy targets that could withstand other types of attack; and retaliation for the use of biological, chemical, or nuclear weapons.

A draft "Doctrine for Joint Nuclear Operations," dated March 15, 2005, and written by the Joint Chiefs of Staff would revise rules and procedures for use of nuclear weapons in accordance with the Bush administration's preemption strategy. It would provide for commanders to seek authority from the president to use nuclear weapons to preempt an attack on the United States with nuclear, chemical, or biological weapons and to destroy enemy stockpiles of these weapons.

Per the NPR, new nuclear capabilities will be required to meet new challenges. They include bombs to destroy deep underground bunkers, precision weapons that inflict little damage to buildings, and weapons designed to be used against small targets. Such weapons would be useful against terrorist organizations, the authors of the report believe.

The administration plans to integrate nonnuclear and nuclear capabilities both by incorporating nonnuclear capabilities into nuclear-strike forces and by introducing nuclear capabilities into conventional weapons systems under development. The report describes a "New Triad," which underscores the integration of the nuclear and the conventional. This triad consists of an "offensive leg" (nuclear and conventional forces), "active and passive defenses" (antimissile systems and other defenses), and "a responsive defense infrastructure" (the ability to resume nuclear testing and the mass production of nuclear weapons).[24]

The United States has withdrawn from the ABM Treaty in order to be free to develop defenses against ballistic missiles. Deterrence depends on the absence of effective missile defenses. Mutual destruction would no longer be assured if one nation could launch a first strike with confidence that it could prevent missiles launched in retaliation from striking. The ABM Treaty was the result of the earliest negotiations on strategic arms reduction. Understandably but regrettably Russia withdrew from the START II arms control agreement following the U.S. withdrawal from the ABM Treaty.

Russia appears to be responding in other ways to the changing U.S. position on nuclear weapons. It is cooperating with the United States to secure its nuclear materials and thus to reduce the possibility that they will fall into the hands of terrorists. However, it desires to maintain a viable nuclear arsenal and has made statements suggesting that the U.S./Soviet arms race could be revived.

President Vladimir Putin stated in a press release dated February 18, 2004, that "successfully concluded experiments . . . enable us to confirm that the Russian Armed Forces, the Strategic Missile Forces, will receive new hypersound-speed, high-precision new weapons systems that can hit targets at intercontinental distance and can adjust their altitude and course as they travel. This is a very significant statement because no country in the world as yet has such arms in their military arsenal."[25]

On July 13, 2004, at London's International Institute for Strategic Studies, Defense Minister S. B. Ivanov stated, "We closely follow what is being done in the sphere of strategic nuclear forces in the USA. Particularly, we take a considerable interest in the progress of the US program of the development of ultra small nuclear charges because each new type of armaments modifies the overall picture of global stability and we must take these modifications into consideration in our military planning."[26]

Russia is arguably not the only nuclear nation that is being affected by U.S. nuclear plans and activities. China, for one, continues to develop its arsenal and means of delivery. Moreover, nonnuclear nations can argue that they need to obtain nuclear weapons in order to deter attacks on themselves.

The leading argument against nuclear weapons has always been that they are immoral because of their indiscriminate destructive power and because of the harm that their development, production, and testing cause to people and the environment. Today another argument is increasingly heard—that the stockpiles of the major nuclear powers are encouraging additional nations to go nuclear and thus are increasing rather than decreasing the nuclear threat to those nations that have long possessed them.

North Korea and Iran

North Korea openly challenged the nuclear nonproliferation regime, and Iran is suspected of having a nuclear weapons program. Should these countries succeed in flouting the Nuclear Non-Proliferation Treaty, other nations may likely seek nuclear weapons.

Although North Korea did not begin working on nuclear weapons until the 1980s, the origin of North Korea's nuclear program dates from 1964, when, with Soviet help, North Korea established a complex for research on nuclear energy at Yongbyon-kun. It obtained a small research reactor from the Soviets the following year. In the 1970s it constructed a five-megawatt (MW) electric research reactor, and in the 1980s, a large plutonium separation plant at the Yongbyon-kun complex.

Under international pressure it acceded to the NPT in 1985, but it did not sign a safeguards agreement with the IAEA until 1992. In spring 1994 North Korea caused an international crisis by unloading fuel from the 5-MW nuclear reactor, apparently for the purpose of separating plutonium from the fuel. This crisis was resolved later in the year when North Korea and the United States signed the Agreed Framework. The agreement included provisions for North Korea to freeze its nuclear program and dismantle the 5-MW reactor, two larger reactors under construction, and its fuel reprocessing plant. In return North Korea would receive shipments of heavy oil and two light water reactors. The light water reactors, the type of reactor operated by U.S. utilities, would be safer and would produce less plutonium than the reactors then under construction.

In October 2002 the United States informed North Korean officials that it knew that North Korea had received materials from Pakistan for a facility to produce highly enriched uranium. North Korea first denied and then admitted the charge. The United States suspended shipments of heavy oil the following month. North Korea declared that it was ending the freeze on its nuclear program. In December it ordered inspectors to leave the country, and on January 10, 2003, it declared its withdrawal from the NPT.

A series of six-party talks to resolve the crisis began in Beijing in April 2003. The United States insisted that North Korea undertake a complete and verifiable dismantlement of all its nuclear facilities before the United States addressed North Korea's concerns about security and economics. Also, the United States refused the one-on-one talks with North Korea that the nation has requested. The third round of multilateral talks was held in June 2004. A fourth round, scheduled for September 2004, was canceled. The six-party talks resumed September 13, 2005. Six days later North Korea agreed to abandon its nuclear weapons and existing nuclear program in return for a nonagression pledge and economic and energy aid from the United States. Details remained to be negotiated.

The Institute for Science and Security (ISIS) estimates that as of 2003, North Korea held 15–40 kilograms of unirradiated plutonium and that with this plutonium it could have produced between two and nine weapons. It may have enriched uranium in centrifuges but, as far as is known, could have produced little, if any, highly enriched uranium. North Korea itself declared in February 2005 that it has manufactured nuclear weapons, but the actual situation is unclear.

Iran acceded to the NPT in 1970. In the mid-1970s, it began a nuclear energy program and possibly research on nuclear weapons in Bushehr. The revolution, which overthrew Shah Mohammad Reza Pahlavi in 1979, resulted in a suspension of nuclear activity. In the Iran-Iraq War, which broke out in 1980, Iraq bombed and damaged two incomplete nuclear power reactors at Bushehr. In 1984 Iran revived its nuclear energy program.

Russia is helping Iran to construct a nuclear power reactor at Bushehr and has agreed to supply it with fuel. Contending that Iran has so much oil that it does not need nuclear energy, the United States has criticized the Russian assistance. The United States believes that the civilian program is a cover for Iran's obtaining sensitive nuclear technology and know-how that it can use to produce weapons. One of Iran's motives for acquiring nuclear weapons is the Arabs' fear of Israel, which is believed to have a secret stockpile of weapons and openly demonstrates its means of delivering them.

In mid-2002 U.S. intelligence learned of two secret nuclear facilities in Iran: a pilot-scale uranium enrichment facility at Natanz and a plant for the production of heavy water near Arak. If Iran used uranium in the enrichment plant for tests before informing the IAEA of the plant's existence, it violated Iran's obligations under the NPT. In February 2003 IAEA inspectors visited the enrichment plant and found that Iran has the ability to build additional centrifuges for enrichment. In February 2004 the IAEA revealed that it had found traces of highly enriched uranium, suitable for weapons, at at least two different sites the previous year. This led Defense Minister Ali Shamkhani to admit that the military had constructed enrichment centrifuges.

Iran stated in 2003 that it wants to operate the complete nuclear fuel cycle in order not to be dependent on other countries for nuclear fuel, but, as of mid-2005, it maintains that its purposes are peaceful. Possibly Iran has ended its covert activities now that it knows that they are liable to be detected and to cause the nation problems with the international community. George Perkovich of the Carnegie Endowment for International Peace points out that the intelligence community should analyze the dates of all available indications of illegal activity in Iran, if it has not done so, to try to determine whether this is the case.

It would be in the interests of Iran to stop any activity explicitly directed at weapons and to adhere to IAEA safeguards as currently interpreted. Current interpretation of the NPT allows a nonnuclear weapon state to acquire uranium enrichment and plutonium separation capabilities. By avoiding illegal activity, Iran could do so without incurring international condemnation and sanctions and then, the technology obtained, could take up the military option at some time in the future.[27] A lack of covert activities as of 2005 would thus not end the threat that Iran poses.

Mohamed ElBaradei has suggested that there be a worldwide moratorium on the construction of new enrichment plants. Such a moratorium would be difficult to achieve—two enrichment plants are in the planning stage in the United States. But such an approach that looks beyond Iran holds promise for a solution to the problem of nations with nuclear ambitions. In return for not enriching uranium themselves, they would be assured access to fuel from outside Iran. The need to stop nations like Iran from acquiring nuclear weapons is urgent. The deadliest combination for the future would be a relationship between a nation with even a rudimentary nuclear infrastructure and a terrorist group.

Terrorist Organizations and the Response to Their Threat

The possibility that terrorist groups could acquire intact nuclear weapons cannot be ruled out. Russia's tactical weapons and Pakistan's weapons are the most likely sources. There is also a possibility that terrorists could acquire fissile materials and manufacture what is known as an "improvised nuclear device." Only about 25 kilograms of highly enriched uranium or five to 10 kilograms of plutonium would be needed, and the technology could be acquired by terrorists with a technical or scientific background who study the available literature.[28] Nevertheless, in terms of terrorism, the detonation of a dirty bomb is a more likely event.

Measures to prevent terrorists from acquiring intact nuclear weapons or nuclear materials must be carried out on three levels. The first and the most important is controlling weapons and materials at their source. As Matthew Bunn and Anthony Wier state in their report *Securing the Bomb 2005*, "The most crucial element in preventing nuclear terrorism "is to lock down every nuclear weapon and every kilogram of potential bomb material everywhere."[29]

Weapons and material worldwide must be thoroughly inventoried so that international authorities know what is where, and they must be secured. In 2004 and early 2005 three steps that lay a foundation for these efforts were taken. The UN Security Council passed Resolution 1540, which legally obligates every nation to account for and secure nuclear stockpiles. The U.S. Department of Energy (DOE) launched the Global Threat Reduction Initiative to speed up and expand efforts to secure potential bomb material now in insecure sites. Moreover, U.S. president George W. Bush and Russian president Vladimir Putin agreed at their February 2005 summit to work together to secure nuclear stockpiles in Russia and to lead in upgrading security elsewhere.

Nevertheless, actual implementation of these efforts on the ground has been slow and, as of mid-2005, continues to be so. To mention only Russia, as of the end of 2004, 46 percent of weapons-usable nuclear material in the former Soviet Union had been subject to a comprehensive security upgrade (26 percent) or at least a rapid security upgrade (20 percent). Only 56 percent of former Soviet buildings containing nuclear material had been secured. Meeting a goal of DOE to finish comprehensive nuclear security upgrades of this weapons-usable material by the end of 2008 would require a dramatic speeding up of the ongoing work. Such an acceleration can only be achieved if Bush and Putin intervene to eliminate such problems as access to sensitive areas.

A second step, which should occur concurrently, is preventing nuclear material from crossing national borders. Progress has been made in this direction. From time to time, the media reports the arrest of a smuggler. However, the technological means to prevent such smuggling worldwide are not available. A third approach is therefore necessary: taking the necessary measures to prevent any nuclear material that enters a country illegally from being used within that country.

On MSNBC's program *Meet the Press*, May 29, 2005, host Tim Russert asked all four of his guests whether they think that it is a "distinct possibility" that a nuclear weapon will be exploded within the United States in their lifetimes. Thomas Kean and Fred Thomson, the chair and vice chair of the 9/11 Commission, said that they believe it to be possible. Former senator Sam Nunn, a Democrat from Georgia, and Senator Richard Lugar, a Republican from Indiana, authors of the Nunn-Lugar Cooperative Threat Reduction Program, agreed that it is possible, but both added that it is preventable. Doing so, they said, will require the public to insist that national leaders put the issue on the front burner and take the steps necessary to prevent terrorists from obtaining nuclear weapons and nuclear materials.

BIOLOGICAL WEAPONS

A biological warfare agent is a living microorganism or a biologically created toxin that causes injury or death.

Intrinsic factors that influence the weapons potential of a given microorganism or toxin include its lethality, availability or ease of production, particle size and weight, ease of distribution, and stability. An agent must be composed of particles that are the right size to be ingested, through breathing deep into the lungs, or that can enter through the skin of victims. The most effective size range for particles to be inhaled is one to five microns because particles of this size reach the lower lung. Furthermore, an agent must survive environmental conditions during delivery and after release. The temperature, ultraviolet radiation, moisture, and atmospheric pressure at the location under attack are among the relevant factors.

Production of an agent requires a seed stock. Some agents, such as anthrax, can conceivably be obtained by isolating them from the natural environment, but most weapons makers turn to culture collections in commercial firms, research institutions, or university or hospital laboratories. The potential agent may then be processed to modify its natural characteristics. This processing and the mating of an agent with a means of delivery are known as weaponization. The end result is a biological weapon.

In processing agents two techniques employed by weapons designers are lyophilization, or freeze-drying, and microencapsulation. When an agent is lyophilized, a solution of the agent and a sugar-like stabilizer are transformed into a small cake, which is then ground to a fine powder. Microencapsulation involves coating the agent with materials that cause the agent to be released within the victim at the part of the body where it will do the most harm. This technique can also produce particles of optimum size and help make the agent stable.

Biological agents are generally delivered by means of aerosols—the dispersion of a liquid suspension or dry powder of the agent in an airborne cloud. This may be achieved by release from aerial bombs, rockets, missiles, or spray tanks, but not all agents can remain potent through a trip on a missile.

Advances in biotechnology are increasing the threat that bioweapons pose. Genetic engineering may be used to increase the virulence of an agent, to make it resistant to known drugs and vaccines, or to increase its resistance to environmental stresses, including those that occur during delivery. Genetic alteration of a microorganism might cause it to create a toxin that was previously difficult to obtain in quantity. The possibilities are varied and ominous.

Types of Biological Warfare Agents

Biological warfare agents can be divided into the following major groups: bacteria, viruses, rickettsias, and toxins, each of which are described briefly below.

Bacteria

Bacteria are free-living microorganisms that reproduce by cell division. Most can be grown on liquid or solid culture media. When subjected to hostile conditions such as heat or sunlight, some form spores (i.e., they protect themselves by building walls around themselves). The diseases that bacteria produce often respond to treatment with antibiotics. Among the bacteria that have been used as weapons are anthrax, tularemia, and plague.

Anthrax is an acute disease caused by a spore-forming bacterium, *Bacillus anthracis.* The spores can survive severe environmental conditions and then, after introduction into a living human body, become active. The disease has three forms determined by its route into the body: cutaneous (through the skin), ingestional, and inhalational. The inhaled form, which results in acute respiratory problems, is the most dangerous. If left untreated, it has a fatality rate of about 100 percent. The cutaneous form, if untreated, has a fatality rate of about 20 percent.

Plague is caused by *Yersinia pestis,* a bacterium that does not form spores but is nevertheless relatively hardy. Under natural conditions, the disease is transmitted to humans by rodents and their fleas. In biological warfare, the bacteria would be delivered by contaminated fleas, which cause bubonic plague or, more likely, by bacteria carried by aerosols, which cause pneumonic plague. If untreated, about 50 percent of the victims of bubonic plague die. The death rate for untreated victims of pneumonic plague is 100 percent. The cause of death is septic shock brought on by the collapse of the respiratory and circulatory systems.

Tularemia is a highly infectious disease caused by the bacterium *Francisella tularensis.* When bacteria are inhaled, they cause severe respiratory problems. If victims are not treated with antibiotics, they may die; but, with treatment, the fatality rate is less than 1 percent.

Viruses

Viruses are subcellular organisms that are dependent on the cells of the host that they infect. The diseases that they cause respond to antiviral compounds rather than to antibiotics, but few antiviral compounds are available. Among the examples of viruses that have been prepared for use as weapons are smallpox and Venezuelan equine encephalitis.

Smallpox was for centuries a dreaded disease, as it kills or permanently disfigures its victims. There is no known effective treatment, and the mortality rate for nonvaccinated humans is around 35 percent. Many countries vaccinated their population against the disease, but smallpox was eradicated in the 1970s and vaccination ceased. People who were vaccinated before the programs ended are believed to no longer be immune. Samples of the virus that causes smallpox are stored at the Centers for Disease Control and Prevention in Atlanta, Georgia, and at a Russian state research center. Secret stocks may be harbored by other nations. Smallpox is highly contagious, and the virus can be deliberately distributed in aerosols.

Venezuelan equine encephalitis is a severe illness in horses, donkeys, and mules. Under natural conditions, humans become ill with the disease after being bitten by mosquitoes that fed on infected animals. The cause is a group of viruses, which the mosquitoes transmit. Dissemination of the viruses as an aerosol would directly affect humans, as virtually 100 percent of those who breathe them in would become ill, along with any horses, donkeys, or mules in the area. Symptoms in humans include high fever and severe headaches. About 4 percent of the human victims of a natural epidemic develop infections of the central nervous system that can cause convulsions or paralysis. The mortality rate for the disease is less than 1 percent in adults but is higher in children. Prior to 1970 the United States and the Soviet Union both weaponized the virus for the purpose of using it to incapacitate victims.

Rickettsias

Rickettsias are microorganisms that combine characteristics of bacteria and viruses. Like viruses, they can grow and replicate themselves only inside living cells, but, like bacteria, they have cell membranes and use oxygen. They respond to broad-spectrum antibiotics. Q fever is an example of a disease caused by a rickettsia. It can be incapacitating because it causes fever and difficulty in breathing, but it does not kill. People can acquire the disease from infected cattle, sheep, and goats by inhaling particles contaminated with the microorganism that causes it, *Coxiella burnetti*. Stocks of this microorganism, which is particularly suitable for dissemination in weapons since it can survive drying, make up part of the U.S. and the Soviet bioweapons arsenals.

Toxins

Toxins are poisonous substances that resemble chemicals but that are ordinarily produced by living plants, animals, or microorganisms. Since toxins are not themselves living organisms, they straddle the line between biological and chemical agents and may be classified as either. They may respond to specific antisera and pharmacologic agents. Examples of toxins used as weapons include botulinum, ricin, and saxitoxin.

The bacillus *Clostridium botulinum* causes botulism poisoning by producing neurotoxins. The toxins are proteins that bind to neurons in such a way as to prevent release of acetylcholine and block neurotransmission. As a bioweapons agent, botulinum toxin can be delivered by aerosol, although the toxin is best known as a contaminant of spoiled food. Whether the toxin is inhaled or ingested, the results are similar. Death, if it comes, is generally from paralysis of the respiratory muscles, causing respiratory failure. With modern medical techniques, the death rate should be less than 5 percent, but lengthy care is necessary if the victim is to recover.

Ricin is a toxin that kills cells by blocking protein synthesis. It is made from seeds of the castor-oil plant, which are widely available. When inhaled, ricin causes sufficient damage to the lungs to kill the victim. It is also usually fatal when ingested.

Saxitoxin is a toxin that attacks the nervous system. It is primarily produced by marine organisms known as dinoflagellates that are found in red tides. People who eat shellfish that have consumed the organisms die of paralytic shellfish poisoning if they are not treated. As a weapon, it would most likely be received into the body by inhalation or on a projectile. The United States stockpiled saxitoxin until President Nixon decided to destroy all toxins in the nation's arsenal.

History of Biological Weapons Use

Humans have understood contagion since at least 1770 B.C., as is indicated by inscriptions on cuneiform tablets from the archives of Mari, an outpost of Sumeria in Mesopotamia. One royal letter orders people from an infected town not to visit a healthy town for fear that they will spread disease. The ancients drew on their understanding to try to defeat their enemies, as did military leaders during the Middle Ages. In 1346 during the siege of Kaffa, a fortress in Genoa, Mongols catapulted the bodies of their own soldiers who had died of bubonic plague over the walls of the city in order to spread the plague to their enemies. The defense of the city eventually collapsed. Later, in the New World during the French and Indian Wars, the British gave to hostile American Indian tribes blankets that had been used by people ill with smallpox.

During World War I the only reported uses of biological weapons involved the contamination of animals and animal feed. The use of biological warfare against people was apparently regarded as inhumane by both sides. In 1915 German-American physician Dr. Anton Dilger produced the biological agents that cause glanders (a virulent disease primarily in equine species) and anthrax at his home in Washington, D.C., from samples supplied to him by the German government. German operatives paid stevedores, men whose job it was to load and unload ships, to infect horses and cattle being dispatched to the Allies in Europe. Evidence exists that French operatives in Switzerland infected horses being shipped to Germany with glanders and that Germans infected horses being used by czarist troops to move artillery supplies to the Eastern Front.

During World War II the Japanese released grain and contaminated fleas above Chinese cities in order to spread bubonic plague and also attacked Chinese cities and troops with various biological agents by means of food, water, and sprayers. The Japanese admit to having killed some 20,000 Chinese as a result of biological warfare; the Chinese have set the toll as high as 200,000. The actual figure will never be known, in part because some of the diseases that the Japanese disseminated were already present in China.[30] The Germans' only known tactical use of a biological agent during World War II was the contamination of a big reservoir in Bohemia with sewage in 1945.

In 1951 and 1952 China, North Korea, and the Soviet Union accused the United States of conducting biological warfare against China and North Korea. In 1951 North Korea accused the United States of using smallpox against the North Korean capital, and in 1952 North Korea claimed that the United States released insects bearing cholera and other diseases from airplanes (over Chinese and North Korean troops). The aim would have been to weaken the troops through illness. The United States has always denied the charge. A commission composed of scientists from six countries and sponsored by the World Peace Council, which interviewed hundreds of witnesses, concluded that the charges were true.[31] Nevertheless, China and North Korea resisted efforts by the World Health Organization and International Red Cross to investigate. No evidence directly implicating the United States has surfaced, and the case is still unsubstantiated.[32]

In September 1984 members of a religious cult from India, the Rajneesh, contaminated salad bars in 10 restaurants in The Dalles, Oregon, with the salmonella bacteria *Salmonella typhimurium* in a test to influence the November 1984 election. Nobody died as a result, but at least 750 people became ill and 40 were hospitalized.

The Aum Shinrikyo cult, which exposed between 5,000 and 6,000 people in a Tokyo subway to the chemical nerve agent sarin in 1995, had earlier tried and failed to produce weapons from botulinum toxin and anthrax. Between 1990 and 1995 members had made up to a dozen unsuccessful attempts to use biological warfare against the public in Japan. The cult believed in Armageddon and its right to hasten the coming of Armageddon by mass killing.

In October 2001 in the wake of the attacks of September 11, 2001, various members of the media and Congress received letters containing anthrax spores. Five individuals—recipients or postal workers—died. As of mid-2005 the perpetrator(s) had not been identified. The anthrax used was of two types: cutaneous (through the skin) and inhalational (through breathing). The latter type is far more deadly than the former. Although a relatively small number of people ultimately were affected, the attacks caused enormous fear, dislocations, and expenditures of money. Measures taken to respond to these attacks included temporarily closing down many federal buildings, decontaminating areas where the letters had been handled, and distributing antibiotics as a precautionary measure.

DEVELOPMENT AND PRODUCTION OF BIOLOGICAL WEAPONS IN THE UNITED STATES

In 1939 as a result of intelligence reports that Germany and Japan were conducting research on biological weapons, American military scientists began to take a serious interest in biological warfare. In 1942 a War Research Service under the chairmanship of George W. Merck was established to oversee the biological warfare program, and the Chemical Warfare Service was put in charge of building and operating laboratory and production facilities.

A research and production facility for bioweapons began operating at Camp Detrick (later Fort Detrick) in Maryland in 1943. Open-air test sites were established at Dugway Proving Ground in Utah and, for a short time, at Horn Island in Pascagoula, Mississippi. A large plant that had been constructed to manufacture conventional munitions, the Vigo Plant, in Terre Haute, Indiana, was converted to work on biological agents, but it was dangerous to operate and produced only biological simulants before it closed at the end of the war.

From 1942 on, the Americans and the British shared their research and their resources on bioweapons. In 1944 the United States began to mass-produce for the British the "N" bomb, a four-pound bomb filled with anthrax spores, intended to be loaded into 500-pound cluster bombs. By the end of the war the United States had brought to an advanced stage of development another antipersonnel weapon. Known as "US," it was designed to spread brucellosis.

Following World War II, research was curtailed at laboratory programs at Fort Detrick, but with the outbreak of the Korean War, the bioweapons program again began to expand. In 1953 a defensive program to develop vaccines and antisera for U.S. troops was established. Technological advances now made possible large-scale production of biological agents, and in 1954 a factory for the production of agents and munitions began operating in Pine Bluff, Arkansas. At

Camp Detrick new biological weapons facilities were constructed; in one of them, Building 470, anthrax and other deadly microbes were produced.

The United States also conducted research on biological agents for use against plants and animals. By 1951 wheat rust had been successfully tested, and bombs to carry it were being manufactured for the U.S. Air Force. By 1958 the United States had built its first missile to carry a biological warhead, the Honest John Rocket, with a range of 25 kilometers and the ability to deliver 356 4.5-inch bomblets. The Sergeant, in service by the early 1960s, had a range of 120 kilometers and could carry 720 bomblets.

In 1969 President Richard Nixon brought the offensive program to a halt by announcing that the United States unilaterally renounced biological warfare. In 1970 he expanded the declaration to include toxins. The United States destroyed its biological weapons in 1971–73 by heating or mixing them with caustic soda (sodium hydroxide).[33]

In 1969 the U.S. Army Medical Research Institute of Infectious Diseases (USAMRIID) was established at Fort Detrick to continue to develop means of defending U.S. troops. Since September 11, 2001, the United States has greatly increased its defensive research.

TESTING BIOLOGICAL WEAPONS

The history of testing biological weapons has at times been quite gruesome and cruel, most noticeably the experimentation the Japanese did during World War II. Below are highlights of the history of biological weapons testing in a number of nations that have or had biological warfare programs.

Iraq

Notes kept by Dr. Rihab Taha, who directed Iraq's biological weapons program, indicate that in 1990 Iraq field-tested botulinum toxin and spores of *Bacillus subtilis* at a facility 300 miles west of Baghdad. *Bacillus subtilis* is similar to anthrax but does not cause disease. The agents were successfully dispersed by 122-millimeter rockets, and the animals used in the test died from the botulinum in significant numbers. In a previous test, she noted, 250-kilogram aerial bombs successfully dispersed biological agents.[34]

Japan

In 1937 Japan established an offensive biological weapons program near Harbin in Manchuria, which Japan was occupying. Unit 731 of the Imperial Japanese Amy set up a laboratory complex. The complex, which also became known as Unit 731, consisted of 150 buildings and five satellite camps and employed more than 3,000 scientists and technicians. They experimented with anthrax, cholera, plague, typhoid, and other pathogens as potential weapons and tested them on prisoners, mostly Chinese, Koreans, Mongolians, and Russians. At least 10,000 prisoners died from disease or were executed after experimentation was completed.

Unit 731 also carried out field trials, which are scarcely distinguishable from outright attacks. At least 11 Chinese cities were subject to releases of biological agents. The first occurred on October 4, 1940, when Japan dropped wheat and fleas inflected with plague into the city of Chuhsien in Chekiang province. The wheat attracted rats, which were then bitten by the infected fleas. A month later, bubonic plague broke out in the area. The toll among Chinese residents of the area is not known.

Following Japan's surrender at the end of World War II, the director of the Japanese biological warfare program, General Ishii Shiro, ordered Unit 731 burned to the ground. The Western Allies did not arraign any member of Unit 731 to stand trial for war crimes, although 12 Japanese prisoners of war were tried in 1949 in the Soviet Union for use of biological weapons. The United States requested and obtained data from the Japanese scientists who had worked at Unit 731.[35]

Soviet Union

From the mid-1930s to the breakup of the Soviet Union, the Soviets tested bioweapons on the southern half of Vozrozhdeniye Island in the Aral Sea. There the Soviets routinely released into the air such lethal organisms as anthrax, brucellosis, plague, and smallpox in order to test the dissemination of aerosols and develop methods for detecting agents. Livestock and laboratory animals were the official targets, but reportedly fish kills and outbreaks of disease among humans in the area occurred. In 1988 the Soviets, trying to hide the fact that they had been stockpiling biological weapons, hastily buried on the island hundreds of tons of anthrax spores in stainless steel canisters. However, the Aral Sea is shrinking and the island is expected to become connected with the mainland eventually. U.S. authorities fear that the anthrax canisters may be leaking and that anthrax from the canisters, as well as other pathogens still on the island, will serve as a source of biological agents for potential users of bioweapons. The site is located in Uzbekistan and Kazakhstan, which refuse to take responsibility for the dump.

United Kingdom

In 1940 the British set up a "biology department" at the chemical weapons facility at Porton Down in Wiltshire. The team was made up of no more than 50 people but included American bacteriologists. The department chose Gruinard, a 522-acre island a few hundred yards from a remote portion of the northwest coast of Scotland for the testing. There in 1942 and 1943, scientists attacked sheep with bombs containing two types of anthrax. In 1946 the government had to acquire the island because it was still contaminated. The island was finally decontaminated in 1987 using 280 tons of a solution of formaldehyde and sea water.

United States

In the 1940s the United States set up two centers where at least some open-air testing of biological agents took place: Camp Detrick in Maryland, primarily a research and development center, and Dugway Proving Ground in Utah, primarily a test center. In addition, the United States cooperated with Canada and the United Kingdom on their testing programs.

Detrick was later enlarged. Among the additions was a hollow metal sphere four stories tall in which bioweapons were exploded. At Dugway, open-air testing involving human volunteers and animals took place. One of the army's tactics was releasing infected insects and other animals to determine whether they would spread the contamination through native populations.

The army tested biological simulants in North American cities. Biological simulants are organisms that are believed not to cause disease but that can be distributed in the same ways as biological agents. A device for spreading an agent can be tested by using it to spread a biological stimulant, for instance; the way that weather conditions affect the spread of an agent can be evaluated by releasing simulants under varying conditions. *Bacillus globigii* and *Serratia marcescens* were sprayed on San Francisco on various occasions between September 1950 and February 1951. The use of *Serratia marcescens* allegedly led to the death of one man, Edward J. Nevin, and the infection of 10 others. Relatives of Nevin later tried unsuccessfully to gain damages in court. In New York City between June 7 and 10, 1966, riders in the subways were exposed to *Bacillus subtilis.* The army wanted to learn whether disease could be spread by breaking globes containing the bacteria over the street-level ventilator grills for the subway system. Among the other cities where the population was subjected to simulants were Washington, D.C., and Winnipeg, Canada.[36] Because public health officials were not notified of the tests, they did not make any effort to evaluate their results. Although the simulants used were believed at the time to be harmless, researchers have since learned that they may develop into harmful strains that are resistant to antibiotics.

The United States also tested outside North America. A group of experiments was conducted off Johnson Atoll in the Pacific, for example. Planes released an agent, which drifted down to monkeys on barges below. Navy personnel in protective clothing monitored the effects. The monkeys usually died, and some navy personnel now claim that they have experienced illnesses because of the tests.

Controlling Biological Weapons

The two basic means of controlling biological weapons are an international ban, the Biological and Toxin Weapons Convention (BWC), and controls on exports, coordinated at the international level by an informal group of nations known as the Australia Group. The group was formed in 1984 to oppose the export of substances used in chemical weapons, but it began restricting exports related to bioweapons in 1993.

The Biological and Toxin Weapons Convention

Attempts to ban biological weapons go back to the Geneva Protocol of 1925. The protocol primarily concerned chemical weapons, but those adhering to the protocol agreed to extend its prohibition on chemical weapons "to the use of bacteriological methods of warfare." This protocol, which went into force in 1928, had severe limitations. It banned the use of chemical and biological agents in warfare, but it did not ban their development, production, or stockpiling; it also did not ban their use against nations that had not ratified the protocol.

Realizing the limitations of the protocol, a group of nations called the Eighteen-Nation Disarmament Committee met in Geneva between 1962 and 1968 to discuss abolition of nuclear, biological, and chemical weapons. In 1969 President Richard Nixon unilaterally renounced use of biological warfare by the United States. The announcement was in part a result of the Disarmament Committee meetings and of world opinion and in part a response to practical considerations—the United States could counter any biological weapons owned by small nations with its overwhelming nuclear force.

Nixon's decision gave renewed impetus to international disarmament negotiations. In 1972 the Conference of the Committee on Disarmament, which developed from the Eighteen-Nation Disarmament Committee, presented a convention on biological weapons to the United Nations General Assembly. After further discussion, a Convention on the Prohibition of the Development, Production and Stockpiling of Bacteriological (Biological) and Toxin Weapons and on Their Destruction (BWC) was opened for signature March 16, 1972. It entered into force on March 26, 1975, after it had been ratified by the United States and the Soviet Union.

State parties to the convention agree not to develop, produce, or stockpile biological agents or toxins and to destroy or divert to peaceful use those that they possess when they ratify the convention. However, the convention makes no provision for monitoring or verification, and, while it requests that members assist victim nations, it specifies no punishment for violators.

There is fairly widespread doubt as to whether all nations who have ratified or acceded to the BWC have declared and destroyed all their biological weapons. U.S. officials are uncertain about China, Iran, and North Korea, in particular. Syria, which has signed but not ratified or acceded to the BWC, may be seeking to establish a program.

To complicate matters, many nations that have ratified or acceded to the BWC do not participate fully in confidence-building measures established at a 1986 review conference. These nations either do not submit an annual report as requested or else submit an incomplete report.

Biodefense Research

It is even more difficult to identify a secret biological weapons program than it is to find a clandestine chemical weapons operation because, apart from the specific microorganism or toxin being weaponized, there are no telltale materials or equipment that are unique to a military program. Even the microorganisms and toxins themselves may well have civilian uses—for example, in preparing vaccines.

Adding to the problem, the line between defensive research and offensive research is very thin. The U.S. National Biodefense Analysis and Countermeasures

Center (NBACC) to be constructed at Fort Detrick, Maryland, will include a Biothreat Characterization Center, which has an agenda that gives the appearance of crossing that line. This agenda was described by Lieutenant Colonel George W. Korch, Jr., deputy director of NBACC, in a public lecture in 2004. He summarized the task areas for biothreat-agent analysis and technical-threat assessment at NBACC as "Acquire, Grow, Modify, Store, Stabilize, Package, Disperse." The center will characterize classical, emerging, and genetically engineered pathogens for their potential as biothreat agents. While doing so, it will undertake "computational modeling of feasibility, methods, and scale of production."[37]

The characterization of genetically engineered pathogens and research on their production could be understood to be part of a defensive program since, it could be argued, that a country cannot defend itself against agents with which it is unfamiliar. However, agents that are modified by genetic engineering for defensive purposes could at some point be given offensive roles. To Milton Leitenberg, Ambassador James Leonard, and Dr. Richard Spertzel, writing in an article in *Politics and the Life Sciences*, Korch's account of the tasks to be performed by the NBACC suggest offensive development of agents "in the guise of threat assessment."[38] Whatever the intentions of the center, foreign countries may interpret the words to indicate development of agents for weapons, a step forbidden by the BWC.

Biodefense research, as described by Korch, creates a risk that the United States will start a bioweapons arms race. If other nations fear that the United States is trying to develop new agents for offensive purposes, they may engage in offensive bioresearch to keep up. This may, in fact, already be occurring, as little is known about the research programs in biodefense in other countries. If the U.S. bioweapons defense program is operated in secrecy, it gives other nations, particularly Russia and China, which are likely to be interested in carrying on offensive programs, an excuse to maintain the secrecy of their bioweapons work. If it is conducted openly, it is likely to give other nations ideas for agents that can be used against the United States.

ARSENALS AND ONGOING PROGRAMS TODAY

Several nations are suspected of having either stockpiles of biological weapons (bioweapons) or offensive bioweapons programs, but proof is generally lacking. A summary of these nations follows. Please note that though Iraq has been proven to not have biological weapons or programs, it is discussed below because it was recently a suspect. Research that may cross the line between development of defensive measures and development of offensive weapons are discussed in the section on "Controlling Biological Weapons" on page 46.

Suspected Stockpiles or Offensive Weapons Programs in the Middle East

Iran: Iran entered upon a bioweapons program during the Iran-Iraq War in the 1980s. It has ratified the Biological and Toxin Weapons Convention (BWC), but

U.S. officials believe that Iran is still engaged in agent production and weaponization under the cover of its large pharmaceutical and biotech industries.

Iraq: Iraq began a bioweapons research program in the mid-1980s after it had obtained bacterial strains from abroad, in particular from a U.S. scientific supply company. In December 1990 it began filling missiles and aerial bombs with anthrax, aflatoxin, and botulinum toxin, and in January 1991 it deployed the missiles. A 1995 United Nations Special Commission (UNSCOM) report stated that agents in Iraq's biological weapons program included "lethal agents, eg anthrax, botulinum toxin and ricin, and incapacitating agents, eg aflatoxin, mycotoxins, haemorrhagic conjunctivitis virus and rotavirus."[39]

As a condition of the ceasefire ending the Gulf War, Iraq ratified the BWC. In April 1991 the United Nations formed UNSCOM to oversee the destruction of Iraq's biological and chemical weapons and production facilities and to monitor related activities. In December 1998 Iraq unilaterally ended the UNSCOM inspections. Renewed UN inspections took place in the months preceding the U.S. attack on Iraq, and the United States and its coalition partners searched for weapons during the war that began in March 2003. The United States abandoned the search for biological and chemical weapons late in 2004, as no evidence of their continued existence had been found.

Israel: Israel may have produced and stockpiled bioweapons agents. It certainly has the technical ability to do so, but no information is available in unclassified documents. Israel has not signed the BWC.

Egypt: According to a Congressional Research Service report, Egypt is known to have biological weapons, but Egyptian officials declare that the country has never produced or stockpiled them.[40]

Syria: Syria is thought to be possibly conducting weapons research programs, though not to have stockpiled agents. Both Egypt and Syria have signed but not ratified the BWC.

Suspected Stockpiles or Offensive Weapons Programs in Asia

China and North Korea: China and North Korea may have produced and stockpiled agents. Experts generally believe that North Korea has had some kind of bioweapons arsenal since the 1970s. The agents that North Korea has most likely produced are anthrax, botulism, and the plague. North Korea acceded to the BWC, and China signed it.

India and Pakistan: India and Pakistan are thought to be possibly conducting weapons research programs, though not to have stockpiled agents. Both are members of the BWC.

Soviet Union and Russia: The Soviet Union signed the BWC in 1972. Nevertheless, in the late 1980s U.S. and British authorities learned from defectors that the Soviets were carrying out a massive offensive biological weapons program, divided among some 50 institutions, under the cover name Biopreparat.

In April 1992 Russian president Boris Yeltsin promised to ban the development of bioweapons and to convert biowarfare installations to peaceful uses. A

Tripartite Agreement signed by Russia, the United States, and the United Kingdom allowed the Western nations to inspect Russian installations and vice versa. However, by 1994 Russia had stopped the on-site visits.

Russia is generally believed to have destroyed its offensive weapons, although the destruction is not subject to independent verification and stocks may remain. Russia reportedly holds thousands of samples of agents that could be used to grow new stocks, and it maintains facilities in which new stocks could be produced. Furthermore, the samples and the scientists who once worked on bioweapons represent a proliferation risk that may be more dangerous than the prospects of Russia's beginning to make offensive weapons again.

Other Nations with Offensive Biological Weapons Programs

Algeria may be conducting research on biological weapons, and Cuba has been reported to have a biological weapons capability. Furthermore, some nations with offensive programs may not have been identified. Weapons programs are difficult to detect because legitimate agricultural, industrial, and medical programs use equipment and materials that can serve military purposes.

DEFENSE METHODS FROM BIOLOGICAL WEAPONS

As the threat of biological warfare has increased, governments have poured money into defending their military and their citizens against bioweapons. Current methods range from detection of agents by means of strips of paper to inoculations against specific agents. More sophisticated techniques are under development. Meanwhile, controversy swirls around such steps in the United States as the government's plans to create new high-containment laboratories.

Methods of Detection and Defense in the Military

The U.S. military has developed systems for defending its troops against the effects of bioweapons. Troops entering situations in which they may be attacked by bioweapons are given protective inoculations and vaccinations before their deployment. They are likely also to be issued gas masks and protective suits.

A few techniques are available to detect bioweapons threats and thus alert troops (or other exposed personnel) to the need to wear protective gear. However, not all are suitable for a military situation. The most precise means of identifying biological agents is culturing—growing microbes on a surface that contains nutrients and studying the resulting colony with the eye or a microscope. This method is reliable and inexpensive but extremely slow. Identification is possible within 12–24 hours for most bacteria but may take more than a week for others.

Remote or standoff detection is the assessment of a biological agent by observing aerosolized masses or clouds from a distance. This may be done with Doppler radar, as in weather reporting, or with LIDAR (Light Detection and Ranging, or Laser Identification and Ranging), which bounces laser-generated high-energy light waves off a target. The U.S. Army's Short Range Biological Standoff Detection System (SR-BSDS), which employs both infrared LIDAR and ultraviolet light reflection, can determine whether an aerosol in a target cloud is biological in origin. In laboratory tests LIBS (Laser-Induced Breakdown Spectroscopy) systems have succeeded in differentiating among bacteriological species in aerosol clouds.

Point detectors necessitate physical contact between the agent and the detection instrument. An Aerosol Particle Sizer (APS) uses particle size and particle concentration to detect biological agents. After an APS detects the presence of an agent, techniques to distinguish among possible agents must be employed. The two basic approaches are immunoassays and genetic analyses.

Immunoassays imitate the body's immune system, which produces antibodies (highly specific proteins) in response to antigens from microbiological organisms. In the detection device an antibody recognizes the antigen that would have produced it in a human infection. An optical signal indicates a "hit." Handheld assay test kits using tickets or test strips are easy to use, but they generate many false responses. Simple ticket detectors are designed to identify only a single pathogen. More complex detectors may identify a variety of pathogens. The U.S. military's Biological Integrated Detection System (BIDS), which is furnished with an array of detectors, includes immunoassay tests for 10 agents.

In detectors based on genetics, DNA or RNA is taken from a sample and exposed to nucleic acid sequences (oligonucleotides) that correspond to selected biological agents. An optical signal indicates a "hit." DNA microarrays in the form of "chips," under study for detection, would compare the suspected agent to hundreds of oligonucleotides at one time.

Mass spectrometry is another detection technology. It fragments a sample of the suspected pathogen into progressively smaller charged pieces, ending with protein pieces. The charged fragments have different masses, which make possible physical differentiation, and the chemical groups have different fragment patterns that can be identified like fingerprints. For large molecules the prints must be compared with patterns in libraries of "fingerprints." If a sample is a mixture of agents, separation is required. This can be accomplished by chromatography, a technique that separates the mixture by slowly passing it through an adsorbing material. Gas chromatography is extremely sensitive, but the instruments are bulky and expensive.

Miniaturization and speed are great needs in detection technology. The above-noted BIDS is characterized as portable. Nevertheless, it weighs 135 pounds and requires reagents, warm-up time, and substantial power. When it travels it moves with a generator mounted on a vehicle.[41]

Defense of Civilians

Although the military must be equipped to defend itself against biological weapons, U.S. civilians may be more likely than the armed forces to be attacked by biological agents. The administration and Congress have both taken steps to prepare for such an attack.

Among the measures taken by federal agencies is Project Biowatch, a program to monitor the air in 31 cities for biological warfare agents. The system uses some 500 air filters that are collected every 12 hours. Genetic-based detection equipment then analyzes the filter content for pathogens.

The presidential directive Biodefense for the 21st Century, issued June 12, 2002, lists Project Biowatch and other accomplishments of the administration. As of that date, the administration had, among other things: "increased funding for bioterrorism research within the Department of Health and Human Services by thirty-fold"; "expanded the Strategic National Stockpile of medicines for treating victims of bioterror attacks, ensuring that the stockpiles . . . push packages. [sic] can be anywhere in the United States within 12 hours"; "stockpiled enough smallpox vaccine for every American, and vaccinated over 450,000 members of the armed services"; and "provided Federal funds to improve the capacities of state and local health systems to detect, diagnose, prevent, and respond to biological weapons attacks."

The "essential pillars" of the U.S. national biodefense program, as outlined in the presidential directive, are "Threat Awareness, Prevention and Protection, Surveillance and Detection, and Response and Recovery." For each of these pillars the directive refers to "aims and objectives for further progress."[42]

Congress, at the urging of the administration, has passed several laws related to biodefense: the Patriot Act; the Public Health Security and Bioterrorism Preparedness and Response Act, known as the Bioterrorism Act; the Homeland Security Act; and the Project Bioshield Act.

A report by the Chemical and Biological Arms Control Institute (CBACI), *Fighting Biotorrism: Tracking and Assessing U.S. Government Programs* (2004), finds that, despite the administration's program and the new legislation, much remains to be done. According to the report, Biodefense for the 21st Century "is an important step in the right direction" but is not a "comprehensive and integrative strategy." Furthermore, the plan "fails to spell out the means for meeting [its] objectives or the metrics for measuring progress." Too much emphasis is put on technology, according to this analysis, and not enough on preparing people and infrastructure. The budget for bioprevention and biopreparedness is not clear. Furthermore, the report states, "public health response systems are still deemed by experts both in and out of government to be incapable of coping successfully with a major bioterrorist attack."[43]

Points made by the CBACI have also been made by others concerned about the federal biodefense program. Some scientists have charged that the government is investing in research without thoroughly evaluating what is needed, and some hospital personnel complain that hospitals are not receiving the financial resources that they must have if they are to prepare for their role in response to an attack.

CBACI recommends several changes in bioprevention and biopreparedness policy, with the emphasis on placing funding on "a more stable and coordinated platform." The nation would benefit from the administration's sending to Congress a single Congressional Justification document that recommends amounts to be spent in the five following years; Congress's appropriating funding for a five-year period, with a "budget wall" around biodefense spending; and the authorities' paying greater attention "to the structure, timing, and coordination of state and local biodefense grant programs."[44]

Controversial Research Laboratories

A point of public controversy in regard to the U.S. biodefense program is the increase in the number of biodefense laboratories, particularly Level 4 National Biocontainment Laboratories (BL-4), which are required for handling the most dangerous biological agents. Four BL-4 laboratories already exist. The Department of Health and Human Services is planning at least six new ones, including facilities at the University of Texas Medical Branch at Galveston and at Boston University. It is also planning up to nine BL-3 regional laboratories. Furthermore, the Department of Energy (DOE) proposed constructing BL-3 laboratories at Livermore National Laboratory and Los Alamos National Laboratory, and various universities are also developing their own research programs related to biodefense.

As the result of litigation, DOE withdrew its proposal for the Los Alamos laboratory. Around at least the Boston site of a BL-4 laboratory and Lawrence Livermore National Laboratory, citizens are, as of 2005, fighting the new laboratories by lawsuits and other means. They maintain that the need for them is unproven and that vaccines developed today may be useless against pathogens modified by genetic engineering. Furthermore, it is argued, the facilities create health risks to their neighboring populations. Some leading biological scientists have questioned the advisability of the proposed laboratories.

Mistakes do occur. Pathogens occasionally leak out or are mistakenly released, as happened in 2004 when the Southern Research Institute apparently sent "live anthrax instead of killed germs" by mistake to the Children's Hospital Oakland Research Institute.[45] Moreover, someone with ill intent may utilize a laboratory to acquire dangerous pathogens. Peter Gilligan, a professor at the Medical School of the University of North Carolina, who has worked on U.S. biodefense strategies, stated in 2004 that from all he knows the anthrax used in a terrorist attack in the United States in 2001 was "a strain that was once in a governmental lab."[46]

The financial outlay is also an important issue. Biodefense research is expensive. Many say that society needs to debate fully how much it wants to spend on vaccines and research on rare illnesses and how much on defeating more common illnesses. Furthermore, the most expensive answer may not be the best even in terms of bioterror. Simple face masks "can filter out most biological agents," but supplying them to the public is apparently not under consideration.[47]

CHEMICAL WEAPONS

A chemical agent is a substance intended to kill, injure, or incapacitate a target population by means of its physiological effect. A chemical weapon combines an agent with a means of delivery. Agents can be described in terms of lethality (likelihood that they will cause death), mode of action (route of exposure, usually through the lungs or the skin), speed of action, toxicity (the amount required to kill), persistency (the length of time the agent remains potent after delivery), and state (whether a solid, liquid, or gas). Most agents are stored and delivered in the form of liquid.

A chemical warfare system needs to generate aerosols (solid or liquid particles suspended in air) from the liquid. Although particles one to five microns in size are most likely to be deposited in the lungs (a micron is one thousandth of a millimeter), particles of 10 microns or more may poison through the linings to the respiratory tract. Means of delivery range from simple cylinders, open to the wind, to cruise and ballistic missiles. Compounds are likely to be added to the agent to stabilize it or to increase the range of temperatures at which it is active.

Below are the basic characteristics of various types of chemical agents. The first four types (choking agents, blister agents, blood agents, and nerve agents) were produced for use in war. The last two types (incapacitating agents and riot-control agents) may be used in war but were developed primarily for use in domestic law enforcement.

The choking agents cause pulmonary edema (retention of fluid in the lungs), asphyxiating the victim in his or her own fluids. The best-known substances, chlorine and phosgene, are used in many industrial processes and are relatively abundant and inexpensive. They are delivered as gases and are not persistent. Chlorine is a greenish yellow gas with a strong odor at room temperature. In the lungs it mixes with moisture to form hydrochloric acid and hypochlorous acid. Phosgene is almost odorless and reacts more slowly than chlorine. Victims may die as much as 24 hours after exposure.

Blister agents are more likely to be used to injure opponents or to cause them to have to wear protective clothing than to kill them. The best known are the mustards and lewisite. Mustard generally kills only a small percentage of its victims. They suffer serious skin damage, temporary or permanent blindness, and damage to the upper respiratory system. It is a yellow-brown, oily liquid when prepared crudely; it is colorless and odorless when pure. Lewisite was manufactured in large quantities but seldom used, and relatively little is known about its effect on humans. The blister agents, like the choking agents, were used in World War I.

Blood agents poison by blocking the use of oxygen or the uptake of oxygen from the blood. Thus they in effect asphyxiate victims. They are highly volatile. Hydrogen cyanide, or prussic acid, was the active ingredient in Zyklon B, used by the Nazis to kill prisoners in the gas chambers of their concentration camps. Arsine, derived from arsenic, is a colorless gas that was studied for use in World War I but that has been little used because of its volatility and chemical instability.

Nerve agents, which were developed just before and during World War II, act by inhibiting the action of acetylcholinesterase throughout the body. This enzyme normally hydrolizes acetylcholine. When the enzyme is inhibited, acetylcholine accumulates, and muscles, including those in the respiratory system, cannot contract and relax normally. Paralysis of the respiratory musculature causes death. Exposure can occur both through the lungs and through the skin. Death may occur in a few minutes, but severe symptoms may not appear for several hours. The V agents (VE, VG, VM, VX) are more lethal and more persistent than the G agents (GA [tabun], GB [sarin], GD [soman], GE, and GF). If 10–15 milligrams of VX (much less than a drop) is placed on the skin of a man of average weight, he will die unless he receives treatment. VX has been applied to roads to block their use for days or weeks. The G and the V agents are related to the organophosphate pesticides.

Incapacitants are designed to prevent temporarily the victims from acting effectively by calming, disorienting, or even paralyzing them. Ideally an incapacitant does not kill or cause permanent injury, produces effects that last for hours or days, and allows for recovery without medical treatment. It should also be potent and easy to store. In practice, incapacitants generally kill a percentage of the victims because different people respond differently to chemicals. They are particularly dangerous in confined areas. As of 2002 the only incapacitant known to have been weaponized for use on the battlefield was BZ (3-quinuclidinyl benzilate), one of the compounds derived from a poisonous plant in the nightshade family called belladonna.

The three main classes of riot-control agents are lacrimators (eye irritants or tear gas), sternutators (an extreme form of tear gas that produces a copious flow of fluids), and vomiting agents (agents that cause pain in the eyes, nose, and throat and, as the name indicates, induce vomiting). All have been used in combat.

History of Chemical Weapons Use

Ingenious uses of what could be called chemical weapons date from before the time of Jesus Christ. In 429 B.C. during the Peloponnesian War, for example, the Spartans at Plataia burned pitch and sulphur to create toxic fumes, and in 80 B.C. the Roman general Quintus Sertorius defeated the Characitani of Spain by piling up caustic soil in front of the caves where they lived.

The first massive use of chemical weapons, however, did not occur until World War I. In 1914 the French attacked the Germans with grenades containing tear gas, and the Germans responded with artillery shells also carrying the gas. Then on April 22, 1915, the Germans used chlorine gas against the French at Ypres. From there the employment of chemical agents escalated. Phosgene mixtures and mustard came into use, and the British, Russians, and Americans joined in the chemical combat. According to some estimates, a total of 1.3 million people were killed or injured by chemical warfare agents.[48]

During the Russian civil war, which followed World War I, the British employed adamsite against the Bolsheviks. Then in the 1920s the British attacked Kurdish villages in Iraq with poison gas in order to demoralize the Kurds, who were resisting the British invasion of Iraq. In 1922 in Spanish Morocco, the Spanish began attacking the Rif rebels with chemical weapons, a practice that continued into 1927.

Japan began producing chemical warfare agents on Okunoshima Island in 1928 or 1929. It used tear gas in 1930 to crush a rebellion in central Taiwan, which at the time belonged to Japan. In 1931 Japan invaded Manchuria, where it attacked soldiers and Chinese civilians with biological and chemical weapons, including phosgene and mustard.

The Italians used mustard gas against Abyssinians in an invasion of their country (now Ethiopia), which began in October 1935. As punishment the League of Nations initiated a partial embargo against Italy.

During World War II the Allies and Germany possessed large stocks of chemical weapons, but the only known use of chemical weapons between combatants in that war were the attacks by the Japanese against the Chinese. They began in 1937 and continued until at least 1942 and, according to a Soviet source, numbered more than 1,000.[49] The United States suffered casualties in December 1943 when the Germans attacked a U.S. ship loaded with mustard bombs off Bari, Italy. Eighty-three men died in the poisoned water. Beginning in 1942, the Germans employed Zyklon B (hydrocyanic acid) in gas chambers to kill prisoners in their concentration camps.

In the 1950s in their war against insurgents in Malaya, the British applied herbicides to clear vegetation along their lines of communication and to destroy crops. The use set a precedent for the Vietnam War, during which the United States, in addition to using tear gas, applied to vegetation the plant growth regulators Agent Orange, Agent White, and Agent Blue. Agent Orange and Agent White both contained 2,4-D. Agent Blue was an organic arsenic compound. The Agent Orange was contaminated by dioxin. The United States also employed a napalm-like incendiary in Vietnam, but incendiaries are not generally considered to be chemical weapons.

During Egyptian intervention in the Royalist and Republican civil war in Yemen, Egyptians used chemical weapons (phosgene and mustard gas) as early as 1963. Journalists reported a chemical attack in 1967 in Yemen, which resulted in more than 100 fatalities. The source of the chemical agents has been variously reported as the United Kingdom and the Soviet Union.

In 1983 Iraq began using chemical weapons (mustard gas), against Iran in the Iran-Iraq War. The following year Iraq employed tabun against Iran, the first use in war of a nerve agent. By 1986, Iran was attacking Iraq with chemical weapons. On March 16–17, 1988, after the Iran-Iraq War, Iraq used mustard gas, nerve agents, and possibly hydrogen cyanide against the Kurdish city of Halabja. The people had sympathized with Iran in the war. Hundreds of people died. When Iraq invaded Kuwait in 1990, it still had stockpiles of chemical weapons, but it elected not to use them in the Gulf War.

Other instances of chemical weapons use occurred in the 1980s and 1990s. Vietnam reportedly employed hydrogen cyanide and phosgene in Cambodia in 1985. Libya reportedly used chemical weapons against Chadian troops in Chad in 1987–88.

The most widely recognized chemical weapons attack in recent years was a terrorist attack with poisonous gas in the Tokyo subway system the morning of March 20, 1995. Members of the Aum Shinrikyo religious cult, which believes in Armageddon, had put containers of sarin that they had made themselves into rail cars. Between 5,000 and 6,000 people were exposed to the nerve agent. Twelve people died and several people suffered permanent brain damage. The cult had already mounted an earlier attack; in June 1994, they had dispersed sarin in the city of Matsumoto to the west of Tokyo. Three hundred people were exposed; seven people died.

On October 26, 2002, a calmative gas (one designed to induce unconsciousness or semiconsciousness as opposed to death) was used by the Russian authorities with disastrous results. Chechen rebels had taken hostage the audience in a Moscow theater. In an attempt to capture the rebels without their having the opportunity to kill their hostages, Russian special forces pumped what was reportedly a derivative of fentanyl into the theater. The hostages as well as the rebels were overcome by the gas and more than 110 hostages died as a result.

Development and Production of Chemical Weapons in the United States

Chemical factories that existed before World War I were the primary source of the chemical agents used by the combatants in that war. Most of the agents could, in fact, be produced on a large scale using the equipment and techniques normally used to make dye. It is no coincidence that the first country to employ chemical weapons in modern warfare was Germany and that Germany had by far the world's largest chemical industry. The chlorine gas employed by the Germans at Ypres in April 1915 came from the concentration of chemical companies in the Ruhr known as the Interessen Gemeinshaft (I.G.). The British had to scramble to catch up with the Germans, and the British war effort became the basis after the war of the Imperial Chemical Industries. Large factories devoted to chemical weapons were constructed in Europe and Asia in the years preceding and during World War II. They included a phosgene factory at Clemency in France, a mustard gas factory at Sutton Oak in England, and factories at Brandyuzhsky, Karaganda, and Kuibyshev in the Soviet Union.

By the time the United States entered World War I, in April 1917, poison gas was being heavily employed on the battlefield. The nation therefore knew the importance of chemical weapons from the outset of its engagement. It established a "Gas Service" as a branch of the American Expeditionary Force in France. This service became the U.S. Army Chemical Warfare Service (CWS); in 1946 it was renamed the Chemical Corps. In June 1918 the United States used gas for the first time in combat. By the end of the war the American First Gas Regiment had employed phosphorous incendiaries and poison gas in some 200 actions.[50]

It also constructed Edgewood Arsenal in Maryland to produce as well as to develop chemical agents. By the end of World War I, Edgewood Arsenal included 218 production buildings and could manufacture 200,000 chemical bombs and shells a day.[51] Between World Wars I and II, the United States produced chemical agents—chlorine, chloropicrin, phosgene, and mustard gas—and accumulated mortars, chemical shells, and portable cylinders.

During World War II the United States manufactured more than 146,000 tons of chemical agents. Nevertheless, President Franklin D. Roosevelt announced a "no–first use" policy, and, like the other combatants, the United States did not use chemical weapons.

The United States in the 1950s concentrated on the weaponization of sarin and the development of cluster bombs to deliver sarin by air. It also began work on VX, a viscous liquid, and in the 1960s developed means of delivering this nerve agent with artillery and rockets. The precursors for sarin and soman were produced at a factory built at Muscles Shoals, Alabama, in 1953. The nerve agents themselves were produced at the Rocky Mountain Arsenal in Denver, Colorado.

The U.S. offensive chemical weapons program ostensibly stopped in 1969 as a result of Public Law 91-121, which restricted the testing, transportation, storage, and disposal of chemical weapons; President Richard Nixon's reaffirmation of Roosevelt's "no–first use" policy; and the submission of the Geneva Protocol to the Senate for ratification. However, the Chemical Corps occupied itself with herbicides, napalm-like incendiaries, and riot-control agents, all of which the United States used in Vietnam.

In 1985 President Ronald Reagan ended the United States's unilateral moratorium on the development and production of offensive chemical weapons. The Chemical Corps concentrated on binary weapons. In 1987 it started production of a binary artillery shell in which the precursors difluor (DF) and isopropyl alcohol mixed in flight to become 70 percent sarin.

The U.S. chemical weapons program came to an official end when Congress passed the Department of Defense Authorization Act of 1986, requiring the destruction of the U.S. chemical weapons stockpile. The United States ratified the Chemical Weapons Convention in 1997.

TESTING CHEMICAL WEAPONS

Chemical weapons, like biological weapons, have been tested extensively, in laboratories and in the field, on volunteers and on unwitting victims. Many details of U.S. programs are still classified, but below are some instances of testing by the United States and its allies.

United States

Early tests took place at Edgewood Arsenal in Maryland, later combined with the Aberdeen Proving Ground to form the Edgewood Chemical Activity (ECA) Aberdeen Proving Ground. In 1942 the United States established Dugway Proving Ground in Utah for testing both biological and chemical weapons. The site, which now totals almost 800,000 acres, is still used for defensive chemical and biological tests. It may be most familiar to the public for a test that went awry. In 1969 VX released from a plane drifted 27 miles to Skull valley, where it killed some 6,000 sheep.

To learn how effective chemical weapons would be in climate extremes, the United States tested them at Fort Greely, Alaska; Camp Tuto, Greenland; and Fort Clayton in the Panama Canal Zone, among other places. With the intention of preparing to attack with chemicals the Japanese occupying Pacific islands during World War II, the United States heavily used San José Island off the coast of Panama for chemical weapons testing. Between 1944 and 1947, with the support of Canada and the United Kingdom, the United States secretly detonated or dropped some 31,000 phosgene and mustard gas bombs and other chemical weapons on San José Island. The Fellowship of Reconciliation, after a study of government records, estimates that one in 10 bombs, or more than 3,000 weapons, remain on the island undetonated.[52]

Behavior-altering drugs were tested on individuals from World War II onward. For example, in a secret Central Intelligence Agency (CIA) program code-named "MKULTRA," a physician reportedly gave drug addicts LSD and then noted the effects of the drug.[53]

Between 1963 and 1969 in Project SHAD (Shipboard Hazards and Defense), the United States subjected sailors on certain ships to biological and chemical agents, including the nerve gases VX and sarin. The U.S. Department of Defense acknowledged the existence of the project in 2002 after the Veterans Administration had begun studying the medical histories of SHAD veterans.

United Kingdom

Porton Down in England was the center of British testing. Before 1953, 1,500 servicemen volunteered for tests of nerve agents. One of them died after a drop of GB liquid was applied to his forearm and covered to prevent evaporation. During World War II Britain conducted field tests in Australia, India, and Canada. After the war, when India was no longer a colony, it moved its tropical testing to Obanokoro, Nigeria.

Canada

Canada has not manufactured chemical weapons, but in 1947 it entered into what was known as the Tripartite Agreement on chemical weapons with the United Kingdom and the United States. The main contribution of Canada to the program was allowing field trials to take place in a large expanse of prairie near Suffield. In return, Canada received research results.

Australia and New Zealand

The British tested gas agents in Australia during World War II. The arrangement ended after the war, but in 1965 Australia entered into a Technical Cooperation Program with the United Kingdom, Canada, and the United States. The director of Porton Down claimed in 1980 that Britain and the United States tested chemical weapons equipment in Australia and New Zealand.

CONTROLLING CHEMICAL WEAPONS USE

Attempts to control chemical weapons date back to the 19th century. Neverthless, despite promises by the major powers to refrain from using these weapons, they were employed on a large scale in World War I and were used sporadically in other 20th-century conflicts. A treaty banning chemical weapons, the Chemical Weapons Convention, was not opened for signature until 1993, and even today implementation of this treaty is beset with problems.

The Chemical Weapons Convention

At the invitation of Czar Nicholas II of Russia, 26 nations came together at The Hague, in the Netherlands, in the International Peace Conference of 1899, now known as the First Hague Conference. A Second Hague Conference, the International Peace Conference of 1907, followed. The conferences resulted in several declarations in regard to chemical warfare, though not all the declarations were signed by all participants. A declaration in 1899, signed and ratified by Germany but not by the United States, included a pledge to "Abstain from the use of projectiles the sole object of which is the diffusion of asphyxiating or deleterious gases." A convention from the 1906 conference stated, "It is expressly forbidden . . . to employ poisons or poisonous weapons."[54]

At the close of World War I, in which some 124,000 tons of chemical agents were released, the Allies banned Germany from producing chemical weapons. At a Conference for the Limitation of Naval Armament in 1921 in Washington, D.C., known now as the Washington Arms Conference of 1922, the participants (France, Great Britain, Italy, Japan, and the United States) made an unsuccessful attempt to reach an agreement not to engage in chemical warfare. The next attempt to limit chemical warfare came at the 1925 Geneva Conference.

The Geneva Conference was convened in May 1925 under the auspices of the League of Nations to limit international trade in conventional weapons. Led by the United States, the delegates agreed, however, to work on the issue of poison gas, and, after a month of debate, the representatives of 38 nations signed on June 17 what is known as the Geneva Protocol, a ban on "the use in war of asphyxiating, poisonous or other gases" and the "use of bacteriological methods of warfare." The ban only extended to the first use of chemical and biological weapons and did not prevent nations from producing or stockpiling them. Nevertheless, while the respective governments were in the process of ratifying the treaty, an anti-gas lobby went to work. Japan did not ratify the treaty until 1970 and the United States not until 1974. Most of the nations that ratified early on added reservations. Belgium, for example, said that the protocol was only binding on Belgium in regard to nations that had signed or ratified the treaty or might accede to it in the future.

During the cold war, disarmament advocates largely concerned themselves with nuclear weapons. The first significant discussion of new agreements to ban chemical weapons did not take place until after the signing of the Biological and Toxin Weapons Convention in 1972. At UN disarmament conferences in Geneva in the seventies, Japan and the United Kingdom proposed initiatives. The main issue of contention in the 1970s and in the 1980s was on-site inspections to verify compliance. A treaty was not possible until both the United States and Russia were able to accept verification procedures. A Chemical Weapons Convention finally went into force in 1997.

The Chemical Weapons Convention (CWC) forbids the "development, production, acquisition, retention, stockpiling, transfer and use of all chemical weapons." It also requires destruction of existing weapons under an agreed upon timetable. Member states must declare their chemical weapons stockpiles and destroy them within 10 years of the treaty's entry into force, that is by 2007. Furthermore, they must destroy or convert to civilian use their chemical weapons production facilities, and they must get rid of chemical weapons that they abandoned in foreign countries. Weapons must be destroyed by methods that do not harm the environment or human health. The last marks a major break with the past, as the United States, United Kingdom, Japan, and other nations disposed of thousands of tons of weapons into the ocean.

The CWC is a stronger treaty than the BWC. Unlike the earlier treaty, the CWC provides for inspection and monitoring. Nevertheless, the treaty is not perfect. There are no stated punishments for nations that violate its provisions, and implementation is proving to be difficult. Four of the problem areas and an aspect of the convention that is causing controversy are discussed below.

Problem Areas Adoption of national laws is proving to be a stumbling block. Member states are required to adopt comprehensive national laws to criminalize the possession and use of chemical weapons. As of 2004 less than 40 percent of the member states had done so.

Another is reports of CWC-related activities. Many members are not submitting timely and accurate declarations of their activities. France is a case in point. Its annual declarations are incomplete and lack transparency.

Verification is a third problem area. The CWC affects the private sector greatly, the U.S. State Department has pointed out, because the United States produces and uses for civilian purposes various chemicals that can be used to produce chemical weapons. The CWC must therefore monitor commercial facilities that produce or use dual-use chemicals to be sure that they are not diverted to military purposes.

The Organisation for the Prohibition of Chemical Weapons (OPCW) has established what the Government Accountability Office (GAO) calls "a credible inspections regime." However, it needs to carry out more inspections than it has the money to finance. Between April 1997 and December 2003 more than half of OPCW inspections took place at military facilities, although commercial facilities may pose a greater proliferation risk. At 167 of 190 declared military sites, 965 inspections were carried out. At 514 of 5,460 commercial facilities, only 634 inspections were carried out. The OPCW is trying to find "more efficient and cost-effective means" of conducting inspections in order to meet the need.

Destruction of chemical weapons is a fourth area in which the CWC is having difficulty. As of December 2004 member states had declared 71,373,000 metric tons of chemical agents worldwide, but only 10,350,000 metric tons of these agents had been destroyed. The agents had been declared by six states. Albania, India, and an unnamed nation were expected to finish destruction of their stockpiles by 2007, and Libya intended to destroy the 23 metric tons of weapons that it declared in 2004, although the destruction schedule was not known.[55] The United States and Russia, who together owned more than 95 percent of the world's declared stockpile, pose a bigger problem. Nations can request a five-year extension to 2012 of the destruction deadline, but any additional request must be approved by all members of the OPCW. The GAO does not believe that either the United States or Russia will finish destroying its stocks by 2012.

United States In 1986 Congress made the U.S. Army responsible for the destruction of U.S. chemical weapons, and in 1995 it forbade the transportation of chemical stockpile munitions across state lines. This meant that the weapons at each storage site must be destroyed in place. The army's Chemical Materials Agency (CMA) operates three programs designed to eliminate the nation's chemical weapons.

The Chemical Stockpile Disposal Program disposes of the agents at Anniston, Alabama; Pine Bluff, Arkansas; Umatilla, Oregon; and Tooele, Utah, sites and has destroyed those at Johnston Island in the Pacific Ocean, using incineration. As of March 2004, Tooele had reduced its stockpile by 47.1 percent, Anniston by 5.1 percent, and Aberdeen by 7.9 percent. Destruction had not yet begun at Umatilla. Initially the army intended to incinerate weapons at every site. However, intense public pressure forced the army to look for alternatives to what the public perceived as a hazardous procedure.

The Alternative Technology and Approaches Program (ATAP) develops alternative approaches. As a result, at the Newport, Indiana, and Edgewood, Missouri, sites, which only store agents in bulk containers, the chemicals will be neutralized by hydrolysis of the agent in water or in sodium hydroxide solution.

The Non-Stockpile Chemical Material Program (NSCMP) disposes of non-stockpile chemical material, using advanced methods that it is developing. The program is already employing assessment systems that allow operators to determine the contents of a weapon without opening it and using mobile treatment systems. The latter include the Explosive Destruction System to destroy chemical-filled, explosively configured munitions and the Rapid Response System to neutralize the contents of Chemical Agent Identification Sets, equipment used to train soldiers and civilians in identification of chemical agents.

An Assembled Chemical Weapons Alternatives (ACWA) program exists within the Department of Defense (DOD) to identify and demonstrate alternatives to incineration for use at the stockpiles in Pueblo, Colorado, and Richmond, Kentucky. This program, which DOD must manage separately from the army, was mandated by Congress in 1996. At Pueblo and Richmond, destruction plants are still in the design stage.

The GAO reports that management problems are in part to blame for the delays. The program is complex, "with multiple lines of authority within the Army and the separation of program components between the Army and DOD." There is no "overarching, comprehensive management strategy." Other causes of delay are incidents during operations, difficulty in obtaining environmental permits, and "unfunded requirements." People living near the sites fear that the weapons will leak deadly gas. They are also afraid of accidents during destruction.

Russia As of September 2003 Russia had destroyed only 1.1 percent of its estimated 40,000 tons of chemical munitions and had only one operating destruction facility. At that time the United States had destroyed 24 percent of its stockpile. The Russian effort is dependent on international funding. The GAO accuses Russia of not having "a credible" weapons destruction plan and of not having worked out a detailed budget and schedule. Meanwhile, Russia's chemical weapons arsenal is not secure and is vulnerable to theft or diversion.

Russia differs from the United States and the OPCW in its definition of destruction. The last two believe that destruction must be irreversible. If agents are neutralized, the resulting hazardous waste must be properly disposed. The OPCW inspects both the neutralization stage and final processing of the waste. Russia contends that weapons should be considered destroyed after neutralization takes place; the toxic waste does not require processing, as the cost to convert the waste into weapons again would be prohibitive.[56]

Japan Japan has no stocks of chemical weapons to declare, but it does have weapons. Although after World War II the military threw most of its nerve agents into the water, remaining weapons have turned up on land in Japan and in China. A total of between 700,000 and 2 million chemical munitions abandoned by Japan remain in China today, and an estimated 2,000 Chinese have been victims of discarded weapons.[57] Japan is gradually retrieving and destroying the weapons, but China would like the program accelerated.

Riot-Control Agents and Incapacitating Agents, a Controversial Subject

Article I of the CWC states that state parties must not prepare to use or use riot-control agents such as tear gas "as a method of warfare," and Article II bans chemicals that "cause incapacitation" except for certain purposes including "law enforcement." Nevertheless, some parties are using or preparing to use riot-control agents and calmatives in military situations. The United States is a case in point.

Under the coordination of the Department of Defense's Joint Non-Lethal Weapons Directorate (JNLWD), created in 1997 to study alternative weapons for low-intensity conflicts, the United States is carrying out research on what are called nonlethal weapons. These weapons include toxic chemical agents such as anesthetics and psychoactive substances, often referred to as "calmatives" or "incapacitants." JNLWD is also developing means of delivery for these chemicals.[58]

The United States blocked discussion of incapacitants at the first CWC review conference in 2003. Furthermore, it appears to be integrating incapacitants into military policy. In 2002 the National Research Council of the National Academy of Sciences released a study that recommended use of nonlethal weapons by the U.S. Navy and development of such weapons for other branches of the service. Among the many weapons it mentions as under study is a sponge projectile with a calmative.[59]

Executive Order 11850, signed by President Gerald Ford on March 29, 1975, allowed the use of riot agents in battle, with advance presidential approval, against human shields during rescue missions, and to save troops from a mob. President George W. Bush has authorized U.S. troops to use tear gas in the war in Iraq, apparently at the discretion of the combatant commander.[60]

Advocates of the use of riot-control agents and calmatives in combat state that these substances will save lives and facilitate the United States' accomplishment of its mission. Critics fear that they will contribute to the undermining of the CWC. Whether or not U.S. research on nonlethal weapons to control hostile crowds is illegal under the CWC—and "as a method of warfare" is not defined in the treaty—it is "at least so close to the borderline as to be destabilizing," arms-control expert Malcolm Dando has stated.[61]

Export Controls

There are also controls set up to limit the exporting of chemical weapons. Under the U.S. Export Administration Act of 1979, the president can control the export of chemicals and equipment that "would assist the government of any foreign country in acquiring the capability to develop, produce, stockpile, deliver, or use chemical or biological weapons."

The Australia Group is an informal group of nations formed to help stop the spread of chemical weapons. Members share information on suspicious activities, coordinate national export controls, and control chemical weapons precursors and, since 1993, certain biological pathogens. As of 2002 their "warning list" included 54 items, many of them dual-use substances not on the CWC's schedules.

ARSENALS AND ONGOING PROGRAMS TODAY

Chemical weapons and chemical weapons programs appear to be more widespread than biological weapons and programs. They are, in fact, often described as the poor nations' counter to nuclear weapons. A list of known arsenals follows. Iraq and Libya are listed below because they recently moved out of the list of suspects.

Stockpiles in Russia and the United States

Soviet Union/Russia: The Soviet Union maintained a strong chemical weapons capability from the end of World War I through the cold war. The stockpile in Russia today is estimated to amount to almost 40,000 metric tons, stored at seven sites. Approximately 81 percent is in the form of nerve agents, including sarin, soman, and VX. Approximately 19 percent is composed of blistering agents, including lewisite, mustard, and mixtures of the two. The agents are stored in munitions containers, such as bombs and spray devices, or in bulk storage containers. Russia ratified the Chemical Weapons Convention (CWC), a treaty aimed at abolishing chemical weapons, in 1997, but as of September 2003, it had destroyed only about 1.1 percent of its chemical arsenal. Although Kazakhstan has ratified the CWC, it reportedly retained chemical weapons stockpiles from the Soviet era.

United States: When the United States, around 1990, stopped producing chemical weapons, it had a stockpile of approximately 31,500 tons of chemical agents, which is now undergoing destruction. As of March 2004 an estimated 8,692 tons (27.6 percent) had been destroyed; an estimated 22,809 tons remain.[62]

The stockpile is composed of unitary (as opposed to binary) chemical munitions (various land mines, projectiles, and rockets) and bulk items containing blister agents and nerve agents (VX and GB). About 60 percent of the nerve agents are in bulk storage containers and the remaining 40 percent in munitions, most of them obsolete. A stockpile at Johnston Atoll in the Pacific Ocean has been destroyed. Eight sites still store portions of the stockpile. As of April 2004 the distribution was as follows: Tooele, Utah, 7,216 tons of mustard, VX, and sarin; Anniston, Alabama, 2,141 tons of mustard, VX, and sarin; Hermiston, Oregon, 3,717 tons of mustard, VX, and sarin; Pine Bluff, Arkansas, 3,850 tons of mustard, VX, and sarin; Newport, Indiana, 1,269 tons of VX; Edgewood, Maryland, 1,511 tons of mustard; Pueblo, Colorado, 2,611 tons of mustard; Richmond, Kentucky, 523 tons of VX and sarin.[63]

Not part of the unitary stockpile declared in 1986 is what is known as non-stockpile chemical materiel. This materiel, which is not included in the above figures, consists of binary chemical weapons (in each weapon, the chemicals are in two compartments and are mixed during delivery), former production facilities, and various chemical warfare materiel, including ampoules, drums, and other containers of chemical agent or industrial chemicals. The non-stockpile materiel is located on active or former military bases. Much of it is buried in scattered sites, as burial used to be considered an acceptable means of disposal.

Stockpiles in the Middle East

Egypt: Egypt, the first Arab nation to use chemical weapons, is believed likely to still possess a chemical weapons capability.[64] Author Eric Croddy states that the evidence suggests that Egypt can produce its own weapons, from raw materials to finished product. Egypt has justified chemical weapons as a counter to Israel's nuclear weapons. It has not signed the CWC.

Iran: Although Iran is a member of the CWC, the U.S. State Department believes that Iran has not declared the full extent of its chemical weapons program. Researchers suspect that Iran has a stockpile of a variety of chemical weapons, including blister agents and nerve agents.

Iraq: Among the Arab states, Iraq once had the largest arsenal of chemical weapons, including mustard, lewisite, and nerve agents, but it apparently destroyed them between the Gulf War and the U.S. invasion of Iraq.

Israel: Israel is believed to be capable of producing chemical weapons, but whether it has a chemical weapons stockpile and, if so, what weapons it contains are not known.[65]

Saudi Arabia: According to unconfirmed reports, Saudi Arabia has developed chemical weapons.

Sudan: Sudan acceded to the CWC. Nevertheless, according to the U.S. director of Central Intelligence, it has been developing a chemical weapons capability. The U.S. Department of State does not believe that Sudan fully declared its chemical weapons program.

Syria: Syria has what Croddy characterizes as a "formidable CW capability." Chemical weapons, including nerve and mustard gases, are reportedly produced at facilities near Damascus and Homs and at Aleppo. Syria has reportedly developed cluster bomblets carrying chemical weapons for long-range Scud missiles and it arms Scud-B missiles, which have a range of only 300 kilometers, with VX and sarin. Like Israel, Syria has not signed the CWC.

Stockpiles in Asia

China: When it ratified the CWC, China declared the existence of production facilities but not of a stock of weapons. Whether or not China has retained any weapons is debatable, but China is believed to be capable of making weapons. The U.S. State Department does not think that China has made a full declaration of its chemical weapons program.

India: India admitted, when it became a state party to the CWC, that it had produced chemical weapons in the past and promised to destroy its production facilities and weapons. It has passed CWC inspections but is believed to at least retain the capability of producing chemical weapons.

Myanmar (Burma): Myanmar has not ratified the CWC and has been identified as probably owning chemical weapons.

North Korea: North Korea is known to have a large stock of chemical weapons composed of at least 14 different agents of varying types. Croddy hypothesizes that, because of the lack of a domestic supply of certain precursors, North Korea has probably concentrated on producing mustard, phosgene, sarin, and V-agents. The stock is estimated to weigh between 2,500 and 5,000 tons.[66] North Korea has not signed the CWC.

Pakistan: Pakistan ratified the CWC but is reported to be conducting research on these weapons and probably has the capability of producing them.

South Korea: In becoming a state party to the CWC, South Korea declared that it had chemical weapons production facilities and some chemical weapons. Under the terms of the convention it was obliged to destroy both. Researcher Joseph Cirincione of the Carnegie Endowment for International Peace, reports that South Korea has been carrying out its obligations. However, like the United

States and Russia, it has asked the Organization for the Prohibition of Chemical Weapons for an extension of a destruction deadline. The Congressional Research Service notes that it is suspected of still having a weapons capability.

Taiwan and Vietnam: Taiwan and Vietnam are "likely" to have a chemical weapons capability.

Stockpiles in Africa

Algeria: Algeria ratified the CWC in 1995. Nevertheless, Algeria is suspected of having a chemical weapons capability.

Libya: Libya operated a chemical weapons plant at Rabta. In December 2003 it announced that it was abandoning its weapons of mass destruction and ballistic missile programs. It has since been destroying its weapons of mass destruction under observation.

Defense Methods from Chemical Weapons

The United States and other countries protect their military forces against chemical attack by means of detection devices, protective clothing, and medicine. Within the United States the main use of equipment to protect the civilian population appears to be the detectors installed around stocks of old chemical weapons to detect leaks

Detection

Chemical weapon detection systems are more highly developed and accurate than biological systems. For remote detection, infrared spectroscopy may be used. This technique is based on the fact that when infrared light is sent through a gas or cloud, the chemical structure of the compounds in the gas or cloud determines which wavelengths of the light are absorbed. The more sophisticated instruments can compare patterns of absorption in the cloud to an entire library of patterns stored in the instrument and rapidly determine the nature of the cloud. The detectors are expensive, complex, and bulky.

For point detection, in which the instrument comes into direct contact with the gas, various techniques are employed. The fastest, lightest, and least expensive are based on visible color change. The U.S. military uses what are known as M8 and M9 detection papers. Both can identify agents only when they are in liquid form and have a tendency to generate false positives, as they mistake pesticides and diesel fumes for chemical agents. Systems of colorimetric detection tubes detect both gases and vapors.

Ion mobility spectrometry is the basis of the Chemical Agent Monitor (CAM) used by the U.S. military. It was the first reliable, handheld instrument that could detect nerve gas and blister agents. A software addition to the original instrument allows it to also detect blood and choking agents. The procedure relies on differences in the speed with which ions pass along a cylindrical tube, a "drift tube," which can be as small as a credit card.

Mass spectroscopy in combination with gas chromatography is the most sensitive and reliable method of detection and is the only method approved for use in on-site challenge inspections under the Chemical Weapons Convention. However, the instruments are large and costly, necessitate the preparation of samples and reagents, and require trained personnel.

Two other types of point detectors are electrochemical, or chemiresistor detectors—in which an electrical current changes when it interacts with a chemical agent—and enzyme-based detectors. A Czech company has developed a nerve-gas detector that depends on the activity of a sample of the enzyme acetylcholinesterase from the brain tissue of cows that has been placed on a strip or in a tube. Nerve gas would reduce the activity.[67]

Protective Clothing

The newest generation of protective suits, examples of what is called Joint Service Lightweight Integrated Suit Technology, are made of a layered and porous material that traps chemicals in tiny beads of carbon. They can be worn for 45 days if not subject to chemical or biological agents but, if they are contaminated, must be replaced within 24 hours. Once the vacuum-sealed package in which a suit has been distributed has been broken open, the suit remains effective for no more than 120 days even if it is not worn.

At nine pounds each, the suits are lighter and more comfortable than the battle dress overgarments used during the Gulf War. They are also more durable. Complete suits are essential in the presence of chemical agents that can poison through the skin, notably nerve gas. Gas masks alone provide considerable protection against agents that are deadly only if inhaled.

Medicine

During the Gulf War U.S. soldiers were supplied with antidotes to chemical weapons composed of atropine and another compound. The antidotes can be furnished in autoinjection delivery systems that enable individuals to rapidly treat themselves or others. Tablets of pyridostigmine bromide (PB) were prescribed as a precautionary means of protection against possible attack with a nerve agent.

RADIOLOGICAL DEVICES AND CONVENTIONAL WEAPONS

Terrorists generally seek to turn into weapons materials that are not extremely difficult to obtain and to use effectively. Hence they are more likely to turn to radioactive sources, computers, and industrial and agricultural chemicals than to plutonium or bacteria when they want to create multiple injuries and panic. The possibilities for doing damage by such relatively available means are virtually limitless.

RADIOLOGICAL EMISSION DEVICES AND RADIOLOGICAL DISPERSION DEVICES

Radiological devices are devices that spread radioactivity by means other than a nuclear reaction. They can be categorized into two main types: radiological emission devices (REDs) and radiological dispersion devices (RDDs). REDs do not utilize any explosives and distribute radioactivity over a localized area through stationary radiation emissions. RDDs, usually relying on explosives, are designed to spread radioactivity over a much wider area.

A suitcase containing material that emits gamma radiation is an example of a RED. Left in a building or train or on a city street, it can irradiate passersby without their knowledge. When the presence of the device comes to light, the public is likely to panic, adding considerably to the device's effectiveness.

The so-called dirty bomb, which has been of particular concern since September 11, 2001, is a leading example of an RDD. A dirty bomb is a bomb made of radioactive materials wrapped around or placed inside conventional explosives. When the explosives are detonated, they scatter the radioactive material into the environment. Since dirty bombs do not involve the splitting or fusing of atoms, they do not generate the intense heat and radiation levels of nuclear weapons.

Effects of Radiological Dispersion Devices

The physical effects of the detonation of a dirty bomb would vary with such factors as the radioactive material involved, the amount of material released, and the direction and speed of wind. People living within range of the bomb would be exposed to radioactive particles inhaled during the first passage of the radioactive cloud, and then to radioactive dust deposited by the cloud. Buildings, pavement, and soil would be contaminated. If cesium 137 were present, it would release gamma radiation and chemically bind to glass, concrete, and asphalt. Decontamination methods for buildings might include sandblasting and demolition.

A study by the Center for Technology and National Security Policy at the National Defense University underscores the potential seriousness of a dirty bomb. Under certain circumstances such a bomb could cause "tens to hundreds of fatalities" as well as generate huge economic losses, possibly greater than those from the September 11, 2001, attacks, and certainly cause great panic.[68]

Availability of Materials for RDDs and REDs

Radioactive materials for an RDD and also for a RED are much more widely available than are materials for a nuclear weapon. High-level radioactive waste in the form of irradiated fuel from a commercial power plant could conceivably become the basis for a potent RDD. However, unless the fuel had been in storage for many years and had lost much of its initial radioactivity, any people, including terrorists, attempting to gain access to and utilize it might die of radiation poisoning before they could complete their work. Fuel from a research reactor, which is generally less radioactive, would be a more likely choice. Low-level waste would be another possibility. Despite the name, such waste can be dangerously radioactive, as it includes such items as ion exchange resins and filter sludge that have absorbed contaminants from reactor cooling water. Like irradiated fuel, low-level waste normally contains a mixture of isotopes.

Commercial radioactive sources arguably pose a greater risk because they are used across the world in hospitals, factories, oil fields, and scientific laboratories and are often not closely guarded or monitored. Most incorporate materials that are produced in nuclear reactors, but only a fraction of the sources would make an effective bomb. Those representing the greatest threat are americium 241, californium 252, cesium 137, cobalt 60, iridium 192, plutonium 238, and strontium 90, in part because they have half-lives of between a couple of months and several hundred years. The amount of radioactivity emitted from a given material depends on its half-life. For a radiological device, material needs to remain radioactive long enough to necessitate decontamination of an area but short enough to give off appreciable radioactivity.

Sources that contain nuclear material in a dispersible form pose a particularly great risk. In large sources cesium 137 often appears as powdered cesium chloride, which is easily disseminated. Whether or not a source is readily transportable is another factor that determines risk.

Defensive Measures

Measures to protect the public from radiological dispersion and emission devices are multifaceted. They include preventing radioactive materials from falling into the wrong hands, detecting any radioactive materials or devices held by terrorists, preparing to respond to an attack, and devising means of cleaning up after an attack.

Securing Radioactive Sources A number of international initiatives aim to increase the safety and security of radioactive sources. They include the model project of the International Atomic Energy Agency, initiated in 1995 to assist governments to improve their respective regulatory infrastructures, and a series of international conferences on the safety and security of radioactive sources. In 1998, at the first conference, work began on a Code of Conduct on the Safety and Security of Radioactive Sources, a nonbinding guide for governments.

Within the United States various measures are also being taken to secure orphan and high-risk disused sources (sources that are no longer wanted by the user). Disused sources that are more radioactive than "low-level" waste are the responsibility of DOE. The agency has established the Off-Site Source Recovery Project (OSR), which is placing these sources in temporary storage. The U.S. Congress requires DOE to set up a permanent repository for them, but it is not expected to be ready until after 2007.

To take care of U.S. orphaned sources, about one of which is reported each day, the Environmental Protection Agency (EPA) is financing the Orphan Source Initiative, under which it is working with the Conference of Radiation Control Program Directors, made up of members of state radiation control agencies. Their first project is securing sources now at scrap sites and steel mills. The Nuclear Regulatory Commission (NRC) has asked entities licensed to use radioactive sources to increase their security measures.

Detecting Radiological Devices and Preventing Their Entry into the United States The federal government has been setting up sensor networks to measure ionizing radiation and wind currents in the Washington, D.C., metropolitan area (DCNet) and elsewhere. As of April 2004 seven sensor towers had been constructed on government buildings. Three more are planned. New York has two towers, and planners have asked for a network of 75–100 towers altogether. The lead federal agency for DCNet is the National Oceanic and Atmospheric Administration. Together with the Department of Homeland Security, this agency is considering whether to extend the network.

On March 1, 2003, the Bureau of Customs and Border Protection in the Department of Homeland Security began screening with radiation detection devices all individuals who enter the United States at border security checkpoints. The main tools of the screeners are handheld detection devices. Inspectors can supplement these with X-ray machines that can determine if heavy shielding is in place to block radioactive emissions and prevent detection. Portal monitors are used to detect radiation in containers brought into the country on trucks and also in ships.

Large containers pose particular concerns because detectors that can check the entire contents of containers are reportedly in short supply. The government attempts to supplement physical detection by checking ships' manifests for suspicious cargo, but this method cannot be relied on to block fully hazardous and radioactive shipments.

The United States is also asking other governments to check ships leaving their ports for the United States. Even if such checks were thorough, however, cargo could possibly be transferred at sea to a ship given a clean bill of health at the port where it left.[69]

Responding to an Attack In addition to trying to prevent use of a radiological dispersion device within this country, the United States has to prepare to respond to such an attack. Exercises staged to evaluate readiness have shown the need for improvement in coordination between federal, state, and local officials; the need for development of decontamination technologies; and the need for a radiological decontamination standard. Some argue that the allowable level of contamination of the environment should be raised, at least in relation to a dirty bomb, to decrease the need for expensive decontamination of roads, buildings, and soil after an attack.

In 2005 the Department of Homeland Security is expected to issue guidelines for responding to a dirty-bomb attack. The guidelines will likely recommend, for long-term remediation, a process by which local stakeholders and decision-makers develop cleanup plans to meet specific local situations. Several public interest groups have protested the expected lack of fixed standards on the basis that without such standards, a thorough cleanup will not be feasible.

Mitigating Impacts Public education should be an important part of any plans to prepare for an attack because one of the main aims of terrorists in releasing a dirty bomb would be to create public panic. Pharmaceuticals can play an important part in mitigating impacts. Drugs designed to lessen or prevent damage from radioactivity are called radioprotectants. They have been developed for use in conjunction with radiotherapy for cancer as well as for treatment for possible bomb victims. Various compounds are known to protect human tissue from the effects of radioactivity if given before exposure, but most have to be injected and have significant side effects. Postexposure medications block absorption of radioisotopes by internal organs or facilitate expulsion of radioisotopes through the gastrointestinal tract. Potassium iodide is an example of the former. This compound, if administered just before or after exposure to radioactive iodine, decreases the risk of thyroid cancer. The thyroid absorbs iodine, and saturating the thyroid with potassium iodide helps to prevent that organ from taking in the radioactive iodine. Radioactive iodine is a likely contaminant in the case of an accident at a nuclear power plant, but is not likely to be a major component of the radiation from a dirty bomb.

Prussian blue is an example of postexposure medication that facilitates expulsion of radioisotopes through the gastrointestinal tract. Sold by a German company (HEYL Chemisch—pharmazeutische Fabrik GmbH & Co. KG.) under the trademark Radiogardase, Prussian blue combines with cesium and thallium in the intestines and allows them to be excreted. Cesium is a likely constituent of a dirty bomb.

Health authorities are looking for drugs to give to first responders as well as to victims. The federal government is cooperating with private companies in this area through research and development agreements. A promising possibility is a drug under development that would strengthen the portion of the immune system that is found in bone marrow.

Effects of Low-Level Radiation

The harm potential of a dirty-bomb attack and the degree of decontamination necessary after such an attack are tied to the question of the effect of low-level doses of radiation on human and ecological well-being, an issue that remains controversial. Differing scientific models, all with their supporters in the scientific community, give different answers. The Linear-No-Threshold (LNT) model holds that the risk of injury is directly related to dose strength, increasing at higher doses and decreasing at lower doses in proportion to the dose. The model also holds that there is no safe dose of radiation (no threshold below which radiation is harmless). The Supralinear model, supported by nuclear critic Dr. John Gofman, among others, holds that as exposure increases, the risk per dose unit decreases. Higher doses cause more harm, but per unit of radiation the damage is greater at lower doses. Researchers who believe in a dose-rate effectiveness factor (DREF) represent an opposite point of view. They hold that short-term high doses of radiation are more effective in causing disease than are longer-term low doses. In other words if the exposed person receives a single high dose, he or she will be more likely to become ill than through receiving the same total dose through lower doses over time.

In 1999 the National Academy of Sciences appointed a Committee on Health Risks from Exposure to Low Levels of Ionizing Radiation (BEIR VI) to analyze data published since 1990 on that subject. In 2005 the committee issued a report, *Health Risk from Exposure to Low Levels of Ionizing Radiation (BEIR VII-Phase 2)*, which supports the LNT model.

Attack on Nuclear Facilities

An attack on a truck or train carrying irradiated fuel or on a nuclear facility could create a de facto RDD. The most potentially vulnerable facilities are those with large inventories of radioactive materials. These include commercial reactors and the pools of irradiated fuel alongside them, plants for reprocessing irradiated fuel, and facilities for storing and handling the waste from reprocessing.

Results of a Nuclear Facility Attack

Fuel in an operating nuclear reactor and fuel that has been recently removed from a reactor must be kept cool. Even after a reactor has been shut down or the fuel taken out of it, the decay of radioactive isotopes in the fuel gives off heat. If the heat is allowed to accumulate, the zircalloy cladding of the fuel element will melt or even burn, releasing volatile radionuclides and possibly setting on fire any older fuel that is present. The severity of the resulting contamination depends on the amount of radioactivity in the fuel and on the percentage that escapes. Calculations are often made in terms of cesium 137, which is volatile, accounts for approximately half of the fission product radioactivity in 10-year-old fuel, and emits gamma radiation.

The accident at reactor 4 at the Chernobyl nuclear plant in the then USSR in 1986 resulted in the release of two megacuries (MCi) of cesium 137. The core of a 1,000-megawatt nuclear power reactor, typical of U.S. reactors, contains 80 tons of fuel with a total of 5 MCi of cesium 137. The typical pool contains 400 tons of fuel, with 35 MCi of cesium 137. The Chernobyl accident contaminated 10,000 square kilometers, half the area of the state of New Jersey, with 15 curies per square kilometer of cesium 137. Residents of the 10,000-square-kilometer area around the facility had to be evacuated. An accident in a U.S. irradiated fuel pool that releases 10–100 percent of the radioactivity in the pool would contaminate 6,000–50,000 square kilometers at above 15 curies per square kilometer.[70]

Fatalities and financial loss, as well as contamination of land, would result from the release of radioactivity. An unclassified study conducted by Brookhaven National Laboratory for the Nuclear Regulatory Commission in 1997 found that the median results of a fire that releases 8–80 MCi of cesium 137 would be 54,000–143,000 extra cancer deaths and $117–566 billion in evacuation expenses as well as contamination of 2,000–7,000 square kilometers of agricultural land.[71]

Points at Which Plants Could Be Attacked

Reactors are enclosed in containment structures intended to prevent the spread of radioactivity in the event that an accident occurs. They are also designed to protect the reactor. However, both the IAEA and the NRC have acknowledged, in response to questions from the public, that plant containment structures were not constructed to withstand attacks by airliners as large as Boeing 757s or 767s. Conflicting reports exist as to whether these airliners or even lighter planes could break through containment. Analysts sponsored by the Nuclear Energy Institute and Electric Power Research Institute found in computer simulations that the crash of a Boeing 767 would not release radioactivity. On the other hand, Ed Lyman of the Nuclear Control Institute calculated that the engines of a jet would penetrate the containment and cause a fire of jet fuel and/or an explosion.

Much more open to attack than the reactors themselves are the auxiliary buildings in a nuclear power complex. The control center for each nuclear plant is generally housed in a separate building that is unhardened. Supplemental control facilities, apart from the main control center, exist, but whether operators would have the presence of mind to manage the reactor while the main control center is under attack is questionable.

The pools in which U.S. utilities store their irradiated fuel are almost always in buildings that are outside the reactor's containment structure. At plants with pressurized water reactors, pools are in industrial-grade auxiliary buildings and are usually below ground level. At boiling water reactors, the pools are aboveground, inside the building that surrounds the primary reactor containment structure but not inside the containment structure itself. A crack in the concrete wall or floor of the aboveground pools would allow water to drain.

The pools were intended to hold only about 100 metric tons of irradiated fuel each. Utilities planned to transfer fuel after a few years in the pool to a reprocessing plant or a central repository, but these facilities have not been constructed. Therefore, the utilities have added racks to their pools to allow them to hold extra fuel. Today the pools are likely to store four or five times more fuel than they were designed to hold. A pool that contained only 100 metric tons of fuel could have been safely cooled by air if it lost its water, but the pools today are safe only if the water in them is continuously cooled. Safer means of storage in dry casks, which are cooled by natural convection, is used in addition to the pools at 32 sites, but the expense of the casks has prevented their wider adoption.

Means of Attack

Nuclear plants are vulnerable to attack by various means. The most likely means of attack is arguably that demonstrated on September 11—airplanes. Jetliners and smaller planes loaded with explosives are both potential threats. Whether or not a small plane could penetrate a containment structure, it could penetrate an auxiliary building. And while the U.S. government has put into effect elaborate measures to prevent the hijacking of jetliners, airports that cater to small, private planes are much less protected.

Other possible means of attack on nuclear power plants include commando-style terrorist attacks, sabotage by plant employees, bombs (suicide or otherwise) brought in on trucks and detonated, and missiles launched from distant boats or automotive vehicles. Even tampering with computer networks presents a potentially destructive means of terrorism. Nuclear plants are very computer-dependent: strategically placed computer tampering (for example, with an undetected virus) could exacerbate any nuclear plant malfunctioning and increase the potential for radioactivity releases.

Defense Methods from a Nuclear Facility Attack

Nuclear facility security systems were originally designed long before September 11, 2001. Thus, while terrorism prevention has always been a nuclear security concern, it has not been an overriding priority. As a consequence, security at reactor sites today is generally inadequate to defend against the kind of attacks from the ground, water, or air that terrorist actions have demonstrated are possible. Utilities tend to subcontract for security services with private security companies, which must prepare to defend a plant against what is called the Design Base Threat, or DBT. The exact nature of a DBT is classified information, but researchers believe that until April 2003, the DBT consisted of a single insider and/or three external attackers. The NRC upgraded the DBT in 2003. However, the nonprofit Project on Government Oversight (POGO), which has conducted numerous interviews with security guards and officers at nuclear power plants across the United States, reported in a March 10, 2004, press release, that "security standards for nuclear power plants are not 'even close' to meeting the threats assessed by the intelligence community. . . . The intelligence community generally advises that terrorists would attack a target with a squad-sized force," that is 12–14 people. From what POGO has learned, NRC's new DBT is "inadequate" to counter such a force.[72]

Attack by Conventional Weapons

The means that could be used to attack nuclear power plants and their fuel pools could also be turned against other parts of the nation's infrastructure. As the media and the Department of Homeland Security have informed the American public, water storage systems, bridges, trains carrying hazardous materials, the electricity grid, tank farms storing petroleum, and chemical and industrial plants all offer tempting targets. The targets that could be used to directly kill or injure the greatest number of people are arguably plants using or storing large quantities of hazardous materials.

Chemical Facilities

What might be achieved in an attack on a chemical plant is sadly suggested by the accident at the Union Carbide pesticide plant at Bhopal, India, in 1984. Water entered a tank storing 40 tons of methyl isocyanate. The uncontrolled reaction that followed blew apart the tank and spewed out a cloud of methyl isocyanate, hydrogen cyanide, and other chemicals. Union Carbide reported that 3,800 people were killed. The Bhopal Medical Appeal states that a total of 20,000 people eventually died, that 120,000 suffer illnesses as a result of the accident, and that local groundwater was severely contaminated.[73]

Under the terms of the Clean Air Act in the United States, companies that use or store extremely hazardous chemicals must file a risk management plan that includes an account of the worst-case scenario that could result from an accident. According to an Environmental Protection Agency (EPA) compilation of these scenarios, an accident or terrorist attack at any one of more than 100 large plants around the United States could endanger more than 1 million people. An attack on any of 3,700 additional sites could threaten at least 10,000 people.[74]

Journalists have found lax security at chemical plants, including those in metropolitan areas. In 2002 Carl Prine, an investigative reporter for the *Pittsburgh Tribune-Review*, visited 60 plants across the country. He found that at many sites he could walk right up to tanks holding hazardous chemicals. Reporters for the CBS television program *60 Minutes*, who went to plants in metropolitan areas a year later, also found open gates and rundown fences.

The American Chemistry Council requires its members to assess the vulnerability of their sites and to improve security as necessary. However, its members own or operate only 1,000 plants and about 7 percent of the facilities that are subject to risk management plan provisions of the Clean Air Act. The Government Accountability Office (GAO) in March 2003 reported that "the federal government has not comprehensively assessed the chemical industry's vulnerabilities to terrorist attacks." Governments at all levels "lack comprehensive information on the vulnerabilities the industry faces." The GAO recommended that the secretary of Homeland Security and the administrator of the EPA develop together a "national chemical security strategy" that both assesses vulnerabilities and improves preparedness.[75] Both Christine Todd Whitman, former director of the EPA, and Tom Ridge, former director of the Department of Homeland Security, have expressed the need for federal regulations to make the industry less vulnerable, and Senator Jon Corzine, a Democrat from New Jersey, has made strenuous efforts to convince Congress to take action to require companies to assess and improve their security. However, no comprehensive assessment of vulnerability has yet been made, and efforts to improve security are still on a voluntary basis.

The Electricity Grid

The results of an attack on the electricity grid might be enormous in terms of loss of life, but they are difficult to estimate. The deaths would be indirect and would depend, in large measure, on the length of time and the size of the area where electricity is lacking. Terrorists might make such an attack through computers. Researchers have identified "back doors" in the digital relays and control-room technologies that increasingly direct electricity flow in North America. Saboteurs or terrorists, they say, could shut down computer systems or change settings in ways that might set off a cascade of blackouts. They might also physically attack a key portion or portions of the grid. Nuclear power plants would be among the facilities that would lose power. If a nuclear plant loses electricity from the grid, it turns to backup generators. If these generators do not function correctly—and backup generators at nuclear plants have a history of problems—a catastrophic accident could result.

Conventional Explosives

Conventional explosives would be easier for terrorists to obtain and use than nuclear, chemical, or biological weapons. In the United States a terrorist willing to commit suicide and planning to drive a truckload of explosives into a chemical storage area or other hazardous component of the nation's infrastructure could obtain material for explosives from a farm supply company.

In 1995 American terrorists Timothy McVeigh and Terry Nichols used 4,000 pounds of ammonium nitrate, a common fertilizer, as the principal ingredient of a truck bomb that blew up the federal building in Oklahoma City, Oklahoma. Ammonium nitrate was also used in a nightclub bombing in Bali in 2002, and the same chemicals were found under railway lines in France in 2003, placed as an apparent bomb. Nevertheless, its sale in the United States is still unregulated. The attractiveness of ammonium nitrate for terrorists is that it is widely available from legitimate sources. Some states require that fertilizer dealers and distributors register their businesses, and the federal Bureau of Alcohol, Tobacco, Firearms, and Explosives; the Fertilizer Institute; and other groups have been trying to educate manufacturers, shippers, sellers, and farmers about the possible use of ammonium nitrate by terrorists. As a result dealers have been motivated to keep tabs informally on who buys fertilizer from them. There are no requirements, however, that they keep records on purchases.

CONTROVERSIES

All fields and disciplines include controversies and divergences of opinion, particularly when public policy concerns are centrally involved. Whether the issue is the degree to which government should support academic research in the sciences or whether the Federal Communications Commission should allow television to air X-rated movies, ongoing debates are likely to rage over in-place or contemplated polices.

Weapons of mass destruction are particularly controversy-intensive because of their intrinsic natures. They do not provide direct scientific insight or entertainment or any other useful product or service. While the argument is put forth that weapons research findings can be applied to peaceful purposes—with the Manhattan Project cited as a leading example—this is clearly an inefficient, as well as a destructive, way to advance scientific understanding.

The purpose of weapons of mass destruction is simply to destroy property and kill living species. The basic controversy surrounding them, then, is simply whether they should exist—whether governments should tolerate their development and proliferation. There have long been opposing, and polarized, sides on this issue, with the deterrence-through-weapons side generally having a sizable advantage.

Deterrence is the overriding argument for their existence: If a nation—or an organization, for that matter—possesses weapons of mass destruction, the argument goes, that will deter its enemies from rendering harm to it. However, the concept of deterrence itself has long been fraught with controversy. Before World War I there was a strong sentiment worldwide that the invention of the Gatling gun—an early version of today's automatic weapons—would prove an overwhelming deterrent to starting a war. The reasoning was simply that no leader would engage in a military campaign in which troops faced the prospect of being cut down in large numbers by weapons that could engage in mass destruction. This clearly did not prove to be the case. Slaughter of troops in World War I by this new weapon became just an accepted fact of military engagement.

The invention of the atomic bomb brought a new, and more intensive, belief in the concept of deterrence through weapons of mass destruction, yet the atomic bomb has been highly controversial virtually since its inception. Opponents of the bomb have argued that the deterrent argument was fatally flawed from the start, since the horrendous destruction resulting from the Hiroshima bombing did not bring about an immediate capitulation of the Japanese. Tens of thousands of additional civilian deaths—through a second atomic bomb in Nagasaki—would be required before the Japanese surrendered.

Apart from the general questions of whether weapons of mass destruction should exist at all and whether deterrence is a useful concept, controversies rage in regard to each type of weapon of mass destruction. The burning question in regard to nuclear weapons in the first decade of the 21st century is how to prevent their spread. Should the Non-Proliferation Treaty be strengthened or discarded and, if it is to be strengthened, how can this be done? Would implementation of Article VI, requiring the nuclear powers to take significant steps toward nuclear disarmament, actually help to deter other nations from developing weapon, or would it weaken the nuclear powers without serving any purpose? Another controversial question, though less discussed, is whether the U.S. and Soviet policies of launching missiles on warning of a nuclear attack should be ended.

In regard to biological weapons, a major controversy within the United States is whether the nation is making adequate preparations to prevent and cope with a biological attack or simply spending money on the problem without first carefully considering how the money is to be used. One particular aspect of this issue is the new laboratories that are being built to conduct research on deadly biological agents. Will the laboratories serve an essential purpose? Also, does any purpose that they are designed to serve outweigh the risk that biological agents will escape from them and contaminate the local population and possibly people in more distant areas? U.S. plans for greatly expanded research in biological warfare are, in principle, directed toward *defensive* objectives of better preparing this country to thwart future biological attacks. The line between defensive and offensive research is, however, a thin one, and many have opposed expanded activity in this area for that very reason. On the international level there is the question of whether the Biological Weapons Convention should be strengthened by mandatory inspections and penalties for violators.

The question of whether an international treaty should be strengthened recurs in terms of the Chemical Weapons Convention. Unlike the Biological Weapons Convention, this treaty provides for mandatory inspections, but it has no meaningful penalties. Should it? Another issue that is coming to the fore is whether signatories of the treaty can use riot-control agents, such as tear gas and chemicals designed to temporarily incapacitate their victims, in military situations. According to the treaty, riot-control agents and incapacitants can legitimately be used in law enforcement. However, a branch of the U.S. Department of Defense is carrying out research on nonlethal weapons, and U.S. troops in Iraq are permitted to use tear gas at the discretion of the combatant commander. Given this, the question sharply emerges as to whether the United States is reinterpreting the convention for military purposes.

In terms of radiological and other nontraditional weapons, two critical points of controversy are how chemical plants should be safeguarded to prevent terrorists from causing a devastating release of chemicals from one or more of them and what the role of nuclear power should be in our energy future. A number of reports indicate that manufacturing and processing facilities in the United States utilizing highly toxic and hazardous materials are generally poorly prepared for attacks by terrorists, or even simple acts of theft of materials. How this situation can be changed, who should manage the change, who should pay for it, and how much should be spent remain highly controversial issues.

Nuclear power provides a visibly controversial set of issues related to weapons of mass destruction for three major reasons: The research and development needed to advance nuclear reactors has applications in nuclear weaponry; dirty bombs can be made out of irradiated nuclear fuel and other radioactive materials from nuclear plants; and the plants themselves might be sabotaged to cause a catastrophic release of radioactivity.

The U.S. nuclear power industry currently is moribund. High costs of operation and maintenance and dozens of aging reactors that need to be upgraded or decommissioned, combined with relatively low growth in electricity demand, have made the economics of nuclear power dismal. In addition, sizable public opposition to siting spent nuclear fuel disposal sites has meant that these materials, scattered across the United States at power plant sites, are not secured.

Americans are sharply divided as to whether the nuclear option should be accelerated or closed. Higher energy prices have added pressure to revive the nuclear option in the United States, and the Bush administration has advocated new programs to support expansion of nuclear power. As it has been for decades, the nuclear power question remains a highly controversial and often polarizing public policy issue.

---

[1] Nina Tannenwald. "Weapons of Mass Definition." *Bulletin of the Atomic Scientists*, vol. 59 (July/August 2003): 4.

[2] Peter Eisler. "Fallout Likely Caused 15,000 Deaths." *USA Today*, February 28, 2002, page 1A.

[3] Atomic Archive. "Basic Effects of Nuclear Weapons." Available online. URL: http://www.atomicarchive.com/Effects. Downloaded February 10, 2005; Carey Sublette. "Effects of Nuclear Explosions." Available online. URL: http://nuclearweaponarchive.org/Nwfaq/Nfaq5.html. Posted May 15, 1997. Unless otherwise indicated, the information in this section is drawn from these two sources.

[4] Harvey Wasserman and Norman Solomon. *Killing Our Own: The Disaster of America's Experience with Atomic Radiation.* New York: Dell Publishing, 1982, p. 113.

[5] James D. Happell. "A History of Atmospheric Tritium Gas (HT) 1950–2002." *Tellus: Series B*, vol. 56 (July 2004): pp. 183ff.

[6] R. P. Turco et al. "Nuclear Winter: Global Consequences of Multiple Nuclear Explosions." *Science*, vol. 222, 1983, pp. 1,283–1,297.

[7] *Columbia Electronic Encyclopedia.* 6th ed., Columbia University Press. Available online. URL: http://www.infoplease.com/cc6/sci/AO836144.html. Downloaded December 16, 2004.

[8] Carey Sublette. "Effects of Nuclear Explosions." Available online. URL: http://nuclearweaponarchive.org/Nwfaq/Nfaq5.html. Posted May 15, 1997.

[9] Ronald E. Powaski. *March to Armageddon: The United States and the Nuclear Arms Race, 1939 to the Present.* New York and Oxford: Oxford University Press, 1987, p. 32.

[10] Powaski. *March to Armageddon*, p. 51.

[11] Unless otherwise indicated, data on the stocks, deployment, and testing of U.S., Soviet/Russian, Chinese, and British nuclear weapons in this chapter are taken from the series Nuclear Notebook, written by Robert S. Norris and Hans M. Kristensen of the Natural Resources Defense Council (NRDC) and published in each issue of the *Bulletin of the Atomic Scientists.* The series is available online at the web site of the NRDC, http://www.nrdc.org. Statistics on stocks of French nuclear weapons are taken from a report of the Centre de Documentation et de Recherche sur la Paix et les Conflits, "Etat des forces nucléaires françaises au 15 août 2004." Available online. URL: http://www.obsarm.org/obsnuc/puissances-mondiales/france-forces2.htm. Statistics on the history of French weapons are from the Nuclear Notebook series.

[12] Jeffrey Lewis. "The Ambiguous Arsenal." *Bulletin of the Atomic Scientists*, vol. 61 (May/June 2005): 52–59.

[13] Unless otherwise noted, data on the nuclear arsenals of nations other than the United States, Russia/Soviet Union, France, China, and the United Kingdom are drawn from Joseph Cirincione, *Deadly Arsenals: Tracking Weapons of Mass Destruction.* Washington, D.C.: Carnegie Endowment for International Peace, 2002; Sharon A. Squassoni. *Nuclear, Biological, and Chemical Weapons and Missiles: Status and Trends.* RL 30699. Washington, D.C.: Congressional Research Service, 2005; and the national profiles on the web site of the Nuclear Threat Initiative (http://www.nti.org).

[14] Missile Threat. "Jane's: North Korea Deploying 2,500 km Range Missile, Capable of Ship-Launch." Available online. URL: http://missilethreat.com/news/200408030854.html. Downloaded February 23, 2005.

[15] Cirincione. *Deadly Arsenals*, p. 87.
[16] *Nuclear Weapon Archive*. "Principles of Nuclear Weapons Security and Safety." Available online. URL: http://nuclearweaponarchive.org/Usa/Weapons/Pal.html. Updated October 1, 1997; Thomas B. Cochran, et al. *Nuclear Weapons Databook*. Vol. 1, *U.S. Nuclear Forces and Capabilities*. Cambridge, Mass.: Ballinger, 1984, p. 30.
[17] Alan Phillips and Steven Starr. "Eliminate Launch on Warning." Available online. URL: http://www.wagingpeace.org/articles/2004/09/00_phillips_eliminate-launch-warning.htm. Posted December 2004.
[18] Robert S. Norris and Hans M. Kristensen. "Dismantling U.S. Nuclear Warheads." *Bulletin of the Atomic Scientists*, vol. 60 (January/February 2004): 72–74.
[19] General Accounting Office. *Nuclear Weapons: Opportunities Exist to Improve the Budgeting, Cost Accounting, and Management Associated with the Stockpile Life Extension Program*. GAO-03-583. Washington, D.C.: General Accounting Office, July 2003, pp. 1–2.
[20] Norris and Kristensen, "Dismantling U.S. Nuclear Warheads," 73.
[21] Linton F. Brooks at a press conference, June 1, 2004, quoted in Thomas Cochran, Robert S. Norris, and Hans M. Kristensen. "Too Many, Too Slow." National Resources Defense Council. Available online. URL: http://www.nrdc.org/nuclear/fstockpile.asp. Last revised June 7, 2004; Robert S. Norris and Hans M. Kristensen, "U.S. Nuclear Forces, 2005." *Bulletin of the Atomic Scientists*, vol. 61 (January/February 2005): 73–75.
[22] David Albright and Kimberly Kramer. "Stockpiles Still Growing." *Bulletin of the Atomic Scientists*, vol. 60 (November/December 2004): 12–16.
[23] Council for a Livable World. "3 Nobel Laureates Criticize Bush Nuclear Posture Review." [Press Release.] March 18, 2002.
[24] William M. Arkin. "Secret Plan Outlines the Unthinkable." *Los Angeles Times*, March 10, 2002. Available online. URL: http://www.latimes.com/news/opinion/la-op-arkinmar 10.story; Center for Nonproliferation Studies. "U.S. Nuclear Posture Review." Available online. URL: http://www.nti.org/f_wmd411/f2c.html. Updated November 2004.
[25] Quoted in the Disarmament Documentation section of The Acronym Institute web site. URL: http://www.acronym.org.uk/docs/0402/doc30.htm.
[26] Quoted in the Disarmament Documentation section of The Acronym Institute web site. URL: http://www.acronym.org.uk/docs/0107/doc04.htm.
[27] George Perkovich. *"Changing Iran's Nuclear Interests."* Available online. URL: http://www.carnegieendowment.org/publications. Posted May 2005.
[28] See Chapter 3, "Seizing the Bomb," and Chapter 4, "Making the Bomb" in Charles D. Ferguson, et al. *The Four Faces of Nuclear Terrorism*. Washington, D.C.: Monterey Institute, Center for Nonproliferation Studies, 2004.
[29] Matthew Bunn and Anthony Wier. *Securing the Bomb 2005: The New Global Imperatives*. Cambridge, Mass.: Project on Managing the Atom, Belfer Center for Science and International Affairs, Harvard University, 2005, p. v.
[30] Eric Croddy. *Chemical and Biological Warfare*. New York: Springer-Verlag, 2002, p. 225.
[31] Jeanne McDermott. *The Killing Winds: The Menace of Biological Warfare*. New York: Arbor House, 1987, pp. 167–169.

[32] Cirincione. *Deadly Arsenals*, pp. 182–183
[33] Cirincione. *Deadly Arsenals*, pp. 181–183; Croddy. *Chemical and Biological Warfare*, pp. 226–229; Robert Harris and Jeremy Paxman. *A Higher Form of Killing*. New York: Hill and Wang, 1982, pp. 96, 105, 160, 218.
[34] Mike Boettcher. "Iraqi Scientist's Notes Reveal Bioweapons Tests." CNN.com. Available online. URL: http://www.cnn.com/2003/WORLD/meast/01/27/sprj.irq.bio.scientist. Posted January 28, 2003.
[35] Robert Hutchinson. *Weapons of Mass Destruction*. London: Weidenfeld and Nicolson, 2003, pp. 245–247; Croddy, *Chemical and Biological Warfare*, pp. 224–225.
[36] McDermott. *The Killing Winds*, pp. 170–188.
[37] Quoted in Milton Leitenberg, Ambassador James Leonard, and Dr. Richard Spertzel. "Biodefense Crossing the Line." *Politis and the Life Sciences*, vol. 22, no. 2 (2004): 1–2.
[38] Leitenberg, Leonard, and Spertzel. "Biodefense Crossing the Line," pp. 1–2.
[39] Cited in Malcolm Dando. *New Biological Weapons*. Boulder, Colo.: Lynne Rienner, 2001, p. 22.
[40] Sharon A. Squassoni. *Nuclear, Biological, and Chemical Weapons and Missiles: Status and Trends*. RL 30699. Washington, D.C.: Congressional Research Service, 2005, p. 8.
[41] Margaret E. Kosal. "The Basics of Chemical and Biological Weapons Detectors." Available online. URL: http://www.cns.miis.edu/pubs/week/031124.htm. Posted November 24, 2003; Jessica Gorman. "Danger Detection." *Science News*, vol. 163, (June 7, 2003): 362ff.
[42] President George W. Bush. "Biodefense for the 21st Century." Available online. URL: http:// www.whitehouse.gov/homeland/20040430.html. Released April 28, 2004. Downloaded January 6, 2005.
[43] Michael Moodie. *Fighting Bioterrorism: Tracking and Assessing U.S. Government Programs*. Washington, D.C.: Chemical and Biological Arms Control Institute, 2004, pp. iv–v.
[44] Moodie. *Fighting Bioterrorism*, p. iv.
[45] Council for Responsible Genetics. "Mistakes Happen: Accidents and Security Breaches at Biocontainment Laboratories." Available online. URL: www.gene-watch.org/bubiodefense/pages/Accidents. Downloaded February 10, 2005.
[46] Laurie Goodman. "Biodefense Cost and Consequences." *Journal of Clinical Investigation*, vol. 114 (July 2004): 3.
[47] Lola Vollen. "Fools Rush In." *GeneWatch*, vol. 16, February 2003. Available online. URL: http://www.gene-watch.org. Downloaded on December 10, 2004.
[48] *Strengthening the Biological and Toxin Weapons Convention: Countering the Threat from Biological Weapons*, Presented to Parliament [United Kingdom] by the Secretary of State for Foreign and Commonwealth Affairs. Cm 5484. April 2002. Available online through the web site of the Federation of American Scientists. URL: http://www.fas.org. Downloaded on December 11, 2004.
[49] Croddy. *Chemical and Biological Warfare*, p. 154.
[50] Croddy. *Chemical and Biological Warfare*, pp. 222–223.
[51] Harris and Paxman. *A Higher Form of Killing*, p. 33.
[52] David Pugliese. "Panama: Bombs on the Beach." *Bulletin of the Atomic Scientists*, vol. 58 (July/August 2002), pp. 55ff.

[53] Harris and Paxman. *A Higher Form of Killing*, pp. 205–206.
[54] Quoted in Croddy. *Chemical and Biological Warfare*, pp. 170 and 171.
[55] General Accounting Office. *Nonproliferation: Delays in Implementing the Chemical Weapons Convention Raise Concerns about Proliferation.* GAO-04-361. Washington, D.C.: General Accounting Office, 2004, pp. 5–7. Downloaded on December 19, 2004.
[56] General Accounting Office. *Chemical Weapons: Destruction Schedule, Delays and Cost Growth Continue to Challenge Program Management.* GAO-04-634T. Washington, D.C.: General Accounting Office, 2004, pp. 3, 24–25. Downloaded on December 19, 2004.
[57] Joel A. Vilensky and Pandy R. Sinish. "The Dew of Death." *Bulletin of the Atomic Scientists*, vol. 60 (March/April 2004): 58.
[58] Sunshine Project. "US Military Operating a Secret Chemical Weapons Program," with related documents. Available online. URL: http://www.sunshine-project.org/publications/pr/pr240902.html. Posted September 24, 2002.
[59] Committee for the Assessment of Non-Lethal Weapons Science and Technology, National Research Council. *An Assessment of Non-Lethal Weapons Science and Technology.* Washington, D.C.: National Academies Press, 2003.
[60] Kerry Boyd. "Military Authorized to Use Riot Control Agents in Iraq. *Arms Control Today*, May 2003. Available online. URL: http://www.armscontrol.org/act/2003_05/nonlethal_may03.asp; Downloaded on December 17, 2004. James Randerson. "US in Danger of Breaking Chemical Weapons Treaty." *New Scientist*, vol. 177 (April 5, 2003): 6. Downloaded on December 17, 2004.
[61] Quoted in Julian Borger. "US Weapons Secrets Exposed." *Guardian*, October 29, 2002.
[62] Raymond J. Decker. *Chemical Weapons: Destruction Schedule Delays and Cost Growth Continue to Challenge Program Management.* GAO-04-634T. Washington, D.C.: General Accounting Office, 2004, p. 1.
[63] Jonas Siegel. "Disposal in the Doldrums." *Bulletin of Atomic Scientists*, vol. 60 (July/August 2004): 9
[64] Unless otherwise stated, data on chemical weapons capability of nations other than the United States and Russia are drawn from Cirincione, *Deadly Arsenals;* Croddy, *Chemical and Biological Warfare;* Squassoni, *Nuclear, Biological, and Chemical Weapons and Missiles;* and the national profiles on the web site of the Nuclear Threat Initiative (http://www.nti.org).
[65] Avner Cohen. "Israel and CBW: History, Deterrence, and Arms Control." *Nonproliferation Review* (Fall 2001): pp. 1–20.
[66] Vilensky and Sinish. "The Dew of Death," p. 60.
[67] Kosal. "The Basics," pp. 7–11; "Briefing: Nuclear, Biological, and Chemical Detection," *Jane's Defence Weekly*, vol. 41 (April 14, 2004): 24.
[68] Quoted by Joby Warwick. "Raises Projection for 'Dirty Bomb' Toll." *Washington Post*, January 13, 2004, p. A2.
[69] Charles D. Ferguson et al. "Dispersing Radiation: Dirty Bombs and Other Devices." In *The Four Faces of Nuclear Terrorism.* Washington, D.C.: Monterey Institute, Center for Nonproliferation Studies, 2004.
[70] Robert Alvarez et al. "Reducing the Hazards from Stored Spent Power-Reactor Fuel in the United States." *Science and Global Security*, vol. 11, (2003): pp. 1–10.

[71] R. J. Travis et al. *A Safety and Regulatory Assessment of Generic BWR and PWR Permanently Shutdown Nuclear Power Plants.* NUREG/CR-6451. Brookhaven National Laboratory, 1997, cited by Alvarez et al. "Reducing the Hazards from Stored Spent Power-Reactor Fuel in the United States," p. 10.

[72] Project on Government Oversight. "Security Still Lax at Nuclear Power Plants: POGO" [Press Release.] March 10, 2004.

[73] Bhopal Medical Appeal. "What Happened in Bhopal?" Available online. URL: www.bhopal.org/whathappened.html. Downloaded January 4, 2005.

[74] General Accounting Office. *Homeland Security: Voluntary Initiatives Are Under Way at Chemical Facilities, but the Extent of Security Preparedness Is Unknown.* GAO-03-439. Washington, D.C.: General Accounting Office, 2003, p. 4; Margaret Kriz. "Bush Not Doing Enough to Protect Chemical Plants, Critics Contend." GOVEXEC.com Daily Briefing, August 7, 2003. Available online. URL: http://www.govexec.com/story_page.cfm?articleid=26308. Downloaded on September 20, 2004.

[75] General Accounting Office. *Homeland Security*, pp. 4–6.

CHAPTER 2

The Law and Weapons of Mass Destruction

This chapter describes in turn the major international treaties and agreements relating to nuclear, biological, chemical, and radiological weapons; a cross section of U.S. laws on these subjects; and a cross section of relevant court cases, including the Advisory Opinion of the International Court of Justice on the Legality of the Threat or Use of Nuclear Weapons. The Advisory Opinion does not relate to a particular *plaintiff v. defendant* case but is included because of the frequency with which it is cited in discussions of nuclear weapons. Materials in the three sections of the chapter are closely related: Many of the laws pertaining to weapons of mass destruction involve the implementation of treaties, and court cases involve the interpretation of laws.

TREATIES AND AGREEMENTS

Listed below in order of their entry into force are the major international treaties and agreements on nuclear, biological, and chemical weapons. Included in this listing are key international export arrangements. Even though they are not formal treaties, they are directly relevant to the international flow of weapons and materials and equipment to make weapons.

Additional treaties prohibit certain nuclear activities in particular geographic areas: the Antarctic Treaty, which prohibited nuclear explosions and other military activities in Antarctica (1959); the Treaty for the Prohibition of Nuclear Weapons in Latin America and the Caribbean (Treaty of Tlatelolco, 1967); the South Pacific Nuclear Free Zone Treaty (Treaty of Rarotonga, 1985); the Southeast Asia Nuclear-Weapon-Free Zone Treaty (Treaty of Bangkok, 1995); and the African Nuclear-Weapon-Free Zone Treaty (Pelindaba Treaty, 1996).

Geneva Protocol (Signed in 1925)

The full name of the Geneva Protocol states its purpose: "Protocol for the Prohibition of the Use in War of Asphyxiating, Poisonous, or Other Gases, and of

Bacteriological Methods of Warfare." The protocol does not include a prohibition on developing, producing, and stockpiling chemical and biological weapons. It goes into force for a given signatory when that country ratifies it and only binds the signatories not to use chemical and biological weapons against each other. The protocol was signed on June 17, 1925, but the United States did not ratify it until December 16, 1974.

Treaty Banning Nuclear Weapons Tests in the Atmosphere, in Outer Space, and under Water (Signed in 1963)

The Treaty Banning Nuclear Weapons Tests in the Atmosphere, in Outer Space, and Under Water, known as the Partial or Limited Test Ban Treaty, was signed by the Soviet Union, the United Kingdom, and the United States on August 5, 1963, and entered into force on October 10, 1963. The treaty was the result of a massive international campaign by citizens to end atmospheric testing. France, nevertheless, continued atmospheric testing until 1974 and China until 1980.

Treaty on Principles Governing the Activities of States in the Exploration and Use of Outer Space, including the Moon and Other Celestial Bodies (Signed in 1967)

Known as the Outer Space Treaty, the Treaty on Principles Governing the Activities of States in the Exploration and Use of Outer Space, including the Moon and Other Celestial Bodies prohibits the placement of nuclear weapons or other weapons of mass destruction in orbit around the Earth. The treaty, which entered into force on October 10, 1967, is ordinarily classified as a nuclear arms limitation treaty.

Nuclear Non-proliferation Treaty (NPT) (Signed in 1968)

The Nuclear Non-Proliferation Treaty (NPT) entered into force on March 5, 1970, after the United States and the Soviet Union ratified the treaty. The treaty has a dual purpose: to encourage the peaceful use of nuclear energy and to keep nonnuclear-weapon states from acquiring nuclear weapons. In terms of the treaty, nuclear-weapon states are countries that exploded a nuclear device before January 1, 1967. The treaty places obligations on parties that are nonnuclear-weapon states and on parties that are nuclear-weapon states.

Nuclear-weapon state parties (signatory nations possessing nuclear weapons) are "not to transfer to any recipient whatsoever nuclear weapons or other nuclear explosive devices" or to help them acquire such weapons and devices (Article I). Nonnuclear-weapon parties are not to receive or develop nuclear weapons (Article II) and are to allow the International Atomic Energy Agency (IAEA), through its safeguards system, to verify that they are not using nuclear materials and facilities for military purposes (Article III). All parties that are in a position to assist in spreading peaceful applications of nuclear energy to nonnuclear-weapon parties should do so (Articles IV and V). Each party to the treaty is to negotiate "in good faith, on effective measures relating to cessation of the nuclear arms race at an early date and to nuclear disarmament, and on a treaty on general and complete disarmament under strict and effective international control" (Article VI).

A review conference was to be held five years after the treaty went into force and could be held every five years thereafter. These conferences have taken place. As of January 2005, 188 states were parties to the treaty. Since 1970, nuclear energy has spread internationally but so have nuclear weapons, although not as fast as might have occurred without the treaty.

The combination of prohibiting nuclear weapons but encouraging nuclear power makes implementation of the treaty difficult to monitor because a civilian nuclear program and a military nuclear program involve many of the same materials and technologies. For implementation, the treaty depends on the IAEA. The IAEA's program, however, is generally not considered strong enough to overcome this inherent difficulty

The IAEA has three objectives: promote the peaceful use of nuclear energy, ensure that the nuclear power industry operates safely, and verify through inspections that states comply with their commitments under the NPT and other nonproliferation agreements.

To achieve the last objective, the IAEA operates a safeguards system based on assessment of the correctness and completeness of declarations by the nations on their nuclear material and nuclear-related activities. Assessments are carried out by means of physical inspections and analysis of data from various sources including computerized monitoring. The NPT requires that its nonnuclear-weapon signatories submit all nuclear material and nuclear activities to IAEA safeguards and conclude a comprehensive safeguards agreement with the IAEA.

After the Gulf War, as the result of special authority given the IAEA by the UN Security Council, the IAEA discovered a clandestine nuclear weapons development program in Iraq. The discovery underscored weaknesses in the IAEA's standard safeguards system, which had failed to detect the program initially. In 1997 a Model Additional Protocol, giving the IAEA broader powers than it previously possessed, was negotiated. The new powers include the authority to make inspections of all buildings at a declared nuclear site on short notice and to take environmental samples (seeking indications of radioactivity, for example) at locations other than declared nuclear sites. However, nonnuclear-weapon signatories of the NPT are not obligated to accept the additional protocol as written. It is only a model, and each party to the NPT is supposed to negotiate its own protocol based on the model. As of mid-2003 only 81 of 187 NPT states had negotiated a new agreement.

The IAEA's safeguards system has other weaknesses. Nuclear material accountancy is the basic means of safeguarding nuclear material. The IAEA monitors the quantity of nuclear material in a facility and any changes in these quantities. However, plutonium is impossible to measure with high accuracy. The precise quantity that arrives at a reprocessing plant cannot be determined until reprocessing is under way, and plutonium sticks to piping and equipment. Enough plutonium to make a nuclear device could conceivably be diverted without the IAEA discovering the loss in time to prevent production of the device.

Since the IAEA is not able to detect all diversions and inspect all possible locations of nuclear materials in a timely manner, the NPT has to rely to a certain extent on the willingness of its members, if not of other nations, to adhere to their obligations. The willingness of nonnuclear-weapon states to do so is being undermined by the failure of the nuclear-weapon states to live up to their obligations to move toward disarmament as stated in the treaty.

Two informal coalitions of nations were set up in the 1970s to assist in curbing nuclear proliferation. Members voluntarily restrict exports of equipment and materials that could be used for nuclear weapons. The first, the Non-Proliferation Treaty Exporters Committee or Zangger Committee was formed in 1971 to establish guidelines for implementing Article III of the Nuclear Non-Proliferation Treaty. In 1974 the committee drew up guidelines, including a list of items that would force recipient states to agree to adhere to IAEA safeguards. The second, the Nuclear Suppliers Group (NSG), was formed in 1974. It adopted guidelines similar to those of the Zangger Committee but added to them restrictions on the exportation of uranium enrichment and plutonium extraction equipment and technology. After the Gulf War the NSG added for the first time dual-use items to its list and required states receiving listed items to acquiesce to full-scope IAEA safeguards, that is, IAEA inspection of all their nuclear activities.

The Non-Proliferation Treaty is reviewed at a conference every five years. Delegates to the 1995 conference agreed that the treaty should remain in force indefinitely. The 2000 conference, among other decisions, listed steps that nations should take to implement Article VI, which states that that each party to the treaty is to negotiate "in good faith, on effective measures relating to cessation of the nuclear arms race at an early date and to nuclear disarmament, and on a treaty on general and complete disarmament under strict and effective international control." The specific steps listed by the review conference included ratification of the Comprehensive Test Ban Treaty and an "unequivocal undertaking" by the nuclear-weapon states to eliminate their nuclear arsenals. The 2005 conference closed without delegates making any new agreements. Nonnuclear-weapon states insisted that the nuclear powers undertake efforts to greatly reduce their nuclear weapons, while the United States tried to focus attention on the nuclear programs of Iran and North Korea.

TREATY ON THE PROHIBITION OF THE EMPLACEMENT OF NUCLEAR WEAPONS AND OTHER WEAPONS OF MASS DESTRUCTION ON THE SEABED AND OCEAN FLOOR AND IN THE SUBSOIL THEREOF (APPROVED BY THE UN GENERAL ASSEMBLY IN 1970)

Known as the Seabed Arms Control Treaty, the Treaty on the Prohibition of the Emplacement of Nuclear Weapons and Other Weapons of Mass Destruction on the Seabed and Ocean Floor and in the Subsoil Thereof bans the placement of nuclear weapons or other weapons of mass destruction outside a 12-mile coastal zone. It was approved by the UN General Assembly on December 7, 1970. Like the Outer Space Treaty, it is usually considered to be a nuclear arms limitation treaty.

CONVENTION ON THE PROHIBITION OF THE DEVELOPMENT, PRODUCTION AND STOCKPILING OF BACTERIOLOGICAL (BIOLOGICAL) AND TOXIN WEAPONS AND ON THEIR DESTRUCTION (BWC) (SIGNED IN 1972)

The Convention on the Prohibition of the Development, Production and Stockpiling of Bacteriological (Biological) and Toxin Weapons and on Their Destruction entered into force on March 26, 1975. The United States had ratified it on January 22, 1975. As of February 2004, 150 nations were parties to the treaty and 14 additional nations had signed it.

State parties to the convention agree never "to develop, produce, stockpile or otherwise acquire or retain" "microbial or other biological agents, or toxins," in types or in quantities not needed for peaceful purposes or means of delivery of such agents for hostile purposes. Parties agree to destroy or divert to peaceful purposes agents or toxins and means of delivery within nine months of the entry into force of the convention. Furthermore, they are not to transfer to or help "any State, group of States or international organizations" to acquire these materials and weapons.

Any party can lodge a complaint with the UN Security Council if it finds another party is acting contrary to its agreement, and each is to cooperate in carrying out any investigation that the Security Council initiates. If the Security Council decides that a party has been endangered because of a violation of the convention, other parties are to support or assist it. Unfortunately no provision is made for monitoring or verification, and, apart from the call to assist victim nations, no punishment for violators is specified.

The convention called for a review conference five years after it went into effect. This conference took place, and subsequent conferences have been held at intervals of approximately five years. At the 1986 conference four confidence-building measures were established. The first measure requires annual reports from member states about any high-containment facilities for work on dangerous biological materials, and the second requires reports of the outbreak of any diseases that could be caused by biological weapons. The third suggests that research related to biological weapons be published and the fourth that scientists discuss their research with other scientists.

The third review conference, held in 1991, set up an Ad Hoc Group of Governmental Experts to Identify and Examine Potential Verification Measures from a Scientific and Technical Standpoint (VEREX). VEREX reported in September 1994 that various potential verification measures were promising but that implementation would be difficult. An ad hoc group open to all state parties was then set up to draft proposals to strengthen the convention, including possibly verification measures. After years of negotiations the group developed a "composite text" for a protocol.

The biotechnology industry finds problems with monitoring and verification in regard to the convention. It holds that much of the technology that would be used in producing biological agents for weapons can be obtained from non-weapons-related activities (e.g., technologies that are needed for fermentation of food and beverages, fuel processing, and civilian research at universities.) Modern cleanup methods on production lines would allow for any indications of weapons work to be removed in as little as one or two hours. Inspections, moreover, would be likely to reveal trade secrets.

On July 25, 2001, the United States, which had participated in the ad hoc group to strengthen the convention, announced in a statement made by Ambassador Donald Mahey at Geneva, Switzerland, that it could not support the composite text "even with changes." John R. Bolton explained the U.S. position in remarks at the Tokyo America Center, Japan, on August 26, 2002. The "traditional arms control measures" on which the text was based would not work with biological weapons because of dual use, he said, and inspections under the text would have made known "trade secrets and sensitive bio-defense information." The U.S. announcement brought to an end negotiations on a protocol.

At the fifth review conference, which was held in 2002, the parties agreed by consensus to meet for a week each year through 2005 to discuss several steps of limited scope: 1) the adoption of national measures to implement the convention; 2) the adoption of national mechanisms to secure pathogenic microorganisms and toxins; 3) the strengthening of international capabilities to respond to, investigate, and decrease the effects of any alleged use of biological or toxin weapons; and 4) the strengthening of international measures to combat infectious diseases. The parties also agreed to hold a sixth review conference by the end of 2006. Meanwhile, international measures to strengthen the prohibitions in the convention are no longer under official consideration.

INTERIM AGREEMENT ON STRATEGIC OFFENSIVE ARMS (SIGNED IN 1972)

The Strategic Arms Limitation Talks (SALT I) extended over two and a half years and ended on May 26, 1972, with President Richard Nixon and General-secretary Leonid Brezhnev signing the Anti-Ballistic Missile Treaty and the Interim Agreement on Strategic Offensive Arms. The interim agreement essentially limited Soviet and U.S. strategic ballistic missile launchers to the number operational or under construction at the time.

Anti-Ballistic Missile Treaty (ABM) (Signed in 1972)

The Anti-Ballistic Missile (ABM) Treaty, which entered into force on October 3, 1972, permitted the United States and the Soviet Union to have only two ABM deployment areas each. The areas were to be so located that they could not provide a nationwide defense or become the basis for such a defense. A protocol that went into effect in 1976 reduced the number of deployment areas to one each. Subsequent amendments further modified the treaty. The United States withdrew from it, effective June 17, 2002.

Treaty on the Limitation of Underground Nuclear Weapon Tests (Signed in 1974)

The Treaty on the Limitation of Underground Nuclear Weapon Tests, also known as the Threshold Test Ban Treaty, prohibits tests having a yield greater than 150 kilotons, the equivalent of 150,000 tons of TNT. This eliminates the possibility of testing new or existing weapons with a yield greater than a fraction of a megaton. A protocol sets forth verification procedures. In Article I the parties obligate themselves to continue negotiations toward a Comprehensive Test Ban Treaty. The Threshold Test Ban Treaty was signed in July 1974 and was submitted to the U.S. Senate for ratification in 1976 but did not enter into force until 1990, after the verification procedures had been agreed upon.

Treaty on Underground Nuclear Explosions for Peaceful Purposes (Signed in 1976)

The Treaty on Underground Nuclear Explosions for Peaceful Purposes governs all nuclear explosions carried out at locations other than the test sites designated in the Threshold Test Ban Treaty. No individual explosion is to have a yield greater than 150 kilotons, and no group of explosions is to have a yield greater than 1,500 kilotons. The treaty was signed May 28, 1976, and entered into force on December 11, 1990.

Strategic Arms Limitation Talks II (SALT II) (Signed in 1979)

The SALT II agreement, signed June 18, 1979, by President Jimmy Carter and Soviet General-secretary Leonid Brezhnev, was to replace the Interim Agreement on Strategic Offensive Arms with a long-term treaty that would limit strategic offensive weapons systems. Because of subsequent disagreements between the United States and the Soviet Union, the U.S. Senate never ratified it, but the agreement was observed.

THE AUSTRALIA GROUP (ESTABLISHED IN 1984)

The Australia Group is an informal group of nations that opposes the proliferation of biological and chemical weapons. It was formed in 1984 after sales by international suppliers made possible the use of chemical weapons in the Iran-Iraq War. Its initial concern was chemical weapons, but it enlarged its efforts to include biological pathogens in 1993. Working on a consensus basis the 33 members coordinate national export controls, share information on suspect activities, and control chemical weapons precursors, biological pathogens, and dual-use equipment.

MISSILE TECHNOLOGY CONTROL REGIME (MTCR) (ANNOUNCED IN 1987)

In July 1987, seven governments announced the Missile Technology Control Regime (MTCR), a policy and the institutional means to put it into effect. The MTCR was initially intended to curb the proliferation of ballistic and cruise missiles that can deliver nuclear weapons. In 1993 the regime was expanded to cover missiles capable of carrying biological and chemical weapons and all unmanned vehicles capable of carrying weapons of mass destruction. Members commit to a common export control policy (MTCR guidelines) and to a common list of controlled items (MTCR annex). Each state implements the guidelines and annex in accordance with its own laws. States seeking membership in the MTCR must meet specified criteria, including having an export control system based on legislation and effectively administered. As of June 1, 2004, the regime had 34 members. Three additional states had unilaterally announced adherence.

INTERMEDIATE-RANGE NUCLEAR FORCES TREATY (SIGNED IN 1987)

The Intermediate-Range Nuclear Forces (INF) Treaty, signed by President Ronald Reagan and Soviet General-secretary Mikhail Gorbachev in 1987, went into effect on June 1, 1988. As a result of the treaty the Soviet Union and the United States eliminated by May 1991 all nuclear-armed ground-launched cruise and ballistic missiles with ranges between 500 and 5,500 kilometers (approximately 300 to 3,400 miles).

STRATEGIC ARMS REDUCTION TREATY I (START I) (SIGNED IN 1991)

The Strategic Arms Reduction Treaty I (START I), signed by President George H. W. Bush and President Boris Yeltsin in 1991, like the INF Treaty, resulted in actual reductions of nuclear forces. The treaty went into effect in December 1994 after ratification by the United States, Belarus, Kazakhstan, Russia, and the Ukraine. It required the reduction of deployed strategic nuclear-delivery vehicles to 1,600 and "accountable" warheads to 6,000, of which no more than 4,900 could be on ballistic missiles. The result was a reduction in strategic warheads of 25–35 percent. In addition Russia cut its SS-18 ballistic missiles by 50 percent. The treaty provides for technical means of verification, on-site inspections, and continuous monitoring.

The Lisbon Protocol to START I, signed in May 1992, named Belarus, Kazakhstan, Russia, and Ukraine as successors to the Soviet Union parties to the treaty. Belarus, Kazakhstan, and Ukraine committed themselves in the protocol to acceding to the Nuclear Non-Proliferation Treaty as quickly as possible. The U.S.'s Cooperative Threat Reduction Program assisted Ukraine and Kazakhstan in eliminating strategic warheads and delivery systems, as required under START I.

Strategic Arms Reduction Treaty II (START II) (Signed in 1993)

START II, signed in 1993 by President George H. W. Bush and President Boris Yeltsin, was to eliminate heavy or multiple-warhead intercontinental ballistic missiles (ICBMs) and to reduce the strategic weapons deployed by each country to two-thirds of pre-START levels over a seven-year period. However, Russia withdrew from the treaty in June 2002 after the United States withdrew from the ABM Treaty. Therefore, its contents are now moot.

Chemical Weapons Convention (CWC) (Signed in 1993)

The Chemical Weapons Convention (CWC) forbids the "development, production, acquisition, retention, stockpiling, transfer and use of all chemical weapons." The United States ratified it April 25, 1997, and it went into effect four days later. Member states must declare their chemical weapons stockpiles and destroy them within 10 years of the entry into force. They must dispose of chemical weapons that they abandoned in foreign countries. Furthermore, they must destroy or convert to civilian use their chemical weapons production facilities. Any state can become a member by signing and ratifying the convention; the possession of chemical arms is not a condition of membership.

Unlike the Convention on the Prohibition of the Development Production and Stockpiling of Bacteriological (Biological) and Toxic Weapons and on their Destruction and also the Geneva Protocol, the CWC provides for inspection and monitoring. State parties (signatory nations) together make up the Organisation for the Prohibition of Chemical Weapons (OPCW), which is based in The Hague, Netherlands. The technical secretariat of the OPCW is in charge of verification. Chemical agents and their precursors are listed on three schedules, based on the risk that each poses. Members must report to the OPCW any substances on the first two schedules that they are making, in what quantities, and for what purposes. The OPCW carries out inspections to verify these statements.

A nation that believes that another state is violating the convention by producing or stockpiling agents or weapons can request a challenge inspection, which, if approved by the OPCW executive council, takes place with brief advance notice to the suspected state. An inspection can also be requested to verify an alleged use of chemical weapons by one state on another state's territory. The convention does not clearly provide for any punitive measures, other than loss of membership in the CWC.

As of February 2005, 166 nations were parties to the treaty.

The Wassenaar Arrangement (Established in 1996)

The Wassenaar Arrangement was established as "a voluntary system for coordinating national controls on exports of conventional arms and dual-use technologies." Control depends on the exchange of information. The dual-use items relate to a great extent to weapons of mass destruction, including nuclear weapons.

Comprehensive Test Ban Treaty (CTBT) (Signed in 1996)

The Comprehensive Test Ban Treaty (CTBT) obligates states that ratify it not to carry out any nuclear weapon test explosion or any other nuclear explosion. Thus it bans both low-yield tests and tests for peaceful purposes. It establishes a Comprehensive Nuclear Test-Ban Treaty Organization, a verification regime, and an international monitoring system.

The treaty was signed on September 24, 1996, by the United States and 70 other nations. As of January 2005 it had been signed by 174 nations and ratified by 120 nations, including the United Kingdom, France, and Russia. However, the U.S. Senate refused in October 1999 to ratify it.

The treaty will enter into force after 44 specified "nuclear-capable" states have deposited their instruments of ratification with the UN secretary-general. The 44 states, listed in Annex 2, are those that have nuclear weapons or nuclear power or research reactors and that participated in the work of the Conference on Disarmament's 1996 session and were members of the Conference on Disarmament as of June 18, 1996. Of the 44 designated states, India, Pakistan, and North Korea have neither signed nor ratified the treaty, and eight additional states have not ratified it. An informal, voluntary moratorium on nuclear testing has been in effect since July 1996, when China ceased testing.

In January 2002, in briefings relating to the Nuclear Posture Review, the Bush administration stated that it continues to oppose the CTBT, continues to adhere to the test moratorium, and is planning to reduce the time necessary to prepare to resume testing. Since President Bush has not withdrawn the treaty from the Senate, the U.S. signature on it is still valid as an expression of support. According to customary international law, a country that has signed but not yet ratified a treaty is bound by it until that country withdraws from the treaty.

Strategic Offensive Reduction Treaty (SORT) (Signed in 2002)

The Strategic Offensive Reduction Treaty (SORT), signed by President George W. Bush and President Vladimir Putin, limits deployed strategic warheads to 1,700–2,200 but has no schedule for implementation other than the expiration date of the treaty and does not require that the warheads that are withdrawn be destroyed. Both nations can store their warheads and take them out of storage in January 2013. The treaty contains no provisions for limiting delivery vehicles. The treaty will be easily reversible. The only verification measure specified in the treaty is an agreement that a bilateral implementation commission meet at least twice a year.

International Code of Conduct against Ballistic Missile Proliferation (2002)

At a conference hosted by the Netherlands at The Hague in 2002, 93 nations subscribed to an International Code of Conduct against Ballistic Missile Proliferation. A voluntary arrangement among member countries, the code is designed to strengthen efforts to curb ballistic missile proliferation worldwide and to delegitimize missile proliferation. Membership in it is not limited and, as of November 2003, 111 countries had subscribed to the international code.

Fissile Materials Cut Off Treaty (Under Consideration as of 2005)

A treaty that would cut off the production of plutonium and highly enriched uranium for weapons could be said to have been in process for a decade. In 1995 and again in 1998 the UN Conference on Disarmament agreed to start negotiations on a fissile material cutoff treaty that would include a verification mechanism. Both mandates expired. The United States called in July 2004 for a new round of negotiations but said that it would not support inspections and verifications. Critics of the administration stated that without them a treaty would be meaningless. Even if enforced, a treaty limited to production of material for nuclear weapons would not affect the five official nuclear weapons states but it could affect India, Israel, Pakistan, and nations bent on acquiring weapons. The fact that civilian fissile materials would be permitted would make enforcement difficult.

UNITED STATES LAWS

The following is a sampling of U.S. laws that relate directly or indirectly to weapons of mass destruction. They include laws controlling exports, compensating radiation victims, and restricting expenditures on biological and chemical agents.

ATOMIC ENERGY ACT (1946)

Signed by President Harry S. Truman on August 1, 1946, the Atomic Energy Act (PL 79-585) transferred control of atomic weapons from the military to civilians. It established a five-member Atomic Energy Commission (AEC), appointed by the president, to replace the U.S. Army's Manhattan Project, which had developed and built the atomic bomb during World War II. It gave oversight of the commission to a group of 18 members of Congress, nine from each House, called the Joint Committee on Atomic Energy (JCAE). The AEC was to own all nuclear materials and the nation's nuclear infrastructure, including the weapons laboratories and all reactors, whatever their function. The AEC was called upon both to promote nuclear energy and to regulate the emerging industry.

ATOMIC ENERGY ACT OF 1954

The Atomic Energy Act of 1954 (PL 83-703, 42 U.S.C. 2011–2259), signed by President Dwight D. Eisenhower on August 30, 1954, amends the Atomic Energy Act of 1946. It was designed to promote the peaceful use of nuclear energy through private enterprise. The Atomic Energy Commission (AEC) was given ownership of all facilities that produce special nuclear materials (plutonium, uranium 233, and uranium 235) but could contract with private entities to operate these facilities. The AEC was charged with issuing licenses to private companies to construct and operate nuclear power plants in the United States. They could use but not own special nuclear material. The AEC was granted permission to cooperate with other nations on nuclear energy provided it acted in each case in accordance with a cooperation agreement that had been submitted by the Department of Defense to the president. The commission could adopt any regulations it believed necessary "to protect the health and safety of the public." The law has since been extensively amended.

FREEDOM OF INFORMATION ACT (1966)

The Freedom of Information Act (5 U.S.C. 552), signed by President Lyndon Johnson on July 4, 1966, specifies that "any person" can request information from the government. All branches of the federal government must adhere to the provisions of the act, with certain restrictions such as for work in progress (early drafts), classified documents, and national security information. Although it has been imperfectly implemented, the Freedom of Information Act is a powerful tool by which individuals and organizations have obtained extensive information about the government's programs in the areas of nuclear, chemical, and biological weapons.

ARMS EXPORT CONTROL ACT (1968)

Signed by President Lyndon Johnson on October 22, 1968, the Arms Export Control Act (AECA) (PL 90-629; 22 U.S.C. 2751 and following), as amended, authorizes U.S. government military sales, loans, leases, and financing and licensing of commercial arms sales to other countries. The AECA coordinates such actions with other foreign policy considerations, including nonproliferation, and determines the eligibility of recipients.

Section 3(f) (Eligibility; 22 U.S.C. 2753(f)) added in 1994, prohibits U.S. military sales or leases to any country that the president determines has broken commitments to the United States in regard to nonproliferation of nuclear explosive devices and unsafeguarded special nuclear material.

Section 40 (Transactions with Countries Supporting Acts of International Terrorism; 22 U.S.C. 2780), added in 1986 and later amended, prohibits facilitating the acquisition of munitions by countries, the governments of which have supported "acts of international terrorism." The act includes in its definition of "acts of international terrorism" "all activities that the Secretary [of State] determines willfully aid or abet the international proliferation of nuclear explosive devices" and "unsafeguarded special nuclear material" or aid individuals or groups to "acquire chemical, biological, or radiological weapons."

Sections 72 and 73 (Denial of the Transfer of Missile Equipment or Technology by U.S. Persons; 22 U.S.C. 2797a; Transfers of Missile Equipment or Technology by Foreign Persons; 2797b), added in 1990 and later amended, require sanctions against any U.S. citizen or foreigner whom the president determines is engaged in exporting or facilitating the export of any equipment or technology identified by the Missile Technology Control Regime (MTCR) that "contributes to the acquisition, design, development, or production of missiles in a country that is not an MTCR adherent."

Section 101 (Nuclear Enrichment Transfers; 22 U.S.C. 2799aa), added by the Nuclear Proliferation Prevention Act of 1994, prohibits foreign economic or military assistance to any country that the president determines delivers or receives nuclear enrichment equipment, materials, or technology. The prohibition is not required if the material, equipment, or technology is to be under multilateral safeguard arrangements or if the recipient has an agreement with the International Atomic Energy Agency (IAEA) regarding safeguards.

Section 102 (Nuclear Reprocessing Transfers, Illegal Exports for Nuclear Explosive Devices, Transfers of Nuclear Explosive Devices, and Nuclear Detonations; 22 U.S.C. 2799a-1), added by the Nuclear Proliferation Prevention Act of 1994, prohibits foreign economic or military assistance to nations that the president determines deliver to another country or receive from another country nuclear reprocessing equipment, material, or technology. It further prohibits assistance, defense sales, and various export licenses and loans with certain exceptions, to any country that the president has determined transfers a nuclear explosive device to a nonnuclear-weapon state or otherwise assists a nonnuclear-weapon state to develop or manufacture a nuclear explosive device.

ARMED FORCES APPROPRIATION AUTHORIZATION ACT FOR FISCAL YEAR 1970

Public Law 91-121 appropriating funds for military purposes for fiscal year 1970 and signed November 19, 1969, contains in Title IV: General Provisions, Section 409, restrictions on the testing, transportation, storage, and disposal of chemical and biological weapons. The secretary of defense must submit semiannual reports to Congress on amounts spent on the "research, development, test and evaluation and procurement of all lethal and nonlethal chemical and biological agents." No funds provided by this or any act can be spent on transportation of any lethal chemical or biological warfare agent or on open air testing of such an agent within the United States unless specific, strict authorization procedures have been followed. No funds authorized by the act can be used for the purchase of any delivery system for chemical or biological warfare agents. Other restrictions apply to U.S. agents and means of delivery that are located outside the United States. The president can suspend the operation of Section 409 during war or national emergency.

ENERGY REORGANIZATION ACT OF 1974

The act (PL 93-438; 42 U.S.C. 5801) abolishes the Atomic Energy Commission (AEC) and creates two new agencies: the Nuclear Regulatory Commission, to take over the "licensing and regulatory functions" of the AEC, and the Energy Research and Development Administration (ERDA), "to bring together and direct Federal activities relating to research and development on the various sources of energy, to increase the efficiency and reliability in the use of energy, and to carry out the performance of other functions, including but not limited to the Atomic Energy Commission's military and production activities and its general basic research activities." The Department of Energy replaced ERDA in 1977.

NUCLEAR NON-PROLIFERATION ACT OF 1978

The Nuclear Non-Proliferation Act of 1978 (PL 95-242; 22 U.S.C. 3201 and elsewhere) states U.S. policy for obtaining more effective international controls over the transfer and use of nuclear materials, equipment, and technology in order to prevent proliferation of nuclear weapons. The act promotes the establishment of a framework for international cooperation for developing peaceful uses of nuclear energy, authorizes the U.S. government to license exports of nuclear fuel and reactors to countries that adhere to nuclear nonproliferation policies, provides incentives for countries to establish joint international cooperative efforts in nuclear nonproliferation, and authorizes export controls.

Section 304(b) (Export Licensing Procedures; 42 U.S.C. 2155a) requires the Nuclear Regulatory Commission to establish procedures for granting, suspending, revoking, or amending nuclear export licenses.

Section 309 (Additional Requirements; 42 U.S.C. 2139a) requires the Department of Commerce to issue regulations relating to items that could be significant for purposes of nuclear explosions.

Veterans Dioxin and Radiation Exposure Compensation Standards Act (1984)

This act (PL 98-542; 38 U.S.C. 354 note), signed by President Ronald Reagan on October 24, 1984, is intended "to ensure that Veterans' Administration disability compensation is provided to veterans who were exposed . . . in Vietnam to a herbicide containing dioxin or to ionizing radiation in connection with atmospheric nuclear tests or in connection with the American occupation of Hiroshima or Nagasaki" and, as a result, suffered a disability that can be linked to the military service by means of "sound scientific and medical evidence." After amendments, the act covers 16 cancers and four illnesses other than cancer. A veteran exposed to radiation must prove that his or her radiation exposure was sufficiently high to have caused the cancer.

Department of Defense Authorization Act (1986)

The U.S. Department of Defense Authorization Act of 1986 (PL 99-145), signed November 8, 1985, contains a section on the destruction of chemical weapons: Title XIV General Provisions, Part B Chemical Weapons, Section 1412 Destruction of existing stockpile of lethal chemical agents and munitions. The secretary of defense was to destroy the U.S. stockpile of lethal unitary chemical agents and munitions. The destruction was to be done in conjunction with the acquisition of binary weapons, which the act refers to as safer. Unless the United States ratified a treaty banning the possession of chemical agents and munitions, the destruction was to be completed by September 30, 1994. If a treaty was ratified, destruction was to be accomplished by the date specified therein. A management organization was to be established within the army to be responsible for the destruction of the agents and munitions.

Radiation Exposure Compensation Act (1990)

The Radiation Exposure Compensation Act (RECA), signed by President George H. W. Bush on October 15, 1990 (PL 106-245; 42 U.S.C. 2210 note), rewards two classes of claimants: people living in certain areas downwind of the Nevada Test Site and uranium miners. The downwinders with any of 13 cancers were to receive lump sum payments of $50,000 each; miners who have severe respiratory illness, lump sum payments of $100,000 each. In return for the payments, recipients waive further claims. In the year of RECA's passage the act was amended by PL 101-510 (the National Defense Authorization Act for Fiscal Year 1991) to add on-site participants: veterans and civilians who worked for nuclear weapons contractors and various government agencies and participated in a test. They receive $75,000 each for any of the 13 cancers.

Amendments to RECA enacted in 2000 (PL 106-245) increase the claimant populations, add additional compensable diseases, lower radiation exposure thresholds, modify medical documentation requirements, and remove certain disease restrictions. Under the amendments there are five categories of claimants: uranium miners, uranium millers, ore transporters, downwinders, and on-site participants. The first three categories are eligible for $100,000 each; the latter two are still eligible for $50,000 and $75,000, respectively. Each category is compensated for any of a list of specified illnesses.

Maintaining sufficient funds in the program has proved to be a problem, and the act still does not provide compensation to possible victims of radioactive fallout who at the time of the tests lived outside the counties in Nevada, Utah, and Arizona named in the original legislation.

Chemical and Biological Weapons Control and Warfare Elimination Act of 1991

The Chemical and Biological Weapons Control and Warfare Elimination Act is Title III of a law that pertains to trade (PL 102-182; 22 U.S.C. 5601 and following), signed December 4, 1991. Title III mandates U.S. sanctions and encourages international sanctions against countries that use chemical or biological weapons in violation of international law or use lethal chemical or biological weapons against their own nations. It also imposes sanctions against companies that aid in the proliferation of chemical and biological weapons, and it supports multilateral efforts to control the proliferation of chemical and biological weapons. A list is to be drawn up of items that would help a foreign government or group to acquire biological or chemical capability. Export of these items will require a validated license.

National Defense Authorization Act for Fiscal Year 1995

Section 1040 (Transportation of Chemical Munitions) of Public Law 103-337, signed October 5, 1994, states that "The Secretary of Defense may not transport any chemical munition that constitutes part of the chemical weapons stockpile out of the State in which that munition is located on the date of the enactment of this Act" or transport any such munition into a state in which it is not located at that time. Weapons not in the stockpile may be transported to the nearest stockpile storage facility if the transportation can be done safely.

Energy Employees Occupational Illness Compensation Act (2000)

The Energy Employees Occupational Illness Compensation Act (EEOICP; PL 106-398; 42 U.S.C. 7384 and following), signed by President Bill Clinton on October 13, 2000, is a federal entitlement program intended to compensate workers in the U.S. nuclear weapons complex for certain illnesses linked to their employment. It establishes a special cohort, which consists of people who worked at one of the three gaseous diffusion plants or at the nuclear test site at Amchitka Island, Alaska. Members of the special cohort are automatically compensated if they have any of a list of specified illnesses. Individuals who believe that they are ill because of work at other weapons sites must prove that their illness "at least as likely as not" resulted from their exposure. The president, on advice from the Advisory Board on Radiation and Worker Health, can add workers from other plants to the special cohort. Awards are a lump sum payment of $150,000 (to the victim or survivors) and coverage of medical expenses connected with the illness. Uranium miners who receive payment of $100,000 under RECA can receive an additional $50,000 in compensation and medical expenses. Except for illnesses from toxics, the Department of Labor is in charge of administering the act. Workers who believe that they became ill because of exposure to toxic chemicals at a Department of Energy (DOE) site are to receive assistance from DOE in obtaining compensation from a state worker compensation program.

EEOICP was significantly amended by PL 108-N375 in 2004. In the amended version the Department of Labor takes over from DOE the responsibility for workers made ill by toxic chemicals and is to provide them federal compensation and medical benefits. As of February 2005 no additional groups of workers had been added to the special cohort.

Public Health Security and Bioterrorism Preparedness and Response Act of 2002

Known as the Bioterrorism Act (PL 107-188), signed June 12, 2002, the act increases control of dangerous biological agents and toxins. Among the actions it requires are assessment and improvement of the integrity and security of vulnerable facilities, systems, and personnel, including hospitals and water supplies; improvement of pathogen security measures (creation of a new select agent list and registration of individuals and facilities working with these agents); establishment of criminal penalties for transfers to unregistered persons and failure to register for possession of listed substances; and improvement of public health capabilities (strengthening of public health response capabilities and creation of a strategic national vaccine supply).

Homeland Security Act of 2002

Signed November 25, 2002, the Homeland Security Act (PL 107-296) gives the secretary of Homeland Security responsibility for developing a national policy and strategic plan to identify and develop countermeasures to biological and other emerging terrorist threats. The secretary is to establish federal priorities for programs and operations to prevent the importation of chemical, biological, radiological, and nuclear weapons and related materials and to protect against terrorist attacks involving these materials. He or she is responsible for coordinating with the secretary of Health and Human Services a strategy relating to countermeasures and response to such threats and for maintaining a stockpile of vaccines and other health supplies that would be needed in an emergency.

PROJECT BIOSHIELD ACT OF 2004

Signed July 21, 2004, the Project Bioshield Act (PL 108-276) is a comprehensive effort to develop and make available drugs and vaccines to protect against attack by chemical, biological, radiological, and nuclear weapons. The secretaries of Homeland Security and of Health and Human Services oversee implementation. The act:

- gives the federal government spending authority for "next-generation" vaccines and countermeasures. The FY 2004 appropriation for the Department of Homeland Security includes an authorization for the government to spend $5.6 billion over 10 years to develop and purchase "huge amounts" of vaccines or drugs and for the purchase of next-generation countermeasures against anthrax and smallpox as well as other chemical, biological, nuclear, and radiological agents;
- gives the National Institutes of Health new authority to bypass traditional procedures when awarding grants and contracts for bioterrorism research; and
- gives the Food and Drug Administration power to authorize the use of experimental drugs in an emergency to make promising treatments quickly available in emergency situations.

COURT CASES

An Advisory Opinion of the International Court of Justice and four U.S. court cases are examples of how court proceedings and resulting judicial decisions have direct and indirect influence on major issues pertaining to development, testing, transport, and storage of weapons of mass destruction. These cases are detailed below.

U.S. SUPREME COURT: *FERES V. UNITED STATES*, 340 U.S. 135 (1950)

Background

The district court dismissed an action by the executrix of *Feres v. United States* (340 U.S. 135, 137) to recover for death caused by negligence. The victim died in a fire in the barracks at Pine Camp, New York, while on active duty in the U.S. military. Allegedly he was housed in barracks that were known or that should have been known to have defective heating equipment. Allegedly also the military did not maintain an adequate fire watch. The executrix of Feres charged negligence. The Court of Appeals, Second Circuit, upheld the dismissal (177 F. 2d 535).

Legal Issues

Under the policy of sovereign immunity, an extension of the English maxim that "the King can do no wrong," the U.S. government was immune from suit until 1946. In that year Congress passed the Federal Tort Claims Act (FTCA) as a response to the public's feeling that the government should be liable for the negligence of its employees and as a means of ending the requests for the passage of private bills in Congress to secure redress for injuries.

The Supreme Court considered the *Feres* case along with two other case—*Jefferson v. United States. United States v. Griggs, Executrix* and (340 U.S. 135, 1950)—because all three turned on a common issue arising out of the FTCA. The *Feres* case alleged negligence in providing a safe living environment, while the *Jefferson* case and the *Griggs* case alleged medical malpractice by army surgeons.

The Supreme Court stated that the common fact underlying the three cases is that each claimant, while on active duty and not on furlough, was injured due to negligence on the part of others in the military. "The only issue of law raised is whether the Tort Claims Act extends its remedy to one sustaining 'incident to the service' what under other circumstances would be an actionable wrong." The test of allowable claims, the Court notes, is that the Federal Tort Claims Act states that, "with certain exceptions not material here," "The United States shall be liable . . . in the same manner and to the same extent as a private individual under like circumstances."

Decision

The Supreme Court concluded that the relationship between the government and its soldiers has no counterpart in private relations between individuals. Congress, in the Federal Tort Claims Act, did not intend the government to be liable to members of the armed forces "for injuries that arise out of or are in the course of activity incident to service." It therefore affirmed the judgment in the *Feres* case.

Impact

The Supreme Court's decision in the *Feres* case has since become known as "the Feres doctrine." The courts have repeatedly referred to this doctrine in denying claims for compensation from members of the military for exposure to radiation and toxic chemicals in the course of their service.

U.S. District Court, Western District of Wisconsin: *United States of America v. Progressive, Inc., Erwin Knoll, Samuel Day, Jr., and Howard Morland,* 467 F. Supp. 990 (W.D. Wis.), 1979

Background

In 1978 the *Progressive* magazine, which is published in Madison, Wisconsin, assigned Howard Morland, a freelance writer, the task of researching and writing an article on the design of the hydrogen bomb. With the permission of the Department of Energy (DOE), Morland toured plants in the weapons complex and talked to DOE scientists. He also studied the open literature. The *Progressive* sent the resulting article and accompanying illustrations to the DOE for verification of technical information. The DOE responded that the article contained restrictive data as defined by the Atomic Energy Act of 1954. The agency offered to help Morland rewrite the article to remove the offending material, but the *Progressive* formally refused the offer. The government then asked the U.S. District Court for the Western District of Wisconsin to enjoin the *Progressive* from publishing, communicating, or otherwise disclosing certain information in the manuscript entitled "The H-Bomb Secret: How We Got It, Why We're Telling It."

Legal Issues

Morland asserted that he wrote the article only to encourage intelligent discussion of nuclear weapons and that the material he used to write the article was in the public domain. The government did not challenge these contentions. Any danger in the article lay not in Morland's intentions nor in his sources but in the conclusions that he reached and the speculations that he made about the design of the hydrogen bomb on the basis of his research. At issue was whether the government can suppress information deduced from materials that are freely available to the public.

In view of the First Amendment the Supreme Court has held that prior restraint on expression must overcome a heavy presumption of invalidity. A key issue was whether the government met the heavy burden of justification for enjoinment of publication.

Specifically, for the article to be enjoined, the government needed to prove that it fell within the national security exception to the rule against prior restraints. The only instance in which the Supreme Court had interpreted the national security exception was *The Pentagon Papers Case—New York Times Co. v. United States.* In that case the Court found that the government failed to overcome the heavy presumption of unconstitutionality that inheres in any system of prior restraint but did not indicate how that could have been done.

Referring to the Atomic Energy Act of 1954, the government argued that national security interests permitted it to classify and censor information originating in the public domain that when brought together presented immediate, direct, and irreparable harm to the United States. The defendants argued that the article does not rise to the level of immediate, direct, and irreparable harm that could justify abridgement of First Amendment freedoms. Even if the article accurately presented the design of a hydrogen bomb, it would not permit production of one. Many variables, including the possession of hard-to-obtain materials, would be involved.

The trial entailed a clear clash of the principles of national security and freedom of the press, but, according to Morland, the case actually came down to whether the three H-bomb concepts that he described were both secret and correct. The defense argued that nothing that he said validated both of these conditions. Its last appeal briefly stated that two of the concepts were publicly known and the third was incorrectly described.

A major part of the trial was conducted by means of secret hearings and exchanges of classified affidavits. The attorneys for the defendants were given security clearances and were told the secret of the hydrogen bomb that the government was trying to hide. The defendants refused clearances because the clearances would have permanently prevented them from speaking out. The secrecy itself eventually became an issue.

Decision

On March 9, 1979, federal judge Robert W. Warren of Milwaukee granted a temporary restraining order blocking publication. He issued a preliminary injunction on March 26, 1979.

He based the preliminary injunction on a finding that publication would cause grave and irreparable injury to the national interest and that the danger posed by the publication would be direct and immediate. He did not, however, find that publication was certain to have consequences. The court order stated that "the article could possibly provide sufficient information to allow a medium size nation to move faster in developing a hydrogen weapon."

Impact

In the months after the court issued the preliminary injunction, attorneys became preoccupied with the question of whether the *Progressive* had been scooped and the case rendered moot. Because of the publicity that the case generated, other journalists began trying to emulate Morland by describing the hydrogen bomb. Chuck Hansen, a nuclear weapons buff, sent Senator Charles Percy of Illinois a letter in which he speculated about the concepts underlying the H-bomb. The DOE classified the letter and demanded surrender of all copies. Nevertheless, the *Madison Press Connection*, a paper published by striking employees of the Madison dailies, published the letter on September 16, 1979. On September 17 the Justice Department held a press conference announcing that it was dropping the case against the *Progressive* because the publication of Hansen's letter had made the issue of the *Progressive's* publication moot.

The *Progressive* published Morland's article as originally written in October 1979. Whether the result of the case can be considered a victory for freedom of expression is, however, debatable. The injunction was the first time that the United States blocked publication of an article on grounds of national security. On September 13 of that year the Seventh Circuit Court of Appeals in Chicago heard oral arguments on the case. The panel of three appellate court judges appeared to be skeptical about the government's claims. Had they clearly disagreed with the decision of Judge Warren, the case would have become a precedent for rejection of prior restraint. The government's dropping the case prevented them from ruling. As it is, the case stands as an important example of the government's using a law—in this case the Atomic Energy Act—to block publication of material on a weapon of mass destruction that it sought to keep out of the public's hands, ostensibly to prevent or retard proliferation of that weapon.

U.S. District Court, District of Hawaii: *Greenpeace U.S.A. v. Stone*, 748 F. Supp. 749 (D. Haw. 1990)

Background

As of 1986 the United States had a stockpile of some 30,000 tons of unitary chemical weapons, nerve and blister agents, which Congress mandated must be destroyed. The weapons were stored at eight locations in the United States, at Johnson Atoll in the Pacific, and at Clausen in Germany. The case concerns the destruction of the weapons stored in Germany.

In 1986 President Ronald Reagan entered into an agreement with Chancellor Helmut Kohl to remove the munitions from Germany by December 1992. By mutual agreement the date was moved to the end of 1990. The U.S. Army and Department of Defense then planned with the German army to remove the stockpile and transport it by ocean to Johnston Atoll for storage and incineration.

The U.S. Army prepared three environmental impact statements (EISs) in regard to the incineration of the nerve agents at Johnston Atoll: one on construction and operation of the facility, one on disposal of its wastes, and one on the destruction of the European stockpile. On July 12, 1990, it released a record of decision announcing its determination to destroy the European stockpile at Johnston Atoll. In compliance with Executive Order 12,114, it prepared a global commons environmental assessment (EA) for the shipment across the ocean but neither an EIS nor an EA for the transportation within Germany.

On August 1, 1990, Greenpeace U.S.A. and other environmental organizations filed a complaint for declaratory judgment and injunctive relief against the secretary of the army and the secretary of defense. The plaintiffs asked the U.S. District Court for the District of Hawaii to enjoin the army's shipment of nerve gas from Germany to Johnston Atoll for destruction and to require the army to compile a comprehensive EIS covering the entire transportation and destruction operation.

Legal Issues

The basic issue in this case was whether the procedural requirements of the National Environmental Policy Act (NEPA) are applicable to actions that federal agencies undertake abroad. The language of NEPA does not state whether the act governs such actions. Furthermore, Executive Order No. 12,114, issued by President Jimmy Carter on January 4, 1979, which established rules for federal agencies to follow in assessing the impact of their projects overseas, is ambiguous in regard to NEPA's applicability outside the United States.

A related issue was whether NEPA requires a comprehensive EIS for federal agency actions that involve foreign countries but have domestic implications.

Decision

The district court held that NEPA applied neither to the movement of the chemical weapons within Germany nor to their transportation over the ocean. It found that the transport within Germany was a nondomestic federal action within the foreign policy power of the president. It held that the army's compliance with Executive Order No.12,114 and the foreign policy power of the president precluded the application of NEPA to the ocean crossing. Because it held that a comprehensive environmental impact statement was not required, the court denied the motion of the plaintiffs for a preliminary injunction. Greenpeace appealed, but the Circuit Court for the Ninth Circuit dismissed the appeal as moot because the chemical weapons had by that time arrived at Johnston Atoll (924 F. 2d 175 (9th Cir. 1991)).

Impact

The case did not resolve the question of whether NEPA applies outside the United States. The district court restricted its ruling to the specific situation presented, as courts have tended to do in previous cases on the subject.

However, the court's piecemeal approach to NEPA varies from the holdings in two prior cases: *Sierra Club v. Coleman I* (405 F. Supp. 53 (D.D.C. 1975)) and *National Organization for the Reform of Marijuana Laws (NORML) v. United States Department of State* (452 F. Supp. 1226, 1232 (D.D.C. 1978)). The court sidestepped the question of whether a comprehensive EIS is required for federal agency actions that involve foreign countries but have domestic implications. Nevertheless, by analyzing each portion of the action separately it gave tacit approval to breaking down an action into units during the EIS process.

Considering each unit separately allowed foreign policy considerations and the power of the president in foreign affairs to dominate decisions on the portions of the action that took place abroad. The court gave more weight to foreign policy considerations than to domestic impacts. From the standpoint of attempting to limit the movement of weapons of mass destruction through environmental regulatory approaches, the case represents a step backward.

U.S. DISTRICT COURT, DISTRICT OF NEVADA: *PRESCOTT V. UNITED STATES*, 858 F. SUPP. 1461, 1464 (D. NEV. 1994)

Background

Prescott v. United States was a negligence action involving 15 consolidated cases and 216 former test-site workers who claimed that the government negligently overexposed workers at the Nevada Test Site to radiation that caused illnesses and deaths. The case is named for Keith Prescott, who sued the U.S. government and Reynolds Electrical and Engineering Company (REECo) in the District Court for the District of Nevada in May 1980. Prescott had worked as a mucking machine and heavy equipment operator at the Nevada Test Site from 1961 to 1971. Resolution of the case was delayed, in part because the district court awaited the final decisions in *Consolidated United States Atmospheric Testing Litigation* (820 F. 2d 982 (9th Cir. 1987)) and *Allen v. United States* (816 F. 2d 1417 (10th Cir. 1987)) on the discretionary function exception in the Federal Tort Claims Act.

In 1985 Judge Roger D. Foley consolidated all the Nevada Test Site worker radiation injury cases pending in his court. After consolidation the government was substituted for the contractor defendants. Six representative plaintiffs, including Prescott, were chosen. They were tunnel walkers, security guards, laborers, radiation safety monitors, and heavy equipment operators employed at the test site from the 1950s through the 1970s. All except Prescott had died of cancer by 1985.

In January 1993 Judge Foley had to withdraw because of poor health, and Judge Philip Pro was assigned to the case. After various delays the trial began on December 13, 1993, and ended on February 1, 1994.

Legal Issues

The government based its defense on the discretionary function exception in the FTCA. This exception does not allow suit under the FTCA when the alleged tort is "based upon the exercise or performance or the failure to exercise or perform a discretionary function or duty on the part of a federal agency or an employee of the Government, whether or not the discretion involved be abused."

At issue was the question of whether the alleged negligent acts were immune under the discretionary function. To reach a decision the court evaluated the government's radiation safety policies at the test site.

The government had to prove that its decisions regarding radiation safety were discretionary. It did this by presenting evidence that on-site officials had been explicitly entrusted with the responsibility of balancing competing political, economic, and social considerations and that they reached decisions regarding radiation safety after analyzing available scientific and medical data.

The court then had to decide whether Congress intended to exempt decisions of this type from the requirements of the FCTA.

Decision

The court concluded that Congress did intend to exempt decisions on radiation standards from the requirements of the FCTA and that therefore the discretionary function barred the claims of the plaintiffs. In making its decision it referred to the Atomic Energy Act. Through the act, Congress delegated to the Atomic Energy Commission responsibility for formulating radiation safety standards to protect health. Because Congress delegated authority for radiation safety standards, the radiation safety decisions made by test site officials were the type of decisions that Congress intended to protect with the discretionary function exception.

Impact

The decision in the *Prescott* case maintained the discretionary function's role in preventing government compensation of alleged victims of the U.S. nuclear testing program. The discretionary function had previously blocked compensation for civilians irradiated by fallout from the tests and for military personnel who participated in military nuclear effects tests.

Because *Prescott* was only a district court decision, other jurisdictions would not be bound by its conclusions. Therefore, other alleged victims might still have the possibility of obtaining compensation through the courts. However, after *Prescott,* it appeared that the best hope for nuclear test victims lay in the enactment by Congress of laws that provide compensation. By the time that the decision was delivered, some on site workers had become entitled to limited monetary compensation through the Radiation Exposure Compensation Act.

ADVISORY OPINION OF THE INTERNATIONAL COURT OF JUSTICE: LEGALITY OF THE THREAT OR USE OF NUCLEAR WEAPONS (1996)

Background

The International Court of Justice (ICJ) was established by Chapter 14 of the UN Charter and is the principal judicial organ of the United Nations. The court is composed of 15 judges, chosen by the General Assembly and the Security Council, voting independently, from a list of candidates nominated by government-appointed national groups of international law experts. No two judges can come from the same state. The court may be asked to rule on certain types of disputes between states. It may also give advisory opinions. Article 96 of the UN Charter states that the General Assembly and Security Council may request an advisory opinion of the ICJ on any legal question and that other UN organs may request opinions on "questions arising within the scope of their activities."

In 1993 the International Physicians for the Prevention of Nuclear War (IPPNW) steered a resolution on nuclear war, cosponsored by 22 countries, through the annual assembly of the World Health Organization (WHO). The resolution asked the ICJ: "In view of the health and environmental effects, would the use of nuclear weapons by a State in war or other armed conflict be a breach of its obligations under international law including the WHO Constitution?" The resolution passed in May 1993 and was received by the court in September 1993.

Meanwhile, the World Court Project (WCP), a network of organizations and individuals with the International Peace Bureau, IPPNW, and the International Association of Lawyers against Nuclear Arms at its core, conducted a campaign to convince the UN General Assembly to seek an advisory opinion from the ICJ also. In plenary session December 15, 1994, the General Assembly adopted a resolution to ask the court for its opinion on the question: "Is the threat or use of nuclear weapons in any circumstance permitted under international law?" The

General Assembly asked that the opinion be given "urgently." Therefore the IJC decided to consider it on the same timetable as the question from WHO. The court responded to both questions on July 8, 1996.

Legal Issues

In its advisory opinion on the request from the UN General Assembly the court took up one by one the legal issues involved in the case, summarized them, and gave an opinion. Each judge wrote a separate declaration or opinion, some of them lengthy. The issues considered included the following:

- Did the court have jurisdiction and, if so, should the court exercise it? Some states argued that the court could not give an opinion on matters unrelated to the work of the General Assembly or Security Council. Others stated that there is no such restriction and that, in any case, the issue is relevant to the work of the General Assembly.
- Was the question a legal question? Some argued that it was essentially a political question and thus not within the scope of the court. Others said that the question was indeed a legal question because it entailed identifying the relevant existing rules and principles of international law, applying them, and giving an answer based on them. The fact that it obviously has political aspects does not destroy its character as a legal question.
- Was the question too vague and abstract for an answer to be useful and within the scope of the court's judicial function?
- Do existing norms and treaties relating to the safeguard of the environment and to human rights make the use of nuclear weapons in any circumstance unlawful? Do principles of human rights and environmental protection designed for times of peace apply to armed conflict? Do they impose restrictions that go beyond the law that treats the conduct of hostilities? In other words, is international law divided into watertight compartments?
- How should the rule, in customary international law, that the right to self-defense is subject to proportionality and necessity be applied to nuclear weapons? Some states argued that because a nuclear conflict is likely to escalate rapidly no use of nuclear weapons could meet the rule of proportionality.
- Were nuclear weapons prohibited by existing treaties? Some states argued that existing treaties that prohibit nuclear weapons in certain locations and conventions that limit and control them "bear witness . . . to the emergence of a rule of complete legal prohibition." Others said that even the Nuclear Non-Proliferation Treaty does not ban the use of nuclear weapons by the five nuclear-weapon states.

Decision

The court declined to give an opinion on the question from WHO. On the request from the General Assembly, the court issued an opinion composed of 105 numbered sections. Section 105 is often cited as the decision, although the court makes clear that this section must be interpreted in the light of the preceding sections. Below, the points made in section 105 are designated by letters, as is customary.

Section 105 opens with a finding by the court that (A) customary and conventional international law does not authorize a nation to use or to threaten to use nuclear weapons; and that (B) this body of law does not set out "any comprehensive and universal prohibition" against the use or threat of use of these weapons. The court then states that (C) any threat or use of nuclear weapons that is contrary to the United Nations Charter is unlawful, and that (D) any threat or use of nuclear weapons must be in accordance with "international law applicable in armed conflict," particularly with international humanitarian law, and with treaty obligations. All members of the court voted for points A, C, and D. The vote on B was split 11 to three.

Statement E, which is divided into two clauses, was also controversial. Clause 1 of this statement states that, given the preceding requirements, the threat or use of nuclear weapons would "generally be contrary to the rules of international law applicable in armed conflict." Clause 2 states that nevertheless, given the status of international law and the facts available to the court, the court cannot say whether the threat or use of nuclear weapons is unlawful when the survival of a nation is at stake. The vote on E was seven to seven, with President Mohammed Bedjaoui casting a deciding vote.

Three of the seven judges who voted against section E were the three judges who voted against section B. Therefore, 10 judges were either in favor of E or went further by holding that there is a comprehensive and universal prohibition against the threat or use of nuclear weapons.

Advocates of a prohibition on the use of a nuclear-weapon state that section E must be read in conjunction with section D. Nuclear weapons cannot be compatible with the principles of humanitarian law as defined by the court. Therefore, the threat or use is contrary to international law. Judge Rosalyn Higgins from the United Kingdom wrote that clause 2 was a refusal to render an opinion because the law was unclear. President Bedjaoui disagreed with this interpretation.

Section 105 concludes with a statement on which all members of the court could agree. Nations are obligated to engage in and conclude "negotiations leading to nuclear disarmament" under international control.

Impact

The UN General Assembly, on December 10, 1996, adopted a resolution that welcomed the ICJ opinion and called on all states to fulfill their obligation to pursue negotiations leading to nuclear disarmament and to immediately begin negotiations leading to a nuclear weapons convention that would provide for the elimination of nuclear weapons. The vote on the resolution showed that the opinion of the ICJ had caused a shift in the opinion of UN members. The vote in 1994 to ask the court to render an opinion was 79 for and 99 against, abstaining, or absent. In 1996 the vote on the resolution was 115 for and 63 against, abstaining, or absent.

When individuals or organizations that commit civil disobedience are brought to trial, they or their lawyers are likely to cite the decision of the International Court of Justice in their defense. Sometimes citing this decision leads to an acquittal. The decision adds to the legal justification for states and interstate organizations to ban nuclear weapons within their regions or jurisdictions. Some believe that states can go farther and, on the basis of the decision, ban the transportation of nuclear weapons through their territorial waters and Exclusive Economic Zones (EEZs). In April 2001 the Inter-Parliamentary Union, composed of more than 130 national parliaments, adopted without dissent a resolution calling on states to ban the transportation of nuclear weapons and other weapons of mass destruction through their EEZs.

Local governments have also used the opinion of the court as one of the bases for setting up local nuclear-free zones or calling for a ban on nuclear weapons

Basing their arguments in part on the finding of the ICJ and the response to it by the UN General Assembly, representatives of many nonnuclear-weapon states and nongovernment organizations lobbied at the Nuclear Non-Proliferation Treaty review conference in 2000 to insist that the nuclear-weapon states negotiate significant steps toward nuclear disarmament.

CHAPTER 3

CHRONOLOGICAL SURVEY

The development and deployment of agents and weapons—both crude and sophisticated—capable of causing widespread death, disease, and destruction are not phenomena of modern society. Our earliest literature does, in fact, record use of what today would be called chemical or biological weapons. The following is a listing of selected events related to weapons of mass destruction in world history.

about 750 B.C.

- Ancient Roman poet Homer, in his epic *The Odyssey*, describes the work's hero Odysseus poisoning his arrows. Ovid and others described Hercules as using arrows dipped in poison. Toxic arrows are the first biological weapons to appear in Western literature.

about 590 B.C.

- The Amphictionic League poisons the water supply of the fortified Greek city Kirrha with hellebore. The Kirrhans become too ill to fight, and the Amphictions easily take the city. The poisoning is the first reported case of the deliberate contamination of drinking water.

429 B.C.

- At Plataia, during the Peloponnesian War, the Spartans create a fire of resin and sulphur that releases toxic fumes. This event, described by Thucydides, is the first documented use of fire to create a poison gas.

331 B.C.

- Scythian archers, riding horses and shooting poisoned arrows, defeat the army of Alexander the Great. To create their poison, they mix decomposed vipers with animal dung and human blood serum. The most inventive and the most feared of the groups fighting with poisoned arrows, the Scythians developed a sophisticated bow and arrow known as a composite reflex bow that projects arrows with greater speed and accuracy than other contemporary weapons, thus making it possible to inflict more casualties in less time.

190 B.C.

- The Carthaginian general Hannibal overcomes the fleet of King Eumenes of Pergamum in Asia Minor by throwing earthen jars filled with poisonous snakes onto the decks of Eumenes' ships. The jars break, and Eumenes' sailors are too busy trying to avoid the snakes to fight. The incident is one of the earliest examples of a general deliberately terrorizing enemy troops in order to keep them from fighting. Hannibal ultimately becomes known for his use of elephants to inflict widespread terror and damage on the enemy. (In a lecture at Cornell University in 1962, historian Donald Kagan called Hannibal's use of elephants "the atomic bomb of his day.")

189 B.C.

- The Greeks in the city of Ambracia contrive to blow noxious fumes, from burning coals and bird feathers, into the tunnel of Roman sappers trying to undermine the city's walls. To do so, they produce the smoke in a container the size of the tunnel. The tactic is one of the earliest, if not the earliest, use of a smoke machine in the West. The sappers are driven away.

80 B.C.

- The Roman general Sertorius defeats the Characitani of Spain by causing fine white soil to blow into the caves that the Characitani inhabit. The caustic soil, likely gypsum or soft limestone, chokes and blinds the Characitani. The event, described by Plutarch, is an early use of a chemical aerosol.

1346

- During the siege of Kaffa, a fortress in Genoa, the Mongols catapult corpses of their own soldiers who have died of bubonic plague over the walls of the city. The defense of the city eventually collapses. Historians generally consider the victory at Kaffa to be the first attempt to win a battle by spreading contagion, but Adrienne Mayor, author of *Greek Fire*, writes that ancient sources describe even earlier instances of this tactic.

1494

- The Spanish poison French wine and chase prostitutes bearing diseases into the camp of the French army during the Naples campaign of Charles VIII of France. The use of plague-infected women in war repeats a tactic employed by the ancient Hittites, 3,000 years earlier.

1710

- In a more recent use of disease as a weapon, Russian troops reportedly throw corpses of plague victims over the walls of the Swedish trading center Reval (Tallinn) during the Great Northern War. The city had as many as 8,000 residents in 1708. By 1710 when it capitulates, it is down to some 2,000 as a result of privation and the plague.

Chronological Survey

1763

- ***June 24:*** Captain Simeon Ecuyer of the Royal Americans, fighting in the French and Indian wars, notes in his journal that two Indian chiefs have been given blankets and a handkerchief from a smallpox hospital. "I hope it will have the desired effect."

1863

- ***April 24:*** The U.S. War Department issues General Order 100, stating that "The use of poison in any manner, be it to poison wells, or foods, or arms, is wholly excluded from modern warfare."

1899

- ***July 29:*** The "Hague Convention (II) with Respect to the Laws and Customs of War on Land" is signed. The convention prohibits the use of "poison or poisoned arms."

1915

- ***April 22:*** The Germans employ chlorine gas against Allied forces at Ypres, France, the first use of a lethal chemical weapon in World War I and the first modern use of gas in warfare.

1917

- The U.S. Army's Edgewood Arsenal in Maryland begins producing chemical agents and munitions.
- ***April 5:*** The United States declares war on Germany.
- ***July:*** Mustard gas is used for the first time in World War I, as the Germans employ it at Ypres.

1918

- ***February 26:*** The Germans attack U.S. troops with phosgene and chloropicrin shells, in the first major use of gas against U.S. forces.
- ***June:*** France uses mustard gas in combat for the first time. The British begin using it in August.
- ***June 28:*** The United States establishes the Chemical Warfare Service, thus beginning its formal chemical weapons program.
- ***November 11:*** A cease-fire goes into effect, ending World War I.

1919

- Russian leader Vladimir Ilyich Lenin establishes the Bacteriological Institute in Saratov. There, infected animals are killed, dried, and ground into powder for biological weapons.

1922

- In Spanish Morocco, the Spanish begin attacking the Rif rebels with chemical weapons.

1925

- ***June 17:*** The "Geneva Protocol for the Prohibition of the Use in War of Asphyxiating, Poisonous, or Other Gases, and of Bacteriological Methods of Warfare" is signed.

1930

- The Japanese use tear gas to crush a rebellion in Wushe in central Taiwan, which belongs to Japan. Local tribal leader Mona Rudo leads the rebellion.

1936

- The Italians use mustard gas against Abyssinians in an invasion of their country (now Ethiopia) that began in 1935.

1937

- The Japanese establish a biological weapons program at Harbin in occupied Manchuria. There, at the research and development complex known as Unit 731, the Japanese experiment on prisoners. The Japanese begin using chemical weapons, including phosgene and mustard gas, against the Chinese. Use continues until at least 1942.

1939

- ***September 3:*** France and the United Kingdom declare war on Germany.
- ***October 11:*** U.S. president Franklin D. Roosevelt receives a letter from Austrian-American Scientist Albert Einstein informing him of German atomic research and the possibility of a new and powerful type of bomb. Einstein urges the United States to secure uranium supplies. As a result Roosevelt appoints a Uranium Committee.

1940

- The Japanese drop ceramic bombs containing rice and wheat mixed with fleas carrying bubonic plague on Manchuria and other regions of China. Their biological attacks continue in 1941.

1941

- ***December 7:*** The Japanese attack the U.S. naval base at Pearl Harbor in Hawaii. The next day the United States declares war on Japan.
- ***December 11:*** The United States declares war on Germany and Italy.

Chronological Survey

1942

- Germany begins killing prisoners in the gas chambers of its concentration camps with Zyklon B (hydrocyanic acid).
- ***May 15:*** At a cabinet meeting President Roosevelt orders the implementation of a National Academy of Sciences report calling for defensive and offensive biological bioweapons research.
- ***August 13:*** The U.S. Army establishes the "Manhattan Engineer District" (Manhattan Project) within its Corps of Engineers to develop an atomic bomb.
- ***September 26:*** British scientists drop a bomb containing anthrax spores from a plane at Gruinard Island off the coast of Scotland. U.S. scientists participate in the experiment.
- ***December 2:*** Scientists initiate the world's first self-sustaining nuclear chain reaction, in a reactor constructed in a squash court under abandoned stands in Stagg Field at the University of Chicago.
- ***December 10:*** George W. Merck, U.S. director of the new federal agency the War Research Service, asks the Chemical Warfare Service to establish a bioweapons program.

1943

- ***March 9:*** Detrick Field, an abandoned airfield outside Frederick, Maryland, is formally acquired as a site for Camp Detrick (later renamed Fort Detrick), a research and development facility for biological weapons. It becomes operational later in the year.
- ***June 8:*** President Roosevelt declares that if the Axis Powers use poison gas, the United States will retaliate in kind upon military objectives.

1945

- ***May 7:*** Germany surrenders unconditionally, ending World War II in Europe.
- ***July 16:*** The United States explodes its first nuclear device, at Alamogordo Air Base in New Mexico.
- ***August 6:*** The B-29 bomber *Enola Gay* drops a uranium bomb, code-named "Little Boy," on Hiroshima in Japan.
- ***August 9:*** The United States drops a bomb constructed from plutonium, code-named the "Fat Man," on Nagasaki.
- ***August 14:*** Japan surrenders, ending World War II. Japanese general Ishii Shiro subsequently orders Unit 731 to be burned down and dumps its remaining chemical weapons into the water off its coast.

1946

- ***July 1:*** A Nagasaki-type bomb with the force of 23,000 tons of TNT is dropped from a Superfortress flying over 73 ships off Bikini Atoll in the Pacific Ocean.

- ***August 1:*** U.S. president Harry S. Truman signs the Atomic Energy Act of 1946, which transfers control of atomic energy from the military to civilians.
- ***August 31:*** *Hiroshima*, a lengthy article by John Hersey, is published in *New Yorker* magazine.

1947

- ***January 1:*** The Atomic Energy Commission takes over control of atomic weapons from the Manhattan Project, as provided for in the Atomic Energy Act.
- ***February 23:*** The Allied Powers take into custody several hundred underground Nazis in the U.S. and British occupation zones in Germany. They include former officers in Germany's bacteriological warfare and intelligence departments. The Nazis claim to have a secret biological weapon that, according to the U.S. army, they hoped to use to free Germany.

1948

- ***January 13:*** In a report entitled *Survival in the Air Age*, the U.S. president's Air Policy Commission warns of the possibility of biological warfare.

1949

- ***September 23:*** President Truman reports that an atomic "explosion" has taken place in the Soviet Union. Two days later the Russian news agency Tass states that the Russians possess "an atomic weapon."

1950

- ***June 25:*** The Korean War breaks out, as North Korean troops invade South Korea.
- ***June 27:*** President Truman orders U.S. forces to give South Korea sea and air support; the UN Security Council, without Russia, calls on member states to support South Korea.
- ***June 30:*** The U.S. Department of Defense's Committee on Chemical, Biological and Radiological Warfare issues the Stevenson Report, which recommends that the United States acquire the capability to employ chemical agents. The report is later withdrawn but is nevertheless influential.
- ***September:*** Biological simulants are sprayed over San Francisco to test the dispersal of biological agents. Another test occurs in February 1951.

1951

- ***January 27:*** The first nuclear test to be held at the Nevada Test Site occurs. A one-kiloton device is dropped from a plane.
- ***September 26:*** It is reported that the U.S. Public Health Service has created an "epidemic intelligence service" to help protect the public against biological attack.

Chronological Survey

1952

- ***October 31:*** The United States carries out its first successful thermonuclear test, at Enewetak in the Pacific.

1953

- ***June 19:*** Purported spies and traitors Julius and Ethel Rosenberg are executed. In 1951 they were found guilty of selling information on nuclear weapons technology to the Soviet Union.
- ***June 27:*** The Korean War officially ends with the signing of a cease-fire agreement.
- ***August 12:*** The Atomic Energy Commission detects in the Soviet Union an explosion involving both fission and thermonuclear reactions. The Soviets announce on August 20 that they have tested a hydrogen bomb, although according to physicist Hans Bethe the test was "not a true H-bomb."
- ***September 15:*** U.S. Army secretary Robert Stevens announces that the United States will deploy in Germany a 280-millimeter atomic cannon with a 20-mile range. The projectile is the first "tactical" nuclear weapon that is not delivered by an aircraft. The first arrives in Bremerhaven on October 9.
- ***December 8:*** President Dwight Eisenhower delivers the "Atoms for Peace" speech, in which the United States promises to share nuclear technology for peaceful purposes.

1954

- ***January 21:*** The U.S. Navy launches the *Nautilus*, the first submarine propelled by nuclear energy, at the Electric Boat Company shipyard in Groton, Connecticut.
- ***February 28:*** The Bravo test, the largest nuclear test ever conducted by the United States, takes place at Bikini Atoll, Marshall Islands, in the Pacific Ocean. It has a yield of 15 megatons. Japanese fishermen on board the *Lucky Dragon*, 70–90 miles from ground zero, are subject to heavy fallout, and one dies later of radiation-related problems.
- ***August 30:*** President Eisenhower signs the Atomic Energy Act of 1954, aimed at promoting the peaceful use of nuclear energy through private enterprise.

1955

- Soviet military intelligence agents steal the structural formula for V-agents (nerve gas) developed by Dr. Ranajit Ghosh in England. Britain has previously given the formula to Canada and the United States.
- ***January 15:*** The Central Secretariat of the Chinese Politburo decides to undertake a nuclear weapons program.

1956

- ***January 19:*** Dr. Willard Libby of the Atomic Energy Commission states in a lecture that "nuclear weapons tests as carried out at present do not constitute a health [or genetic] hazard to the human population."
- ***December 10:*** The National Committee on Radiation Protection recommends that the allowable exposure for atomic industry workers be reduced to five roentgens a year or a lifetime exposure of 260 roentgens, about one-third the dosage permitted in 1956.

1957

- ***July 29:*** The statute of the International Atomic Energy Agency enters into force.
- ***September 19:*** The United States sets off its first underground nuclear test, at the Nevada Test Site, a hundred miles from Las Vegas.
- ***September 29:*** A tank containing highly radioactive waste from plutonium production explodes at a Soviet nuclear weapons plant near Chelyabinsk. The Soviet Union covers up the accident, although it results in the evacuation of more than 10,000 people.
- ***October 4:*** The Soviets launch the *Sputnik* satellite.

1958

- ***July 3:*** The United Kingdom and the United States sign the 1958 Mutual Defense Agreement on cooperation on the uses of atomic energy for mutual defense purposes.

1959

- ***January 26:*** Three editors of the *China Monthly Review of Shanghai* go on trial in San Francisco, charged with sedition for allegedly printing false statements during the Korean War. The statements include charges that the United States used germ warfare, a charge the United States denies.
- ***December 1:*** Defense Secretary Neil McElroy reports that the United States and the Soviet Union each have about 10 combat-ready intercontinental ballistic missiles.

1962

- U.S. troops on a training mission in Vietnam are instructed to retaliate if fired upon. A military assistance command is set up in South Vietnam, which the United States is supporting against the Soviet-backed North Vietnam.
- The United States begins employing tear gas and defoliants, including Agent Orange, in Vietnam. Use of Agent Orange continues into 1970.
- ***October 22:*** U.S. president John F. Kennedy announces the discovery of Soviet-supplied missiles in Cuba, imposes a naval "quarantine" around Cuba, and warns Soviet premier Khrushchev that a missile attack on the United

States from Cuba would provoke full-scale retaliation by the United States against the Soviet Union.

- ***October 28:*** After negotiations, Khrushchev announces that the Soviet Union is withdrawing "offensive" weapons from Cuba in return for a U.S. pledge not to invade Cuba.

1963

- ***August 5:*** The United States, the Soviet Union, and the United Kingdom sign the Limited [Partial] Test Ban Treaty, prohibiting nuclear testing in the atmosphere, in outer space, and underwater. France and China continue atmospheric testing.

1964

- ***October 16:*** China detonates its first nuclear device, which is exploded on the top of a tower.

1966

- ***June:*** The United States releases a biological simulant in the New York subways to test the city's vulnerability to a bioweapons attack.
- ***July 2:*** France conducts the first of 41 nuclear atmospheric tests in Polynesia.

1967

- Egyptians reportedly kill more than 100 people in a chemical attack during their military intervention in the Royalist and Republican civil war in Yemen.

1968

- ***March 13:*** The U.S. Army conducts a test of VX nerve gas at Dugway Proving Ground in Utah. The gas kills more than 6,400 sheep in Skull valley, 27 miles away, reportedly because of an unexpected shift in the wind.
- ***July 1:*** The United States, United Kingdom, Soviet Union, and 59 other countries sign the Nuclear Non-Proliferation Treaty.

1969

- ***July 8:*** In Okinawa, Japan, 23 American soldiers and a U.S. civilian are exposed to sarin while refurbishing chemical munitions. In August the Okinawan legislature demands that the United States remove all nerve gas stocks from the island, and the Pentagon agrees to do so.
- ***November 25:*** U.S. president Richard Nixon announces that "the United States unilaterally renounces first use of lethal or incapacitating chemical agents and weapons and unconditionally renounces all methods of biological warfare." He tells the Department of Defense to draw up a disposal plan for biological weapons.

1970

- ***February 14:*** The White House announces extension of the U.S. ban on biological warfare to cover toxins.
- ***March 5:*** The Nuclear Non-Proliferation Treaty enters into force.

1972

- ***April 10:*** The "Convention on the Prohibition of the Development, Production and Stockpiling of Bacteriological (Biological) and Toxin Weapons and on Their Destruction" (referred to as the Biological and Toxin Weapons Convention [BTWC]) is opened for signature and signed in London, Moscow, and Washington.
- ***May 26:*** The Soviet Union and the United States sign the Treaty on the Limitation of Anti-Ballistic Missile Systems (the Anti-Ballistic Missile Treaty, or ABM Treaty) and the Interim Agreement on Certain Measures with Respect to the Limitation of Strategic Offensive Arms. These agreements are known as SALT I.

1973

- ***January 27:*** The United States, North Vietnam, South Vietnam, and the Provisional Revolutionary Government (the Vietcong) sign peace accords, ending U.S. involvement in Vietnam.

1974

- ***May 18:*** India conducts its first nuclear detonation, which it describes as a peaceful nuclear explosion.
- ***December 16:*** The U.S. Senate unanimously votes for ratification of the BTWC and the Geneva Protocol.

1975

- ***March 26:*** The Biological and Toxin Weapons Convention enters into force. Under its terms, stockpiles of biological agents and toxins not needed for peaceful purposes, as well as biological weapons, are to be destroyed within nine months.
- ***December 26:*** Heads of U.S. federal departments and agencies certify that they have complied with the terms of the BTWC in regard to destruction of biological agents and weapons.

1977

- ***August 4:*** U.S. president Jimmy Carter signs legislation abolishing the Energy Research and Development Administration and creating the Department of Energy.
- ***September 21:*** Fifteen nuclear supplier countries, known as the Nuclear Suppliers Group or the London Club, reach agreement in London on a set of

principles and guidelines to govern the transfer of nuclear materials, equipment, and technology.

1978

- ***March 10:*** President Carter signs the Nuclear Non-Proliferation Act, which sets forth conditions for U.S. nuclear export in order that material not be diverted to weapons.

1979

- ***April:*** Near Sverdlosk in the Ural Mountains, an escape of anthrax from a military facility causes human deaths. The Soviets cover up the true cause, and the amount of anthrax involved remains uncertain.

1980

- ***May 8:*** Member states of the World Health Organization unanimously accept the conclusions of its Global Commission for the Certification of Smallpox Eradication: Smallpox has been eradicated and will not return as an endemic disease.

1981

- ***June 7:*** Israel bombs Iraq's Osiraq research reactor. Iraq purchased the reactor from France and planned to produce military plutonium in it.

1984

- For the first time the nerve gas tabun is used in combat—Iraq employs it against Iran in the Iran-Iraq War.
- ***April:*** The United States signs a nuclear trade pact with China (the U.S.-SINO Nuclear Trade Pact) after Peking agrees to join the International Atomic Energy Agency (IAEA) and accept IAEA inspection of any exported nuclear equipment and material.
- ***September 9:*** Members of the Rajneeshee religious cult contaminate the salad bar at Shakey's Pizza in The Dalles, Oregon, with salmonella bacteria. This is one of a series of attacks with chemicals and bacteria carried out by the cult in Oregon in 1984 and 1985.

1985

- ***August 6:*** By the South Pacific Nuclear-Free Zone/Rarotonga Treaty, eight members of the South Pacific Forum, including Australia and New Zealand, establish a nuclear-free zone in the South Pacific.

1986

- ***Spring:*** Iran makes extensive use of chemical weapons in fighting around Basra in the Iran-Iraq War.

1987

- ***December 8:*** U.S. president Ronald Reagan and Soviet president Mikhail Gorbachev sign the Treaty on the Elimination of Intermediate-Range and Shorter-Range Missiles (INF Treaty).

1988

- Some 500,000 steppe antelope die in one hour because of a release of biological agents near the Soviet biological storage/testing site of Vozrozhdeniye Island in the Aral Sea.
- ***March 16–17:*** Iraq uses mustard gas and nerve agents against the Kurdish city of Halabja, where the chemical agents kill hundreds of civilians.
- ***September 29:*** The American Type Culture Collection, a private scientific supply company, ships 11 strains of germs, including a type of anthrax developed for biological warfare, to Iraq.

1989

- ***February 23:*** The U.S. Commerce Department bans the sale of anthrax and many other pathogens to Iran, Iraq, Libya, and Syria, all known to have or suspected of having germ warfare programs.
- ***Autumn:*** Vladimir Pasechnik, a Soviet defector, reveals for the first time to the West the scope of the Soviets' biological weapons program.

1990

- ***August 2:*** Iraq invades Kuwait. The country is quickly occupied. The UN Security Council subsequently condemns the occupation, imposes a trade embargo, and gives Iraq an ultimatum to withdraw by January 15, 1991.
- ***late September:*** The United States removes its last intermediate-range nuclear missile from Europe.
- ***October 15:*** U.S. president George H. W. Bush signs the Radiation Exposure Compensation Act.

1991

- ***January 17:*** With Iraq occupying Kuwait, an international coalition led by the United States begins a massive air assault on Iraq. A land offensive begins on February 24. Iraq's chemical and nuclear facilities are heavily damaged.
- ***March 3:*** Iraqi forces having been driven out of Kuwait, Iraq agrees to the cease-fire conditions laid down by the coalition.
- ***July 31:*** After 10 years of difficult negotiations, presidents George H. W. Bush and Mikhail Gorbachev sign the initial Strategic Arms Reduction Treaty I (START I).
- ***September 27:*** President Bush announces that the United States, in a unilateral initiative, will eliminate its entire worldwide inventory of ground-launched tactical nuclear weapons.

- ***December 12:*** President Bush signs the Soviet Nuclear Threat Reduction Act (Nunn-Lugar Legislation), which provides for U.S. funding of nonproliferation activities in the Soviet Union, including destruction of nuclear and chemical weapons.
- ***December 25:*** Mikhail Gorbachev resigns as president of the USSR and hands over to Boris Yeltsin the Soviet nuclear war codes. A Commonwealth of Independent States composed of 11 of the 12 former Soviet constituent republics replaces the Soviet Union.

1992

- ***April 25:*** *Izvestia* reports that Boris Yeltsin has issued a decree banning in Russia all biotechnology research that is not permitted by the BWTC.
- ***July 13:*** President Bush announces that the United States will no longer produce plutonium or highly enriched uranium for explosive purposes.
- ***September 3:*** The "Convention on the Prohibition of the Development, Production, Stockpiling and Use of Chemical Weapons and on Their Destruction" (known as the Chemical Weapons Convention or CWC) is approved by the United Nations.
- ***September 14:*** The United States and Russia announce that Russia has agreed to allow U.S. and British inspectors to visit its biological research facilities. The Russian deputy foreign minister reads a statement admitting that the Soviet Union carried out until March 1992 activities banned by the BWTC.
- ***September 23:*** The United States conducts its last nuclear test to date.

1993

- ***January 3:*** Presidents Bush and Boris Yeltsin sign the Treaty on Further Reduction and Limitation of Strategic Offensive Arms Treaty II (START II).
- ***January 13:*** The United States signs the Chemical Weapons Convention.
- ***February 8:*** Officials of the UN organization inspecting Iraq nuclear facilities (UNSCOM) announce that Iraq's nuclear weapons program has been destroyed, although long term monitoring to ensure compliance should continue.
- ***February 18:*** The United States and Russia sign an agreement committing the United States to purchase from Russia over the coming 20 years low-enriched uranium blended down from 500 metric tons of weapons uranium.
- ***March 24:*** President F. W. de Klerk announces that South Africa developed "a limited nuclear deterrent capability" but dismantled its six fission devices before joining the NPT.

1994

- ***November 23:*** The United States removes nearly 600 kilograms of highly enriched uranium from Kazakhstan in a secret operation named Operation Sapphire.

1995

- ***March 1:*** U.S. president Bill Clinton announces the permanent withdrawal of 200 tons of fissile material from the U.S. nuclear stockpile.
- ***March 20:*** A religious cult, Aum Shinrikyo, attacks passengers in a Tokyo subway with sarin gas.
- ***May 11:*** The Review and Extension Conference of the Parties to the Nuclear Non-Proliferation Treaty decides to extend the treaty indefinitely and without conditions.

1996

- ***January 26:*** The U.S. Senate ratifies START II without amendment.
- ***January 27:*** France conducts its 210th and final nuclear test.
- ***April 11:*** Forty-three African states sign the Pelindaba Treaty, establishing a nuclear-free zone in Africa (AFNWFZ). The United States signs two protocols to the treaty.
- ***July 8:*** The International Court of Justice issues an advisory opinion on the legality of the threat or use of nuclear weapons. It is decided unanimously that "there exists an obligation to . . . bring to a conclusion negotiations leading to nuclear disarmament."
- ***July 29:*** China conducts its 45th known nuclear test and announces a unilaterial moratorium on testing pending the conclusion of a Comprehensive Test Ban Treaty.
- ***September 24:*** The Comprehensive Test Ban Treaty is opened for signature in New York. Seventy-one countries, including the five declared nuclear-weapon states, sign the treaty.

1997

- ***April 25:*** The United States ratifies the Chemical Weapons Convention.

1998

- ***May 11:*** India claims it has detonated three underground nuclear tests, one a thermonuclear test.
- ***May 28:*** Pakistan announces that it has successfully conducted five nuclear tests.
- ***August 11:*** The Conference on Disarmament establishes an ad hoc committee to begin negotiations on a ban on the production of fissile material.
- ***August 31:*** North Korea tests a Taepo Dong I missile/space-launch vehicle. The missile travels 1,320 kilometers. Although the test is only partially successful, the fact that the rocket has three stages has a major impact on estimates of the future threat to the United States from countries like North Korea.

Chronological Survey

1999

- ***October 6:*** A silo to launch the Minuteman III missile is blown up at Grand Forks Air Force Base in South Dakota. All 150 launch facilities for the Minuteman III at the base are to be destroyed by December 1, 2001, according to the terms of START I.
- ***October 13:*** The U.S. Senate rejects the Nuclear Comprehensive Test Ban Treaty in a 48 to 51 vote.
- ***November 13:*** The first remanufactured Minuteman III missile, with a new guidance and propulsion system, is fired successfully from Vandenberg Air Force Base to the Kwajalein Missile Range in the Pacific Ocean.

2000

- ***March 23:*** Peace activist Philip Berrigan is sentenced to 30 months in prison for conspiring to damage U.S. fighter aircraft at a U.S. national guard base in 1999.
- ***November 30:*** The U.S. Army completes destruction of the chemical weapons stored on Johnston Atoll in the Pacific Ocean.

2001

- ***July 25:*** The United States announces that it cannot support, even with changes, the negotiated text of a protocol designed to strengthen compliance with the Biological Weapons Convention.
- ***September 11:*** Terrorists hijack four U.S. cross-country passenger planes. They apparently take over the controls of the planes, purposely crashing two into the World Trade Center towers and the third, into the Pentagon. The fourth plane crashes in a field in Pennsylvania after passengers apparently fight to prevent the plane's takeover.
- ***October:*** Various members of the media and Congress receive letters containing anthrax. Five recipients die, and 18 others are infected. As of early 2005 the perpetrator(s) has not been identified.
- ***December 5:*** The Russian Federation and the United States announce that they have completed the arms reduction required by START I and reached the level of 6,000 deployed warheads each.
- ***December 13:*** U.S. president George W. Bush serves formal notice to Russia that the United States is withdrawing from the Anti-Ballistic Missile (ABM) Treaty and deploying the National Missile Defense (NMD) system, which would violate the terms of the treaty.

2002

- ***January 9:*** The U.S. administration delivers to Congress a classified version of its recently completed Nuclear Posture Review, a blueprint for the changing role of U.S. strategic nuclear forces.

- ***January 10:*** U.S. Department of Energy secretary Spencer Abraham recommends that Yucca Mountain, Nevada, become the site of the country's first repository for highly radioactive waste.
- ***May 24:*** Presidents Bush and Vladimir Putin (of the United States and Russia, respectively) sign the Moscow Treaty, the Strategic Offensive Reductions Treaty (SORT).
- ***August 31:*** In a secret operation the United States helps remove highly enriched uranium (HEU) from the Vinca research reactor, a poorly secured facility in Belgrade, Yugoslavia.
- ***October 2:*** Deactivation of the 50-missile MX/Peacekeeper Intercontinental Ballistic Missile force begins with the removal of W87 warheads from a missile at F. E. Warren Air Force Base in Wyoming.
- ***October 26:*** Russian special forces pump a derivative of the calmative gas fentanyl into a Moscow theater to incapacitate Chechen rebels who have taken hostage the audience. More than 110 hostages die.
- ***November 25:*** The United Nations monitors, led by UN chief inspector Hans Blix and Mohamed ElBaradei of the International Atomic Energy Agency, resume Iraqi weapons inspections, the first since the UN inspection regime collapsed in 1998.
- ***December 27:*** North Korea orders the expulsion of IAEA weapons inspectors and announces that it will reactivate a facility capable of extracting weapons-grade plutonium from irradiated fuel rods.

2003

- ***January 10:*** North Korea announces that it is withdrawing from the Nuclear Non-Proliferation Treaty.
- ***March 19:*** The administration of George W. Bush announces the start of war against Iraq. It begins with the firing of cruise missiles against Baghdad.
- ***September 30:*** The National Institute of Allergy and Infectious Diseases announces the funding of nine Regional Biocontainment Laboratories and of two National Biocontainment Laboratories.
- ***December 19:*** Libya announces that it will dismantle its weapons of mass destruction and ballistic missile program.

2004

- ***January 12:*** Germany's Federal Environmental Ministry confirms that the companies that manage the countries' nuclear power plants are considering installing artificial fog machines to prevent terrorist attacks on the plants from the air.
- ***January 23:*** David Kay, head of the Iraq Survey Group responsible for searching for proscribed weapons in Iraq, resigns. He testifies before the Sen-

ate Armed Services Committee on January 28 that no weapons of mass destruction have been found and that he expects none to be found in Iraq.

- ***February 2:*** Ricin is found on a mail-opening machine in the office of U.S. senator majority leader Bill Frist, in the Dirksen Senate office building.
- ***February 4:*** Pakistani nuclear scientist Abdul Qadeer Khan signs a confession to the effect that he provided Iran, North Korea, and Libya with designs and technology for the production of fuel for nuclear weapons.
- ***March 5:*** Libya discloses that it has stockpiled 44,000 pounds of mustard gas and declares the location of a production plant.
- ***March 9:*** Pakistan tests its nuclear-capable Shaheen II missile, which has a range of 1,240 miles and could hit targets deep in India.
- ***May 7:*** The 2004 Preparatory Committee (PrepCom) meeting of parties for the 2005 Review Conference to the Nuclear Non-Proliferation Treaty (NPT) ends in disarray. State parties to the treaty adopt only parts of a final report containing the most minimal agreements to enable the 2005 Review Conference to take place.
- ***May 25:*** A subcritical nuclear test, named "Armando," is conducted at the Nevada Test Site. It is the 21st U.S. subcritical test since 1997, the Department of Energy announces.
- ***July 21:*** President George W. Bush signs into law a bill establishing Project BioShield, aimed at developing and making available drugs and vaccines.
- ***July 29:*** An Israeli Arrow 3 interceptor launched from the U.S. Navy's Naval Warfare Center at Point Mugo, California, successfully intercepts a live short-range ballistic missile. Israeli defense sources say that the test proves that Israel can defend itself.
- ***October 4:*** The federal government halts design work on a plant in Pueblo, Colorado, to neutralize stored chemical weapons.
- ***November 20:*** Congressional conferees to the Fiscal Year 2005 Omnibus appropriations bill eliminate funding for the Robust Nuclear Earth Penetrator and for the Advanced Concepts Initiative to design new kinds of nuclear warheads.
- ***December 15:*** A U.S. interceptor missile fails to launch from Kwajalein Atoll in the Pacific, in a test of a new antiballistic-missile system designed to destroy enemy warheads in mid-flight. As part of the same test, a target missile armed with a mock warhead launches successfully from Kodiak Island, Alaska.

2005

- ***January 6:*** A train derailment in South Carolina results in a release of chlorine, which kills nine people, hospitalizes 58, and necessitates the evacuation of thousands of people. The incident highlights the possibility that terrorists may turn rail cars carrying hazardous material into weapons.

- ***January 13:*** The *New York Times* reports that "at some point late last year" the United States, without public announcement, ended its search for weapons of mass destruction in Iraq.
- ***January 27:*** U.S. Attorney General John Ashcroft tells the Associated Press that the possibility that terrorists could obtain a nuclear bomb is the greatest terrorist threat to the United States.
- ***February 10:*** The government of North Korea declares publicly for the first time that it has nuclear weapons.
- ***March 2:*** At Kiev airport the Ukraine security service arrests a man who has a case containing 582 grams of uranium 238 in his car.
- ***March 28:*** The Government Accountability Office releases a report on the screening of airline passengers. It states that the U.S. Transportation Security Administration is behind schedule in developing a program to assess the risk posed by individual airline travelers in order to determine how much screening each person should undergo, and it questions whether the program will work.
- ***April 6:*** The Senate Appropriations Committee approves a requirement that Defense Department officials move forward on their plan to begin destruction of nerve gas at Kentucky's Blue Grass Army Depot in 2010. The Pentagon, in December 2004, had announced that it would delay the project because of a funding shortfall.
- ***April 11:*** A shipment of mixed oxide (MOX) fuel arrives in South Carolina from France, where it was fabricated from excess U.S. weapons plutonium. The fuel is to be used in the Catawba nuclear power plant to help determine the feasibility of employing MOX as a means of rendering plutonium useless for weapons.
- ***April 19:*** The last shipment of plutonium-contaminated waste from Rocky Flats nuclear weapons plant leaves Colorado for disposal in the Waste Isolation Pilot Project (WIPP) in New Mexico. The cleanup of Rocky Flats is scheduled to be officially completed by November 2005.
- ***May 15:*** The Bush administration warns North Korea that if it conducts a nuclear test, the United States and several Pacific nations will take punitive action. It does not state what that action would be.
- ***May 15:*** The Iranian parliament votes to force the Iranian government to develop the full nuclear fuel cycle.
- ***May 27:*** The 2005 review conference on the Nuclear Non-Proliferation Treaty ends without delegates having made any decision about how to strengthen the treaty or otherwise stop the spread of nuclear weapons.
- ***June 29:*** The National Academies' National Research Council releases a report entitled *Health Risks from Exposure to Low Levels of Ionizing Radiation (BEIR VII-Phase 2)*, which supports the "linear, no-threshold" risk model, ac-

cording to which even the smallest levels of ionizing radiation pose a risk to human health.

- ***August 29:*** Hurricane Katrina strikes the Gulf Coast with disastrous force. The obviously inadequate response of government agencies to the devastation throws doubt on the ability of authorities to assist Americans in the wake of an attack by nuclear, chemical, or biological weapons.
- ***September 11:*** The media calls attention to a draft "Doctrine for Joint Nuclear Operations" written by the Pentagon's Joint Chiefs of Staff and dated March 15, 2005. The document would revise rules and procedures for use of nuclear weapons in accordance with the George W. Bush administration's preemption strategy. It envisions use of nuclear weapons to preempt an enemy attack or to destroy enemy stockpiles of nuclear, biological, or chemical weapons.
- ***September 19:*** North Korea promises to dismantle its nuclear weapons and existing nuclear program and return the Nuclear Non-Proliferation Treaty in return for a nonaggression pledge and economic and energy assistance from the United States. Difficult negotiations on implementation of the agreement lie ahead.
- ***November 13:*** An explosion at a chemical plant in northeastern China pollutes the Songhua River with nitrobenzene. The pollution forces Harbin, a city of 4 million people in northeastern China, to go without a water supply for several days. The spill, which illustrates the potential for chemical terrorism, eventually moves north toward Russia, threatening water supplies on an international scale.
- ***December 8:*** The Armenian parliament ratifies the Comprehensive Nuclear Test Ban, which brings to 127 the total number of ratifying nations. Haiti ratified it the previous week.
- ***December 9:*** Nations belonging to the Biological and Toxin Weapons Convention approve a report that encourages scientists across the world to develop codes of conduct aimed at reducing the risk of biological terrorism. The original proposal before the nations would have encouraged governments to participate in developing, adopting, and promulgating codes of conduct.
- ***December 12:*** North Korea suspends multilateral talks on its nuclear program "for an indefinite period" because the United States is imposing financial sanctions on eight North Korean companies.
- ***December 13:*** Speaking in Sweden, the director of the International Atomic Energy Agency, Mohamed ElBaradei, predicts that within the next two decades up to 30 nations could have nuclear weapons.
- ***December 14:*** U.S. Representative David Hobson (R-Ohio) promises to continue opposing any attempts by the Bush administration to revive research on the Robust Nuclear Earth Penetrator. Hobson is chairman of the House Appropriations Energy and Water Subcommittee.

2006

- ***February 6:*** U.S. Senator Richard Lugar (R, Ind.) tells the UN Security Council that the world needs an international accountability system for weapons of mass destruction. Such a system would require that every nation that has "weapons and materials of mass destruction" account for what it has, store the weapons and materials safely, and prove that it will not allow cells and other nations access to them.

CHAPTER 4

BIOGRAPHICAL LISTING

The following is a list of a few of the individuals who have figured prominently in the area of weapons of mass destruction—from development, proliferation, and use to control and elimination. Their widely varying backgrounds and beliefs illustrate the complexity of issues in this area.

Ken Alibek, high-ranking administrator in the Soviet biological weapons program who defected to the United States. He was born a Kazakh, Kanatjan Alibekov. He became fascinated with biological weapons in military medical school, which he entered in 1973. After rising through the ranks of the Biopreparat—nominally civilian facilities engaged in research, development, and production of bioweapons—he became its first deputy director. He defected in 1992, changed his name, and began publicizing the Soviet bioweapons program. In 1999 he published an autobiography, *Biohazard.*

Ira Baldwin, professor of bacteriology at the University of Wisconsin who was chosen to head the biological warfare effort at Camp Detrick. He became the facility's first technical director and played a key role in developing methods that made possible the safe production of bioagents on a large scale. He returned to the university in 1945 and remained there until his retirement. He died in 1999 at the age of 103.

Wouter Basson, cardiologist and military officer who headed the secret chemical and biological warfare program of South Africa's apartheid government, Project Coast, during the 1980s and early 1990s. F. W. de Klerk, after he became South Africa's president, pressured Basson to retire. Subsequently, as a consultant, Basson traveled frequently, including to Libya. The Nelson Mandela government rehired him, within the medical section of the military, in 1995 to try to prevent him from spreading information about chemical and biological weapons.

Mohammed Bedjaoui, president of the International Court of Justice when, in 1996, it handed down its advisory opinion on the legality of the threat or use of nuclear weapons. An Algerian, Judge Bedjaoui devoted his life to the study and practice of international law. He edited for UNESCO *International Law: Achievements and Prospects* (1992), with contributions from every continent, analyzing the state of international law at the time. He resigned from the court in 2001.

Philip Berrigan, peace activist. He and his brother Daniel Berrigan were the first Catholic priests to receive federal prison sentences for peace agitation in the United States. They engaged in civil disobedience against the Vietnam War and later cofounded Ploughshares, a movement that carries out symbolic vandalism against military targets involving nuclear weapons. Philip Berrigan married Elizabeth McAlister, a former nun, for which he was excommunicated. They turned their home into a communal residence and training center for peace activists. He died in 2002 at the age of 79.

Hans Bethe, wartime director of the Theoretical Division at Los Alamos, where the first atomic device was assembled and detonated. He was born in Strassburg in 1906 but left Europe in 1933. From 1935 until his retirement in 1975 he held the chair of physics at Cornell University. He died March 5, 2005, after surviving longer than the other great leaders of the Manhattan Project.

Osama bin Laden, an Islamic fundamentalist leader believed to be responsible for several terrorist attacks on the United States. Born in 1957, he was raised in Saudi Arabia, where his father owns a large construction company. He founded the group Al Qaeda, initially to support resistance to the Russians in Afghanistan but later largely directed against the United States and its allies. The most devastating action of bin Laden and Al Qaeda was the attack on the New York City World Trade Center and the Pentagon on September 11, 2001. As of early 2005 Bin Laden was hiding from U.S. forces presumably in or near Afghanistan.

Hans Blix, Swedish lawyer and diplomat who directed the International Atomic Energy Agency from 1981 until 1997. In 2002 the United Nations appointed him to head the UN Monitoring, Verification, and Inspection Commission (UNMOVIC) on Iraq. In 2004 he published the book *Disarming Iraq*, giving his view of the search for weapons of mass destruction in that country.

Niels Bohr, Danish physicist who produced a new model for the atom and helped validate the quantum theory. In 1922 he received a Nobel Prize in physics for explaining the process of fission. During World War II he worked on the atomic bomb in the United States, but he later became passionate about the need to control nuclear weapons. He died in 1962.

Linton F. Brooks, administrator of the U.S. Department of Energy's National Nuclear Security Administration. His previous positions have included serving as vice president of the Center for Naval Analyses and assistant director for strategic and nuclear affairs at the U.S. Arms Control and Disarmament Agency. As the chief Strategic Arms Reduction Treaty (START) negotiator, he was responsible for final preparation of the START I and START II Treaties.

George Herbert Walker Bush, vice president of the United States under Ronald Reagan and president from 1989 to 1993. Bush signed and obtained the ratification of the Treaty on the Elimination of Intermediate-Range and Shorter-Range Missiles (INF Treaty), signed the Strategic Arms Reduction Treaty (START 1), and undertook a unilateral initiative whereby the United States eliminated its worldwide inventory of ground-launched tactical nuclear weapons and withdrew all sea-based tactical nuclear weapons from ships, submarines, and naval aircraft.

Biographical Listing

Vannevar Bush, electrical engineer and scientist who served as scientific adviser to President Franklin D. Roosevelt in World War II. He was instrumental in setting up the Manhattan Project, which built the atomic bomb. After the war he greatly influenced the development of science and engineering in the United States.

Helen Caldicott, Australian-born pediatrician and antinuclear activist opposed to both nuclear power and nuclear weapons. She was president of Physicians for Social Responsibility from 1978 to 1983 and founded Women's Action for Nuclear Disarmament (WAND). In 2002 she founded the Nuclear Policy Research Institute in Washington, D.C., of which she is president. She was cowinner of the 1985 Nobel Peace Prize.

Jimmy Carter, president of the United States from 1977 to 1981. During his single term he took a number of steps to combat nuclear proliferation. He announced that the United States would defer indefinitely the reprocessing of irradiated fuel, played a key role in the demise of the Clinch River breeder reactor, and signed the Nuclear Non-Proliferation Act, setting forth conditions for U.S. nuclear exports. He also signed the SALT II Treaty. Since 1981 he has devoted himself to peacemaking and humanitarian efforts, largely through the Carter Center, which he established.

Albert Einstein, German-born, U.S. physicist famous for his formulation of two theories of relativity. During World War II he used his reputation to draw the attention of President Franklin D. Roosevelt to the possibility that Germany might be developing atomic weapons, which eventually led to U.S. production of the bomb (he did not participate in its creation). After the war he was active in the effort to abolish nuclear weapons.

Dwight David Eisenhower, American general and, from 1953 to 1961, president of the United States. His "Atoms for Peace" speech in 1953 paved the way for U.S. export of nuclear technology for peaceful purposes and to the creation of the International Atomic Energy Agency. The Atomic Energy Act of 1954, which he signed, set the stage for promoting the peaceful use of nuclear energy through private enterprise. He took a position against use of nuclear weapons during the Korean War.

Samuel S. Epstein, physician, pathologist, and environmental scientist. He was born in England in 1926 and moved to the United States in 1960. He received the Society of Toxicology's Achievement Award in 1969 for efforts to alert the public to the hazards of various poisons. His testimony before Congress on the health hazards of the chemicals in Agent Orange was instrumental in persuading Congress to ban the military use of that agent in 1972.

Enrico Fermi, physicist who built the first nuclear reactor, created the first self-sustaining chain reaction in uranium, and worked on the atomic bomb at Los Alamos. He later helped to develop the hydrogen bomb and served on the General Advisory Committee of the U.S. Atomic Energy Commission. He was born in Italy and came to the United States in 1938 after he had made significant contributions to what is now known as nuclear physics.

Sheri Garman, native of Emmett, Idaho, who in summer 2004 called the attention of a state legislator and the public to the fact that many residents of southern Idaho are suffering from cancer that may be attributable to fallout from aboveground nuclear testing. Garman grew up on a dairy farm where the cows ate grass that, it is now presumed, was contaminated. She overcame thyroid cancer but in fall 2004 was gravely ill with breast and bone cancer.

John W. Gofman, professor emeritus of molecular and cell biology at the University of California at Berkeley. He founded, at the request of the U.S. Atomic Energy Commission, the Biomedical Research Division at the Lawrence Livermore National Laboratory, for the purpose of evaluating the health effects of all types of nuclear activities. Gofman and his colleague, Dr. Arthur Tamplin concluded in 1969 and 1971 that human exposure to ionizing radiation was much more serious than previously recognized. Their critically acclaimed book *"Population Control" through Nuclear Pollution* was the first major nationally (and internationally) recognized work documenting public health risks of nuclear-related activities.

Leslie Richard Groves, officer in the U.S. Army Corps of Engineers who was appointed in September 1942 to direct the Manhattan Engineering District, later known as the Manhattan Project. The district was an office established within the army to develop the atomic bomb. This task was assigned to the army because it involved large-scale construction projects, and Groves had managed the building of the Pentagon. Groves had a major influence on the choice of the Japanese cities Hiroshima and Nagasaki as bomb targets.

Fritz Haber, German chemist regarded as inventing chemical warfare. He persuaded Germany to attack the Allied Powers with toxic gas for the first time, in 1915; in 1916 he was made chief of Germany's chemical warfare service. He also was the inventor of a chemical fertilizer. In 1919 he was awarded the Nobel Prize in chemistry, but, because of his war work, the prize was controversial. After Adolf Hitler came to power in 1933, Haber, a Jew, left Germany; he died in 1934.

Orrin G. Hatch, U.S. senator who, with the late Wayne Owens, pushed through Congress in 1990 the Radiation Exposure Compensation Act (RECA). He later prodded Congress to pass the Radiation Exposure Compensation Act Amendments of 2000 to enlarge the original program. A Republican living in Salt Lake City, Utah, Hatch was first elected to the Senate from Utah in 1976 and has been reelected to successive terms since.

Riley D. Housewright, microbiologist who was scientific director of the Army Biological Laboratories at Fort Detrick from 1956 to 1970. He went to Fort Detrick in 1943 when research was being conducted to counter potential biological attacks from Germany and Japan. During the Cuban missile crisis he directed research into the possible use by the United States of biological warfare in Cuba. He died in 2003 at the age of 89.

Saddam Hussein, president of the Republic of Iraq from 1979 to 2003. He came to power as the result of a military coup. In the 1980s his forces used chemical weapons against Iran in the Iran-Iraq War and then against the

Kurds. Iraq had stocks of chemical and biological weapons at the time of the Persian Gulf War but did not use them. He was overthrown in 2003, when the United States and its allies invaded Iraq.

Ishii Shiro, Japanese general who directed his country's biological weapons program during World War II. Ishii established Unit 731 in Manchuria, where gruesome experiments on human subjects were carried out. He died in 1959 without having been prosecuted for war crimes.

Hussein Kamal, son-in-law of Saddam Hussein who defected to Jordan in 1995. He had run Iraq's biological and chemical weapons program for almost 10 years and possessed documents about the program. In Jordan he was debriefed by representatives of the International Atomic Energy Agency, Central Intelligence Agency, and United Nations. Hours after Kamal fled the country, Iraq said that it found documents about the germ warfare program on a farm that Kamal owned and showed the documents to the press. Kamal returned to Iraq in 1996 and was reportedly murdered by Saddam Hussein.

David A. Kay, former special adviser for strategy regarding Iraqi weapons of mass destruction programs. The Central Intelligence Agency appointed him to this post in June 2003. In January 2004 he resigned, testifying that no weapons of mass destruction had been found. In 1991–92 he had been the chief nuclear weapons inspector for the United Nations in Iraq. Later in the 1990s he was a senior fellow at the Potomac Institute for Policy Studies.

David Kelly, microbiologist who served as a consultant on arms control to British and international government agencies. He led inspections of Russian biological warfare facilities from 1991 to 1994; from 1991 to 1999 he was senior adviser on biological warfare for the United Nations in Iraq. He committed suicide in 2003 after he was publicly identified as the source of a British Broadcasting Company (BBC) report that alleged that the British government had falsified reports about Iraq's weapons of mass destruction.

Abdul Qadeer Khan, father of Pakistan's nuclear weapons program. A metallurgist educated in Germany, he worked in the 1970s in the Netherlands for a subcontractor to URENCO, a uranium-enrichment consortium. He took information from URENCO to Pakistan in 1976 and succeeded in constructing a uranium-enrichment plant, which enabled Pakistan to build nuclear weapons. In 2004, following investigations of Pakistan's nuclear program, Khan confessed on television that he had sold nuclear technology to Iran, Libya, and North Korea. Pakistan's president pardoned him.

Kim Jong Il, chief of state in the Democratic People's Republic of Korea (DPRK), known as North Korea. Born in northern Korea in 1942 and educated in part in China, he rose to power through the Korean Workers' Party. He succeeded his father, who died in 1994, as leader of North Korea. His official positions are chairman of the National Defense Commission, the highest North Korean administrative authority, and general-secretary of the Korean Workers' Party. His determination to pursue a nuclear program with military implications has put him at cross-purposes with the United States.

Joshua Lederberg, U.S. geneticist and the first scientist to manipulate genetic material. He shared the 1958 Nobel Prize for Physiology or Medicine with Edward Tatum and George Beadle for work on biochemical genetics. Concerned with the dangers inherent in research on biological warfare agents, he is scientific adviser on biological warfare to the World Health Organization and lectures and writes on the relationship between science and society.

David Lilienthal, director of the Tennessee Valley Authority (TVA) in its formative years and the first chairman of the Atomic Energy Commission. TVA was established in 1933. The inexpensive electricity that it generated made possible the creation in World War II of the Oak Ridge nuclear research and production center, where uranium was enriched. Lilienthal died in 1981.

Sultan Bashir-ud-Din Mahmood, Pakistani nuclear scientist reported to have passed information on making nuclear weapons to Osama bin Laden and the Taliban. Mahmood studied nuclear engineering in Britain in the 1960s. After his return to Pakistan, he held a variety of senior positions in that nation's nuclear program. He resigned from the program in 1999. In June 2000 he and Chaudiri Abdul Majeed founded Ummah Tameer-e-Nau, known as UTN, to conduct relief efforts in Afghanistan. In December 2001 the George W. Bush administration added UTN to the list of entities supporting terrorism.

Thomas Mancuso, researcher and physician at the University of Pittsburgh who, at the request of the Atomic Energy Commission, studied for 15 years the radiation exposure records of thousands of workers in the U.S. nuclear weapons complex. After he reported that "low-level" exposure can cause cancer and that exposure standards were too high, the government cut his funds and removed him from the study. Hanford in Washington State was the only site that he had time to analyze in detail before his termination.

Edward J. Markey, member of the U.S. House of Representatives who has worked on nuclear issues ever since his election to the post in 1976. He has pushed for increased security at civilian and military nuclear facilities and steps to prevent radiological and nuclear devices from entering the United States. He is from Malden, Massachusetts, and received B.A. and J.D. degrees from Boston College.

John Marquand, U.S. novelist who was in charge of biological warfare intelligence from 1944 to 1945, as special consultant to the Secretary of War. He received a Pulitzer Prize in fiction for his novel *The Late George Apley.*

George W. Merck, president of Merck Pharmaceutical Company. Secretary of War Henry Lewis Stimson appointed him chairman of the civilian War Research Service (WRS) to oversee preparations for offensive and defensive biological warfare activities during World War II. The agency was under the Federal Security Agency in the Department of Agriculture.

Matthew Meselson, professor of molecular and cellular biology at Harvard University who has worked for some 40 years against production of chemical and biological weapons. In 1967 he and John Edsall, another Harvard professor, put together a petition that 5,000 scientists signed, asking President Lyndon Johnson to stop the production and use of these weapons. He later wrote a letter to President Richard Nixon urging him to ban biological toxins, which Nixon had neglected to cover in his ban on lethal biological agents. In 2002 he received the Public Service Award from the American Society for Cell Biology.

Karl Z. Morgan, considered the "father of health physics." Morgan was hired by the Manhattan Project to be director of health physics at Oak Ridge National Laboratory, where he helped to establish exposure limits to radiation for workers on the first atomic bombs. By 1949 he and some other researchers had learned that there is no safe level of exposure. He founded and was president of the Health Physics Society and was the first president of the International Radiation Protection Association. Before his work on the Manhattan Project he studied radiation from cosmic rays.

Nursultan Nazarbayev, president of Kazakhstan. He climbed to power through the Communist Party and became president of the Soviet Socialist Republic of Kazakhstan in 1990 when the Soviet Union was going through a period of change. He is interested in economic development and the maintenance of stability; he agreed to rid Kazakhstan of the nuclear weapons that it inherited when the Soviet Union broke up. With the help of the United States, Kazakhstan was free of nuclear weapons by November 1996.

Richard Nixon, 37th president of the United States. In 1969, his first year as president, Nixon secured the ratification by the Senate of the Nuclear Non-Proliferation Treaty and announced a unilateral ban by the United States on the first use of lethal or incapacitating chemical agents and on all methods of biological warfare. He instructed that biological agents were to be destroyed. In 1970 he extended the ban to cover toxins, a potential loophole. He resigned from office in 1974 to avoid impeachment and died in 1994 at the age of 81.

Sam Nunn, cochairman and chief executive officer of the Nuclear Threat Initiative, a nonprofit organization created by media mogul Ted Turner and himself. He served as a U.S. senator from the state of Georgia from 1973 to 1996. While a senator, he concentrated on defense issues and became chairman of the Senate Armed Services Committee and the Permanent Subcommittee on Investigations. He is a professor in the Sam Nunn School of International Affairs at the Georgia Institute of Technology and chairman of the board of the Center for Strategic and International Studies in Washington, D.C.

Hazel O'Leary, secretary of energy from 1993 to 1997 in the Bill Clinton administration. She inaugurated a new openness policy at the Department of Energy; during her tenure the declassification of government documents proved for the first time that underground nuclear tests had released radiation into the atmosphere. O'Leary had previously served in positions relating to energy in the Gerald Ford and Jimmy Carter administrations.

Robert Oppenheimer, physicist selected by General Leslie Groves to be scientific director of the Manhattan Project. After World War II he became chairman of the Atomic Energy Commission. In the summer of 1954 he lost his security clearance and his contract as adviser to the Atomic Energy

Commission because of alleged communist leanings. His condemnation has been described as removing a "voice of reason and restraint." In 1963 President Lyndon Johnson presented him with the commission's Enrico Fermi Award, an effort to publicly clear him.

Wilfred Owen, British poet most completely identified with World War I. In his poem "Dulce et Decorum Est" he gave an unforgettable description of a soldier suffering from an attack of chemical gas. He served with a regiment under fire for six months in France in 1917, was sent to a hospital in England because of injuries, and was returned to France, where he was killed in action shortly before the armistice.

Linus Pauling, U.S. theoretical chemist and biologist. He was awarded the 1954 Nobel Prize in chemistry for his work on the chemical bond and the 1962 Nobel Peace Prize for his role in bringing about the Limited [Nuclear] Test Ban Treaty, forbidding testing in the atmosphere. His work against nuclear testing included presenting to the United Nations a petition against atmosphere testing and what he regarded as excessively large nuclear arsenals, signed by more than 11,000 scientists.

C. J. Peters, director of biodefense for the University of Texas Medical Branch's Center for Biodefense and Emerging Infectious Diseases in Galveston and director of its biosafety Level-4 laboratory. He is a member of the World Health Organization Collaborating Center for Tropical Diseases. For more than 30 years he has conducted research on hemorrhagic fever viruses. In 1997 he and Mark Olshaker published *Virus Hunter: Thirty Years of Battling Hot Viruses around the World.*

Stanislav Petrov, lieutenant colonel in the Soviet military who prevented the Soviet Union from launching a missile attack against the United States on September 26, 1983. Petrov was in charge of the Soviet Union's early warning system, when a Soviet satellite reported that five U.S. missiles were heading for Moscow. Petrov declared the alarm to be false. Soviet engineers later determined that the satellite had seen sunlight reflected off clouds.

Eugene Rabinowitch, founder, with physicist Hyman Goldsmith, of the *Bulletin of Atomic Scientists.* He was the editor-in-chief from its creation in 1945 until his death in 1973. A Russian-born scientist, he had served as a senior chemist with the Manhattan Project but became horrified at the threat that he believed nuclear weapons posed. The bulletin's purpose was to make the public understand the reality of these weapons. He died in 1973 while drafting a book to be titled "The Scientific Revolution and Its Social Consequences."

Bhagwan Shree Rajneesh, religious leader also known as Osho who was involved in the use of biological agents. He moved to the United States from his native India in 1981 and established the Rajneesh community in Oregon. Cult members poisoned food at restaurants with salmonella bacteria in 1984 and 1985. Accusations by the Bhagwan of criminal activity on the part of several cult members led state officials to discover the deliberate poisoning. He was deported from the United States in 1986 for violating immigration laws and died in India in 1990.

Jeremy Rifkin, founder and president of the Foundation on Economic Trends, which works to ensure responsible government policies on issues relating to science and technology. Biotechnology and the dangers of biological weapons are a major concern. The foundation, for example, obtained a permanent injunction against a plan by the Department of Defense to test biological aerosols at Dugway Proving Ground in Utah; Rifkin warned about biological weapons in his 1998 book *The Biotech Century.*

Julius Rosenberg, with his wife Ethyl, was executed on June 19, 1953, for giving nuclear weapons secrets to the Soviet Union. He had earned a degree in electrical engineering and worked as a civilian employee of the U.S. Army Signal Corps. He and his wife became full members of the American Communist Party in 1942 but dropped their membership in 1943. Although he and Ethyl were found guilty of espionage, they maintained their innocence through their trial and subsequent appeals.

Joseph Rotblat, Polish-born physicist and leader who made efforts to abolish nuclear weapons. He worked on the Manhattan Project in the United States but returned to England in 1944 when it was confirmed that Germany was not making atomic weapons. He founded the Pugwash Conference and became its first secretary-general, cofounded the U.K. Campaign for Nuclear Disarmament, and was the initiator and a member of the governing board of the Stockholm International Peace Research Institute. He and the Pugwash Conference were awarded the Nobel Peace Prize in 1995.

Glenn Seaborg, U.S. physical chemist who created the synthetic element plutonium by bombarding uranium with neutrons in a cyclotron at the University of California, Berkeley. In 1952 he shared the Nobel Prize in chemistry with Edwin McMillan. He became chair of the Atomic Energy Commission in 1961, a post he held for 10 years. He died in 1999.

Major General William L. Sibert, known as the father of the Chemical Corps. Upon his graduation from the U.S. Military Academy in 1984, Sibert was commissioned in the U.S. Army Corps of Engineers. He held various responsible positions in the United States and overseas. In 1918 he was nominated by General John J. Pershing to head the newly established Chemical Warfare Service. Bringing together disparate elements of the former Gas Service, he directed the Chemical Service from May 1918 to February 1920,when he retired from active duty.

Alice Stewart, British physician and epidemiologist who spent much of her life studying and publicizing the effects of low-level radiation. Her first major publication was a report of her findings in the Oxford Study of Childhood Cancer, published in the *Lancet* in 1956. She and her statistician George Kneale later served as consultants to T. F. Mancuso on a major investigation of the health of workers at the Hanford nuclear site in the United States. She received the Right Livelihood Award, the so-called alternative Nobel Prize, in 1986. She was 95 when she died in 2002.

Henry Lewis Stimson, American lawyer and statesman and secretary of war from 1940 to 1945. He was named to President Franklin D. Roosevelt's advisory committee on atomic energy in fall 1941 and served as top adviser to Roosevelt and Harry S. Truman on the military use and postwar control of the weapon. He believed that the United States should share information on atomic energy with the Soviet Union and recommended that the United States negotiate directly with the Soviet Union to control and limit the use of the atom for war and to encourage its use for peaceful purposes. Truman did not follow this advice.

Leo Szilard, physicist who first conceived the idea of a nuclear chain reaction. He was born in Budapest, Hungary, in 1898 and came to the United States by way of London in 1938. Worried that Germany would discover the atomic bomb, he persuaded Albert Einstein to send a letter of warning to President Franklin D. Roosevelt. He worked on the Manhattan Project; in 1944, however, he argued on moral grounds against using the bomb. After World War II he organized opposition to a bill that would have placed atomic energy under military control.

Edward Teller, Hungarian-born American physicist who was instrumental in making possible the first explosion by the United States of a hydrogen bomb, in 1952. During World War II he conducted research on the atomic bomb at Columbia University. Subsequently, he was associated with the thermonuclear research program at Los Alamos, New Mexico, from 1949 to 1951 and directed the Livermore Radiation Laboratory of the University of California at Los Angeles from 1952 to 1960. He is credited with inspiring Ronald Reagan with the idea of a space-based defensive shield against nuclear missiles.

Harry S. Truman, president of the United States who oversaw the end of World War II and authorized the dropping of atomic bombs on the Japanese cities of Hiroshima and Nagasaki. Born in 1884, he was elected senator in 1934 and 1940 and vice president in 1944. He assumed the presidency on April 12, 1945, at the death of Franklin D. Roosevelt, who had not told him about the atomic weapons program. He was reelected president in 1948. In 1950 he announced that he had ordered the U.S. Atomic Energy Commission to develop a hydrogen bomb.

Mordechai Vanunu, Israeli nuclear technician who revealed to the world Israel's secret nuclear weapons program. He had worked at Israel's Dimona Nuclear Power Plant from 1976 to 1985. On October 5, 1986, the *London Sunday Times* published a story on Israel's arsenal based on information and photographs from Vanunu. He was sentenced in Israel to 18 years of imprisonment for espionage and treason. As a condition of his release in April 2004, he was forbidden to speak to foreign journalists, a condition he has allegedly violated. As of autumn 2004, he was not free to leave Israel.

James Dewey Watson, American microbiologist who, with Francis Crick and Maurice Wilkins, received the 1962 Nobel Prize in physiology or medicine for the discovery of the structure of DNA. He became director and then president of Cold Spring Harbor Laboratory on Long Island, which became a center of DNA science. In 1989 he was appointed director of the National Center for Human Genome Research at the National Institutes of Health, from which he launched a worldwide effort to map the human genome.

Gregg S. Wilkinson, epidemiologist with a special interest in the effects of low doses of radiation. As a scientist at Los Alamos National Laboratory, he studied workers exposed to plutonium and external radiation at Rocky Flats. He found more cancers in exposed than in unexposed workers. Although reportedly pressured to alter his findings, he published them in 1987 without changes and left Los Alamos. As of 2004, he was an adjunct professor in the School of Public Health at the University of Massachusetts.

Herbert York, nuclear physicist who helped to develop and implement arms-control policy in both Republican and Democratic administrations. He was the first director of Lawrence Livermore National Laboratory and later the first director of Defense Research and Engineering at the U.S. Department of Defense. From 1979 to 1981 he was ambassador to the Comprehensive Test Ban Treaty Talks. In 1982 he founded the Institute of Global Conflict and Cooperation at the University of California, San Diego. His books include *Making Weapons, Talking Peace: A Physicist's Journey from Hiroshima to Geneva* (1987).

CHAPTER 5

GLOSSARY

Nomenclature and terminology in the field of weapons of mass destruction is eclectic. From *ABM* and *Agent Orange* to *vitrification*, *warhead*, and *yield*, the language is mixed with acronyms and terms that draw from a number of areas of policy and technology. Sometimes words have special meaning when applied to the field of weapons of mass destruction. *Fertile material* is a good example. By itself, *fertile* refers to the ability to reproduce, while a *material* is simply a substance that can be shaped into an object. In nuclear parlance, though, a *fertile material* is a substance that readily absorbs neutrons and decays into other elements, producing fissionable material that can be used for weapons production. The following is a glossary of commonly used terms in the literature of nuclear, biological, chemical, and radiological weapons.

aerosol Fine, suspended particles that remain in the air for a significant time period.

Agent Orange A defoliant widely applied by the United States in the Vietnam War. It was contaminated with dioxin. A number of crippling effects and premature deaths have been ascribed to Agent Orange.

alpha radiation A particle radiation in which particles consist of two protons and two neutrons bound together (a helium nucleus). Alpha radiation is given off by the decay of uranium, plutonium, and many other elements. Alpha particles cannot penetrate a sheet of paper or the outer layer of skin, but, once inside the body, they can be very harmful.

anthrax An acute disease caused by a spore-forming bacterium, *Bacillus anthracis.* The disease has three forms, determined by its route into the body: cutaneous (through the skin), ingestional, and inhalational. If left untreated, the inhaled form is the most dangerous, with a fatality rate of about 100 percent.

antiballistic missile (ABM) system A system to attack strategic ballistic missiles in flight. It consists of interceptor missiles, launchers, and radars.

asymmetrical warfare Warfare between forces that differ greatly from each other in size, technological expertise, and even goals.

atmospheric testing The aboveground explosion of a nuclear device to test it or its effects.

Glossary

atom The smallest part of an element that has all the chemical properties of that element. With the exception of hydrogen, an atom consists of a nucleus composed of protons and neutrons and surrounded by electrons.

atomic bomb A bomb in which the energy is produced by the fissioning of uranium or plutonium.

atomic number The number of protons in the nucleus of each of an element's atoms. It determines the chemical properties of the element. A different atomic number means a different, and unique, set of chemical properties of an element.

atomic weight The nominal atomic weight of an isotope is the sum of the number of neutrons and protons in each nucleus. (The exact weight is slightly different from the nominal weight.) The atomic weight of an element is based on the combination of the isotopes of that element found in nature.

bacteria Free-living microorganisms, composed of cytoplasm, nuclear material, and a cell membrane. They reproduce by cell division. Most can be grown on solid or liquid culture media. Antibiotics are often effective against the diseases they produce.

ballistic missile A guided rocket that is powered only during the initial portion of its flight. It then coasts to its target on a ballistic path, mostly above the atmosphere. Long-range ballistic missiles have a range greater than 5,500 kilometers; intermediate-range, a range of 3,000–5,500 kilometers; medium range, 1,000–3,000 kilometers; and short-range, under 1,000 kilometers.

ballistic trajectory The trajectory that is traced after the propulsive force has ceased and only gravity and aerodynamic drag act on the body.

becquerel A unit of radioactivity equal to one disintegration per second. It is a tiny unit, equaling about 27 picocuries.

beryllium A toxic steel-gray metal that does not readily absorb neutrons. In nuclear weapons it is placed around the fissile material, where it reflects neutrons back into the nuclear reaction.

beta radiation Consists of a high-speed electron or positron. Emitted in the radioactive decay of many isotopes, it has a short range in air and a low ability to penetrate other materials. Aluminum shielding a few millimeters thick will typically block it.

binary chemical munition A munition in which chemical substances contained in separate compartments combine to cause a reaction when the munition is fired or otherwise initiated.

bioaccumulation The accumulation of radionuclides or other substances in a living organism.

biological agent A living microorganism or a toxin. Many of the disease-producing microorganisms are bacteria or viruses. Toxins, although not alive, are produced by certain species of microorganisms, plants, or animals.

biological simulant Chemical markers or bacteria believed to be harmless; as airborne particles they act like toxic biological agents. A biological simulant is used for open-air testing.

biological weapon A biological agent combined with the means of distributing it.

biosafety level (BL) A term for classifying laboratories according to the virulence of the pathogens that they are equipped to contain. BL-4 indicates a maximum containment facility, equipped to handle the most dangerous pathogens currently known. The other biosafety levels are BL-3, BL-2, and BL-1, with 1 referring to the least dangerous pathogens.

blister agent See **vesicant.**

blood agents Agents that prevent the transfer of oxygen to the body tissues. They in effect asphyxiate victims and are highly volatile. Hydrogen cyanide or prussic acid and arsine are examples of blood agents.

carcinogen A substance with the ability to cause cancer.

cesium A metallic element with a metabolic effect similar to potassium. The isotope cesium-137, an emitter of beta and gamma radiation, is a fission product with a half-life of 30 years.

chain reaction A self-sustaining series of nuclear fission reactions. Neutrons produced by fission cause more fission. Chain reactions are essential to the operation of nuclear weapons and nuclear reactors.

chemical agent A chemical compound that, when suitably distributed, produces incapacitating, damaging, or lethal effects on people, animals, or plants. People may be contaminated by inhalation, ingestion, or absorption of chemicals through the skin.

chlamydia Microorganisms that are incapable of generating their own energy source and are obliged to live and multiply within living cells. They respond to broad-spectrum antibiotics.

chlorine A choking agent that mixes with moisture in the lungs to form hydrochloric acid and hypochlorous acid.

choking agent An agent that primarily attacks the respiratory track and the eyes, causing pulmonary edema known as dry drowning. The best-known agents, chlorine and phosgene, are used in many industrial processes and are relatively abundant and inexpensive. They are delivered as gases and are not persistent.

ciprofloxacin An antibiotic that is effective against anthrax if given soon enough.

counterproliferation A U.S. policy, first set forth in 1993 by then defense secretary Les Aspin, to use U.S. weapons to destroy weapons of mass destruction in other countries that are a threat to the United States.

critical mass The amount of a fissile substance that will allow a self-sustaining chain reaction. The amount depends on the properties of the fissile element, the shape of the mass, and other factors.

cruise missile An unmanned missile that is propelled all the way to its target through jet or rocket propulsion and that sustains flight through the use of aerodynamic lift.

curie The traditional unit of radioactivity equal to the radioactivity of one gram of pure radium. It equals 37 billion disintegrations per second, or 37 billion becquerels.

decay products The isotopes produced by the decay of an unstable atom; also known as daughter products.

Glossary

decontamination Removal of unwanted radioactive or hazardous contamination by a mechanical or a chemical procedure.

deuterium A stable (not radioactive) isotope of hydrogen; used in fusion reactions.

dirty bomb A radiological dispersion device consisting of radioactive material wrapped in or around a conventional explosive.

dual-use Suitable for use for both legitimate commercial purposes and military purposes. The term is applied to materials, equipment, and technology.

electron A light, negatively charged subatomic particle. Electrons surround the nucleus of an atom.

enrichment The process of increasing the proportion of a particular isotope in a given element. In the case of uranium, the proportion of uranium 235 in uranium is increased.

external radiation dose The dose from sources of radiation located outside the body. Most frequently the dose is from gamma rays, although beta rays can add to the dose to the skin and tissues near the skin. Neutrons may also be an external source.

fallout The descent to Earth of radioactive particulate matter from a nuclear cloud or the particulate matter itself.

fertile material A nuclear material that readily absorbs neutrons and decays into other elements, producing fissionable material.

fissile material A substance that can be split into lighter elements by slow (low-energy) neutrons as well as by fast neutrons.

fission The splitting of the nucleus of an element into fragments. Heavy elements release large amounts of energy when split.

fissionable material A substance whose atoms can be split into lighter elements when struck by fast neutrons. Fissile material is a category of fissionable material.

fission product An atom created by the fissioning of a heavy element. These products are usually radioactive.

fungi Primitive organisms that do not carry out photosynthesis and can grow without oxygen. They obtain their nutrients only by absorption; many are parasites. Most form spores. Various antimicrobial substances may be effective against fungal diseases.

fusion The merging of two nuclei to form a nucleus that is heavier than either. Fusion of the isotopes of light elements such as hydrogen generally releases energy.

gamma radiation High-energy electromagnetic radiation produced by radioactive disintegration. It is the most penetrating type of ionizing radiation and, as a general rule, can be blocked only by thick pieces of lead or concrete. X-rays are identical to low-energy gamma rays and can ionize atoms.

gas-centrifuge process A method of enriching uranium based on the fact that when uranium hexafluoride is spun rapidly in a recipient turning on an axis, the atoms of uranium 238 tend to go to the sides; those of uranium 235 tend to collect in the center. This process must be repeated in a series of recipients (centrifuges).

gaseous diffusion A method of enriching uranium based on the fact that uranium 235 passes through a porous barrier more readily than uranium 238. The method involves forcing uranium hexafluoride through hundreds of barriers, one after the other.

gene splicing Inserting one or more genes of one species of organism into the genome of another.

genetic engineering Direct manipulation of genetic information or the transfer of genes from one type of organism to another.

genome A complete haploid set of chromosomes (the chromosomes in a normal germ cell). The genome is thus an organism's complete genetic information.

glanders A disease, caused by *Burkholderia mallei*, which usually infects donkeys, horses, and mules. Distribution of the bacteria as an aerosol could result in a high mortality rate among humans, even with treatment.

gray A unit of absorbed radiation dose equal to 100 rads.

G-series nerve agents A series of nerve agents that is generally nonpersistent. It includes tabun, sarin, and soman.

half-life The time required for half the atoms of a radioactive substance to disintegrate to the point where it leaves half the original amount of that substance. Half of the remaining substance will disintegrate in another equal period of time. Thus after two half-lives, one-fourth of the original amount remains, and so on.

haploid set A single set of unpaired chromosomes.

heavy water Water containing a significantly greater proportion of heavy hydrogen (deuterium) atoms to ordinary hydrogen atoms than does ordinary water.

Hiroshima bomb The atomic bomb dropped on Hiroshima, Japan, on August 6, 1945. It had a yield of approximately 15 kilotons. Other bombs are frequently compared to the Hiroshima bomb in yield.

hydrogen bomb See **thermonuclear weapon.**

improvised nuclear device (IND) A crude nuclear fission bomb, such as might be built by a terrorist group.

inertial confinement fusion (ICF) The fusion reaction produced by focusing the energy of lasers, electrical-pulse power machines, or ion beams on a tiny cylindrical target containing a droplet of heavy hydrogen isotopes (deuterium and tritium). The density and temperature of the target is raised sufficiently to ignite the fusion reaction in the target.

internal radiation dose The dose to organs of the body from radioactive material inside the body. It can be composed of any combination of alpha, beta, and gamma radiation.

ionize To split off one or more electrons from an atom, giving it a positive charge.

ionizing radiation Radiation that is capable of breaking apart atoms. The four types of ionizing radiation that are important from the point of view of weapons effects are alpha and beta particles, neutrons, and gamma rays.

irradiate To expose to ionizing radiation.

isotope A form of a given element that is identical chemically to, but differs in its physical properties from, other isotopes of that element. Atoms of any specific element all have the same number of protons, and thus the same chemical properties, but may differ in the number of neutrons and thus in weight. Some isotopes are stable and some are unstable or radioactive.

kiloton A unit (1,000 tons) used to describe the explosive power of nuclear weapons. One kiloton equals the explosive power of 1,000 tons of TNT.

laser A device that creates a concentrated beam of light, called a laser beam. The term is an acronym for light amplification by stimulated emission of radiation.

lethality The amount of a substance required to kill.

lewisite A blister agent based on arsenic. Lewisite has been produced in large quantities but has seldom been used; relatively little is known about its effect on humans.

light water Ordinary water (H_2O) as compared to heavy water (D_2O). The nuclear power reactors that operate in the United States use light water; production reactors for radioactive materials often use heavy water.

lithium A naturally occurring light metal used in the production of tritium.

lyophilization Freeze drying, used in the preparation of biological agents to enable them to be stored without losing their virulence. Lypholization can reduce a solution of bacteria and a stabilizer to a dried cake, which can then be made into a powder.

megaton (Mt) A unit of measurement of nuclear yield that equals the energy given off by 1 million tons of TNT.

microencapsulation A process used in preparing biological agents, involving coating liquid or dry agents with materials that will slow or target release of the agent within the victim. It can also produce particles of an optimum size and increase the agent's stability.

mixed oxide (MOX) Nuclear reactor fuel composed of uranium oxide and plutonium oxide.

multiple independently targetable reentry vehicle (MIRV) Multiple reentry vehicles carried by a single missile. Each of the reentry vehicles can be directed to a separate target.

mustard gas A vesicant (blister-producing) chemical agent that was extensively used in World War I. Mustard gas generally kills only a small percentage of its victims, but those who live may suffer serious skin damage, temporary or permanent blindness, and damage to the upper respiratory system. It is a yellow-brown, oily liquid when prepared crudely; it is colorless and odorless when pure.

nanoscience Generally, the manipulation of individual atoms and molecules to create larger structures.

nerve agents Chemical substances that block the enzyme acetylcholinesterase, which is necessary for the functions of the central nervous system. Though commonly referred to as nerve gases, they are liquids at room temperature. They are chemically related to the organophosphate insecticides.

neutron An elementary uncharged particle that is found in the nucleus of every atom heavier than hydrogen. It is slightly heavier than a proton. Uranium 235 and plutonium 239 atoms fission when they absorb neutrons. Thus, chain reactions depend on neutrons.

nonproliferation Efforts to stop or slow the spread of weapons of mass destruction and the materials and technologies that produce them.

nuclear reactor A device that sustains a controlled nuclear fission chain reaction. The main three types are power reactors, production reactors, and research reactors.

nuclear weapons complex The chain of facilities that produce, maintain, and dismantle nuclear weapons.

nucleus The central core of an atom that comprises almost all the weight of the atom. Every atomic nuclei, with the exception of ordinary hydrogen, contains protons and neutrons.

pathogens Organisms or substances that cause disease.

pit The metal-encased plutonium or highly enriched uranium core of a nuclear weapon.

plutonium A highly toxic, heavy, radioactive metallic element that exists in nature only in traces.

plutonium 239 The isotope of plutonium most suitable for nuclear weapons.

positron An elementary particle identical to an electron except that it has a positive rather than a negative charge.

power reactor A reactor designed primarily to produce heat to generate electricity.

precursors In relation to chemical weapons, ingredients.

primary A core of plutonium or highly enriched uranium that is imploded to produce the fission reaction that initiates fusion in a thermonuclear weapon.

production reactor A reactor designed primarily to produce human-made isotopes: plutonium 239 by the irradiation of uranium 238, or tritium by the irradiation of lithium 6.

propellant The source of the energy for propelling a projectile, an explosive charge, or a solid or liquid fuel.

prophylaxis Measures designed to preserve health and prevent the spread of disease.

Q fever A disease that can be incapacitating because it causes fever and difficulty in breathing but does not kill. The microorganism that causes it, *Coxiella burnetii*, has in the past been processed for use in warfare.

rad (radiation absorbed dose) The old unit of absorbed dose of radiation, defined as the deposition of 100 ergs of energy per gram of tissue.

radiation Energy transferred through space or other media in the form of particles or waves. Ionizing radiation, which is the radiation referred to in this book, is capable of breaking up atoms or molecules. The splitting, or decay, of unstable atoms emits ionizing radiation.

radiation equivalent man (rem) A unit of equivalent absorbed dose of radiation, taking into account the relative biological effectiveness of the specific radiation. It is the amount of ionizing radiation necessary to produce the same biological effect as one roentgen of X-rays. The term has been replaced by the sievert. One sievert is equal to 100 rems.

radioactive decay Spontaneous disintegration of the nucleus of an unstable atom, which causes particles and energy to be emitted.

radioactive source As defined by the International Atomic Energy Agency, radioactive material that is permanently sealed in a capsule or closely bonded and in a solid form and not exempt from regulatory control. Radioactive sources are commonly used in certain industries and in the medical sector.

radioisotope An unstable isotope.

radiological dispersion device (RDD) A device containing radioactive material that is designed to spread the radioactivity over a wide area. It may or may not use explosives. A dirty bomb is a type of RDD.

radiological emission device (RED) A device containing radioactive material that is intended to spread radiation over a localized area. It does not contain explosives.

radionuclide A radioactive species of an atom; for instance, strontium 90 and uranium 235.

reentry vehicle The part of a ballistic missile that carries the nuclear warhead. Its name comes from the fact that it reenters the Earth's atmosphere in the last portion of the missile trajectory.

reprocessing The process of extracting substances, usually plutonium and uranium, from irradiated fuel and irradiated targets that have been dissolved in acid. The process is also known as chemical separation.

research reactor A nuclear reactor primarily intended to furnish neutrons for experimental purposes. Common uses are training, testing materials, and producing radioisotopes.

ricin A biological agent that is made from castor seeds. The substance is usually fatal when ingested and has no known antidote.

rickettsias Microorganisms that combine characteristics of bacteria and viruses. Like viruses, they can grow and replicate only inside living cells, but, like bacteria, they have cell membranes and metabolic enzymes and use oxygen. They are likely to respond to treatment with antibiotics.

robust nuclear earth penetrator (RNEP) A high-yield nuclear weapon that the George W. Bush administration is developing to destroy deeply buried targets.

roentgen The old unit of radiation exposure. In non-bony biological tissue, one roentgen delivers a dose approximately equal to one rad.

sarin A nerve agent of the organophosphate group that inhibits acetylcholinesterase, an enzyme that is essential to normal muscular contraction.

science-based stockpile stewardship (SBSS) A term used by the Department of Energy to refer to the maintenance of nuclear weapons without nuclear testing.

sievert A unit of equivalent absorbed dose equaling 100 rems.

signature Any or all the properties of a substance that may be used to detect, identify, or engage it or its origin.

smallpox A virus-caused disease that kills or permanently disfigures its victims. The mortality rate for nonvaccinated humans is 30 percent. It can be distributed in aerosols and is contagious.

specific activity The number of disintegrations over a given period of time (the activity) per unit mass of a radioisotope. It is expressed in becquerels or curies per gram.

spore A dormant bacterium that has grown a thick wall around itself to protect itself from environmental extremes.

stockpile Stored weapons; the total number of nuclear, chemical, or biological weapons that a state maintains in storage at all sites and potentially available for deployment.

strategic In terms of weapons and delivery systems, missiles or bombers deployed for nuclear deterrence or retaliation, or for defense against such an attack. The term is usually used for long-range weapons, but in regions made up of small states, shorter-range offensive systems that are equipped with nuclear weapons and are capable of striking deep inside an enemy's territory may be considered strategic.

subcritical experiment An experiment involving fissile materials and chemical high explosives in configurations and quantities that do not produce a self-sustaining chain reaction.

tactical In terms of weapons and delivery systems, relatively short-range missiles and bombers and corresponding defensive systems. Tactical weapons are likely to be used on the battlefield between the front lines of opposing forces. However, weapons systems that a large state may consider to be tactical may be considered by a small state to be strategic.

target In the context of weapons production, material placed in a nuclear reactor to be bombarded by neutrons in order to produce a new, human-made radioactive material.

theater A geographic area outside the continental United States for which a commander of a unified or specified command has military responsibility.

thermonuclear weapon A nuclear weapon that uses fission to start a fusion reaction, from which it derives most of its energy. It is often referred to as a hydrogen bomb, or H-bomb.

TNT equivalent The weight of TNT (trinitrotoluene) that would release the same amount of energy as a given nuclear or other explosion. One ton of TNT releases approximately 1.2 billion calories (i.e., 5.1 kilojoules per gram). The energy released by nuclear explosions is usually stated in kilotons (kt) or megatons (Mt).

toxic warfare Use in war or acts of terror of hazardous substances, including waste and inexpensive, relatively easily obtainable chemicals (not the banned materials incorporated in what are defined as chemical weapons).

toxins Poisonous substances that resemble chemicals but that are ordinarily produced by biological or microbic processes. Specific antisera and pharmacological agents are used against them.

transuranics Elements that have a higher atomic number and thus are heavier than uranium. Among them are americium, curium, neptunium, and plutonium. Except for trace quantities found in nature, transuranics are manufactured.

transuranic waste Radioactive waste that contains more than 100 nanocuries of transuranic nuclides per gram of material. In the United States, where commercial fuel has seldom been reprocessed, nearly all transuranic waste is of military origin.

tritium An isotope of hydrogen with two neutrons and one proton in its nucleus. With deuterium or alone, it is used to produce the fusion reaction.

tularemia A highly infectious disease caused by the bacterium *Francisella tularensis*. When bacteria are inhaled, they cause severe respiratory problems. If victims are not treated with antibiotics, they may die.

unmanned aerial vehicle (UAV) An aircraft that is remotely piloted or self-controlled. UAVs are generally powered by jet or propeller engines and carry cameras, sensors, communications equipment, or other material.

uranium The basic material for nuclear technology. It is a slightly radioactive, naturally occurring heavy metal that is denser than lead. Uranium is chemically toxic as a heavy metal in addition to being toxic as a radioisotope.

uranium mill tailings The voluminous solid waste resulting from the milling and other processing of uranium ore to concentrate the uranium. It includes 5 to 10 percent of the original uranium, uranium decay products, heavy metals, and chemical residues from the treatment process.

vaccine A preparation introduced into a person's or animal's bloodstream to cause the recipient to resist a future infection. As a result of the vaccine, the body produces antibodies that fight the infectious agent.

vadose zone The soil between the surface of the ground and the water table.

vesicant A chemical agent that inflicts painful burns and blisters that require medical attention even when the dose is low; also known as blister agents. Blister agents are more likely to be used to injure opponents or to cause them to have to wear protective clothing than to kill. The best known are mustard gas and lewisite.

viruses Subcellular organisms that are dependent on the cells of the host that they infect. Antibiotics are not effective against the diseases that they produce. They may respond to antiviral compounds but few of these are available. They are difficult to cultivate.

vitrification The process of converting into glass. It often refers to the stabilization of nuclear waste by mixing it with molten glass to reduce its solubility. The glass is poured into canisters, where it hardens.

V-series nerve agents A series of nerve agents that are generally persistent. The most familiar is VX (methylphosphonothioic acid).

warhead The part of a missile, projectile, or other munition that contains materials intended to cause damage (i.e., the nuclear or thermonuclear system, biological or chemical agents, high-explosive systems, or inert materials).

yield The energy released in a nuclear explosion. It is usually described in terms of the quantity of TNT (trinitrotrinoluene) necessary to produce the same amount of energy.

PART II

GUIDE TO FURTHER RESEARCH

CHAPTER 6

How to Research Weapons of Mass Destruction

The subject of weapons of mass destruction involves a wide variety of fields of knowledge ranging from virology to political science. No single chapter could describe the research tools specific to all the relevant areas. This chapter will discuss basic types of reference tools and, where possible, give examples of sources directly relevant to weapons of mass destruction.

The most helpful starting points for research present both an overview and sources of further information. This book, which gives both, is designed to serve as such a starting point. If unfamiliar with weapons of mass destruction, read the relevant background information before using suggested reference tools. Alternative or supplemental starting points include encyclopedias, books that present an overview of a type or types of weapons, and certain web sites. One helpful Web resource for the novice is WMD 411, located on the site for the Nuclear Threat Initiative (http://www.nti.org/). Designed as an introduction, it gives brief, understandable presentations of the main aspects of chemical, biological, and nuclear weapons, along with links to additional information.

Using the World Wide Web

Web sites provide access to a variety of types of material. On a single site the researcher may find reports from government agencies and nongovernmental organizations, newspaper and journal articles, and copies of treaties and laws. The majority of the material on the Web was generated within the last 10 or 15 years, although, increasingly, older material is being linked to the Web. To identify web sites, the researcher can use search engines, directories, guides to research, and links provided by the sites themselves, among other resources.

Search Engines

Search engines use what is called a web crawler to seek matches in millions of web pages for the user's search terms. The references retrieved serve as links to the corresponding web pages.

Among the most widely used general search engines are:

- Google (http://www.google.com)
- Yahoo! (http://www.yahoo.com)
- Ask Jeeves (http://www.askjeeves.com)
- Teoma (http://www.teoma.com)

A few search engines that draw results from several other general engines include:

- All the Web (http://www.alltheweb.com)
- Metacrawler (http://www.metacrawler.com)
- Hotbot (http://www.hotbot.com) (Note: Hotbot does not merge the results into one list.)

In using a search engine, be as precise as possible in the choice of terms in order to limit the results as far as possible to useful references. Most search engines support what are called Boolean operators (i.e., the words AND, OR, and NOT). Use these words to connect terms in order to broaden or limit search results. References retrieved are normally listed in order of their perceived relevance. If one does not find useful pages among the first 10 or 20 references, trying other search terms is likely to prove more useful than combing through the remainder of the results.

The web site Search Engine Watch (http://www.searchenginewatch.com) compares search engines based on the views of Search Engine Watch readers. Because search engines differ in their coverage, using more than one for a given search is advisable.

DIRECTORIES

Directories or web indexes are, in effect, catalogs of web pages. The web pages are arranged by subject in hierarchies that are compiled by information specialists. Thus, a human editor has approved the pages referenced in a web index. The user can enter terms in a search engine and retrieve a list of references drawn from the catalog, or work through the hierarchy of subjects to find the needed pages.

For years, the best-known directory has been Yahoo! In 2002 Yahoo! began using crawler-based technology to search millions of web pages to produce its main results, but it retained its directory. Thus, the difference between the results achieved by a crawler and those from a directory are well illustrated on http://www.yahoo.com. For example, entering the term *chemical weapons* into the search box and clicking on "Directory," just above the box, yields approximately 90 references. Entering the same term but clicking on "Web" (the default position) yields thousands of references.

The Yahoo! Directory can still be searched manually. To find it, scroll down the home page at http://www.yahoo.com to Yahoo! Web Directory and click on it. For *weapons of mass destruction*, click on "Government" as the starting point. Then narrow down the search step by step: "Military>Weapons and Equipment>Weapons of Mass Destruction." Another good general directory is LookSmart (http://search.looksmart.com).

INTERNET GATEWAYS AND PORTALS

The home pages of the major Internet services such as AOL, Earthlink, and Yahoo! are also considered portals to the Internet, as they provide quick access to sources of information on a wide variety of topics. More specialized gateways also exist. One of possible value to the researcher on weapons of mass destruction is the Air War College Military Quick-Portal (http://www.au.af.mil/au/awc/awcgate/awc-port.htm). It provides access to many military and other government sites but also has links to national and international news services.

METASITES

A metasite brings together and organizes much information about a given topic. The best sites give a permanent home to material that would otherwise be hard to find. They are good starting points for research for a person who is already knowledgeable on the subject but may prove confusing to the uninitiated because of the wealth of material presented.

On some metasites, as information has accumulated, the organization of the information has grown increasingly complex. The user may not be able to access everything on the site by clicking on the categories listed on the home page and making subsequent selections. If there is a site map, go to it to see the arrangement of the site as a whole and obtain a detailed list of topics. Most important, use the search engine to the site if one exists. As with a search engine to the Web as a whole, be precise in the choice of search terms.

When useful material is identified, make a note of the URL for that specific item. Otherwise the item may be very difficult to find again. One way to do this is to print the first page of a given web page and, if the URL is not automatically printed, write it on the page.

Below are a few metasites on the topic of weapons of mass destruction:

- Carnegie Endowment for International Peace (http://www.ceip.org): Material listed under "Proliferation News and Resources," is of special interest. Find this section by clicking on "Non-Proliferation" under "Carnegie Programs>GlobalPolicy" on the home page. In Proliferation News and Resources, users can choose among countries and types of weapons to retrieve up-to-date articles and reports. The site has a searchable news archive with articles from major newspapers, other institutes, and government agencies.

- Center for Nonproliferation Studies (CNS) of the Monterey Institute of International Studies (http://www.cns.miis.edu): CNS maintains four databases: the WMD Terrorism Database, the WMD Country Profiles Database, the NIS Proliferation Databases, and the China WMD and Arms Control Database. The WMD Terrorism Database is available on the CNS web site to subscribers only. The other three databases are available to the public as part of the Nuclear Threat Initiative Research Library. This library may be accessed at http://www.nti.org/e_research/e_index.html. The CNS web site also offers a variety of other resources grouped by subject (including Chem/Bio, Missiles, Nuclear, and Terrorism) and by region. The Chem/Bio section includes resources on proliferation and terrorism.
- Federation of American Scientists (http://www.fas.org): This site offers a wealth of information and useful links, but the site was reorganized in 2004 and some of the long-standing files on weapons of mass destruction are now hard to find. The offering includes a special weapons primer, with sections on nuclear, chemical, and biological weapons.
- Military Education and Research Library Network (MERLN) (http://merln.ndu.edu): A comprehensive web site by a consortium of military education research libraries, this site includes a series of MiPALs (Military Policy Awareness Links), one of which is on weapons of mass destruction. Each MiPAL groups and presents links to recent documents from nongovernmental organizations, U.S. civilian agencies, and the U.S. military. The "Rich Site Summary," located in the menu bar at the top of the screen, lists, day by day, items newly added to the MiPALs. The site offers national and international catalogs of materials in member libraries.
- Nuclear Threat Initiative (http://www.nti.org): Includes WMD 411, mentioned above. To find "WMD 411," scroll down the home page and look for the title on the right. The site also offers country profiles, interactive tutorials, issue briefs and databases from CNS, a wealth of source documents, and *Global Security Newswire* (a daily online newsletter). The newsletter covers nuclear, biological, and chemical weapons; terrorism; and related subjects. Back issues to 2001 can be viewed and searched.

OTHER USEFUL WEB SITES

A helpful guide to research in the area of weapons of mass destruction is *National Security Research on the Internet*, by William M. Arkin (http://www.sais-jhu.edu/centers/cse/internet_guide), and its supplement (http://www.sais-jhu.edu/centers/cse/online-supplement). The guide discusses the research process and the various types of information sources. The supplement lists, with brief annotations, a multitude of sources, grouped by type. Links are also provided. The guide was copyrighted in 2000. Therefore it is somewhat out of date and some of the links have broken, but for anyone wanting to do in-depth research, it is still a valuable resource.

A few more examples of the many other web sites potentially useful to researchers of nuclear, chemical, biological, and radiological weapons are listed below. Some other potentially valuable web sites charge for use; those are not listed below.

- All the Virology on the WWW (http://www.virology.net/garryfavwebindex.html): Provides annotations on and links to sites relating to virology. Under "Biological Weapons and Warfare" are sites from nongovernmental organizations and government bodies, including branches of the military.
- Arms Control Association (ACA; http://www.armscontrol.org): Furnishes access to its own news stories, fact sheets, issue briefs, articles in its periodical *Arms Control Today*, and important documents from other sources. "Subject Resources" include "Biological Weapons," "Chemical Weapons," "Export Controls," "Fissile Material," and "Missile Defense."
- Center for Defense Information (http://www.cdi.org): Presents information and documents on what it calls "hot spots," which include missile defense, nuclear issues, space security, and terrorism. The site offers free of charge a variety of e-mail newsletters, including a daily and a weekly on Russia and the monthly *Missile Defense Updates*. Its main periodical, *The Defense Monitor*, is available in paper by subscription.
- Central Intelligence Agency (CIA; http://www.foia.cia.gov): An electronic reading room on this site provides an overview of access to CIA information, including electronic access to previously released documents. Declassified intelligence reports on various countries are among the material available. A section highlights frequently requested records. The site also tells users how to file a Freedom of Information Act (FOIA) request to try to obtain hitherto unreleased records.
- GlobalSecurity.org (http://www.globalsecurity.org): Presents guides and directories, primary documents, news archives, and analysis. John Pike, who used to be responsible for the web site of the Federation of American Scientists is director of Global Security. He posts news with background information as events unfold.
- Institute for Energy and Environmental Research (IEER) (http://www.ieer.org): Posts its many publications on nuclear and energy issues. They include books, fact sheets, periodicals, reports, and comments on proposed actions and environmental impact statements and are searchable by subject and keyword.
- Nuclear Weapon Archive (http://nuclearweaponarchive.org): A site by a knowledgeable individual, Carey Sublette. His Nuclear Weapons Frequently Asked Questions page furnishes detailed, technical information on such topics as nuclear materials, engineering and design of nuclear weapons, and effects of nuclear explosions.
- Stockholm International Peace Research Institute (http://www.sipri.org): Includes a database on chemical and biological warfare and a database of facts on international relations and security trends (FIRST). The site offers excerpts from its many publications, helpful fact sheets, and other resources.

- United Nations Official Documents System (http://documents.un.org): Contains official records, speeches, and background documents published by the United Nations from 1993. The web site can be searched by document number, subject, date, session, and agenda item.
- University of Bradford, Department of Peace Studies (http://www.bradford.ac.uk/acad/sbtwc/home.htm): Provides access to a database on the Biological and Toxin Weapons Convention, which includes the official texts from conferences, meetings, and negotiations aimed at strengthening the convention.

In conducting research, resources of all types should be evaluated before using information from them. This is particularly true of online resources, as the material on the Web varies greatly in quality. A researcher who uses a search engine or follows a link may arrive in the middle of a web site, where there is no indication as to the author or the origin of the site. In such a case, go to the site's home page or to an "About Us" page or even, as a last resort, to a "Contact Us" page. On any credible site, a user should be able to find what entity created and owns the site. The purpose of its work on the site should also be presented. In addition, look for the date when the material in question was created or posted. As with a book, check any notes and bibliography. Does the writer back up statements by referring to reliable sources?

Be aware of the difference between primary and secondary materials. Primary sources are original documents such as legislative bills, agency reports, laboratory studies, and eyewitness accounts. Secondary sources are usually based on primary sources. The site should state the origin of each material posted.

FINDING BOOKS AND REPORTS

LIBRARY CATALOGS

Library catalogs list with bibliographic information the books that a library or group of libraries owns. Today most library catalogs are available online. Online catalogs can usually be searched by author, title, and subject and/or keyword. A keyword search looks for the words that the researcher specifies in the titles, subject headings, and perhaps the tables of contents of the listed books. A subject search looks for the specified subject among the subject headings that catalogers assign to the listed books. Catalogers in U.S. libraries normally draw these subject headings from a list of subjects maintained by the Library of Congress. Specialized libraries may use their own subject lists. A list of subject headings or index terms is often called a thesaurus.

Consulting a thesaurus can help the user find the correct term or terms under which to search. Another means of finding the terms is to look in the catalog at the entry for a familiar book on the topic in question. Note the list of subjects "headings" for that book. Then use those subjects for searches.

When researching, obtain books not available locally through the interlibrary loan service at a local library. To access information on all books published, check out the catalog of the Library of Congress (http://catalog.loc.gov), the largest collection of library materials in the United States.

Particularly helpful for studies of weapons of mass destruction are catalogs of military libraries. The Military Librarians Division of the Special Libraries Association lists and provides links to military libraries (http://www.sla.org/division/dmil/millib.html). Two individual military libraries are the Air University Library (http://www.au.af.mil/au/aul/lane.htm) and Dudley Knox Library at the Naval Postgraduate School (http://library.nps.navy.mil/home/resources.html), which has particularly good information on technology.

WorldCat, available online in many libraries, provides bibliographic information on books and other materials cataloged by libraries that belong to the Online Computer Library Center (OCLC), an international library consortium.

BOOKSTORE CATALOGS

Online store catalogs are a means of identifying books available for purchase and obtaining information about their contents. Both Amazon (http://www.amazon.com) and Barnes and Noble (http://www.barnesandnoble.com) provide, for many of the books that they contain in their catalog, tables of contents, excerpts, publishers' descriptions, book reviews, and readers' comments.

BIBLIOGRAPHIES

Bibliographies or lists of books and other materials about specific subjects appear as separate books, reports, and articles at the end of many other publications. Scanning bibliographies and footnotes for items of interest is an excellent way of finding additional material. The *Bibliographic Index* lists more than 270,000 bibliographies in books, pamphlets, and periodicals. It is available through libraries in print and in an electronic version.

BOOK REVIEWS

Book reviews help the researcher to evaluate, and sometimes to identify, sources of information. For book reviews, consult *Book Review Digest*, *Book Review Digest Plus*, and *Book Review Index*, available in paper and online, or scan the book review section of relevant journals.

FINDING ARTICLES IN PERIODICALS

Indexes to periodicals may cover all or selected periodicals in a given subject area or only a single periodical. The index always used to appear as sets of paper issues. Now many libraries subscribe only to the online versions of indexes but keep the paper sets for the indexing of back issues. The researcher will be restricted to using the indexes to which a given library chooses to subscribe, whether in paper or online. Some online indexes offer full-text copies of all or a portion of the articles indexed. E-mailing texts to a home computer is a quick way of obtaining copies for personal use. Examples of indexes particularly relevant to weapons are:

- Air University Library Index to Military Periodicals (AULIMP; http://www.dtic.mil/dtic/aulimp). An index to English-language military journals from 1989 to the present. Unlike the two sources listed below, this index is available from a home computer by the Web.
- *General Science Index:* Indexes nearly 280 periodicals and is available in printed form and in an online version through libraries.
- *Public Affairs Information Service* (PAIS) *International:* Indexes citations to articles and also books, conference proceedings, government documents, book chapters, and statistical directories. It is available online from 1972 to the present through libraries. *Public Affairs Information Service International Archive*, a cumulation of the numbers that appeared from 1915 to 1976, is also available.

Many periodicals have their own web sites and offer all or a portion of the articles that they have published to users. The main web site of the *Bulletin of Atomic Scientists*, at http://www.thebulletin.org, allows readers to search for and obtain copies of key articles from the *Bulletin*, including the various issues of "Nuclear Notebook," compiled by the Natural Resources Defense Council, and regularly updates information on nuclear arsenals. A supplemental web site, http://www.bulletinarchive.org, allows users to search and download in PDF format all the articles published in the *Bulletin* since 1945. The archive is available only by subscription, but the annual fee for individuals is modest.

Another helpful journal with its own web index is *The Nonproliferation Review* from Monterey Institute of International Studies' Center for Nonproliferation, at http://cns.miis.edu/pubs/npr. The tables of content of the issues for the current and past year can be viewed and selected articles downloaded. Prior volumes can be searched by subject and any article downloaded.

Jane's is a highly regarded commercial publisher of information on armaments and the military worldwide. *Jane's Defence Weekly* places only summaries or excerpts from selected articles on the nonpaying portion of its web site: http://www.janes.com. Searches without charge are restricted to these summaries. The paper edition of *Jane's Defence Weekly* is available in many libraries.

Newspapers of national and international interest and also many local and regional newspapers index their own issues online. Policies on consultation and downloading vary. Newspapers tend to allow viewers to read and download recent articles for free, but charge for copies of back articles.

FINDING U.S. GOVERNMENT DOCUMENTS

Many of the research tools concerned with government documents provide access to only one of the three branches of government: legislative, executive, or judicial. Others refer to materials from all three branches.

The *U.S. Government Manual*, available in print or online, provides comprehensive information on the agencies of the three branches of the government. It also includes information on quasiofficial agencies, international organizations in which the United States participates, and boards, commissions, and committees. The current edition can be searched or browsed online at http://www.gpoaccess.gov/gmanual.

RESEARCHING MATERIAL FROM THE LEGISLATIVE BRANCH

Legislation is generally organized under the number of the Congress during which it was considered. Based on the terms of members of the House of Representatives, each Congress covers two sessions of one year each. The 109th Congress takes place during 2005–06. The numbers of the other Congresses can be calculated by counting backward.

The first two digits in the number of a public law is the number of the Congress that passed it. Unless a bill is defeated, it is generally available for action throughout an entire Congress. To be considered in another Congress, it must be reintroduced.

Status of Legislation

The basic source on the Internet for the status of legislation in the U.S. Congress is a service of the Library of Congress called THOMAS (http://thomas.loc.gov). Directions for use are posted on the site under "THOMAS FAQ." Bills introduced in the current Congress can be searched by keyword or by bill number. For each bill, THOMAS provides a summary, text of the legislation, and status, including committees through which it has passed and floor actions.

Public Laws

After bills have become law, they are published in the *U.S. Statutes at Large* in the order of their passage, which is also the order of their numbers. This publication can be found in printed form in law and government depository libraries but is not available in electronic form.

Public laws as passed by Congress are available through THOMAS. Those passed by past sessions of Congress are online in full text from 1989 (101st Congress) to the present and in summary form since 1973 (93rd Congress). The drawback to THOMAS is that laws can only be searched by the number of the Congress and public law number. They are also available through the Government Printing Office's GPO Access (http://www.gpoaccess.gov). This site provides access to public laws by subject as well as by public law number and gives the citation in the *U.S. Statutes at Large*. However, only laws from 1995 to 1996 (104th Congress) to the present are posted.

U.S Code

The U.S. Code is a consolidation and codification by subject matter of the "general and permanent" laws of the United States. The Office of the Law Revision Counsel of the U.S. House of Representatives prepares and publishes it. At the web site http://uscode.house.gov, the U.S. Code can be searched by subject, and titles and chapters can be downloaded. The U.S. Code is available in print in federal depository libraries and in many other large libraries.

The codification of laws may involve splitting the law as passed and placing the parts in separate Titles of the Code. Titles are the main divisions in the U.S. Code. Each Title is divided into chapters and perhaps subchapters. Each chapter or subchapter is divided into sections. The sections are numbered sequentially, so one need only know the title and section to find a specific passage.

Additional Sources on Congressional Activity

GPO Access provides acccss, for limited time spans, to the Congressional Record (the official record of the proceedings and debates of the U.S. Congress) by date or keyword from 1944 to the present; selected congressional hearings by subject and date from 1994 to the present; committee prints (publications issued by congressional committees on topics related to their legislative or research activities) from 1997 to the present; congressional reports; congressional documents; and the U.S. Congressional Serial Set (House and Senate documents and House and Senate reports bound by session of Congress). Documents for earlier years must be consulted on paper at a government documents repository. A list of repositories can be found on GPO Access.

Three offices that report or reported to Congress are valuable sources of information.

- **Congressional Research Service:** Reports produced by the staff of the Congressional Research Service (CRS) are written in response to requests for information from members of Congress. As a matter of congressional policy, the reports are not directly available to the general public, although individual reports may be requested from a member of Congress. Various unofficial collections are found online. The Federation of American Scientists (http://www.fas.org) posts online the reports relating to national security policy. To access them, type in a topic under "search."
- **Government Accountability Office (GAO):** Formerly the General Accounting Office, the GAO is the investigative arm of Congress in charge of examining all matters relating to the receipt and disbursement of public funds. Most of its reviews are made in response to requests from members of Congress. They are available through the GAO web site, http://www.gao.gov, which is well indexed. They can also be ordered on paper. The office is under the control and direction of the comptroller general of the United States. The legal name became the Government Accountability Office in July 2004.

- **Congressional Office of Technology Assessment (OTA):** The OTA provided objective and authoritative analysis of scientific and technical issues from 1974 to 1995. It closed in September 1995 after Congress stopped funding it. The reports are still available online at http://www.wws.princeton.edu/~ota/ and http://www.access.gpo.gov/ota and can be purchased from the Government Printing Office on CD-ROM.

RESEARCHING MATERIALS FROM THE EXECUTIVE BRANCH

Federal Register

Rules proposed or recently adopted by executive departments and agencies of the federal government and executive orders and other presidential documents are printed in the *Federal Register*, which is published every weekday. It is available online through GPO Access (http://www.gpoaccess.gov/fr), and in print at libraries.

Code of Federal Regulations

The Code of Federal Regulations (CFR) is a codification of the general and permanent rules published in the *Federal Register*. It is divided into 50 titles, each of which represents a broad subject area. The CFR is updated each year, according to a quarterly schedule, with one-fourth of the titles updated every three months. Paper copies of CFR are available in many libraries. The current edition of each title and previous editions back through 1997 can be accessed online at http://www.gpoaccess.gov/cfr/about.html.

Presidential Documents

The Weekly Compilation of Presidential Documents, published every Monday, is the official publication of presidential statements, messages, remarks, and other materials released by the White House press secretary. The publishers are the Office of the Federal Register (OFR) and the National Archives and Records Administration (NARA). Publication began in 1965. The compilation from 1993 to the present is available at the Government Printing Office's web site, http://www.gpoaccess.gov/wcomp. Issues prior to 1993 are available at federal depository libraries. Selected presidential documents are also available on the Web at http://www.whitehouse.gov.

Treaties

Beginning with the 94th Congress (1975–76), treaties are available through THOMAS. Legislative action on ratification is provided as well as the texts.

RESEARCHING MATERIALS FROM THE JUDICIAL BRANCH

In brief, courts at both the federal and state levels are arranged in hierarchies: trial court, appellate (appeals) court, and Supreme Court. At each level, the courts publish their opinions in official reporters. Commercial entities also publish reporters. Digests index the reporters. As a general rule, the cases on web sites on which researchers can search free of charge, such as Findlaw (http://findlaw.com) and Cornell Legal Information Institute (http://www.law.cornell.edu), do not go back more than 10 years. LexisNexis provides cases, but it is only available at large libraries, and the portion of the service available to nonstudents is limited. For older cases, a visit to a law library is essential.

Supreme Court cases are a partial exception. Under Federal Government Resources on the Web, the University of Michigan Documents Center, web site, http://www.lib.umich.edu/govdocs/federal.html, spells out the options for obtaining Supreme Court documents. FindLaw (see URL above) has Supreme Court decisions from 1893 onward. GPO Access (http://www.gpoaccess.gov/judicial.html) provides them from 1937 to 1975 and 1992 onward. The web site of the Supreme Court is limited to 2000 onward.

For the layperson, articles about cases may be more accessible and at least as helpful as the cases themselves. Articles are indexed and sometimes can be retrieved through LexisNexis and the following online services:

- **Index to Legal Periodicals Full Text:** Indexes more than 200 periodicals back to 1981. Full text of the articles indexed is available back to 1994. This database also indexes nearly 300 law reviews and some 1,400 monographs each year.
- **Index to Legal Periodicals Retrospective 1918–81:** Indexes more than 500 periodicals on an international basis but does not provide the full text of articles.
- **Legaltrac™:** Located on Infotrac Web, it includes articles in general magazines as well as law reviews and legal newspapers. Full text of selected articles is included.

In some law libraries, *Index to Legal Periodicals* and *Current Legal Index* are available in paper.

RESEARCH MATERIALS ACROSS ALL THREE BRANCHES OF THE GOVERNMENT

Search Engines

The search engines listed below differ from the general search engines named previously in that their web crawlers only seek matches in government documents.

- **SearchGov** (http://www.searchgov.com): This search engine obtains results from federal, state, and local government sites and also from various federal agencies.

- **Google's Uncle Sam** (http://www.google.com/unclesam): This search engine is a special edition of Google that searches only U.S. government web site.
- **National Technical Information Service Library** (NTIS; http://www.ntis.gov): NTIS searches scientific and technical documents from government agencies published since 1990. For earlier years, search the NTIS index on paper in a large library.
- **Scientific and Technical Information Network** (STINET; http://stinet.dtic.mil): A service of the Defense Technical Information Center, STINET exists in both public and private versions; both provide citations and abstracts. Users of the public version must follow a link to the National Technical Information Service to order the cited documents that are available.
- **SearchMil** (http://www.searchmil.com): This search engine concentrates on military materials.

Gateways to the Internet

The sites below provide quick access to a variety of government sources.

- **Air War College Gateway to the Internet** (http://www.au.af.mil/au/awc/awcgate/awcgate.htm): Categories include "Homeland Security," "Military Index to the Internet," and "USAF Counterproliferation Center"—the last with "Nukes," "Biological," "Chemical," "Missiles," and "War on Terrorism" among the subheadings.
- **FedWorld.gov** (http://www.fedworld.gov): A gateway to government information, managed by the National Technical Information Service (NTIS). Established in 1992, this site was to serve as a locator to all information disseminated by the federal government. However, it falls far short of comprehensiveness but is nevertheless still useful.
- **FirstGov** (http://www.fedworld.gov/firstgov.html): One of the sites to which FedWorld.gov provides entry; allows searches of 30 million government web pages.
- **University of Michigan Government Documents Library** (http://www.lib.umich.edu/govdocs): A gateway to federal documents and, to a much more limited extent, to state and local documents. Some material listed is not available to people outside the university.

An Index to U.S. Government Publications

The Catalog of U.S. Government Publications (CGP) indexes print and electronic material created by federal agencies. It can be used to identify and link to federal agency online resources or to identify materials that agencies have distributed to federal depository libraries. The catalog can be accessed through GPO Access (http://www.gpoaccess.gov/cgp), under "Legislative Branch." It goes back only through 1994.

The print version of CGP began publication in 1895 under the name *Monthly Catalog of United States Government Publications* and is found in depository libraries. In 1994 the Government Printing Office (GPO) began producing a CD-ROM version of the catalog. Since 1999, GPO has used its bibliographic database to put out an abridged print edition of the monthly catalog, a CD-ROM, and the Web edition.

CHAPTER 7

ANNOTATED BIBLIOGRAPHY

This bibliography presents a cross section of the wealth of materials available on nuclear, biological, chemical, and radiological weapons. It is divided into four main sections: weapons of mass destruction in general, including means of delivery; nuclear weapons; biological and chemical weapons; and radiological and other nontraditional weapons. Within each of these sections, books and reports are listed first, followed by articles, and finally by Web documents, if any.

WEAPONS OF MASS DESTRUCTION IN GENERAL (INCLUDING MEANS OF DELIVERY)

BOOKS AND REPORTS

Angelo, Acquisto. *Survival Guide: What to Do in a Biological, Chemical, or Nuclear Emergency.* New York: Random House, 2003. By the medical director of the New York City mayor's Office of Emergency Management, step-by-step instructions to individuals and families on how to protect themselves in emergencies caused by the use of weapons of mass destruction.

Bowen, Wyn Q. *The Politics of Ballistic Missile Nonproliferation.* New York: St. Martin's Press, in association with the Mountbatten Centre for International Studies, 2000. The story of the George H. W. Bush administration's increasing awareness of the threat of missile proliferation and its strengthening of the Missile Technology Control Regime that had been initiated during the 1980s.

Cirincione, Joseph, ed. *Repairing the Regime: Preventing the Spread of Weapons of Mass Destruction.* New York: Routledge, 2000. Opens with a global assessment, followed by sections on Russia, Asia, and the Middle East. The book closes with a chapter on international law and agreements that looks to the future. Essays included in the book are by established researchers.

Cirincione, Joseph, Jon B. Wolfsthal, and Miriam Rajkumar. *Deadly Arsenals: Tracking Weapons of Mass Destruction.* Washington, D.C.: Carnegie Endowment for International Peace, 2002. A basic source on the proliferation of nuclear, chemical, and biological weapons, including delivery systems. The book begins with an overview of the situation as of 2002. It then presents country-by-country analyses, with countries grouped according to their status in regard to nuclear weapons. The book includes numerous maps and tables, texts of relevant documents, a glossary, and a detailed index.

Cordesman, Anthony H. *Strategic Threats and National Missile Defense.* Westport, Conn.: Praeger, 2001. Advocates defend against intercontinental ballistic missiles by linking a national missile-defense program, a counterproliferation policy, increased homeland defense, and a sane approach to arms control and national security.

Crosby, Alfred W. *Throwing Fire: Projectile Technology through History.* Cambridge: Cambridge University Press, 2002. An entertaining history that describes in detail the development of projectile devices.

Davis, Lynn E., ed. *Individual Preparedness and Response to Chemical, Radiological, Nuclear, and Biological Terrorist Attacks.* Santa Monica, Calif.: RAND Corporation, 2003. Describes how individuals should prepare for and respond to the four types of terrorist attacks. The book points out that government and business must play a role by facilitating individuals' responses.

Einhorn, Robert J., and Michèle A. Flournoy. *Protecting against the Spread of Nuclear, Biological, and Chemical Weapons. Vol. 1: An Agenda for Action.* Washington, D.C.: Center for Strategic and International Studies, 2003. A comprehensive analysis of efforts to secure sensitive materials and recommendations for future action drawn up jointly by recipients and givers of aid.

Falkenrath, Richard A., Robert D. Newman, and Bradley A. Thayer. *America's Achilles' Heel: Nuclear, Biological, and Chemical Terrorism and Covert Attack.* Cambridge, Mass.: MIT Press, 1998. From the senior director of policy and plans at the Office of Homeland Security, a comprehensive evaluation of weapons of mass destruction and their potential use against the United States.

Goldblat, Jozef. *Arms Control: The New Guide to Negotiations and Agreements.* London: SAGE Publications, in cooperation with the International Peace Research Institute, 2002. A historical overview covering all arms-control agreements from the latter part of the 19th century through mid-1993. Goldblat presents their historical context and significance as well as their terms. The book includes complete texts or selected excerpts of each agreement.

Huisken, Ronald. *The Origin of the Strategic Cruise Missile.* New York: Praeger, 1981. Relates the exploration of the concept of the cruise missile in the 1950s and the abandonment of this weapon in favor of the ballistic missile; then examines the reasons for the comeback of the cruise missile in the 1970s.

Hutchinson, Robert. *Weapons of Mass Destruction: The No-Nonsense Guide to Nuclear, Chemical, and Biological Weapons Today.* London: Weidenfeld and Nicolson, 2003. Centers in the background and history of the development of weapons of mass destruction since World War II. More information is included on nuclear than on chemical or biological weapons. The book includes a bibliography and glossary but no index. The author has worked as publishing director of Jane's Information Group.

Annotated Bibliography

Lake, Anthony. *6 Nightmares: Real Threats in a Dangerous World and How America Can Meet Them.* New York: Little, Brown, 2000. The nightmares, which include cyberterrorism, are real threats to the United States, presented by President Clinton's National Security Advisor. Lake advocates increased protection by such means as more covert operations to penetrate terrorist groups and closer cooperation between law enforcement officials and national security officials.

Langford, R. Everett. *Introduction to Weapons of Mass Destruction: Radiological, Chemical, and Biological.* Hoboken, N.J.: John Wiley and Sons, 2004. An overview of weapons of mass destruction by a former commander of the army's Toxicology Research Laboratory. For each weapons type, Langford includes history, agents, delivery mechanisms, detection procedures, and results of exposure, decontamination, and treatment. The book is understandable to the general reader but can serve as a source of information for the professional.

Larsen, Jeff, James Wirtz, and Eric Croddy. *Weapons of Mass Destruction: An Encyclopedia of Worldwide Policy, Technology, and History.* 2 vols. Santa Barbara, Calif.: ABC-CLIO, 2004. Coverage in general language of the history, technology, and current issues involving weapons of mass destruction. The first volume is devoted to chemical and biological weapons; the second, to nuclear weapons. The more than 500 entries are by 95 international experts. Arrangement is alphabetical, but each volume ends with an index. A chronology and excerpts from documents are also included.

Lodal, Jan. *The Price of Dominance: The New Weapons of Mass Destruction and Their Challenge to American Leadership.* New York: Council on Foreign Relations Press, 2001. A comprehensive study by the deputy undersecretary of defense in the Clinton administration. The key premise is that other nations are building weapons of mass destruction to counter the dominance of the United States.

National Intelligence Council. *Foreign Missile Developments and the Ballistic Missile Threat through 2015. Unclassified Summary of a National Intelligence Estimate.* Washington, D.C.: Central Intelligence Agency, 2002. Includes an examination of future ballistic missile capabilities of several countries that have ballistic missiles and programs to develop such missiles. For each country, theater-range systems and current and projected long-range systems are discussed.

Office of the Secretary of Defense. *Proliferation. Threat and Response.* 3rd ed. Washington, D.C.: Department of Defense, January 2001. Describes the security challenge posed by the proliferation of nuclear, biological, and chemical weapons and their delivery systems and the Defense Department's response to the challenge. The book includes updated information on the countries that have or may be developing chemical, biological, and nuclear weapons and their means of delivery.

Schell, Jonathan. *The Unconquerable World: Power, Nonviolence, and the Will of the People.* New York: Metropolitan Books, 2003. Traces little-noticed seeds of nonviolence in human history. Schell suggests that the antidote to weapons of mass destruction is peace founded on nonviolence.

Stern, Jessica. *The Ultimate Terrorists.* Cambridge, Mass.: Harvard University Press, 1999. An attempt to examine the problem of international terrorism at the turn of the century. Stern, a former staffer with the National Security Council, discusses the technology and the materials that terrorists would need to act within the United States. She suggests giving the Federal Bureau of Investigation and the Justice Department more leeway to infiltrate and investigate terrorist groups in the United States.

Stockholm International Peace Research Institute. *SIPRI Yearbook 2004: Armaments, Disarmament and International Security.* London: Oxford University Press, 2004. A basic resource that includes three chapters that center on weapons of mass destruction: two surveying developments in 2003 in regard to biological, chemical, and nuclear weapons, and one on biological weapons and potential indicators of biological weapons activity. For developments in previous years, see earlier yearbooks.

Turner, Stansfield. *Caging the Genies: A Workable Solution for Nuclear, Chemical, and Biological Weapons.* Boulder, Colo.: Westview, 1999. Urges the United States to take the lead in international disarmament. Turner, a former director of the Central Intelligence Agency, thinks that public opinion is one of the major obstacles. The book has three parts: the problem, the theory, and the solution.

U.S. Congress, Office of Technology Assessment. *Technologies Underlying Weapons of Mass Destruction.* OTA-BP-ISC-115. Washington, D.C.: Government Printing Office, 1993. A summary of the basic technologies for producing biological, chemical, and nuclear weapons; the means by which states may acquire these weapons; the indicators that inspection or intelligence agencies can look for when attempting to detect their production; and the ways in which producers can hide the evidence.

ARTICLES

Bermudez, Joseph S. "North Korea Deploys New Missiles." *Jane's Defense Weekly,* vol. 41, August 4, 2004, p. 6. Gives evidence that North Korea is developing and deploying at least two new ballistic missile systems, one land-based and one ship-based, each with a range of 2,500 or more kilometers.

Carter, Ashton B. "How to Counter WMD." *Foreign Affairs,* vol. 83, September/October 2004, pp. 72ff. An analysis of ways to fight weapons of mass destruction. The main emphasis of counterproliferation policy should be nuclear and biological weapons. Terrorists should be prevented from obtaining nuclear materials, and preparations should be made to limit the most likely forms of bioterrorism to small outbreaks.

"CBRN Terrorism: How Real Is the Threat?" *Military Technology,* vol. 26, September 2002, pp. 8ff. Looks at the threat of chemical, biological, radiological or nuclear weapons, including the problems in disseminating chemical and biological agents.

Annotated Bibliography

Cirincione, Joseph. "Can Preventive War Cure Proliferation?" *Foreign Policy*, no. 137, July/August 2003, pp. 66ff. Preventive war alone cannot cure proliferation, Cirincione argues. A whole range of treatments is necessary.

Cooper, Mary H. "Weapons of Mass Destruction." *CQ Researcher*, vol. 12, March 8, 2002, entire issue. Like other issues of the *CQ Researcher*, this issue includes an abstract, overview, background information, current situation, outlook, special focus, pro/con arguments, contacts, chronology, and bibliography on a specific issue. A handy starting point for research.

Easterbrook, Gregg. "Term Limits—The Meaninglessness of "WMD." *New Republic*, vol. 227, October 7, 2002, pp. 22ff. Expresses the view that chemical and biological weapons are not as powerful as nuclear weapons and that therefore lumping them together is misleading.

Ellis, Jason. "The Best Defense: Counterproliferation and U.S. National Security." *Washington Quarterly*, Spring 2003, p. 115. A discussion of counterproliferation as a key element of U.S. foreign policy, by a professor at the National Defense University.

Garwin, Richard L. "The Many Threats of Terror." *New York Review of Books*, vol. 48, November 1, 2001, pp. 16–19. Looks at the consequences if terrorists had attacked the World Trade Center with more powerful weapons.

Heidenrich, John G. "Under the Radar Screen? The Cruise Missile Threat to the U.S. Homeland." *Comparative Strategy*, vol. 23, January–March 2004, pp. 63ff. Discusses the emerging threat to the U.S. homeland from cruise missiles. Even a single, short-range missile launched from a ship or plane could inflict enormous damage. Cutting-edge technology is necessary for defense against them.

Leibstone, Marvin. "Missiles and the Global Game-Board." *Military Technology*, vol. 28, June 2004, p. 9. Argues that an "escalating Cold War" in regard to ballistic missiles is in progress. It involves countries like Syria and North Korea as well as Russia and the United States. Carefully crafted diplomacy is a necessity.

Lin, Tony C. "Development of the U.S. Air Force Intercontinental Ballistic Missile Weapon Systems." *Journal of Spacecraft and Rockets*, vol. 40, July 2003, pp. 491ff. A short history of the development of air force intercontinental ballistic missiles, with emphasis on the technology. The author regards the program as one of the most successful programs of the Department of Defense.

Mark, David. "Homeland Security Spending 'Sniffs Out' New Tech Tools." *Electronic Design*, vol. 52, March 29, 2004, pp. 17ff. Reviews the electronic antiterrorism equipment that had been purchased with funding from the U.S. Department of Homeland Security by March 2004.

Ripley, Amanda. "How We Get Homeland Security Wrong." *Time*, March 29, 2004, pp. 32–37. In terms of potential insured losses, a convenient way to assess the terrorist threat is to realize that California, Illinois, and New York are the states at greatest risk, although these states lag behind in federal funding for homeland security. A map ranks the risk state by state.

Szulc, Tomasz. "A Brief History of 'Thunders.'" *Military Technology*, vol. 27, November 2003, pp. 32ff. The history of Chinese air-to-air missiles, including recent updates in technology.

Wirtz, James J., and James A. Russell. "U.S. Policy on Preventive War and Preemption." *Nonproliferation Review*, vol. 10, Spring 2003, pp. 113–124. Finds that the end result of the George W. Bush administration's emphasis on preventive war and preemption may be the strengthening of deterrence and existing international institutions.

NUCLEAR WEAPONS

BOOKS AND REPORTS

Ackland, Len. *Making a Real Killing: Rocky Flats and the Nuclear West.* Albuquerque: University of New Mexico Press, 1999. Relates the troubled history of Rocky Flats, which made plutonium pits for nuclear weapons between 1952 and 1989. The plant experienced a series of fires, some of which sent plutonium to Denver, directly downwind.

Albright, David, Frans Berkhout, and William Walker. *Plutonium and Highly Enriched Uranium 1996: World Inventories, Capabilities and Policies.* London: Oxford University Press, in association with the Stockholm International Peace Research Institute, 1997. Assesses the amounts of plutonium and highly enriched uranium and the capabilities for producing these materials worldwide. Many of the statistics are now out of date, but the histories of fissile materials production in the various nations remain of great value.

Alexander, Brian, and Alistair Millar. *Tactical Nuclear Weapons: Emergent Threats in an Evolving Security Environment.* Washington, D.C.: Brassey's, 2003. Emphasizes policy in regard to tactical nuclear weapons. The writers believe that the United States has largely ignored the threat posed by tactical weapons but that it should not produce a new generation of such weapons itself.

Allison, Graham. *Nuclear Terrorism: The Ultimate Preventable Catastrophe.* New York: Times Books, 2004. Argues that the United States is likely to experience a terrorist nuclear attack in the next decade and that over the long term such a catastrophic attack is inevitable if strict measures are not taken on an international basis. There must be no unsecured nuclear material, no new facilities for processing uranium or plutonium, and no new nuclear states.

Arkin, William M., and Richard Fieldhouse. *Nuclear Battlefields: Global Links in the Arms Race.* Cambridge, Mass.: Ballinger, 1985. Documented for the first time in a book, the deployment of U.S. nuclear weapons overseas. The book shows that the global nuclear infrastructure is itself a source of tension that could result in war.

Baylis, John, and Robert O. Neill. *Alternative Nuclear Futures: The Role of Nuclear Weapons in the Post Cold-War World.* London: Oxford University Press, 2000. Points out that, since the end of the cold war, the debate on the future of nuclear weapons has largely been carried on in private. The book is composed of contributions from well-known academics on the issues that have emerged.

Bergeron, Kenneth D. *Tritium on Ice: The Dangerous New Alliance of Nuclear Weapons and Nuclear Power.* Cambridge, Mass.: MIT Press, 2002. A detailed criticism, on the basis of both nonproliferation and safety, of the U.S. Department of Energy's decision to produce tritium in commercial reactors owned by the Tennessee Valley Authority. Ferguson is a physicist who worked on nuclear safety issues at Sandia National Laboratories for 25 years.

Bernstein, Jeremy. *Oppenheimer: Portrait of an Enigma.* Chicago: Ivan R. Dee, 2004. By a writer of profiles of scientists for the *New Yorker* and in the style of those profiles. This book, a biography of J. Robert Oppenheimer, is for the general reader rather than for the scholar of nuclear history.

Blair, Bruce G. *The Logic of Accidental Nuclear War.* Washington, D.C.: Brookings Institution Press, 1993. An analysis of the command and control systems of the former Soviet Union and the United States.

Blix, Hans. *Disarming Iraq: The Search for Nuclear Weapons.* New York: Pantheon, 2004. Written in an objective tone, an account of the search for nuclear weapons in Iraq by the head of the UN weapons inspection team. He believes that the team would have proven that Iraq no longer had chemical, biological, and nuclear weapons if the Bush administration had postponed invasion.

Boisson de Chazournes, Laurence, and Philippe Sands, eds. *International Law, the International Court of Justice and Nuclear Weapons.* Cambridge: Cambridge University Press, 1999. An analysis of all aspects of the International Court of Justice's advisory opinion on the legality of nuclear weapons. Contributors include lawyers, professors, diplomats, and advisers to international bodies.

Breyman, Steve. *Why Movements Matter: The West German Peace Movement and U.S. Arms Control Policy.* Albany: State University of New York Press, 2001. A well-documented account of the influence of the German peace movement on U.S. nuclear policy during the struggle against deployment of the Euromissiles.

Broad, William J. *Teller's War: The Top-Secret Story behind the Star Wars Deception.* New York: Simon and Schuster, 1992. Relates how Teller "sold" the Star Wars concept while vigorously attacking those who criticized it.

Brown, Archie. *Ending the Cold War: The Gorbachev Factor.* London: Oxford University Press, 1996. A positive analysis of Gorbachev. Brown describes him as playing the main role in ending the cold war—Gorbachev made efforts to reduce international tensions, which gave a basis for limiting the importance of the military and security forces.

Bunn, Matthew, and Anthony Wier. *Securing the Bomb: An Agenda for Action.* Washington, D.C.: Nuclear Threat Initiative, 2004. An assessment of global efforts to secure materials for nuclear weapons and an action plan for accelerating this work. The book notes that less has been secured since 9/11 than in the two years preceding 9/11.

Bunn, Matthew, Anthony Wier, and John P. Holdren. *Controlling Nuclear Warheads and Materials: A Report Card and Action Plan.* Washington, D.C.: Nuclear Threat Initiative, 2003. Asks why there is such a gap between threat and response. The book examines what is being done and should be done to secure warheads and materials, stop smuggling, end production, and reduce stockpiles.

Burroughs, John. *The Legality of Threat or Use of Nuclear Weapons: A Guide to the Historic Opinion of the International Court of Justice.* Münster, Germany: LIT, 1997. A concise presentation of the case in the International Court of Justice, written by an attorney with the nonprofit Western States Legal Foundation in California.

Caldicott, Helen. *The New Nuclear Danger: George W. Bush's Military-Industrial Complex.* New York: New Press, 2002. A warning from a veteran antinuclear activist of the dangers of allowing weapons manufacturers to determine foreign policy. The book includes lists of major U.S. nuclear weapons manufacturers, U.S. nuclear weapons control centers, U.S. nuclear weapons sites, and major antinuclear organizations.

Campbell, Kurt M., Robert J. Einhorn, and Mitchell Reiss, eds. *The Nuclear Tipping Point: Why States Reconsider Their Nuclear Choices.* Washington, D.C.: Brookings Institution Press, 2004. Asks whether the world has reached a point at which nuclear proliferation will become rampant. The book looks at the factors that might cause a state that has foresworn nuclear weapons in the past to develop them now and also at ways of preventing this from happening.

Clearwater, John Murray. *Canadian Nuclear Weapons: The Untold Story.* Toronto: Dundurn Press, 1998. The previously untold history of U.S. warheads on Canadian weapons systems deployed in Canada and West Germany from 1963 to 1984. The book includes a detailed discussion of the nuclear weapons in question.

———. *Nuclear Weapons Databook*, vol. 2, *U.S. Nuclear Warhead Production*, and vol. 3, *U.S. Nuclear Warhead Facility Profiles.* Cambridge, Mass.: Ballinger Publishing Company, 1987. The facts on warhead production and on the major facilities where warheads were produced as of the 1980s. These volumes of the *Nuclear Weapons Databook*, like the first volume, contain many photographs, tables, and diagrams. Volume two, but not volume three, is indexed.

———. *Nuclear Weapons Databook.* Vol. 4, *Soviet Nuclear Weapons.* New York: Ballinger, 1989. A detailed analysis of the Soviet nuclear arsenal. The book is largely based on official Western sources.

Cochran, Thomas B., et al. *U.S. Nuclear Forces and Capabilities.* Vol. 1. Cambridge, Mass.: Ballinger Publishing Company, 1984. This basic reference tool by the Natural Resources Defense Council begins with an overview of the U.S. nuclear weapons system and a primer on the production and operation of nuclear weapons. Then the book describes the warheads in the U.S. nuclear stockpile, the role of nuclear weapons in the U.S. military, and finally, weapon by weapon, the weapons themselves.

Cohen, Avner. *Israel and the Bomb.* New York: Columbia University Press, 1998. Reads like a thriller although it is based on material from government archives. Cohen underlines the issues in regard to the bomb that Israeli strategists and politicians have had to face. He also asks under what circumstances Israel would consider using nuclear weapons.

Annotated Bibliography

Cooper, John R., Keith Randle, and Ranjeet S. Sokhi. *Radioactive Releases in the Environment: Impact and Assessment.* Hoboken, N.J.: John Wiley and Sons, 2003. Presents in one volume the fundamentals of radioactivity. The book includes radioactivity's origin from natural and anthropogenic sources, the effects of radiation on biological organisms, and the management of radioactive waste. It is written by three British scientists for students of radioactivity.

Coyle, Dana, et al. *Deadly Defense: Military Radioactive Landfills.* New York: Radioactive Waste Campaign, 1988. Describes, with clear diagrams, sites in the nuclear weapons complex; gives basic facts about waste at the sites, as of 1988.

Danger Lurks Below: The Threat to Major Water Supplies from Department of Energy Nuclear Weapons Plants. Washington, D.C.: Alliance for Nuclear Accountability, April 2004. A report prepared by Radioactive Waste Management Associates for the Alliance for Nuclear Accountability, it describes the contamination and the threat of contamination of underground water caused by each of the 13 major Department of Energy weapons production sites.

Day, Samuel H., Jr. *Crossing the Line: From Editor to Activist to Inmate: A Writer's Journey.* Baltimore: Fortkamp Publishing Company, 1991. Presents the author's journey from his boyhood in South Africa, through his struggles as a journalist in rural America and his editorship of the *Bulletin of Atomic Scientists* and the *Progressive*, to his years of protest and imprisonment as an antinuclear activist.

Defense Threat Reduction Agency. *Defense's Nuclear Agency, 1947–1997.* Washington, D.C.: Department of Defense, 2002. Recounts the development of the Armed Forces Special Weapons Project and the government organizations that descended from it. The project was formed to furnish training in nuclear weapons operations after the Manhattan Project was disbanded.

Del Tredici, Robert. Introduction by Jonathan Schell. *At Work in the Fields of the Bomb.* New York: Harper and Row, 1987. Striking black-and-white photographs of places and people involved in the history of the atomic bomb. The book closes with interviews and field notes giving background information.

Eden, Lynn. *Whole World on Fire: Organizations, Knowledge, and Nuclear Weapons Devastation.* Ithaca, N.Y.: Cornell University Press, 2003. Shows that for more than 50 years the U.S. government underestimated the results of a nuclear explosion by taking into consideration only the blast, not the fire, although fire damage is predictably far greater than blast damage. Eden looks into why this critical oversight occurred.

Ellis, Jason D. *Defense by Other Means: The Politics of US-NIS Threat Reduction and Nuclear Security Cooperation.* Westport, Conn.: Praeger, 2001. Presents the evolution, the accomplishments, and the challenges and prospects of the Nunn-Lugar Cooperative Threat Reduction Program by which the United States funds the cooperative dismantling of weapons from the old Soviet nuclear arsenal.

Feiveson, Harold A., ed. *The Nuclear Turning Point: A Blueprint for Deep Cuts and De-alerting of Nuclear Weapons.* Washington, D.C.: Brookings Institution Press, 1999. A "detailed political and technical blueprint for very deep" cuts in nuclear weapons arsenals by six researchers and two former ambassadors. The cuts are designed to greatly reduce the danger of nuclear war. Appendixes by other authors approach the issue from regional perspectives.

Ferguson, Charles D., et al. *The Four Faces of Nuclear Terrorism.* Washington, D.C.: Monterey Institute, Center for Nonproliferation Studies, 2004. Examines the growing threat of nuclear terrorism by four means: seizing a nuclear weapon, fabricating an explosive nuclear device, releasing radiation from a major source such as a power plant, or making a radiological dispersion device such as a dirty bomb. The book concludes with recommendations for combatting terrorism.

Freedman, Lawrence. *Deterrence.* Themes for the 21st Century. Malden, Mass.: Polity Press, 2004. A book on policy. Freedman examines the history of deterrence, the meaning of deterrence, and the movement from deterrence to preemption and strategic coercion. He finally considers the future of deterrence.

Gaddis, John Lewis, et al. *Cold War Statesmen Confront the Bomb: Nuclear Diplomacy since 1945.* London: Oxford University Press, 1999. A series of essays by varied authors on 10 statesmen who led their nations during the nuclear era. Harry S. Truman, John Foster Dulles, Dwight D. Eisenhower, and John F. Kennedy are the American leaders presented. The authors speculate as to whether the avoidance of nuclear war was caused by the leaders' fear of such a war or by other factors.

Gallagher, Carole. *American Ground Zero: The Secret Nuclear War.* Cambridge, Mass.: MIT Press, 1993. Interviews with and photographs of people in Utah and other western states whose lives were affected by radioactive fallout from U.S. nuclear atmospheric tests between 1951 and 1963.

Garwin, Richard L., and Georges Charpak. *Megawatts and Megatons: The Future of Nuclear Power and Nuclear Weapons.* Chicago: University of Chicago Press, 2002. An exposition of the dangers of nuclear weapons and the benefits of nuclear energy by two eminent scientists. The writers include an explanation of the principles of fission and fusion.

Gephart, R. E. *Hanford: A Conversation about Nuclear Waste and Cleanup.* Columbus, Ohio: Battelle Press, 2003. The history of contamination at the Hanford plant and a discussion of how it is being and should be cleaned up. Though the book is by a geohydrologist at Pacific Northwest National Laboratory, it is accessible to the general public.

Ginger, Ann Fagan, ed. *Nuclear Weapons Are Illegal: The Historic Opinion of the World Court and How It Will Be Enforced.* New York: Apex, 1998. The opinion of the World Court on nuclear armaments and the separate opinions and dissents of the individual judges, presented with additional material that sets the opinions in context and facilitates the lay reader following the arguments.

Gofman, John W. *Radiation-Induced Cancer from Low-Dose Exposure: An Independent Analysis.* San Francisco, Calif.: Committee for Nuclear Responsibility, 1990. Gofman raises important issues about the risks of exposure to low doses of radiation.

Goldstein, Avery. *Deterrence and Security in the 21st Century: China, Britain, and France and the Enduring Legacy of the Nuclear Revolution.* Stanford, Calif.: Stanford University Press, 2000. A survey of the security policies of China, Britain, and France in the last half of the 20th century and an assertion that their experience will help us to predict the future role of nuclear weapons. The three national studies are well done, but the ability of their experience to predict the future is questionable.

Goodchild, Peter. *Edward Teller: The Real Dr. Strangelove.* Cambridge, Mass.: Harvard University Press, 2004. An in-depth examination of the life of Teller, the "father of the H-bomb," that aims to explain why some viewed him as a thoughtful scientist and others regarded him as a menace to humanity.

Greene, Gayle. *The Woman Who Knew Too Much: Alice Stewart and the Secrets of Radiation.* Ann Arbor: University of Michigan Press, 1999. Recounts the life of a woman scientist who studied and fought to make public the effects of low doses of radiation.

Gusterson, Hugh. *Nuclear Rites: A Weapons Laboratory at the End of the Cold War.* Berkeley: University of California Press, 1996. An ethnographic study of Lawrence Livermore National Laboratory by an anthropologist.

Hacker, Barton C. *The Dragon's Tail: Radiation Safety in the Manhattan Project, 1942–1946.* Berkeley: University of California Press, 1987. Documents the development of radiological safety practices in the early years of the atomic era. The study received institutional and financial support from the U.S. Department of Energy.

Hamza, Khidhir, and Jeff Stein. *Saddam's Bombmaker: The Terrifying Inside Story of the Iraqi Nuclear and Biological Weapons Agenda.* New York: Scribner, 2000. The memoirs of an atomic scientist who describes how he helped Saddam Hussein to work toward a nuclear bomb over a 22-year period. He escaped from Iraq in 1994; thus he has no first-hand knowledge of later events there, including whether or not Iraq continued to build and maintain weapons of mass destruction.

Hansen, Chuck. *U.S. Nuclear Weapons: The Secret History.* New York: Aerofax, dist. by Orion Books, 1988. An excellent sourcebook on developments during and after World War II, including technical details of weapons. The book includes an understandable section on the nuclear physics of bombs.

Harwell, M. A., and T. C. Hutchinson. *Environmental Consequences of Nuclear War (SCOPE 28).* Vol. 2, *Ecological and Agricultural Effects.* New York: John Wiley and Sons, on behalf of the Scientific Committee on Problems of the Environment (SCOPE), 1985. Like the first volume by A. B. Pittock, et al., a detailed, peer-reviewed, assessment of an aspect of the results of nuclear war. Both volumes have extensive lists of references.

Harwit, Martin. *An Exhibit Denied: Lobbying the History of the Enola Gay.* New York: Springer-Verlag, 1996. A chronicle of events leading up to the cancellation of a display of the *Enola Gay* in the National Air and Space Museum by a former director of the museum.

Hecker, JayEtta Z. *Container Security: Current Efforts to Detect Nuclear Materials, New Initiatives, and Challenges.* GAO 03-297T. Washington, D.C.: General Accounting Office, 2002. Evaluates U.S. efforts to prevent radioactive materials from being smuggled into the country in cargo containers. Hecker finds that improvements are needed.

Heller, Bill. *A Good Day Has No Rain: The Truth about How Nuclear Test Fallout Contaminated Upstate New York.* Albany, N.Y.: Whitston Publishing, 2004. Describes the U.S. nuclear test Simon, held April 25, 1953; the fallout from the test; and the reaction to it. The test, held at the Nevada Test Site, went awry, and exposure to the fallout was unexpectedly heavy in Troy, New York.

Herf, Jeffrey. *War by Other Means: Soviet Power, West German Resistance, and the Battle of the Euromissiles.* New York: Free Press, 1991. A well-researched history of the fight within Germany over whether to host U.S. medium-range ballistic missiles. The author believes that this battle, which ended in acceptance of the missiles, made a significant contribution to ending the cold war.

Herken, Gregg. *The Brotherhood of the Bomb: The Tangled Lives and Loyalties of Robert Oppenheimer, Ernest Lawrence, and Edward Teller.* New York: Henry Holt, 2002. The story of the choices that three scientists largely responsible for the development of nuclear weapons had to make and of the rivalry between the three of them.

Hersey, John. *Hiroshima.* New York: Bantam Books, [1948]. A vivid description of the suffering caused by the dropping of an atom bomb on Hiroshima.

Hersh, Seymour M. *The Samson Option: Israel's Nuclear Arsenal and American Foreign Policy.* New York: Random House, 1991. Analyzes Israel's nuclear weapons program and its impact on diplomatic relations between the United States and Israel. Hersh holds that officials in Washington chose to ignore Israel's nuclear program for more than 30 years. The book includes annotated chapter bibliographies.

International Physicians for the Prevention of Nuclear War and the Institute for Energy and Environmental Research. *Plutonium: Deadly Gold of the Nuclear Age.* Cambridge, Mass.: International Physicians Press, 1992. Discusses production, use, dangers, and management of plutonium. The book makes recommendations that are still valid.

Krepon, Michael. *Cooperative Threat Reduction, Missile Defense, and the Nuclear Future.* Houndmills, Basingstoke, England: Palgrave Macmillan, 2002. Facing the threat of nuclear weapons falling into the hands of rogue nations or terrorist groups, Krepon advocates cooperative threat reduction as a replacement for the concept of mutual assured destruction and a means of furthering national security.

Kuletz, Valerie L. *The Tainted Desert: Environmental and Social Ruin in the American West.* New York and London: Routledge, 1998. By the daughter of a weapons scientist, a book that documents the damage being caused by radioactive waste, particularly in the western United States.

Lambers, William. *Documents, Video and Audio CD-ROMS. A Study Supplement for the Book Nuclear Weapons.* Cincinnati: Lambers Publications, 2003. As the title indicates, a companion to Lambers's *Nuclear Weapons* (below).

———. *Nuclear Weapons.* Cincinnati: Lambers Publications, 2002. A history of the nuclear era, with reproductions of relevant government documents.

Langton, Christopher. *The Military Balance: 2003–2004.* London: Oxford University Press for the Institute for Strategic Studies, 2003. A country-by-country accounting of defense expenditures and military forces and summaries of trends in both areas. This is an authoritative resource published periodically.

Lanouette, William, with Bela Silard. *Genius in the Shadows: A Biography of Leo Szilard: The Man behind the Bomb.* New York: Charles Scribner's Sons, 1993. A biography of Leo Szilard, a Hungarian physicist who persuaded Albert Einstein to write to President Franklin D. Roosevelt about the new type of weapon that the Germans might be making.

Lewis, John Wilson, and Xue Litai. *China Builds the Bomb.* Stanford, Calif.: Stanford University Press, 1988. Shows clearly the challenges that Chinese scientists had to face in creating the bomb, in particular the difficulties in gathering materials and in quality control.

Lifton, Robert Jay, and Greg Mitchell. *Hiroshima in America: Fifty Years of Denial.* New York: G. P. Putnam's Sons, 1995. Argues that although U.S. government censorship prevented the American people from seeing images of the toll of the Hiroshima bomb, knowledge of the bombing gave Americans a devastating sense of "futurelessness." Not all readers will agree with this book's opinions.

Light, Michael. *100 Suns.* New York: Knopf, 2003. One hundred full-page color photographs on glossy paper of U.S. nuclear explosions between 1945 and 1962. Each photo is identified by the name of the test, the date, and the number of kilotons of energy released. Notes on the tests and the photographs and a bibliography are printed at the back of the book.

Lovins, Amory B., and L. Hunter Lovins. *Energy/War: Breaking the Nuclear Link.* San Francisco: Friends of the Earth, 1980. A cogent discussion of the relationship between nuclear weapons and nuclear power and an appeal to end reliance on both, by two writers well known for their work on alternative energy.

Lueders, Bill. *An Enemy of the State: The Life of Erwin Knoll.* Monroe, Maine: Common Courage Press, 1996. Includes five chapters that tell the story of the periodical *Progressive* bringing information on thermonuclear weapons to the general public. The periodical wanted to challenge the secrecy surrounding nuclear weapons and to make possible open debate. The government sued, but in court the *Progressive* gained the right to publish.

Makhijani, Arjun, and Annie Makhijani. *Fissile Materials in a Glass, Darkly: Technical and Policy Aspects of the Disposition of Plutonium and Highly Enriched Uranium.* Takoma Park, Md.: IEER Press, 1995. Makes the case for the disposition of plutonium as glass, as opposed to its use in reactor fuel.

Makhijani, Arjun, and Michele Boyd. *Nuclear Dumps by the Riverside: Threats to the Savannah River from Radioactive Contamination at the Savannah River Site.* Takoma Park, Md.: Institute for Energy and Environmental Research, 2004. This report concludes that waste disposal at the Savannah River Site has contaminated portions of the surface and groundwater on the site, with tritium, trichloroethylene, and other substances, and that this contamination has impacted the river.

Makhijani, Arjun, Howard Hu, and Katherine Yih, eds. *Nuclear Wastelands: A Global Guide to Nuclear Weapons Production and Its Health and Environmental Effects.* Cambridge, Mass.: MIT Press, 1995. As its title indicates, the book discusses the impact of nuclear weapons production on the environment and health and then describes weapons production facilities nation by nation.

Manning, Robert A. *China, Nuclear Weapons, and Arms Control: A Preliminary Assessment.* New York: Council on Foreign Relations Press, 2000. A short book aimed at policy makers.

McKinley, Wes, and Caron Balkany. *The Ambushed Grand Jury: How the Justice Department Covered up Government Nuclear Crime: And How We Caught Them Red Handed.* New York: Apex Press, 2004. The story of a 1989–92 grand jury investigation into the Rocky Flats Nuclear Weapons Plant, an alleged cover-up of the jury's conclusions by the U.S. Justice Department, and a citizen investigation of the situation.

McNamara, Robert S. *Blundering into Disaster: Surviving the First Century of the Nuclear Age.* New York: Pantheon, 1986. Looks for, without finding, a way to gain military advantage from the use of nuclear weapons, finds the Strategic Defense Initiative unpromising, and judges that the total elimination of nuclear weapons is unrealistic. McNamara concludes that such weapons should be used only for deterrence.

McPhee, John. *The Curve of Binding Energy.* New York: Farrar, Straus and Giroux, 1974. An overview of the military and civilian nuclear industry, clearly presenting the threat posed by fissile materials, as seen through the eyes of Theodore Taylor, former weapons designer and disarmament advocate.

Miller, Richard L. *Under the Cloud: The Decades of Nuclear Testing.* New York: Free Press, 1986. An in-depth history of U.S. aboveground nuclear testing. In addition to the basic facts about each explosion, Miller includes the paths of the resulting radioactive clouds and the location and character of the fallout. He also describes cover-ups of harm to people and animals. Appendixes have maps and lists of affected communities.

National Academy of Sciences, Committee on International Security and Arms Control. *Management and Disposition of Excess Weapons Plutonium.* 2 vols. Washington, D.C.: National Academy Press, 1994. Examines in detail the various options for the disposition of plutonium in the short and long term. The book includes a wealth of technical information about various aspects of plutonium and waste disposal.

National Academy of Sciences, Committee on Technical Issues Related to Ratification of the Comprehensive Nuclear Test Ban Treaty. *Technical Issues Related to the Comprehensive Nuclear Test Ban Treaty.* Washington, D.C.: National Academy Press, 2002. An analysis leading to the conclusion that the United States can maintain its nuclear stockpile without testing and that the worst-case scenario without a test ban is worse than the worst-case scenario with one.

National Research Council, Board on Radioactive Waste Management, Committee on the Remediation of Buried and Tank Wastes. *Long-Term Institutional Management of U.S. Department of Energy Legacy Waste Sites.* Washington, D.C.: National Academy Press, 2000. Examines the subject of long-term management of sites from a variety of angles. The book concludes with design principles and criteria for an effective system.

National Research Council, Committee on Science and Technology for Countering Terrorism. "Nuclear and Radiological Threats," chapter 2 in *Making the Nation Safer: The Role of Science and Technology in Countering Terrorism.* Washington, D.C.: National Academy Press, 2002. Looks at three categories of nuclear terrorism and radiological terrorism: "stolen state-owned nuclear weapons or weapons components," improvised nuclear devices, and "attacks on reactors or spent nuclear fuel or attacks involving radiological devices."

Natural Resources Defense Council. *Nuclear Insecurity: A Critique of the Bush Administration's Nuclear Weapons Policy.* New York: Natural Resources Defense Council, September 2004. An assessment of the George W. Bush administration's nuclear weapons policies. The authors report that they have made the United States less secure rather than more secure, as, for instance, it flouts the Nuclear Nonproliferation Treaty by continuing to develop nuclear weapons.

———. *The U.S. Nuclear War Plan: A Time for Change.* New York: Natural Resources Defense Council, June 2001. An assessment of the U.S. nuclear war planning process and the assumptions and logic of the Single Integrated Operational Plan (SIOP). This report includes policy recommendations.

Niedenthal, Jack. *For the Good of Mankind: A History of the People of Bikini and Their Islands.* 2nd ed. Majro, Marshall Islands: Micronitor/Bravo Publishers, 2001. The nuclear testing at Bikini, from the perspective of the islanders, whose stories are presented by means of interviews and vignettes of the islands.

Nolan, Janne E. *An Elusive Consensus: Nuclear Weapons and American Security after the Cold War.* Washington, D.C.: Brookings Institution Press, 1999. Traces the development of U.S. nuclear policy in the administrations of George H. W. Bush and Bill Clinton. Makes the point that delegation of authority for nuclear weapons and policy makes fundamental change extremely difficult to achieve. Nolan is director of international programs at the Century Foundation.

Norris, Robert S. *Racing for the Bomb: General Leslie R. Groves, the Manhattan Project's Indispensable Man.* South Royalton, Vt.: Steerforth Press, 2002. A biography of the general who managed the army's Manhattan Project to develop an atomic bomb in World War II. The author is a nuclear specialist at the Natural Resources Defense Council.

Norris, Robert S., Andrew S. Burrows, and Richard W. Fieldhouse. *Nuclear Weapons Databook.* Vol. 5, *British, French, and Chinese Nuclear Weapons.* Boulder, Colo.: Westview Press, 1994. A comprehensive study of the arsenals of

Britain, France, and China. This book by the National Resources Defense Council gives the history and production and the forces and capabilities for each country. It includes lists of nuclear tests and is a detailed, authoritative source of information.

Paine, Christopher E. *Weaponeers of Waste: A Critical Look at the Bush Administration Energy Department's Nuclear Weapons Complex and the First Decade of Science-Based Stockpile Stewardship*. Washington, D.C.: Natural Resources Defense Council, April 2004. Describes the facilities being added to the U.S. nuclear weapons complex, with an emphasis on their cost.

Palevsky, Mary. *Atomic Fragments: A Daughter's Questions*. Berkeley: University of California Press, 2000. From the daughter of scientists who worked on the Manhattan Project, the story of how she came to understand the project and her parents' role in it. She also relates in-depth conversations she had with other nuclear scientists.

Perkovich, George. *India's Nuclear Bomb: The Impact on Global Proliferation*. Los Angeles: University of California Press, 1999. A definitive account of the evolution of India's nuclear arsenal from 1947 to 1988. Perkovich believes that India developed nuclear weapons, not from military need, but as a result of pressure from a few politicians and the scientific community.

Pittock, A. B., et al. *Environmental Consequences of Nuclear War (SCOPE 28)*. Vol. 1, *Physical and Atmospheric Effects*. New York: John Wiley and Sons, on behalf of the Scientific Committee on Problems of the Environment (SCOPE), 1986. A scientific presentation of an aspect of the effects of nuclear war, to which hundreds of scientists contributed. The book avoids use of the term *nuclear winter*, which the authors feel oversimplifies a complex situation, but regards the effects as nonetheless grave.

Podvig, Pavel, ed. *Russian Strategic Nuclear Forces*. Cambridge, Mass.: MIT Press, 2001. A team of seven Russian researchers, using Russian sources, describes the Russian nuclear weapons production complex and Russian weapons. The original book was published in Russian in 1998. The English translation is a revised and updated version.

Polenberg, Richard, ed. *In the Matter of J. Robert Oppenheimer: The Security Clearance Hearing*. Ithaca, N.Y.: Cornell University Press, 2002. An edited transcript of the dramatic hearing that stripped Oppenheimer of his security clearance as a result of his alleged left-wing leanings.

Project on Government Oversight. *U.S. Nuclear Weapons Complex: Security at Risk*. Washington, D.C.: Project on Government Oversight, October 2001. Results of an investigation by the Project on Government Oversight that showed that the Department of Energy is not adequately protecting its nuclear weapons facilities from a terrorist attack.

Rhodes, Richard. *Dark Sun: The Making of the Hydrogen Bomb*. New York: Simon and Schuster, 1995. Starting in 1945–46, this book tells the story of the making of the hydrogen bomb in both the United States and Russia. Russia, Rhodes reports, infiltrated every facility of the Manhattan Engineer District and learned how to make the bomb from the United States.

———. *The Making of the Atomic Bomb.* New York: Simon and Schuster, 1986. A detailed but readable history of the nuclear fission bomb from 1933 to the Japanese surrender in World War II. An epilogue relates the follow-up to Hiroshima and Nagasaki. This book is also well indexed.

Robinson, Paul. *Uranium Mill Tailings Remediation Performed by US DOE: An Overview.* Albuquerque: Southwest Research and Information Center, 2004. An overview of the first radioactive waste management program completed by the Department of Energy. The department has spent almost $2 billion to clean up 22 sites, but groundwater contamination continues at most of them.

Roche, Douglas. *Re-nuclearization or Disarmament: A Fateful Choice for Humanity: A Political Analysis of the Third Preparatory Committee Meeting for the 2005 Review Conference of the Non-Proliferation Treaty.* San Francisco, Calif.: Middle Powers Initiative, May 2004. A factual report of the discussion at the 2004 preparatory committee meeting. The report notes that disagreement at the meeting between the major nuclear states and the nonnuclear states augurs ill for the 2005 review conference. The report includes a diagram of the effect of a Hiroshima-size bomb dropped on the site of the World Trade Center.

Rose, Kenneth D. *One Nation Underground: The Fallout Shelter in American Culture.* New York: New York University Press, 2001. Recounts the history of the national debate on civil defense in the 1960s.

Roy, Arundhati. *War Talk.* Cambridge, Mass.: South End Press, 2003. Six political essays, one of which is about nuclear weapons in India and Pakistan, by the author of *The God of Small Things.*

Sagan, Carl, and Richard Turco. *A Path Where No Man Thought: Nuclear Winter and the End of the Arms Race.* New York: Random House, 1990. A presentation of the concept of nuclear winter for the nonscientist, followed by a plea to reduce the global nuclear arsenal to 300 warheads for reasons of economics, strategic stability, and the threat of nuclear winter.

Sagan, Scott D. *The Limits of Safety: Organizations, Accidents, and Nuclear Weapons.* Princeton Studies in International History and Politics. Princeton, N.J.: Princeton University Press, 1993. An examination of the safety record of the Strategic Air Command. Sagan reveals near-catastrophes with nuclear weapons. The book is based on formerly classified government documents.

Sagan, Scott D., and Kenneth N. Waltz. *The Spread of Nuclear Weapons: A Debate Renewed, with New Sections on India and Pakistan, Terrorism and Missile Defense.* 2nd ed. New York: Norton, 2003. A discussion by two scholars of international relations, each expressing a different point of view. They consider whether the spread of nuclear weapons to new states will make the international situation more stable or less stable in the future.

Schwartz, Stephen I. *Atomic Audit: What the U.S. Nuclear Arsenal Really Cost.* Washington, D.C.: Brookings Institution Press, 1995. Calculates the cost of the U.S. atomic arsenal. As of 1995, one-fourth to one-third of all U.S. military spending—$4 trillion—had gone to nuclear weapons and their infrastructure.

Shambroom, Paul. *Face to Face with the Bomb: Nuclear Reality after the Cold War.* Baltimore: Johns Hopkins University Press, 2003. Composed of photographs of U.S. nuclear weapons and maintenance operations at bases in the United States and the Pacific between 1992 and 2001. The photographs were made with permission of the U.S. Department of Defense.

Shute, Neville. *On the Beach*. London: William Heinemann, 1957. Fiction that brings home the realities of nuclear war. Set in Australia, it shows the victims of an accidental war as the world as we know it nears its end.

Smith, Alice Kimball. *A Peril and a Hope: The Scientists' Movement in America, 1945–47*. Cambridge, Mass.: MIT Press, 1965. Presents the debate over the use of nuclear weapons against Japan at the end of World War II.

Sokolski, Henry D. *Best of Intentions: America's Campaign against Strategic Weapons Proliferation*. Westport, Conn.: Praeger, 2001. Examines various U.S. initiatives, finishing with the counterproliferation initiative. Sokolski asks how future campaigns could be more effective.

Sokolski, Henry D., and Thomas Riisager, ed. *Beyond Nunn-Lugar: Curbing the Next Wave of Nuclear Proliferation Threats from Russia*. Carlisle Barracks, Pa.: U.S. Army War College, Strategic Studies Institute, 2002. The product of a yearlong study of U.S.-Russian nonproliferation cooperation based on competitive strategies analysis. In such analysis, researchers determine how the parties' goals and strategies differ, identify each nation's relevant strengths and weaknesses, and determine how to create new forms of cooperation from them.

Stephenson, Michael, and Roger Hearn. *Nuclear Case Book*. London: F. Muller, 1983. A basic source of information on nuclear weapons.

Teller, Edward, with Judith Shoolery. *Memoirs: A Twentieth-Century Journey in Science and Politics*. Cambridge, Mass.: Perseus Books, 2001. An autobiography by the man known as the father of the hydrogen bomb.

Toscano, Louis. *Triple Cross: Israel, The Atomic Bomb, and The Man Who Spilled the Secrets*. Secaucus, N.J.: Carol Publishing Group, 1990. An account of the life of Mordechai Vanunu, who told the world about Israel's nuclear weapons, and of the attitude of the Israeli government to his revelations. According to Toscana, a veteran reporter, the government decided to allow Vanunu to tell his tales because they wanted the Arab world to know that Israel had the bomb.

U.S. Congress, Office of Technology Assessment. *Complex Cleanup: The Environmental Legacy of Nuclear Weapons Production*. OTA-O-484. Washington, D.C.: U.S. Government Printing Office, 1991. A call for attention to contamination and health problems at federal sites, with suggestions for remedies. The report was comprehensive and groundbreaking in 1991. It has handy summary descriptions of the main sites in an appendix.

U.S. Congresss. Office of Technology Assessment. *The Effects of Nuclear War*. Montclair, N.J.: Allanheld, Osmun and Co., 1980. Examines the range of effects that nuclear warfare would have on civilians.

U.S. Department of Energy, Office of Environmental Management. *Closing the Circle on the Splitting of the Atom: The Environmental Legacy of Nuclear Weapons Production in the United States and What the Department of Energy Is Doing about*

It. Washington, D.C.: U.S. Department of Energy, 1995. An illustrated survey designed for the general public as part of Secretary of Energy Hazel O'Leary's "Openness Initiative." The report estimated that, as of 1995, it would cost $500 billion and take 75 years to clean up the nuclear weapons complex.

———. *Linking Legacies: Connecting the Cold War Nuclear Weapons Production Processes to Their Environmental Consequences.* DOE/EM-0319. Washington, D.C.: U.S. Department of Energy, 1997. Useful as a source of information on weapons production processes and history, although its account of environmental consequences is incomplete. The book includes photographs, diagrams, and a large, removable chart.

U.S. Department of Energy, Office of Inspector General, Office of Audit Services. *Audit Report: The Department's Basic Protective Force Training Program.* DOE/IG-0641. Washington, D.C.: U.S. Department of Energy, March 2004. Reports that the core training program has been applied inconsistently within the complex.

U.S. Department of Energy, Office of Inspector General, Office of Inspections and Special Inquiries. *Protective Force Performance Test Improprieties.* DOE/IG-0636. Washington, D.C.: U.S. Department of Energy, January 2004. Identification by the Department of Energy of improprieties in the tests of its readiness to defend weapons complex sites from terrorist attack.

Vanderbilt, Tom. *Survival City: Adventures among the Ruins of Atomic America.* Princeton, N.J.: Princeton Architectural Press, 2002. Describes travels to sites that show the influence of the cold war on the American landscape.

Wasserman, Harvey, and Norman Solomon. *Killing Our Own: The Disaster of America's Experience with Atomic Radiation.* New York: Dell Publishing, 1982. Presents a series of documented accounts of the contamination and suffering of various groups of Americans as a result of exposure to radioactivity. The first five chapters relay the experiences of victims of nuclear testing.

Weisbrot, Robert. *Maximum Danger: Kennedy, the Missiles, and the Crisis of American Confidence.* Chicago: Ivan R. Dee, 2001. A synthesis of earlier works on the Cuban missile crisis, which points the way for further research.

Weisgall, Jonathan M. *Operation Crossroads: The Atomic Tests at Bikini Atoll.* Annapolis, Md.: Naval Institute Press, 1994. The first account of the U.S. testing at Bikini in 1946 from a nongovernment source. The author has represented the people of Bikini in suits against the U.S. government.

Weissman, Steven, and Herbert Krosney. *The Islamic Bomb: The Nuclear Threat to Israel and the Middle East..* New York: Times Books, 1981. Weissman and Krosney tell how Iraq and Pakistan undertook the development of nuclear weapons more than 20 years ago.

Welsome, Eileen. *The Plutonium Files: America's Secret Medical Experiments during the Cold War.* New York: Dial Press, 1999. Recounts experiments with radioactivity carried out on individuals by the Manhattan Project and the Atomic Energy Commission. The experiments continued into the 1970s and were designed to show the effect of radiation on the human body.

Wenger, Andreas. *Living with Peril: Eisenhower, Kennedy, and Nuclear Weapons.* Lanham, Md.: Rowman and Littlefield, 1997. Evolution of the thinking about nuclear weapons in the Eisenhower and Kennedy administrations and the responses of these administrations to the Berlin and Cuba crises.

Wilcox, Fred A. *Uncommon Martyrs: The Berrigans, the Catholic Left, and the Plowshares Movement.* Reading, Mass.: Addison-Wesley, 1991. Portrays people who have carried out symbolic civil disobedience "actions" against nuclear weapons. Wilcox regards them as heroic.

Winkler, Allan M. *Life under a Cloud: American Anxiety about the Atom.* London: Oxford University Press, 1993. An evaluation of the successes and the shortcomings of citizen action on nuclear weapons issues. Winkler feels that the modest success of such action in the past offers one hope for the future.

Wittner, Lawrence S. *One World or None: A History of the World Nuclear Disarmament Movement through 1953.* Stanford, Calif.: Stanford University Press, 1993. The first volume of a trilogy, *The Struggle against the Bomb*, it won the Warren Kuehl Prize of the Society for Historians of American Foreign Relations. Wittner argues that "the largest grassroots struggle in modern history, one that mobilized millions of people around the globe: the world nuclear disarmament movement," has helped to prevent nuclear war since 1945.

———. *Resisting the Bomb: A History of the World Nuclear Disarmament Movement, 1954–1970.* Stanford, Calif.: Stanford University Press, 1997. Like the other volumes in the *The Struggle Against the Bomb* trilogy, this second volume presents disarmament efforts around the globe; the history of the U.S. efforts is of particular interest.

———. *Toward Nuclear Abolition: A History of the World Nuclear Disarmament Movement, 1971 to the Present.* Stanford, Calif.: Stanford University Press, 2003. Argues that pressure from the antinuclear movement has affected policy. In this third volume of his *The Struggle Against the Bomb* trilogy, Wittner keeps his eyes on grassroots organizations.

Articles

Albright, David, and Holly Higgins. "A Bomb for the Unmah." *Bulletin of the Atomic Scientists*, March/April 2003, pp. 49ff. Discusses attempts by a Pakistani organization to transfer sensitive information on nuclear, chemical, and biological weapons to the Taliban and Al Qaeda.

Allison, Graham. "Tick, Tick, Tick." *Atlantic Monthly*, vol. 294, October 2004, pp. 58–60. Describes Pakistan as a nuclear time bomb that must be defused. Allison suggests ways of doing that, including working through China.

Badkhe, Anna. "Nuclear Theft Case Raises Fears about Russia." *San Francisco Chronicle*, November 23, 2003, p. A16. The theft of six pounds of uranium by a Russian official raises fears about nuclear security in Russia.

Bailey, Kathleen. "Why We Have to Keep the Bomb." *Bulletin of the Atomic Scientists*, vol. 51, January/February 1995, pp. 30–37. Nuclear disarmament is neither practical nor useful. For the government to clearly state this view would not, in Bailey's opinion, increase the risk of nuclear proliferation.

Annotated Bibliography

Bailey, Kathleen, and Robert Barker. "Why the United States Should Unsign the Comprehensive Test Ban Treaty and Resume Nuclear Testing." *Comparative Strategy,* vol. 22, April–June 2003, pp. 131ff. Argues that testing is needed to determine the reliability of existing warheads, to make these warheads safer by implementing new technologies, and to design new warheads to meet emerging needs.

Bleek, Philipp C. "Project Vinca: Lessons for Securing Civil Nuclear Material Stockpiles." *Nonproliferation Review,* vol. 10, Fall–Winter 2003, pp. 1–23. An analysis of the removal of highly enriched uranium from the Vinca Institute in Bulgaria to illustrate how to proceed at other civilian facilities. Bleek urges that civilian stocks of highly enriched uranium in institutions worldwide be secured.

Bohlen, Avis. "The Rise and Fall of Arms Control." *Survival,* vol. 45, Autumn 2003, pp. 7ff. A short history of strategic arms control from the Strategic Arms Limitation Talks in 1969 through the U.S. withdrawal from the Anti-Ballistic Missile Treaty in June 2002.

Bowen, Wyn Q., and Joanna Kidd. "The Iranian Nuclear Challenge." *International Affairs,* vol. 80, March 2004, pp. 257–276. A look at conditions that must be achieved if Iran is not to become a nuclear-weapon state.

Broad, William J. "Addressing the Unthinkable, U.S. Revives Study of Fallout." *New York Times,* vol. 153, March 19, 2004, p. A1. Reports that in a program that began in 1999 but was long secret, U.S. weapons laboratories are refining their ability to detect the source of a nuclear explosion or of another type of radiological event.

Broad, William J., and Patrick Tyler. "Dispute over Russian Testing Divides U.S. Nuclear Experts," *New York Times,* March 4, 2001, p. 14. Reports that U.S. intelligence experts disagree about whether Russia has been testing for the past several years but agree that Russia has been more active than it has admitted.

Brown, S. C., et al. "Lung Cancer and Internal Lung Doses among Plutonium Workers at the Rocky Flats Plant: A Case-Control Study." *American Journal of Epidemiology,* vol. 160, July 15, 2004, pp. 163–172. Presents the results of a study of the association between death from lung cancer and cumulative internal doses to the lung from radioisotopes among a cohort of workers at the Rocky Flats Plant. An elevated lung cancer risk was found among workers with cumulative internal lung doses of more than 400 millisieverts.

Carter, Luther J. "Let's Use It." *Bulletin of the Atomic Scientists,* vol. 50, May/June 1994, pp. 12–15. Argues for the use of weapons plutonium in mixed oxide fuel in U.S. and Russian power plants as a means of rendering the plutonium unusable for weapons.

Clarke, Michael. "Does My Bomb Look Big in This? Britain's Nuclear Choices after Trident." *International Affairs,* vol. 80, January 2004, pp. 49–62. A discussion of the debate Britain will face when the minimal nuclear force of four missile-launching submarines that it now maintains approaches retirement. Nuclear deterrence will be compared with other forms of deterrence.

Cooper, Mary H. "Nuclear Proliferation and Terrorism." *CQ Researcher,* vol. 14, April 2, 2004, entire issue. The basic question examined by this issue of the

Researcher is whether rogue states and terrorists can get hold of nuclear weapons. The pro and con section asks whether U.S. policies will keep nuclear weapons away from terrorists; the special focus section presents a chronology of close calls.

Dasher, Douglas, et al. "An Assessment of the Reported Leakage of Anthropogenic Radionuclides from the Underground Nuclear Test Sites at Amchitka Island, Alaska, USA to the Surface Environment." *Journal of Environmental Radioactivity*, vol. 60, pp. 165ff. Results of a study to determine the validity of charges by Greenpeace of leakage of radionuclides at Amchitka Island. The leakage is not confirmed.

Dunn, F. B. "Government Sets Compensation Guidelines for Radiation Exposure." *Journal of the National Cancer Institute*, vol. 94, June 5, 2002, pp. 797ff. Reports the establishment of radioactive exposure guidelines for weapons workers seeking compensation. Dunn also gives background information on the compensation issue.

Eichenseher, Tasha. "Haste Makes Waste." *E Magazine: The Environmental Magazine*, vol. 14, November–December 2003, pp. 16ff. Describes the cleanup at Rocky Flats nuclear facility as an illustration of the Department of Energy's approach to cleanup in general. Eichenseher raises the question of whether a dramatic cut in the cost of the cleanup at Rocky Flats means that work will be incomplete and shoddy.

Eisler, Peter. "Fallout Likely Caused 15,000 Deaths." *USA Today*, February 28, 2002, p. 1. A short report on an unreleased federal study that shows that fallout from tests across the world probably caused 15,000 U.S. residents to die of cancer.

Elegant, Robert. "Fallout." *National Review*, vol. 54, September 2, 2002, pp. 30ff. A vivid depiction of the effects on human health and the environment of Soviet nuclear testing in Kazakhstan.

Epstein, William. "Indefinite Extension—with Increased Accountability." *Bulletin of the Atomic Scientists*, vol. 51, July/August 1995, pp. 27–30. Reviews negotiations at and the results of the Nuclear Non-Proliferation Treaty Review and Extension Conference of 1995.

Findlay, Trevor, and Oliver Meier. "In Verification We Trust." *Bulletin of the Atomic Scientists*, vol. 57, January/February 2001, pp. 13–15. An Independent Commission on the Verification of the Comprehensive Test Ban Treaty, made up of experts from varied backgrounds, concluded that any nuclear tests are highly likely to be detected, located, and identified.

Frantz, Douglas. "Observers Fault U.S. for Pursuing Mini-Nukes." *Los Angeles Times*, December 23, 2003, p. A1. Relays criticism of the George W. Bush administration's push for new nuclear weapons. Frantz says this push will hurt the nation's efforts to stop nuclear proliferation.

Frieman, Wendy. "New Members of the Club: Chinese Participation in Arms Control Regimes 1980–1995." *Nonproliferation Review*, vol. 3, Spring–Summer 1996, pp. 15–30. Examines the constraints on China's past participation in arms-control regimes and asks whether in the future China will succeed in participating more fully.

Gaddis, John Lewis. "Hanging Tough Paid Off." *Bulletin of the Atomic Scientists*, vol. 45, January/February 1989, pp. 11–14. Makes the case that President Ronald Reagan presided over the greatest improvement in relations between the United States and the Soviet Union and the "most solid progress in arms control" since the beginning of the Cold War.

Goin, Peter. "Nuclear Landscapes." *Grand Street*, Spring 2002, vol. 18, pp. 180ff. Photographs and brief descriptions of the status of sites where the United States conducted nuclear tests.

Goldberg, Stanley. "Groves Takes the Reins." *Bulletin of the Atomic Scientists*, December, vol. 48, December 1992, pp. 32ff. The key role played by General Leslie R. Groves in the Manhattan Project, which produced the first atomic bombs. Groves was not the automaton he is often held to be.

Guinnessy, Paul. "NAS Finds No Flaws in Nuclear Treaty." *Physics Today*, vol. 55, October 2002, pp. 25ff. A summary of and background on the National Academy of Sciences' report on technical issues related to the comprehensive test ban treaty.

———. "Pentagon Revamps Nuclear Doctrine." *Physics Today*, vol. 56, May 2003, pp. 27ff. Surveys the position of the George W. Bush administration on development of new nuclear weapons and the arguments of the opposition.

Happell, James D. "A History of Atmospheric Tritium Gas (HT) 1950–2002." *Tellus*, Series B, vol. 56, July 2004, pp.183ff. Presents data that show that the maximum atmospheric concentration of tritium gas occurred in the early to mid-1970s, when many large underground nuclear tests were occurring. Current data suggest that the major source of tritium today is the commercial nuclear power industry.

Hayes, Peter, and Nina Tannenwald. "Nixing Nukes in Vietnam." *Bulletin of the Atomic Scientists*, vol. 59, May/June 2003, pp. 52–59. The classified report "Tactical Nuclear Weapons in Southeast Asia," produced by scientists in 1966, analyzed the military and political effect of the possible use of tactical weapons in Vietnam. This article summarizes the findings of the report—that use would be ill-advised—and notes that the findings would be valid for other wars today.

Holdstock, Douglas. "Nuclear Weapons: A Continuing Threat to Health." *Lancet*, vol. 355, April 29, 2000, pp. 1544–1547. Discusses the effect on human health of a nuclear weapons explosion, nuclear testing, and the nuclear fuel cycle and states that the solution to the risk that they pose is the elimination of nuclear weapons and nuclear power plants.

Hutchins, Julie. "Bombs Away." *Colorado Business Magazine*, vol. 20, April 1993, pp. 12ff. A presentation of the philosophy of the manager of the Rocky Flats weapons production site, a practicing Episcopal priest. Reconciling his religious views with his work, he implements a policy of openness and caring for the public, the author says.

Jardine, Roger, J. W. de Villers, and Mitchell Reiss. "Why South Africa Gave up the Bomb." *Foreign Affairs*, vol. 72, November/December 1993, pp. 98ff. Celebrates the first instance of a state with nuclear bombs voluntarily giving them up. The article also gives a brief history of the South African nuclear program and the nuclear agenda of the African National Congress and calls attention to such lingering questions as how much foreign assistance with its program South Africa received.

Kang, J., et al. "Storage MOX: A Third Way for Plutonium Disposal." *Science and Global Security*, vol. 10, May 2002, pp. 85ff. Suggests an alternative way of disposing of excess weapons and civilian plutonium: making it into mixed oxide (MOX) fuel containing plutonium and uranium oxides, and mixing this fuel with irradiated fuel in final disposal casks.

Keller, Bill. "The Thinkable." *New York Times* Magazine, vol. 152, May 4, 2003, pp. 48ff. Discusses the growing number of countries who have or want to have weapons of mass destruction. Keller also discusses how nuclear power is part of international relations and of many governments' foreign policy.

Kershaw, Sarah, and Matthew L. Wald. "Lack of Safety Is Charged in Nuclear Site Cleanup." *New York Times*, vol. 153, February 20, 2004, p. A1. Reports on the cleanup of the nuclear reactors at the Hanford nuclear weapons production complex in Washington State.

Koch, Andrew. "Regime Repair" and "No Quick Fix." *Jane's Defense Weekly*, vol. 41, July 7, 2004, pp. 20–21. Companion articles on the endangered nuclear nonproliferation regime. The first article conveys the situation and various proposals for strengthening the regime; the second is devoted to the views of Mohamed El Baradei of the International Atomic Energy Agency. Both note that a security strategy not dependent on nuclear weapons is needed in the Mideast.

———. "Washington Cuts Nuclear Arsenal." *Jane's Defense Weekly*, vol. 41, June 9, 2004, p. 8. Reports on an announcement by Ambassador Linton Brooks that the United States will halve the number of nuclear weapons in its arsenal.

Kristensen, Hans M. "Preemptive Posturing." *Bulletin of the Atomic Scientists*, vol. 58, September/October 2003, pp. 54–59. Comments on the George W. Bush administration's Nuclear Posture Review, with emphasis on the nuclear situation in North Korea. Kristensen does not find the position, as leaked to the press, helpful in that regard.

Lancaster, John. "India, Pakistan to Set up Hotline." *Washington Post*, June 21, 2004, p. A12. Summarizes India's and Pakistan's movement in the direction of peace with one another.

Lanouette, William. "Ideas by Szilard, Physics by Fermi." *Bulletin of the Atomic Scientists*, vol. 48, December 1992, pp. 16ff. The roles played by Leo Szilard and Enrico Fermi leading to the world's first reactor criticality. The article is written in a conversational style.

Larin, Vladislav. "Mayak's Walking Wounded." *Bulletin of the Atomic Scientists*, vol. 55, no. 5, September/October 1999, pp. 20–27. After an overview of the situation at Mayak, former workers at the Soviet plutonium production complex talk about their experiences.

Annotated Bibliography

Lawren, Bill. "Rosalie Bertel." *Omni*, vol. 9, September 1987, pp. 96–97. A sketch in a special section of *Omni* on activist scientists. Rosalie Bertell is a nun and an epidemiologist who has devoted herself to studying and warning about the dangers of low-level radiation and toxic waste.

Lee, Christopher. "DOE Bomb Squads' Exacting Mission: Team Hunting for Radioactive Explosives Faces Aging Equipment, Talent Shortage, Analysts Say," *Washington Post*, March 9, 2004, p. A21. Points out, among other problems, the difficulty of detecting shielded sources of radioactivity.

Levi, Michael A., and Henry C. Kelly, "Nuclear Bunker Buster Bombs." *Scientific American*, vol. 291, August 2004, pp. 66ff. Delineates some of the problems with using nuclear bunker busters and looks at the types of practical alternatives. Nuclear bunker busters have some advantages over conventional arms, the authors conclude, but they are fewer than is often stated. Creative conventional alternatives merit exploration.

Long, Michael E. "Half Life." *National Geographic*, vol. 202, July 2002, pp. 2ff. Discusses the nuclear waste problem in the United States, with emphasis on Department of Energy weapons complex sites and on the proposed Yucca Mountain repository for high-level waste.

Makhijani, Arjun. "Forgotten Exposures: Worker Doses at Three Nuclear Materials Processing Plants in the 1940s and 1950s." *Science for Democratic Action*, vol. 9, December 2000, pp. 1–7. Describes worker exposure to radiation at three now-forgotten plants that processed uranium: in Lockport and Niagara Falls, New York, and Cleveland, Ohio.

———. "Japan: 'Always' the Target?" *The Bulletin of the Atomic Scientists*, vol. 51, May/June 1995, pp. 23–27. Shows that scientists working on the atomic bomb became involved in the program in order to beat Germany to the weapon, but military planners apparently had Japan in mind as a target all along.

———. "Nuclear Targeting: The First 60 Years." *Science for Democratic Action*, vol. 12, March 2004, pp. 1, 12–14. Surveys the history of the threat of the use of nuclear weapons. Makhijani concludes that the idea that instruments of terror can deter terror is an illusion; the policy of deterrence has furthered proliferation.

Mark, J. Carson. "Explosive Properties of Reactor-Grade Plutonium" *Science and Global Security*, vol. 4, 1993, p. 3. Makes clear that reactor-grade plutonium can be used to produce a nuclear device. Thus it must be guarded from terrorists and rogue states as carefully as weapons grade plutonium.

McGregor, Jena. "Rocky Mountain High." *Fast Company*, no. 84, July 2004, pp. 58ff. An explanation of how management persuaded employees to work themselves out of jobs, in order to clean up Rocky Flats nuclear weapons production site faster and at less cost than had been deemed feasible.

McNamara, Robert. "Averting the Apocalypse." *Time*, vol. 161, March 31, 2003, p. A45. A look back at the Cuban missile crisis by one of the leaders involved. McNamara relates conflicting views on the best way for the United States to stop nuclear proliferation, whether to use a conciliatory or a tough approach.

Nelson, Robert W. "Nuclear Bunker Busters, Mini-Nukes, and the US Nuclear Stockpile." *Physics Today*, vol. 56, November 2003, pp. 32–38. Assesses plans of the George W. Bush administration to develop new types of nuclear weapons. Nelson states that these weapons would likely produce massive radioactive fallout and that their development would likely require the resumption of underground nuclear testing.

Norris, Robert S., and Hans M. Kristensen. "Dismantling U.S. Nuclear Warheads." NRDC Nuclear Notebook. *Bulletin of the Atomic Scientists*, vol. 60, January/February 2004, pp. 72–74. Centers on the Pantex Plant, which assembles and disassembles nuclear warheads, but includes facts about the history of weapons production and stockpiles in the United States and about the transportation of weapons. The NRDC Nuclear Notebook, an authoritative source of facts on nuclear arsenals, appears in each issue of the *Bulletin*.

Norris, Robert S., Hans M. Kristensen, and Joshua Handler. "North Korea's Nuclear Program, 2003." *Bulletin of the Atomic Scientists*, vol. 59, March/April 2003, pp. 74ff. A summary of what was known of the status of North Korea's nuclear program, with emphasis on its development of missiles, as of early 2003.

Norris, Robert S., William M. Arkin, and William Burr. "Where They Were." *Bulletin of the Atomic Scientists*, vol. 55, November/December 1999, pp. 26–35. Drawing on a 1978 government document obtained through the Freedom of Information Act, the article tells for the first time where the United States based nuclear weapons between 1951 and 1977 and discusses the secrecy surrounding their deployment.

"Not Iran, Not North Korea, Not Libya, But Pakistan." *London Review of Books*, vol. 26, September 2, 2004, pp. 32ff. A discussion of the nuclear threat to international security with emphasis on uranium enrichment programs and information on the Khan Research Laboratories in Pakistan.

Ortmeyer, Pat, and Arjun Makhijani. "Worse Than We Knew." *Bulletin of the Atomic Scientists*, vol. 53, November/December 1997, pp. 46–50. Argues that almost everyone in the United States was exposed to fallout from nuclear testing and that the government knew what was happening.

Paine, C. E. "A Case against Virtual Nuclear Testing." *Scientific American*, vol. 281, no. 3, September 1999, pp. 64ff. Comments on the Department of Energy's plan to replace nuclear tests with three-dimensional computer simulations. Paine discusses the program in regard to disarmament diplomacy, computing power, the technology, and the financial cost.

Paine, Christopher. "The Moscow Treaty: Making Matters Worse." *Bulletin of Atomic Scientists*, vol. 58, November/December 2002, pp. 19ff. Argues that the Moscow Treaty is a case of "less verification, less cooperative inspection, less warhead and launcher destruction, and less accountability [which means] less security."

Pasternak, Douglas, and Eleni Dimmler. "A Home-Grown Nuclear Threat." *U.S. News and World Report*, September 23, 2002, p. 40. The authors discuss the prospect that nuclear materials that the United States sent to foreign countries in an effort to encourage the use of nuclear energy for civilian purposes may become instruments of terror. The article discusses, in particular, a theft of uranium from the Democratic Republic of the Congo.

Pincus, Walter. "$27 Million Sought for Nuclear Arms Study." *Washington Post*, March 20, 2004, p. A04. Discusses the George W. Bush administration's continuing program to study a nuclear weapon to attack buried bunkers and presents contrasting views of this program.

"Plutonium Cancer Risk Questioned." *Cancer Weekly*, August 3, 2004, p. 58. Discusses that a leaked report by U.K. radiation experts warns that the cancer risk from exposure to plutonium inside the body may be 10 times higher than previously thought.

Potter, William C., and Elena Sokova. "Illicit Nuclear Trafficking in the NIS: What's New? What's True?" *Nonproliferation Review*, vol. 9, summer 2002, pp. 112–120. Trying to compare nuclear trafficking from 1998 to 2001 to that from 1992 to 1997, the authors find information lacking because of shortcomings in its collection and analysis. The article makes recommendations for stopping nuclear trafficking.

Richelson, Jeffrey. "Verification: The Ways and Means." *Bulletin of the Atomic Scientists*, vol. 54, November/December 1998, pp. 52–56. Describes the means of detecting nuclear tests over one kiloton in yield. Richelson makes the case that the seismic, hydroacoustic, and satellite monitoring techniques in use will be sufficient to detect any violations of the Comprehensive Test Ban Treaty.

Robock, Alan. "New Models Confirm Nuclear Winter." *Bulletin of the Atomic Scientists*, vol. 45, September 1989, pp. 32–35. Summarizes the research on nuclear winter produced between 1982 when the concept was introduced to 1989. Robock finds it supports the threat.

Russell, James A. "Nuclear Strategy and the Modern Middle East." *Middle East Policy*, vol. 11, fall 2004, pp. 98–117. An examination of the implications of the George W. Bush administration's Nuclear Posture Review for U.S. security strategy in the Middle East.

Sanger, David E. "Diplomacy Fails to Slow Advance of Nuclear Arms." *New York Times*, vol. 153, August 8, 2004, p. N1. Reviews the conclusions of administration and intelligence officials about Iran's and North Korea's nuclear forces and the problems these conclusions pose for the administration of George W. Bush.

Small, Nancy. "Is Nuclear Deterrence Still Moral?" *America*, vol. 189, September 29, 2003, pp. 14ff. Examines the ethical issues at stake in regard to the pre-emptive military strike doctrine of President George W. Bush. Small asks Catholic bishops to change their stance on nuclear weapons, which relies on their possession as a deterrent.

Smith, D. K., D. L. Finnegan, and S. M. Bowen. "An Inventory of Long-Lived Radionuclides Residual from Underground Nuclear Testing at the Nevada Test Site, 1951–1992." *Journal of Environmental Radioactivity*, April 2003, vol. 67, p. 35ff. An inventory of long-lived radionuclides produced by underground nuclear testing at the Nevada Test Site. Activities are reported for specific portions of the site for 1992, the date of the last test, and, looking ahead, 2492.

Smith-Norris, Martha. "The Eisenhower Administration and the Nuclear Test Ban Talks, 1958–1960: Another Challenge to 'Revisionism.'" *Diplomatic History*, vol. 27, September 2003, pp. 503ff. Examines the nuclear test–ban talks in the historical context of the American position on testing.

Spector, Leonard S. "Interview: Ambassador Linton Brooks on U.S. Nuclear Policy." *Nonproliferation Review*, vol. 9, fall/winter 2002, pp. 1ff. The views of the Acting Administrator of the U.S. National Nuclear Security Administration on such questions as dismantling nuclear weapons and restarting nuclear testing.

Sterngold, James. "Bush's Buildup Begins with Little Debate in Congress." *San Francisco Chronicle*, December 7, 2003, p. A1. Reports that Congress in 2003 voted for more than $6 billion for research on and expansion and modernization of the nation's nuclear weapons arsenal. The allocation marked a radical change in nuclear policy, little recognized or debated by Congress or the public.

———. "Noted Scientists Reject Nuclear Quest. U.S. Research Would Give Legitimacy to Others to Develop Low-Yield Bombs, Letter Says." *San Francisco Chronicle*, May 20, 2003, p. A5. Reports that eight eminent scientists closely involved with the U.S. nuclear weapons program wrote a letter urging Congress not to lift a ban on developing "usable" warheads with a yield of five kilotons or less.

Tavernise, Sabrina. "Cold War Legacy." *New York Times*, vol. 151, May 19, 2002, p. 5. Describes the effects of Soviet nuclear tests on residents of Semipalatinsk, Kazakhstan.

Turco, R. P., et al. "Nuclear Winter: Global Consequences of Multiple Nuclear Explosions." *Science*, vol. 22, 1983, pp. 1283–1297. The report that initially laid out the theory that a nuclear war could result in a "nuclear winter." It is often referred to as TTAPS, the initials of the last names of the authors.

Turner, William D. "Japanese Plutonium Stockpiles: A Transportation, Storage, and Public Relations Challenge." *Journal of Environment and Development*, vol. 12, March 2003, pp. 99ff. Considers the pros and cons of mixed oxide (MOX) fuel, which is now being used in Japan and which the George W. Bush administration would like to use in the United States in the future.

Wald, Matthew L. "Energy Dept. Seeks Power to Redefine Nuclear Waste." *New York Times*, October 1, 2003, p. A17. Reports that the U.S. Department of Energy has asked Congress to grant it authority to redefine certain nuclear waste. The agency would reclassify what has constituted high-level nuclear waste to low-level waste, which would permit it to leave the waste in place rather than transport it to a high-level waste disposal site.

———. "U.S. to Make First Payment in Death Tied to an A-Plant." *New York Times*, vol. 150, August 9, 2001, p. A15. Reports on the presentation of a check by Secretary of Labor Elaine L. Chao to the widow of Jim Harding, a worker at the uranium enrichment plant in Paducah who died of cancer in 1980.

Walker, J. Samuel. "The Atomic Energy Commission and the Politics of Radiation Protection, 1967–1971. *Isis*, vol. 85, March 1994, pp. 57–78. A presentation of the debate on radiation protection in the United States between 1967 and 1971. Walker writes that the Atomic Energy Commission, the agency that exercised primary jurisdiction for radiation safety from 1947 to 1975 did not maintain public confidence about the safety of nuclear energy.

Wilson, A. H. "Nuclear Technology: Arms Control in Perspective." *Contemporary Review*, vol. 280, June 2002, pp. 354ff. Looks at key points in the history of nuclear weapons and arms control, including the testing of the hydrogen bomb and the deployment of intercontinental ballistic missiles.

Winslow, Pete. "Fallout from the Peaceful Atom." *Nation*, vol. 212, May 3, 1971, pp. 557–561. Reviews the dispute between the Atomic Energy Commission and two scientists at the Lawrence Radiation Laboratory, John W. Gofman and Arthur R. Tamplin.

Yost, David. "The U.S. Nuclear Posture Review and the NATO Allies." *International Affairs*, vol. 80, July 2004, pp. 705–729. Implications of the U.S. Nuclear Posture Review for NATO allies and relations between the United States and its allies. Yost notes that U.S. public information concerning the review has been inadequate, which has caused misunderstandings.

Zachary, G. Pascal. "Vannevar Bush Backs the Bomb." *Bulletin of the Atomic Scientists*, vol. 48, December 1992, pp. 24ff. Sketch of the scientist who in the 1940s almost single-handedly convinced the government that technical innovation could be the most important factor in national security.

Zimmerman, Peter D., and Charles D. Ferguson. "Sweeping the Skies." *Bulletin of the Atomic Scientists*, November/December 2003, vol. 59, pp. 57ff. Discusses the effectiveness of nuclear-tipped missiles in intercepting incoming ballistic missiles carrying weapons of mass destruction and the likely results of their use. Concludes that if a practical and politically acceptable defense is needed, nuclear-tipped missiles are not the best tactic.

WEB/INTERNET DOCUMENTS

Behrens, Carl E. "Nuclear Nonproliferation Issues." Available online. URL: http://www.fas.org/spp/starwars/crs/I B10091.pdf. Posted in an updated version June 21, 2004. An overview of nonproliferation issues from a U.S. perspective. The report has three parts: international nonproliferation structures and organizations, U.S. nonproliferation policy, and nuclear proliferation in specific regions.

Eisler, Peter. "Poisoned Workers and Poisoned Places." *USA Today*, September 6–8, 2000. Available online. URL: http://www.usatoday.com/news/poison/cover.htm. Updated June 24, 2001. A series of articles describing past work for the government on weapons-usable materials at privately owned companies across the United States. The articles are the result of a 10-month investigation. The web site lists more than 550 sites where this work was or may have been carried out.

Ledwidge, Lisa, and Arjun Makhijani. "Letter to the BEIR VII Committee (Biological Effects of Ionizing Radiation) of the National Academy of Sciences." (Signed by 133 organizaitons and individuals from 13 countries worldwide.) Available online. URL: http://www.ieer.org/comments/beir/ltr0999.html. Posted September 3, 1999; updated December 20, 1999. Contains a list of key issues that IEER and the signers want the committee to address.

Makhijani, Arjun, David Close, and Lisa Ledwidge. "IEER Letter to the BEIR VII Committee (Biological Effects of Ionizing Radiation) of the National Academy of Sciences." Available online. URL: http://www.ieer.org/comments/beir/ltr0503.html. Posted May 23, 2003. Inquires as to the committee's progress and requests consideration of two more issues.

Medalia, Jonathan. "Nuclear Weapon Initiatives: Low-Yield R&D, Advanced Concepts, Earth Penetrators, Test Readiness." CRS [Congressional Research Service] Report for Congress RL32130. Available online. URL: http://www.fas.org/spp/starwars/crs/RL32130.pdf. Posted in an updated version March 8, 2004. A report on the George W. Bush administration's four nuclear weapons initiatives, as reflected in its budget requests for fiscal years 2004 and 2005. This report includes the policy context for the four, and for each, the technical background, history, and issues involved.

———. "Robust Nuclear Earth Penetrator: Budget Request and Plan, FY2005-FY2009." CRS Report for Congress RL32347. Available online. URL: http://www.fas.org/spp/starwars/crs/RS21762.pdf. Created April 9, 2004. Explains the budget request and presents details on the plan. It is designed to complement RL32130 (previous entry) and will be updated as developments occur.

National Institute for Public Policy. "Rationale and Requirements for U.S. Nuclear Forces and Arms Control." Vol. 1, Executive Report. Available online. URL: http://www.nipp.org/Adobe/volume%201%20complete.pdf. Posted January 2001. Advocates a flexible nuclear policy rather than reliance on static arms-control agreements. The position is reportedly close to that of the George W. Bush administration's Nuclear Policy Review, which is classified.

Riccio, Jim. "Risky Business: The Probability and Consequences of a Nuclear Accident." Greenpeace. Available online. URL: http://www.greenpeaceusa.org/multimedia/download/1/573123/0/risky_business.pdf. Posted 2001. Discussion of the estimated consequences of nuclear accidents (or terrorist attacks) at U.S. nuclear power plants. Riccio includes statistics from the official Calculation of Reactor Accident Consequences for U.S. Nuclear Plants.

Schwartz, Stephen I. "U.S. Nuclear Weapons Research, Development, Testing, and Production, and Naval Nuclear Propulsion Facilities." The Brookings Institution. Available online. URL: http://www.brook.edu/fp/projects/nucwcost/sites.htm. Updated August 16, 2002. A list of U.S. military nuclear facilities with basic information (establishment date, size, budget, employees, function, radioactive materials on site, contractors) on each.

Woolf, Amy. "U.S. Nuclear Weapons: Changes in Policy and Force Structure." CRS Report for Congress RL31623. Available online. URL: http://www.fas.org/spp/starwars/crs/RL31623.pdf. Posted in updated version March 8, 2004. An overview of the U.S. nuclear posture to point out areas of change and areas of continuity. This report is regularly updated as needed.

OTHER DOCUMENTS

Hansen, Chuck, ed. *The Swords of Armageddon: U.S. Nuclear Weapons Development since 1945.* Sunnyvale, Calif.: Chuckelea Publishing, 1995. A compilation of information on nuclear weapons technology, policy, and history, largely based on documents that Hansen obtained under the Freedom of Information Act. The 2,500 pages are on CD-ROM. Information is available at http://www.uscoldwar.com.

National Security Archives, comp. *U.S. Nuclear History: Nuclear Arms and Policy in the Missile Age, 1955–1968.* Cambridge: Chadwyck-Healey, Inc., 1998. A collection of 1,441 declassified documents on 358 microfiche. A printed guidebook/index accompanies the microfiche. In addition to a document catalog, this book includes an overview of U.S. strategic policy between 1955 and 1968, an 85-page chronology, a glossary, and a list of defense and governmental organizations. The guidebook is available separately from the microfiche. Ordering information can be obtained at http://www.chadwyck.com, but the cost is too high for most individual researchers. The collection can be accessed electronically at libraries with a subscription to the Digital National Security Archives. To find out which libraries subscribe, call the National Security Archives at (202) 994-7000. Chadwyck-Healey also offers a compilation by the National Archives, entitled *U.S. Nuclear Non-Proliferation Policy, 1945–1991.*

Nuclear Policy Insitute. *Three Minutes to Midnight: The Impending Threat of Nuclear War. Proceedings of a Conference Held in Washington, D.C., January 25–27, 2004.* Washington, D.C.: Nuclear Policy Institute, 2004. Available on audio CD or DVD from the Nuclear Policy Institute. This recording has presentations by scientists and experts from Russia and America at a conference sponsored by the Nuclear Policy Institute. Speakers include William Arkin, Jacqueline Cabasso, General Charles Horner Bruce, and Professor Anatoly Diakov.

BIOLOGICAL AND CHEMICAL WEAPONS

BOOKS AND REPORTS

Alibek, Ken, with Stephen Handelman. *Biohazard: The Chilling True Story of the Largest Covert Biological Weapons Program in the World—Told from Inside by the Man Who Ran It.* New York: Random House, 1999. The autobiography of Kanatjan Alibekov (now Ken Alibek), the first deputy director of the Soviet

Biopreparat facilities engaged in research, developing, testing, and producing biological weapons. The book sheds light on the Soviet biological weapons complex.

Balmer, Brian. *Britain and Biological Warfare: Expert Advice and Science Policy, 1930–65.* Houndmills, Basingstoke, England: Palgrave, 2001. Based on documentary evidence, the book describes the British government's work on biological weapons. The United States cooperated with the British. The book is packed with details, but without context.

Bicknell, William J., and Kenneth D. Bloom. *Smallpox and Bioterrorism: Why the Plan to Protect the Nation Is Stalled and What to Do.* Cato Institute Briefing Papers, no. 85. Washington, D.C.: Cato Institute, September 2003. The Centers for Disease Control and Prevention overestimate the risk of side effects from smallpox vaccination and underestimate the difficulty of vaccinating Americans after an attack.

Brankowitz, W. R. *Chemical Weapons Movement: History Compilation.* SAPEO-CDE-IS-87001. Aberdeen Proving Ground, Md.: Office of the Program Manager for Chemical Munitions, June 1987. A historical record that provides evidence of the presence of chemical weapons at specific sites.

British Medical Association. *Biotechnology, Weapons and Humanity.* Amsterdam: Harwood Academic Publishers, 1999. On weapons and the new biology, a British Medical Association report on the peculiar dangers and difficulties of biological warfare. The book explains how research like the Human Genome Project could aid terrorists.

Brown, Frederic J. *Chemical Warfare: A Study in Restraints.* Princeton, N.J.: Princeton University Press, 1968. Examines the reasons why chemical warfare was little used during World War II. Brown provides a detailed history of the status of chemical warfare between the two world wars.

Burck, Gordon M., and Charles C. Flowerree. *International Handbook on Chemical Weapons Proliferation.* New York: Greenwood Press, 1991. A broad overview of the character of chemical warfare, its development over time, and the state of chemical weapons proliferation and ways to curb it.

Carus, W. Seth. *The Genie Unleashed: Iraq's Chemical and Biological Weapons Program.* Washington, D.C.: Washington Institute for Near East Policy, 1989. Compilation of evidence indicating that in 1989 Iraq was on the verge of being capable of independently producing large quantities of chemical and biological weapons. Carus describes how mustard gas and tabun are produced. The book has extensive footnotes.

Christoff, Joseph A. *Delays in Implementing the Chemical Weapons Convention Raise Concerns about Proliferation.* GAO-04-361. Washington, D.C.: U.S. General Accounting Office, March 2004. A review of the efforts of members of the Chemical Weapons Convention to implement its key requirements and of efforts by the Organization for the Prohibition of Chemical Weapons to carry out inspections to ensure compliance.

Clarke, Robin. *The Silent Weapons.* New York: David McKay, 1968. An overview of biological weapons by a writer for *Science Journal.* She closes by asking scientists to refuse to support any offensive or defensive work on chemical or biological weapons as a means of making amends for scientists' work on atomic weapons.

Cole, Leonard A. *Clouds of Secrecy: The Army's Germ Warfare Tests over Populated Areas.* Savage, Md.: Rowman and Littlefield, 1990. Describes the army's open-air tests with biological simulants within the United States. Cole treats at length the suit brought by descendants of Edward J. Nevin against the U.S. government as a result of his death, allegedly because of testing in San Francisco.

———. *The Eleventh Plague: The Politics of Biological and Chemical Warfare.* New York: W. H. Freeman and Co., 1996. Discusses U.S. efforts to develop means of defense against chemical and biological agents that, Cole says, endanger U.S. citizens; "moral failures" in the Western countries that have encouraged the spread of chemical and biological weapons; and means of preventing their spread.

Compton, J. A. F. *Military Chemical and Biological Agents: Chemical and Toxicological Properties.* Caldwell, N.J.: Telford Press, 1987. A basic source of information on the properties of chemical and biological agents.

Covert, Norman M. *Cutting Edge: A History of Fort Detrick, Maryland, 1943–1993.* Fort Detrick, Md.: U.S. Army, 1997. A short history of Fort Detrick, with some interesting details—such as the fact that three employees had died from contamination prior to 1997: two from anthrax and one from the bite of an animal with *Machupo virus.* The book is illustrated with photographs.

Croddy, Eric. *Chemical and Biological Warfare: A Comprehensive Guide for the Concerned Citizen.* New York: Copernicus Books, 2002. A readable introduction to chemical and biological warfare and, at the same time, a source of considerable information on the subject. The book has useful endnotes, a bibliography, and an index.

Crone, Hugh D. *Banning Chemical Weapons: The Scientific Background.* Cambridge: Cambridge University Press, 1992. Assesses how advances in biotechnology and neuroscience can be used in weapons systems and considers how these developments can be brought under international control.

Dando, Malcolm. *New Biological Weapons: The Threat, Proliferation, and Control.* Boulder, Colo.: Lynne Rienner Publishers, 2001. A discussion of the threat posed by biological weapons and the future of biological arms control, with emphasis on the new midspectrum agents—those "that fall between living biological weapons and classical chemical agents on the spectrum of chemical and biological threats." The book includes technical information.

Defense Intelligence Agency: *Soviet Biological Warfare Threat.* Washington, D.C.: U.S. Department of Defense, 1986. An assessment of the Soviet threat made before Soviet defectors revealed the extent of the Soviet biological warfare program.

Drell, Sidney D., Abraham B. Sofaer, and George D. Wilson, eds. *The New Terror: Facing the Threat of Biological and Chemical Weapons.* Stanford, Calif.:

Hoover Institution Press, 1999. Surveys the threat posed by biological and chemical weapons and discusses what the United States can do to protect itself against them.

Drexler, Madeline. *Secret Agents: The Menace of Emerging Infections.* Washington, D.C.: The National Academy Press, 2002. Brings to light the clandestine war on infectious diseases that is being fought by researchers on many fronts. Drexler includes a chapter on bioterrorism with information on anthrax and smallpox, among other threats.

Endicott, Stephen, and Edward Hagerman. *The United States and Biological Warfare: Secrets from the Early Cold War and Korea.* Indianapolis: Indiana University Press, 1999. Presents the case that the United States engaged in biological warfare during the Korean War, although U.S. efforts were more experimental than strategic in nature. The authors draw on newly declassified U.S., Canadian, and British documents and on interviews with Chinese who were in North Korea during the war. The United States has always denied that it used biological warfare in Korea.

Evans, Rob. *Gassed: British Chemical Warfare Experiments on Humans at Porton Down.* London: House of Stratus, 2000. Evans looks in detail at activities at the Porton Down chemical and biological research center in Wiltshire, England. There, nearly 30,000 servicemen were guinea pigs in tests of chemical weapons between 1916 and 1989.

Fenn, Elizabeth Anne. *Pox Americana: The Great Smallpox Epidemic of 1775–82.* New York: Hill and Wang, 2001. Shows that smallpox played a crucial role in the shrinking of the Native American population of North America and in the outcome of the Revolutionary War.

Frazier, Thomas W., and Drew C. Richardson, eds. *Food and Agricultural Security: Guarding against Natural Threats and Terrorist Attacks, Affecting Health, National Food Supplies, and Agricultural Economics.* Annals of the New York Academy of Sciences, vol. 894. New York: New York Academy of Sciences, 1999. Presents papers from the International Conference on Food and Agricultural Security, including an industry-government dialogue.

Garrett, Laurie. *Betrayal of Trust: The Collapse of Global Public Health.* New York: Hyperion, 2001. Describes the collapse of public health systems in the United States and across the globe. This collapse, if not corrected, will exacerbate the effects of any bioterrorist attacks.

———. *The Coming Plague: Newly Emerging Diseases in a World out of Balance.* New York: Farrar, Straus, and Giroux, 1994. A thorough study of newly emerging diseases. The thesis is that changes in human habitat and the environment destroy the ecological balance, with dangerous results.

Geissler, Erhard, and John Ellis van Courtland Moon, ed. *Biological and Toxin Weapons: Research, Development and Use from the Middle Ages to 1945.* New York: Oxford University Press, in association with Stockholm International Peace Research Institute, 1999. A frequently cited history of biological and toxin weapons.

Gold, Hal. *Unit 731 Testimony.* Tokyo: Yen Books, 1996. The shocking story of Japanese experimentation with biological agents on humans during World

War II. The first part is a history; the second presents the words of former unit members.

Guillemin, Jeanne. *Anthrax: The Investigation of a Deadly Outbreak.* Berkeley: University of California Press, 1999. The experience of a member of an international team of scientists that visited Russia to investigate an outbreak of anthrax in 1979 in the Ural Mountains region; the result, it turned out, of work on bioweapons.

Haber, L. F. *The Poisonous Cloud: Chemical Warfare in the First World War.* Oxford: Clarendon Press, 1986. A scholarly history of the use of chemical weapons in World War I. Toward the end, the author asks whether gas was a failure. His answer is a qualified yes. The book has detailed notes and index.

Hammond, Peter, and Gradon Carter. *From Biological Warfare to Healthcare: Porton Down 1940–2000.* Houndmills, Basingstoke, England: Palgrave, 2002. The first well-documented history of microbiological science at Porton Down, owned by the British Ministry of Defense until 1979. The United States was involved in Porton Down's experimentation.

Harigel, Gert G. *Chemical and Biological Weapons: Use in Warfare, Impact on Society and the Environment.* Washington, D.C.: Carnegie Endowment for International Peace, 1998. Concise information on chemical and biological weapons, with the greater attention paid to the former.

Harris, Robert, and Jeremy Paxman. *A Higher Form of Killing: The Secret Story of Chemical and Biological Warfare.* New York: Hill and Wang, 1982. Begins with World War I and examines programs worldwide. The book includes examples of bioweapons accidents. The authors, two reporters at the British Broadcasting Company (BBC), interviewed soldiers and scientists and drew on previously classified documents.

Harris, Sheldon H. *Factories of Death: Japanese Biological Warfare, 1932–45, and the American Cover-Up.* New York: Routledge, 1994. Pulls together a wealth of information on the Japanese biological warfare program and the U.S. response. Harris indicates that some scientists at Fort Detrick as well as General Douglas MacArthur were interested in granting immunity to the Japanese who conducted human experimentation, in return for information from the experiments.

Haselkorn, Avigdor. *The Continuing Storm: Iraq, Poisonous Weapons, and Deterrence.* New Haven, Conn.: Yale University Press, 1999. Covers the Persian Gulf War and its aftermath, 1990–98. Haselkorn includes an enlightening chapter on "The Hidden Role of Mass Destruction Weapons" in the Gulf War.

Haugen, David, ed. *Biological and Chemical Weapons.* San Diego, Calif.: Greenhaven Press, 2001. A small volume, composed of a series of articles by experts in biological and chemical warfare plus a short bibliography and list of relevant organizations. The writers were chosen for their contrasting views.

Heller, Charles E. *Chemical Warfare in World War I: The American Experience, 1917–1918.* Washington, D.C.: Government Printing Office, 1984. Drives home the point that 27.3 percent of all American Expeditionary Force deaths and injuries in World War I were caused by gas, but that the military had failed to prepare for gas warfare.

Hersh, Seymour M. *Chemical and Biological Warfare: America's Hidden Arsenal.* Indianapolis: Bobbs-Merrill, [1968]. A comprehensive and well-documented history of the U.S. chemical and biological programs to the late 1960s. Hersh tells which military bases, universities, and corporations conducted research.

Institute of Medicine. *Chemical and Biological Terrorism: Research and Development to Improve Civilian Medical Response.* Washington, D.C.: National Academy Press, 1999. An assessment of civilian capabilities in regard to detecting potential agents and protecting and treating both victims and health-care providers. The book also gives recommendations for priority research and development.

Kaplan, David E., and Andrew Marshall. *The Cult at the End of the World: The Incredible Story of Aum.* New York: Crown Publishers, 1996. Analyzes the Aum cult, a global cult based in Japan, and draws lessons from its terrorist agenda.

Knobler, Stacey L., et al. *Biological Threats and Terrorism: Assessing the Science and Response Capabilities: Workshop Summary.* Washington, D.C.: National Academy Press, 2002. Summarizes the discussion in a workshop, convened by the Institute of Medicine's Forum on Emerging Infections, to consider what steps need to be taken to strengthen the nation's ability to respond to bioterrorism. Participants identified gaps in the public health infrastructure and countermeasure capabilities that need to be addressed.

Kortepeter, Mark, ed. *USAMRIID's Medical Management of Biological Casualties Handbook.* 4th ed. Frederick, Md.: USAMRIID, [2001]. Intended for medical professionals but includes information of general interest, including characteristics of biological warfare agents and vaccines.

Krause, Joachim, and Charles K. Mallory. *Chemical Weapons in Soviet Military Doctrine: Military and Historical Experience: 1915–1991.* Boulder, Colo.: Westview Press, 1992. A standard history of Soviet chemical weapons for the period covered.

Layne, Scott P., Tony J. Beugelsdijk, and C. Kumar N. Patel, eds. *Firepower in the Lab: Automation in the Fight against Infectious Diseases and Bioterrorism.* Washington, D.C.: National Academy Press, 2001. Looks into how the United States can counter the threat posed by infectious diseases, contamination of food and water, and bio attacks by increasing its ability to detect, measure, and monitor harmful biological agents. In particular, it discusses the potential application of laboratory automation and computer technologies.

Lederberg, Joshua, ed. *Biological Weapons: Limiting the Threat.* BCSIA Studies in International Security. Cambridge, Mass: MIT Press, 1999. A collection of thoughtful essays, most of which were first printed in the August 1997 issue of the *Journal of the American Medical Association.* Lowe, Pearson, and Utgoff make a point not often heard. Simple masks are effective against biological weapons. If distributed and if the public is educated in their use, they could provide considerable protection to populations at little cost.

Lefebure, Victor. *The Riddle of the Rhine: Chemical Strategy in Peace and War.* New York: E. P. Dutton, 1923. Lefebure's aim is to present a reasoned account of the development of chemical warfare in World War I. He analyses the German chemical industry and finds the Treaty of Versailles inadequate in regard to chemical disarmament.

Mangold, Tom, and Jeff Goldberg. *Plague Wars: The Terrifying Reality of Biological Warfare.* New York: St. Martin's Press, 2000. A comprehensive account of biowarfare and preparations for biowarfare from the 1930s to 1999. The Soviet and the South African programs are covered particularly well.

Mauroni, Albert J. *America's Struggle with Chemical-Biological Warfare.* Westport, Conn.: Praeger, 2000. Mauroni does not think that the use of chemical weapons in warfare is immoral. He argues that they should be used, not because they can win a war, but because they reduce the efficiency of the enemy in combat. The book contains detailed descriptions of chemical warfare equipment, which will not interest the general reader but the point of view may.

———. *Chemical-Biological Defense: U.S. Military Policies and Decisions in the Gulf War.* Westport, Conn.: Praeger, 1998. An account by a former U.S. Army Chemical Corps official of the efforts of the United States to prepare to defend itself against chemical and biological weapons in the Gulf War. The author makes the mistake of lumping chemical and biological weapons together as though they present identical challenges. Furthermore, the book has been criticized for presenting only the view of the Chemical Corps, as opposed to those of other military services.

Mayor, Adrienne. *Greek Fire, Poison Arrows, and Scorpion Bombs.* Woodstock and New York, N.Y.: Overlook Duckworth, 2003. Explores the roots of today's biological and chemical weaponry in the ancient world. The book covers the period from 1770 B.C. through A.D. 1300.

McBride, David, ed. *Bioterrorism.* 2 vols. New York: Routledge, 2003. A collection of essays on the challenges in regard to bioterrorism that U.S. society and institutions face. The first volume covers epidemics, bioweapons, and policy history. The second covers public health, law enforcement, and minority issues.

McCarthy, Richard D. *The Ultimate Folly: War by Pestilence, Asphyxiation, and Defoliation.* New York: Knopf, 1969. Emphasizes the wide gap between what the author believed were the wishes of Americans at the time of the Vietnam War and the Department of Defense's policy on biological weapons. McCarthy describes this policy as a "policy of default."

McDermott, Jeanne. *The Killing Winds. The Menace of Biological Warfare.* New York: Arbor House, 1987. An exposé of the history and status of U.S. biological warfare research as of the mid-1980s. Intended to open debate when it was published, the book is today useful as a historical account.

McKibben, Bill. *Enough: Staying Human in an Engineered Age.* New York: Times Books, 2003. An exploration of the frontiers of robotics, genetic engineering, and nanotechnology and a plea to turn away from them, in recognition of our humanity. The technologies described could greatly increase the threat that biological and chemical weapons pose.

Miller, Judith, William Broad, and Stephen Engelberg. *Germs: Biological Weapons and America's Secret.* New York: Simon and Schuster, 2001. By three journalists, a survey of the development and use of biological weapons and a warning of the danger to come. This book is frequently cited by other writers.

Milne, Hugh. *Bhagwan: The God That Failed.* New York: St. Martin's Press, 1986. About the Rajneeshees, a cult that poisoned salad bars in Oregon.

Mole, Robert L., and Dale M. Mole. *For God and Country: Operation Whitecoat, 1954–1973.* Brushton, N.Y.: Teach Services, 1998. Tells the story of Seventh Day Adventists who volunteered to be victims in germ warfare experimentation.

National Research Council. Committee on Research Standards and Practices to Prevent the Destructive Application of Biotechnology. *Biotechnology Research in an Age of Terrorism: Confronting the Dual Use Dilemma.* Washington, D.C.: National Academy Press, 2004. Reviews and evaluates the current regulations and institutional arrangements in regard to biotechnological research security. The report identifies deficiencies and recommends steps to increase biosecurity.

National Research Council. Committee on the Effects of Herbicides in Vietnam. *The Effects of Herbicides in Vietnam. Part A: Summary and Conclusions.* Washington, D.C.: National Academy of Sciences, 1974. Summarizes the use and the results of use of herbicides in South Vietnam. The mangrove forests suffered most heavily and, as of 1974, were not growing back.

Norris, John, and Will Fowler. *NBC, Nuclear, Biological and Chemical Warfare on the Modern Battlefield.* Herndon, Va.: Brassey's Inc., 1997. A reference book, with numerous diagrams and black-and-white photographs.

Osterholm, Michael T., and John Schwartz. *Living Terrors: What America Needs to Know to Survive the Coming Bioterrorist Catastrophe.* New York: Delacorte Press, 2000. A warning, from an epidemiologist and a reporter for the *Washington Post,* on the likelihood of a biological attack. The book examines the extent to which America, as of 2000, was prepared to cope with such an emergency and explains what could and can be done to increase preparedness.

Piller, Charles, and Keith R. Yamamoto. *Gene Wars: Military Control over the New Genetic Technologies.* New York: Morrow, 1988. By an investigative journalist and a molecular biologist, an explanation of the implications of genetic engineering for biological warfare. For the general reader, they outline the process of genetic engineering, give a glimpse of future wars, and look ahead to future genetic arms control.

Preston, Richard. *The Demon in the Freezer: A True Story.* New York: Random House, 2002. The exciting story of the eradication of smallpox from nature and a look into the frightening question of what has been and is being done with the remaining stockpiles.

Price, Richard M. *The Chemical Weapons Taboo.* Ithaca, N.Y.: Cornell University Press, 1997. A history and an analysis of the taboo on chemical warfare and the banning of chemical weapons, in the context of reflections on the relationship between morality and technology. Price gives an account of international law and legal norms but is more concerned with the societal and humanitarian basis of what he calls a taboo.

Regis, Ed. *The Biology of Doom: The History of America's Secret Germ Warfare Project.* New York: Henry Holt, 1999. Examines the U.S. offensive germ-warfare program beginning with its origins in the late 1930s. The book is based on extensive documentation obtained through the Freedom of Information Act and provides a readable overview.

Roberts, Brad, ed. *Hype or Reality? The "New Terrorism" and Mass Casualty Attacks.* Alexandria, Va.: Chemical and Biological Arms Control Institute, 2000. A collection of essays, which, before September 11, 2001, looks at the threat of terrorism against the United States and means to counter it. The threat is real, the authors say, but preventive measures need honing.

Ross, Steven, ed. *CBW: Chemical and Biological Warfare.* Boston: Beacon Press, 1968. Based on papers delivered to the Conference on Chemical and Biological Warfare in London, February 22 and 23, 1968. The book goes into detail about the use of biological weapons in Vietnam and possibly also in Yemen.

Rothschild, J. H. *Tomorrow's Weapons: Chemical and Biological.* New York: McGraw-Hill, 1964. By a former brigadier general in the U.S. Army Chemical Corps, a discussion of the moral and political aspects of chemical and biological warfare and how these weapons can be employed and defended against. Rothschild includes the prospect of the use of incapacitating weapons in time of peace by an international police force.

Schuck, Peter H. *Agent Orange on Trial: Mass Toxic Disasters in the Courts.* Rev. ed. Cambridge, Mass.: Belknap Press, 1987. An in-depth analysis of the class-action suit brought by Vietnam veterans against the companies that made the dioxin-contaminated herbicide Agent Orange. Schuck looks at the complex relationships among the veterans' lawyers as well as at the legal strategies employed.

Sidell, Frederick R., T. Takafuji, and David R Franz, ed. *Medical Aspects of Chemical and Biological Warfare.* Washington, D.C.: Borden Institute, Walter Reed Army Medical Center; Falls Church, Va.: Office of the Surgeon General, United States Army, 1997. Includes a review of the history of chemical and biological warfare, emphasizing the United States.

Stearn, E. Wagner, and Allen E. Stearn. *The Effect of Smallpox on the Destiny of the Amerindian.* Boston: Bruce Humphries, 1945. A chronological narrative on the fate of the American Indian, as influenced by smallpox, from the 16th century to its eradication in the 20th century.

Stockholm International Peace Research Institute. *The Problem of Chemical and Biological Warfare.* 6 vols. Stockholm: Almqvist & Wiksell, 1971–75. Highly regarded as the best overview of the field to the time of publication.

Timmerman, Kenneth R. *The Death Lobby: How the West Armed Iraq.* New York: Houghton Mifflin, 1991. Argues persuasively that the United States played a key role in arming Iraq, as a result of its desire to build a counterweight to Iran's fundamentalist Islamic regime.

Tucker, Jonathan B. *Biosecurity: Limiting Terrorist Access to Deadly Pathogens.* Peaceworks 52. Washington, D.C.: United States Institute of Peace, November

2003. Assesses current efforts to prevent terrorists from obtaining dangerous pathogens and urges that there be a set of global biosecurity standards.

———. *Scourge: The Once and Future Threat of Smallpox.* New York: Atlantic Monthly Press, 2001. Recounts the eradication of the disease of smallpox from the Earth under the auspices of the World Health Organization and how the Soviet Union violated the Biological Weapons Convention by carrying on a major biological warfare program that included developing smallpox as a weapon.

Tucker, Jonathan B., ed. *Toxic Terror: Assessing Terrorist Use of Chemical and Biological Weapons.* BCSIA Studies in International Security. Cambridge, Mass.: MIT Press, 2000. Analysis by experts of the 12 cases of reported chemical or biological terrorism most frequently referred to in academic literature prior to 2001. They find that three of the cases did not occur and that most of the remainder could not be described as major terrorist incidents. Tucker concludes that we should perhaps be less concerned with chemical and biological terrorism per se and more "with mass-casualty terrorism from any source."

U.S. Army. *U.S. Army Activities in the U.S. Biological Warfare Programs.* 2 vols. Washington, D.C.: Department of the Army, 1977. An official account and a basic source for information on U.S. biological weapons development, testing, and production during World War I and the cold war.

Watson, James D. *A Passion for DNA: Genes, Genomes, and Society.* Cold Spring Harbor, N.Y.: Cold Spring Harbor Laboratory Press, 2000. Reprints 25 talks and articles by Watson between 1966 and 1999. The book includes his views on the social implications of the Human Genome Project and the recombinant DNA controversies.

Westing, A. H. *Herbicides in War: The Long-term Ecological and Human Consequences.* London: Taylor and Francis, in association with the Stockholm Institute for Peace Research, 1984. Funded by the Stockholm Institute for Peace Research and the United Nations Environment Programe, the book evaluates the long-term effects of herbicide use in war, with particular attention to Vietnam. Westing points out that it is difficult to separate direct from indirect effects. He calls for more research on the effects in Vietnam.

Whitby, Simon M. *Biological Warfare against Crops.* Houndmills, Basingstoke, England: Palgrave, 2002. A thorough study of past and potential use of biological agents against crops. Whitby makes the argument that warfare against crops could have "potentially devastating consequences" and may well be used in the future.

Wilcox, Fred. *Waiting for an Army to Die: The Tragedy of Agent Orange.* Cabin John, Md.: Seven Locks Press, 1989. A new edition of a volume that was well received in 1983. Wilcox combines the original text with an introduction on the class-action suit brought by Vietnam veterans.

Williams, Peter, and David Wallace. *Unit 731: Japan's Secret Biological Warfare in World War II.* New York: Free Press, 1989. An account of the Japanese bioweapons program before and during World War II and of the American cover-up. The book concludes with a look at what became of leaders of the Japanese program.

Wise, David. *Cassidy's Run: The Secret Spy War over Nerve Gas.* New York: Random House, 2000. An established writer on intelligence and espionage describes an espionage operation carried out by the United States against the Soviet Union that lasted for more than two decades. The thoroughly indexed book is both a true account and a "good read."

World Health Organization, Global Commission for the Certification of Smallpox Eradication. *The Global Eradication of Smallpox. Final Report of the Global Commission for the Certification of Smallpox Eradication, Geneva, December 1979.* Geneva: World Health Organization, 1980. Presents the evidence that smallpox has been eradicated and will not return as an endemic disease. It does note that samples have been retained in seven laboratories, from which smallpox could conceivably be deliberately released.

Wright, Susan. *Molecular Politics: Developing American and British Regulatory Policy for Genetic Engineering, 1972–1982.* Chicago: University of Chicago Press, 1994. In the 1970s, when genetic engineering began to be practiced, public debate in the United States and the United Kingdom led to regulations. These have since been almost completely abandoned. Wright traces this history and looks into the reasons for the decline in regulations.

Wright, Susan, ed. *Preventing a Biological Arms Race.* Cambridge, Mass.: MIT Press, 1990. Opens with a history of U.S. policy on biological warfare and, after discussing ethics, biological defense in the military, and international agreements and their violations, the book ends with suggestions for preventing a biological arms race. An appendix gives definitions and uses of biological and chemical warfare agents and prints more than a dozen relevant documents.

Zilinskas, Raymond A., ed. *Biological Warfare: Modern Offense and Defense.* Boulder, Colo.: Lynne Rienner, 1999. A collection of articles by knowledgeable authors. The main aim of the book is to assess the impact of the biotechnology revolution on biological warfare and defense.

ARTICLES

Auer, Catherine. "Killer 'Non-Lethals.'" *Bulletin of the Atomic Scientists,* vol. 59, January/February 2003, pp. 42ff. Outlines the implications of the use by Russian special forces of a calmative gas to overcome the Chechen rebels who took the audience of a Moscow theater hostage in October 2002.

Barletta, Michael, Amy Sands, and Jonathan B. Tucker. "Keeping Track of Anthrax: The Case for a Biosecurity Convention." *Bulletin of the Atomic Scientists,* vol. 58, May/June 2002, pp. 57–62. Summarizes the threat posed by biological agents, the status of control efforts, and, since the Biological and Toxin Weapons Convention lacks formal means of enforcement, the need for a more effective biosecurity convention.

Bauman, Joe. "Cold War Left Utah a Contaminated Legacy." *Deseret News,* February 28, 1998, p. A1. Describes the contamination caused by tests at the army's Dugway Proving Grounds.

Begley, Sharon, et al. "Unmasking Bioterror." *Newsweek*, October 8, 2001, pp. 20ff. While presenting the threat of chemical and biological weapons, the article notes that they are technically difficult to use and that, on occasion, terrorists have tried and failed to use them.

Bismuth, Chantal, et al. "Chemical Weapons: Documented Use and Compounds on the Horizon." *Toxicology Letters*, vol. 149, April 2004, pp. 11ff. Reviews currently employed chemical weapons and toxins plus potential future weapons and counterterrorism tools. The article notes that chemical weapons must be seen in the context of effective conventional weapons.

Black, John Logan, III. "Genome Projects and Gene Therapy: Gateways to Next Generation Biological Weapons." *Military Medicine*, vol. 168, November 2003, pp. 864ff. A peer-reviewed, scientific article discusses in-depth the fact that genomic and gene therapy is making possible genomic warfare, a new form of biological warfare. Black includes a review of relevant literature.

Broad, William J., and Judith Miller. "Government Report Says 3 Nations Hide Stocks of Smallpox." *New York Times*, vol. 148, June 13, 1999, p. A1. Relates that, according to government officials who refer to a secret federal intelligence study, Iraq, North Korea, and Russia probably have secret stocks of smallpox for military use. Other nations may also have stocks.

Budowle, Bruce, et al. "Building Microbial Forensics as a Response to Bioterrorism," *Science*, vol. 301, September 26, 2003, pp. 1852ff. Looks at the need to develop microbial forensics as a protection against bioterrorism. The article also discusses the way in which U.S. law enforcement agencies investigate crimes related to bioterrorism.

Cameron, Gavin, Jason Pate, and Kathleen Vogel. "Planting Fear: How Real Is the Threat of Agicultural Terrorism?" *Bulletin of the Atomic Scientists*, vol. 57, September/October 2001, pp. 38–44. Gives an overview of the possibility of terrorist attacks aimed at agricultural production and the means to prevent such attacks.

"Chemical Weapons Suspect in Gulf Syndrome." *Veterans of Foreign Wars Magazine*, September 1996, p. 9. The Department of Defense has admitted that chemical weapons may be the cause of Gulf War syndrome. Previously, the department had denied any link.

Chepesiuk, Ron. "A Sea of Trouble?" *Bulletin of the Atomic Scientists*, vol. 53, September/October 1997, pp. 40–44. More than 200,000 tons of chemical weapons are resting on the bottom of the ocean. Nobody knows what risks these weapons pose. They are not covered by the Chemical Weapons Convention.

Choffnes, Eileen. "Germs on the Loose: Bioweapons Tests Tainted Sites around the Globe." *Bulletin of the Atomic Scientists*, vol. 57, March/April 2001, pp. 57–61. Presents the problem posed by sites around the world that were formerly used for testing biological weapons and have not been cleaned up.

Cieslak, Theodore J., et al. "Immunization against Potential Biological Warfare Agents." *Clinical Infectious Diseases*, vol. 30, June 1, 2000, pp. 843–850. Reviews the status of vaccines against 10 of the most credible terrorist threats. Vaccines against smallpox, plague, and anthrax are already licensed.

Annotated Bibliography

Cohen, Avner. "Israel and CBW: History, Deterrence, and Arms Control." *Nonproliferation Review*, vol. 8, fall 2001, pp. 27–53. Reviews Israel's changing attitude to nonconventional weapons, attempts to trace Israeli activities in regard to chemical and biological weapons, looks at these weapons in the context of Israel's defense policy, and makes suggestions for modifications in Israel's approach over the long term.

Cooper, Mary H. "Chemical and Biological Weapons." *CQ Researcher*, vol. 7, January 31, 1997, entire issue. A handy introduction to the subject of chemical and biological weapons, including background information, contacts, and a bibliography. A special focus section presents the deadliest weapons, and a pro/con section asks whether exposure to chemical weapons explains Gulf War syndrome.

Coupland, Robin. "Incapacitating Chemical Weapons: A Year after the Moscow Theatre Seige." *Lancet*, vol. 362, October 25, 2003, p. 1,346. Raises the question of how physicians should be involved in the debate about the use of nonlethal weapons.

Coupland, Robin, et al. "No Nonlethal Chemical Weapons." *Issues in Science and Technology*, vol. 20, fall 2003, pp. 9ff. Prints four letters to the editor responding to Mark Wheelis's article "'Nonlethal' Chemical Weapons: A Faustian Bargain," which appeared in the spring issue of the journal. Three expand on his argument that the weapons are more likely to be "useful" to terrorists than to enforcers of the law. One corrects a point.

Dalton, Rex. "US Selects Regional Biodefence Hubs." *Nature*, vol. 425, September 11, 2003, p. 110. Reports on the National Institutes of Health's award to eight university consortia to establish research programs on biological weapons defense.

Dickey, Christopher, and Colin Soloway. "The Secrets of Dr. Germ." *Newsweek*, vol. 140, December 9, 2002, pp. 40–43. The authors write that the removal of individuals capable of rebuilding a weapons program would be likely to provoke a response from Saddam Hussein because he knows that he cannot replace them. One such scientist is Rihab Taha of Iraq's biological weapons program.

Ember, Lois R. "Treaty Compliance Raises Concerns." *Chemical and Engineering News*, vol. 82, April 10, 2004, pp. 33ff. Comments on the problems with implementation of the Chemical Weapons Convention that the U.S. General Accounting Office presents in J. A. Christoff's report, "Delays in Implementing. . .," GAO-04-361.

Fenn, Elizabeth. "Biological Warfare in Eighteenth-Century North America: Beyond Jeffery Amherst." *Journal of American History*, vol. 86, March 2000, pp. 1,552–1,580. Written to broaden the discussion of the connection between Jeffery Amherst and the smallpox from which Native Americans near Fort Pitt suffered in 1763 and 1764.

Finnegan, William. "The Poison Keeper." *New Yorker*, January 15, 2001, pp. 58–64. The story of Dr. Wouter Basson, called "Dr. Death" by Africans, a skilled cardiologist who organized Project Coast, a secret biological and chemical warfare program. Finnegan covers the early part of his trial in Pretoria High Court.

Fong, Tony. "Preparing for a Disaster." *Modern Healthcare*, vol. 33, September 8, 2003, pp. 6ff. Points out that U.S. hospitals are trying to prepare to help the victims of a chemical or biological attack, but they must do so without sufficient financial assistance from the federal government.

Foxell, Joseph W., Jr. "U.S. Policymaking Approaches to Remedying International Security Deficiencies in Bioweapons Materials Controls." *American Foreign Policy Interests*, vol. 26, February 2004, pp. 43ff. Discusses remedies for the lack of protection of bioweapons materials, ways of dealing with terrorists and rogue states that have acquired them, and the steps needed to obtain structural reforms to protect the materials.

Freeman, Karen. "The VA's Sorry, The Army's Silent." *Bulletin of the Atomic Scientists*, vol. 49, March 1993, pp. 39ff. Reports that after 50 years, the U.S. Department of Veterans Affairs has agreed to facilitate compensation for U.S. military personnel who served in tests of chemical agents in World War II. The tests exposed more than 150,000 American servicepeople, usually to mustard gas but also to other chemicals.

Glaberson, William. "Agent Orange, the Next Generation." *New York Times*, August 8, 2004, sec. 1, p. 25. Describes a new wave of suits from people who claim to be victims of the herbicide Agent Orange. The cases raise important legal issues including whether the U.S. government or its contractors can be sued.

Goodman, Laurie. "Biodefense Cost and Consequence." *Journal of Clinical Investigation*, vol. 114, July 1, 2004, pp. 2–3. Reports the views of several people on the costs and benefits to the U.S. population and the world of the immense expansion of biodefense research in the wake of 9/11.

Gorman, Jessica. "Danger Detection." *Science News*, vol. 163, June 7, 2003, pp. 362ff. Briefly surveys the various means of detecting chemical and biological weapons, including the M-8 and M-9 indicator papers.

Hsin, Honor. "Lethal Strains." *Harvard International Review*, vol. 24, Winter 2003, pp. 42ff. An overview of the threat of biological weapons to security. The article includes a comparison of biological and nuclear weapons.

Kelly, Marylia, and Jay Coghlan. "Mixing Bugs and Bombs." *Bulletin of the Atomic Scientists*, vol. 59, September/October 2003, pp. 25–31. Presents the danger inherent in siting biowarfare agent facilities at nuclear weapons design sites.

Kiziah, Rex R. "The Emerging Biocruise Threat." *Air and Space Power Journal*, vol. 17, Spring 2003, pp. 81ff. Shows the need for the United States to develop means of countering the threat that nations will mount biological weapons on cruise missile delivery systems. By 2005 one or more states, such as Iran, Iraq, and North Korea, may well possess biocruise weapons with a range of 500 to 1,000 kilometers.

Koblentz, Gregory. "Pathogens as Weapons: The International Security Implications of Biological Warfare." *International Security*, vol. 28, winter 2003/2004, pp. 84ff. Assesses the implications of biological weapons for international security and looks at the difficulty of preventing the spread of these weapons.

Kohn, Carol, and C. W. Henderson. "U.S. State Governments Receive Antidotes against Chemical Weapons." *Bioterrorism Week*, August 2, 2004, pp. 9ff. Reports on the shipment of chemical weapons antidotes by the Centers for Disease Control and Prevention (CDC) to state governments. The article includes remarks from an official in the CDC.

Kosal, Margaret E. "Is Small Scary?" *Bulletin of the Atomic Scientists*, vol. 60, September/October 2004, pp. 38–47. Describes possible civilian and military applications of nanoscience, outlines the risks in its use, and urges scientists to consider these risks and develop and implement policies and protocols to prevent misuse.

Leitenberg, Milton. "Distinguishing Offensive from Defensive Biological Weapons Research." *Critical Reviews in Microbiology*, vol. 29, September 2003, pp. 223–257. Examines the characterization in the past of various biological weapons programs as offensive or defensive. Leitenberg finds that there are no "internationally recognized boundaries between 'offensive' and 'defensive.'" He also notes that an increase in biodefense research and development in the United States may well encourage research for offensive purposes elsewhere.

Leitenberg, Milton, James Leonard, and Dr. Richard Spertzel. "Biodefense Crossing the Line." *Politics and the Life Sciences*, vol. 22, no. 2, 2004, pp. 1–2. Analyses and comments on the new National Biodefense Analysis and Countermeasures Center (NBACC). The center's tasks include growing, storing, stabilizing, packaging, and dispersing genetically engineered pathogens.

Lugar, Richard, and Joseph Biden. "An End to Chemical Weapons," *Christian Science Monitor*, vol. 89, February 28, 1997, p. 19. A plea to the U.S. Senate to vote for the ratification of the Chemical Weapons Convention, with reasons why the authors believe that they should do so.

Madden, L. V., and M. Wheelis. "The Threat of Plant Pathogens as Weapons against U.S. Crops." *Annual Review of Phytopathology*, vol. 41, issue 1, 2003, pp. 155ff. Addresses the vulnerability of U.S. crops to bioweapons attacks and describes how the nation could prepare itself to counter bioterrorism. Measures to be taken include increasing our understanding of molecular biology and of the epidemiology of agents.

Malakoff, David. "Pentagon Biodefense Program Critiqued." *Science*, vol. 303, January 30, 2004, pp. 607ff. Presents the conclusions of a report from the Institute of Medicine, stating that the Pentagon needs to strengthen its biodefense research program within three years or hand it over to a civilian agency.

Manley, R. G. "Verification under the Chemical Weapons Convention. A Reflective Review." *Pure and Applied Chemistry*, vol. 74, December 2002, pp. 2235ff. States that the inspections regime for the Chemical Weapons Convention has proven to be a success but that, nevertheless, certain problems regarding industry declarations, the approved list of inspection equipment, and on-site sampling and off-site analysis need to be resolved. The article was delivered at a meeting on the Impact of Scientific Developments on the Chemical Weapons

Convention, June 30–July 3, 2002, in Norway. Other papers from the meeting are published in this issue of *Pure and Applied Chemistry.*

Mauroni, Al. "Weapons of Mass Delusion?" *Armed Forces Journal,* March 2004, pp. 36–39. By a senior policy analyst for Innovative Emergency Management Inc. He presents his view that the term *weapons of mass destruction* is not useful. He finds that the risk of chemical and biological weapons to civilians has been inflated and that, although U.S. military forces need protection from these weapons, the weapons can best be discussed apart from the term.

Mehta, Pushpa S., et al. "Bhopal Tragedy's Health Effects." *Journal of the American Medical Association,* vol. 264, December 5, 1990, pp. 2781ff. Calculates the impact of the Bhopal poisoning—at least 2,500 dead and thousands more with permanent injuries.

Meier, Oliver. "Neither Trust Nor Verify, Says U.S." *Bulletin of Atomic Scientists,* vol. 57, Nov.–Dec. 2001, pp. 19–21ff. Evaluates the Geneva talks on a bioweapons treaty verification protocol in 2001.

Meselson, Matthew. "Bioterror: What Can Be Done?" *New York Review of Books,* vol. 48, December 20, 2001, pp. 38ff. A review of the book *Germs* by Judith Miller, Steven Engelberg, and William Broad, with comments on the bioweapons threat by the author. The author of the review is a professor at Harvard engaged in research on molecular genetics and evolution.

Meselson, Matthew, et al. "The Sverdlovsk Anthrax Outbreak of 1979." *Science,* November 18, 1994, pp. 1,202–1,208. The final conclusions of a team that investigated the anthrax outbreak at Sverdlovsk in Russia—inhaled anthrax escaped from the military facility caused human deaths.

Mesler, Bill. "The Pentagon's 'Nonlethal' Gas." *Nation,* vol. 276, February 17, 2003, pp. 19ff. Makes the case that a fascination with calmatives on the part of the Pentagon is encouraging a biological arms race.

Milhollin, Gary, and Kelly Motz. "The Means to Make the Poisons Came from the West." *New York Times,* vol. 152, April 13, 2003, sec. 4, p. 5. Presents the origins of Iraq's chemical weapons program, as stated by Iraq in submissions to United Nations inspectors in the 1980s.

Miller, Judith. "Bush Issues Directive to Bolster Defense against Bioterrorism." *New York Times,* vol. 153, April 28, 2004, pp. A17ff. Reports on a series of initiatives by President George W. Bush to strengthen the nation's defenses against biological weapons.

———. "Libya Discloses Production of 23 Tons of Mustard Gas." *New York Times,* vol. 153, March 6, 2004, pp. A5ff. Discusses Libya's renunciation of biological and chemical weapons and the U.S. government's reaction to Libya's initiative.

———. "New Biolabs Stir a Debate over Secrecy and Safety." *New York Times,* February 10, 2004, p. F1. Presents government plans for several high-containment biodefense laboratories and the varying views of them held by scientists and area residents.

Miller, Judith, Stephen Engelberg, and William J. Broad. "U.S. Germ Warfare Research Pushes Treaty Limits," *New York Times,* vol. 150, September 4, 2001,

p. A1. Reports that the United States is carrying on secret research on bioweapons, which some officials believe violates the Biological Weapons Convention. President Bush plans to expand the research, the authors indicate.

Newman, Richard J., Mike Tharp, and Timothy M. Ito. "Gulf War Mysteries." *U.S. News and World Report*, November 25, 1996, pp. 36–38. According to testimony in Congress, Iraqi chemical weapons may be the cause of the health problems about which many Gulf War veterans complain, but it may never be possible to confirm the link.

Olsnes, Sjur. "The History of Ricin, Abrin and Related Toxins." *Toxicon*, vol. 44, September 2004, pp. 361ff. Presents the history of ricin, abrin, and related toxins in clinical medicine and biomedical research. They have been used for medical treatment since early times, and they have played an important role in immunological research. Ricin is also an instrument of bioterrorism, Olsnes notes.

Oppenheimer, Andy. "To Detect and Protect." *Jane's Defense Weekly*, vol. 41, April 14, 2004, pp. 22–29. A report on recent improvements in systems for detecting biological, chemical, and radiological weapons.

Orent, Wendy. "A Most Dangerous Game." *Natural History*, vol. 113, July/August 2004, pp. 38ff. Calls attention to the fact that the technology and the knowledge to produce a genetically modified smallpox virus that can overcome immunity exists. A U.S. scientist created a mousepox virus with this ability after he set out to develop an antidote to another engineered virus. The author asks whether such research is safe.

Pala, Christopher. "Anthrax Island." *New York Times* Magazine, January 12, 2003, pp. 36–39. A vivid account of a trip by Pala to Vozrozhdeniye Island in the Aral Sea, where the Soviet Union tested bioweapons. He emphasizes that the island is today a potential source of bioweapons agents.

Pinson, Robert D. "Is Nanotechnology Prohibited by the Biological and Chemical Weapons Conventions?" *Berkeley Journal of International Law*, vol. 22, issue 2, 2004, pp. 279ff. Reviews developments in nanotechnology and the relationship of nanotechnology to the biological and chemical conventions, and recommends means of regulating it.

Pugliese, David. "Panama: Bombs on the Beach." *Bulletin of the Atomic Scientists*, vol. 58, July/August 2002, pp. 55–60. Relates that, as part of a program to test the effectiveness of chemical weapons in jungle warfare, the United States, Canada, and Britain exploded thousands of mustard gas and phosgene bombs on San José Island. In 2001, unexploded bombs were found there. Pugliese discusses the history and the cleanup.

Read, Timothy D., et al. "Comparative Genomic Sequencing for Discovery of Novel Polymorphisms in Bacillus anthracis." Science, vol. 296, June 14, 2002, pp. 2,028–2,033. An analysis of anthrax specimens that suggests that the anthrax spores mailed to members of the media and Congress in 2001 came from the U.S. Army Medical Research Unit.

Regis, Ed. "Our Own Anthrax: Dismantling America's Weapons of Mass Destruction." *Harper's* Magazine, vol. 309, July 2004, pp. 69ff. Describes the dismantling of a building at Fort Detrick, Maryland, that produced anthrax and compares the dismantling to the administration's effort to rid Iraq of biological weapons.

Reppy, Judith. "Regulating Biotechnology in the Age of Homeland Security." *Science Studies*, vol. 16, December 2003, pp. 14ff. Summarizes the new regime regulating biological research and looks at the impact that the regime is likely to have on the research community.

Robinson, Julian, Jeanne Guillemin, and Matthew Meselson. "Yellow Rain: The Story Collapses." *Foreign Policy*, vol. 68, Fall 1987, pp. 100–117. Reviews the evidence indicating that yellow rain in Laos and Kampuchea was caused by the defecation of bees rather than by the use of chemical agents, as alleged.

Rosenau, William. "Aum Shinrikyo's Biological Weapons Program: Why Did It Fail?" *Studies in Conflict and Terrorism*, vol. 24, July 2001, pp. 289ff. Finds that cultlike terrorist organizations, like Aum Shinrikyo, may be ill-suited to carrying out a successful bioweapons program.

Salem, Harry. "Issues in Chemical and Biological Terrorism." *International Journal of Toxicology*, vol. 22, November 2003, pp. 465ff. From a staff member of the Edgewood Chemical Biological Center at Aberdeen Proving Ground, an account of the overview of chemical and biological weapons presented at the 2002 meeting of the American College of Toxicology.

Santora, Marc. "Power Fails for Three Hours at Plum Island Infectious Disease Lab." *New York Times*, 20 December 2002, p. B1. Report on a power failure that caused the failure of containment at an infectious disease laboratory. Workers had to seal off doors with duct tape to prevent the escape of germs.

Scherer, Michael. "The Next Worse Thing." *Mother Jones*, vol. 29, March/April 2004, pp. 17ff. Raises the question of whether research funded by the U.S. government is paving the way for a new generation of biological weapons. The National Academy of Sciences, he points out, has warned that the government is without a mechanism to prevent the application of the research to offensive military or terrorist efforts.

Schnabel, Jim. "Spurious Premise behind Gulf War Syndrome." *Houston Chronicle*, November 19, 1996, p. A19. Leaks from a panel of experts indicate that Gulf War syndrome may not even exist, Schnabel reports.

Shoham, Dany. "Chemical and Biological Weapons in Egypt." *Nonproliferation Review*, vol. 5, Spring–Summer 1998, pp. 48–58. Recounts the history of Egypt's chemical weapons program. Then Shoham looks at the evidence that it has a biological weapons program, although the evidence for a biological program is more tenuous than that for chemical weapons.

———. "Chemical/Biological Terrorism: An Old, But Growing Threat in the Middle East and Elsewhere." *Politics and the Life Sciences*, vol. 15, September 1996, pp. 218ff. Prospects for the growth of chemical and biological terrorism. Shoham cites cases in which Arab terrorists used biological weapons against Israel.

Siegel, Jonas. "Disposal in the Doldrums." *Bulletin of the Atomic Scientists*, vol. 60, July/August 2004, pp. 7ff. Reports on the delay in the destruction of U.S. and Russian chemical weapons and remarks on the reasons for the delay.

Simons, Marlise. "Discarded War Munitions Leach Poisons into the Baltic." *New York Times*, June 20, 2003, p. A8. Reports the results of the dumping of chemical weapons in the Baltic Sea and eastern Atlantic after World War II.

Smithson, Amy E. "Chemical Weapons: The End of the Beginning." *Bulletin of the Atomic Scientists*, vol. 48, October 1992, pp. 36–40. A summary of the steps that led up to the successful conclusion of the Chemical Weapons Convention, written shortly before the treaty was opened for signature.

Steinbruner, John D., and Elisa D. Harris. "Controlling Dangerous Pathogens." *Issues in Science and Technology*, vol. 19, Spring 2003, pp. 47ff. States that more systemic protection is needed to guard against the deliberate or unintentional creation of advanced biological agents.

Stone, Richard. "Royal Society Says Panel Needed for Bioweapons Treaty." *Science*, vol. 303, January 23, 2004, pp. 447ff. Reports that the Royal Society argues that a science panel could guide governments in developing means of enforcing the provisions of the Biological and Toxin Weapons Convention.

Taylor, David A. "Japan's Toxic Past Resurfaces." *Environmental Health Perspectives*, vol. 112, June 2004, pp. A465ff. Relates that a recent report from Japan's Ministry of the Environment states that at 81 sites along Japan's shoreline, stocks of chemical munitions or damage caused by shells have been found. A 1973 government report had cited only eight locations. The main chemicals found were mustard gas and lewisite. Some sites must be cleaned immediately to protect residents.

Tracy, Hampton. "Ricin Vaccine Developed." *Journal of the American Medical Association*, vol. 292, September 22, 2004, p. 1419. Announcement of a vaccine of potential use against a biological warfare agent.

Tucker, Jonathan B. "The BWC New Process: A Preliminary Assessment." *Nonproliferation Review*, vol. 11, Spring 2004, pp. 26–39. Reviews the history of efforts to strengthen the Biological Weapons Convention and the current situation in regard to the convention. Tucker closes the article with policy recommendations.

———. "Chemical Weapons: Buried in the Backyard." *Bulletin of the Atomic Scientists*, vol. 57, September/October 2001, pp. 51–56. Presents the problems posed by chemical weapons buried on land outside military bases, as at Spring Valley, Maryland, or dumped at sea and the attempts to deal with them.

Venkatesh, S., and Ziad A. Memish. "Bioterrorism—A New Challenge for Public Health." *International Journal of Antimicrobial Agents*, vol. 21, February 2003, pp. 200ff. From an international perspective, the article surveys the threat of bioterrorism, the results of its use and the likely agents, and discusses the presentation and management of the diseases most likely to be caused by terrorists.

Vilensky, Joel A., and Pandy R. Sinish. "The Dew of Death." *Bulletin of the Atomic Scientists*, vol. 60, March/April 2004, pp. 54–60. Argues that production of lewisite as a chemical warfare agent was a mistake, as it was not suited for use on the battlefield. Now old lewisite stocks and sites are necessitating major cleanup programs in the United States and other countries.

Vogel, Steve. "Army Studies Safety at Fort Detrick Lab; Scientists Contracted Potentially Fatal Disease at Biological Defense Center." *Washington Post*, May 16, 2000, p. B3. Reports three occasions on which a worker in a Biosafety Level 3 facility at Fort Detrick, Maryland, contracted an infectious disease while on the job.

Volans, Glyn N., and Lakshman Karalliedde. "Long-Term Effects of Chemical Weapons." *Lancet*, vol. 360, December 21, 2002, supplement, pp. 35ff. Examines the long-term effects of nerve agents, including the results of exposure to mustard gas in World War I.

Weitzel, Kristin Wisanen, and Jean-Venable R. Goode. "Vaccines in an Era of Bioterrorism." *Drug Topics*, vol. 147, February 17, 2003, pp. 58ff. Furnishes information on the principles of vaccines and on their application to prevent biological terrorism.

Wheelis, Mark. "Biological Warfare at the Siege of Caffa." *Emerging Infectious Diseases*, vol. 8, September 2002, pp. 971–975. Drawing on 14th-century documents, concludes that the use of biological warfare at the siege of Caffa is plausible and provides the best explanation for the entry of plague into the city. However, the movement of plague from the Crimea into Europe was probably the result of other events.

———. "Biotechnology and Biochemical Weapons." *Nonproliferation Review*, vol. 9, Spring 2002, pp. 48–53. Summarizes the advances in biotechnology that are leading to the development of large numbers of new biological weapons. Wheelis also examines problems caused by the development of nonlethal weapons.

———. "'Nonlethal' Chemical Weapons: A Faustian Bargain." *Issues in Science and Technology*, vol. 19, Spring 2003, pp. 74ff. Argues that incapacitants, though developed for use by law enforcement, are likely to be used by criminals, dictators, or terrorists. The benefits will be temporary; the costs, high.

Wheelis, Mark, and Malcolm Dando. "Back to Bioweapons?" *Bulletin of the Atomic Scientists*, January/February 2003, vol. 59, pp. 40ff. Explores the reasons why the United States, in summer 2001, rejected the protocol to the Biological Weapons Convention, which would have established legally binding measures to promote compliance with the convention. The authors theorize that the United States did so because it is committed to continuing and expanding secret bioweapons programs.

———. "New Technology and Future Developments in Biological Warfare." *Military Technology*, vol. 27, May 2003, pp. 52ff. In language understandable to the nonspecialist, the authors describe future biowarfare possibilities, such as weapons that would cause victims' own immune system to turn against them and toxins that might weaken victims' immune systems so that the victims would die from illnesses with which they naturally come into contact.

Yergler, Marilyn. "Nerve Gas Attack." *American Journal of Nursing*, vol. 102, July 2002, pp. 57ff. Discussion of the effects of chemical warfare and the responsibilities of nurses in case of a nerve gas attack.

Annotated Bibliography

Internet/Web Documents

Boettcher, Mike. "Iraqi Scientist's Notes Reveal Bioweapons Tests." CNN.com. Available online. URL: http://www.cnn.com/2003/WORLD/meast/01/27/sprj.irq.bio.scientist. Posted January 28, 2003. Summarizes accounts of Iraqi bioweapons field tests by the director of its biological weapons program.

Cook, Michelle Stem, and Amy F. Woolf. "Preventing Proliferation of Biological Weapons: U.S. Assistance to the Former Soviet States." CRS Report for Congress. Available online. URL: http://www.fas.org/spp/starwars/crs/RL31368.pdf. Posted April 10, 2002. Describes the four kinds of cooperative projects in which the United States is engaging the biological research and production centers throughout the former Soviet Union and the lessons learned from the cooperative projects.

Keppel, David. "A Tale of Two Treaties." *GeneWatch*, vol. 15, March–April 2002. Available online. URL: http://www.gene-watch.org/genewatch/articles/15–2two-treaties.html. Posted March 2002. An examination of the similarities in background and possible consequences of the Bush administration's rejection of the Anti-Ballistic Missile Treaty and of international efforts to strengthen the Biological Weapons Convention.

Kosal, Margaret E. "The Basics of Chemical and Biological Weapons Detectors." Available online. URL: http://www.cns.edu/pubs/week/031124.htm. Posted November 24, 2003. Groups and describes the various types of detectors that are now in use or under development.

Potter, William C. "Prospects for International Cooperation on Biological Security." Available online. URL: http://cns.miis.edu/research/globpart/pottertalk.htm. Posted July 19, 2004. Remarks by Dr. Potter at a conference held at the PIR Center (Center for Policy Studies in Russia) in Moscow, April 2004. Notes that less than 1 percent of the funds pledged for the Global Parternship by the G-8 nations have been committed to biological security. Potter gives reasons why and suggests ways to improve.

Roberts, Guy B. "Arms Control without Arms Control: The Failure of the Biological Weapons Convention Protocol and a New Paradigm for Fighting the Threat of Biological Weapons." INSS Occasional Paper 49. United States Air Force Academy, Colo.: United States Air Force Institute for National Security Studies, March 2003. Available online. URL: http://www.nti.org/e_research/official.docs/other_us/INSSMarch.pdf. Posted March 2003. Advocates that the United States, instead of signing on to a new protocol to the Biological and Toxic Weapons Convention, adopt a flexible approach, based on "the numerous multilateral mechanisms and on-going initiatives" by international governmental organizations, regional security cooperation organizations, and others.

U.S. Department of Health and Human Services. "HHS Fact Sheet—Project Bioshield." Available online. URL: http://www.hhs.gov/news/press/2004pres/20040721b.html. Posted July 21, 2004. This press release is a useful summary of the provisions of Project Bioshield and of steps already taken to strengthen U.S. protections against biological attack.

U.S. Department of State. "U.S. Efforts to Combat the Biological Weapons Threat." U.S. Delegation to the 5th Review Conference of the BWC, Geneva, Switzerland. Available online. URL: http://www.state.gov/t/ac/rls/fs/15150pf.htm. Posted November 14, 2002. This fact sheet summarizes steps taken within the United States and in concert with other nations and international organizations to combat the threat posed by biological weapons.

Vollen, Laurie. "Fools Rush In." *GeneWatch*, vol. 16, February 2003. Available online. URL: http://www.gene-watch.org/genewatch/articles/16–2lola.html. Posted February 2003. Evaluation of what is being done to protect us from bioweapons. Vollen also gives suggestions about what could and should be done to increase protection.

Zilinskas, Raymond A., and Jonathan B. Tucker. "Limiting the Contribution of the Scientific Literature to the BW Threat." Available online. URL: http://cns.miis.edu/pubs/week/021216a.htm. Posted December 16, 2002. A summary of the discussion in a workshop on means of limiting the risk posed by publication of scientific research. The workshop, held in August 2002 and organized by the Center for Nonproliferation Studies, brought together scientists and security experts.

RADIOLOGICAL AND OTHER NONTRADITIONAL WEAPONS

BOOKS AND REPORTS

Ferguson, Charles D., et al. *Commercial Radioactive Sources: Surveying the Security Risks.* Washington, D.C.: Monterey Institute, Center for Nonproliferation Studies, January 2003. Numerous sources of commercial radioactive material could be stolen by terrorists. The public should be educated about the possibility of an attack with a dirty bomb.

General Accounting Office. *Nuclear Regulatory Commission: Oversight of Security at Nuclear Plants Needs to Be Strengthened.* GAO-03-752. Washington, D.C.: General Accounting Office, September 24, 2003. Finds three types of weaknesses in the Nuclear Regulatory Commission's oversight of security at nuclear plants, including problems with the tests of preparedness by means of mock terrorist attacks.

Karasik, Theodore. *Toxic Warfare.* Santa Monica, Calif.: RAND Corporation, 2002. Examines the threat from weapons that incorporate inexpensive and relatively easy-to-obtain chemicals and industrial waste. These weapons are not officially classified as chemical weapons that incorporate banned materials. However, they are a danger for military forces and for civilians in their home countries.

Krepon, Michael. *America at Risk: A Homeland Security Report Card.* Washington, D.C.: Progressive Policy Institute, 2003. Describes radioactive materials security in the United States as poor. The book cites the large number of radioactive sources and the lack of proper security at the facilities that contain them.

Annotated Bibliography

ARTICLES

Alvarez, Robert, et al. "Reducing the Hazards from Stored Spent Power-Reactor Fuel in the United States." *Science and Global Security,* vol. 11, January–April 2003, pp. 1–51. Discusses the danger posed by irradiated fuel stored in pools at nuclear power plants. The article suggests that the fuel would present less of a threat if stored in aboveground casks, as is already done at a few plants.

———. "Response by the Authors to the NRC Review of "Reducing the Hazards from Stored Spent Power-Reactor Fuel in the United States." *Science and Global Security,* vol. 11, May 2003, pp. 213–223. Answers four criticisms by the Nuclear Regulatory Commission, including the claim that they exaggerated the likelihood of a fire in an irradiated fuel storage pool.

Ballard, James David, and Kristine Mullendore. "Weapons of Mass Victimization, Radioactive Waste Shipments, and Environmental Laws: Policy Making and First Responders." *American Behavioral Scientist,* vol. 46, February 2003, pp. 766ff. Examines several of the legal and practical issues relating to the possible use of radiological weapons. The authors make suggestions on policy at the local level.

Berkowitz, Bruce, and Robert W. Hahn. "Cybersecurity: Who's Watching the Store?" *Issues in Science and Technology,* vol. 19, spring 2003, pp. 55ff. An assessment of the vulnerability of electronic communications, which could, among other things, lead to nuclear disaster. Bruce and Hahn do not think that the government is doing all that it could and should to protect the system.

Bunn, George, et al. "Research Reactor Vulnerability to Sabotage by Terrorists." *Science and Global Security,* vol. 11, May 2003, pp. 85ff. A consideration of the possibility that terrorists might be able to inflict "significant doses of radioactivity" on a local population by sabotaging a research reactor. Regulators need to take precautions to prevent such sabotage and also to plan to cope with such an emergency should it occur.

Chase, Marilyn, and Rachel Zimmerman. "If 'Dirty Bomb' Hits, Hospitals Must Improve," *Wall Street Journal,* June 12, 2002, p. B1. Evaluates the procedures that hospitals must follow if a dirty bomb explodes. The article asserts that hospitals will have to improvise and gives the steps that some have taken.

Davidson, Keay. "Dirty Bomb Called 'All But Inevitable.'" *San Francisco Chronicle,* September 5, 2004, p. A1. Assesses the likelihood of a dirty-bomb attack. Davidson notes that industry and the medical establishment are cutting the quantity of radioactive material that they handle but that nevertheless radioactive materials are readily available to terrorists.

Elcock, Deborah, Gladys A. Klemic, and Anibal L. Taboas. "Establishing Remediation Levels in Response to a Radiological Dispersal Event (or 'Dirty Bomb')." *Environmental Science and Technology,* vol. 38, May 1, 2004, pp. 2,505ff. Current laws and regulations concerning radiological cleanup are not designed for cleanup after an attack with a radiological dispersal device. To thwart terrorists, the elements of a response to such an attack must be set up rapidly and must include methods for developing cleanup criteria.

Hall, Mimi. "Officials Trying to Reduce Holes in Security Net." *USA Today*, September 14, 2004, pp. 9ff. The top concerns of experts in homeland security are holes in aviation security, a lack of security for ground transportation, inadequate preparation for bioterrorism, insufficient inspection of cargo from abroad, and lack of security in the private sector, in particular at chemical plants, many of which are located in densely populated areas.

Hirsch, Daniel. "The NRC: What Me Worry?" *Bulletin of the Atomic Scientists*, January/February 2002, pp. 38–44. Decries the inadequate security against terrorists and the inadequate tests of that security at U.S. nuclear power plants.

Lenzner, Robert, Nathan Vardi, and N. V. Forbes. "The Next Threat." *Forbes*, vol. 174, September 20, 2004, pp. 70ff. Discusses terrorist attacks by means of computer hacking. The next major attack on the United States could be a cyber attack, but neither the government nor private industry is doing much to fix flaws in the Internet. The question of who will pay to increase protection looms large.

Levi, Michael A., and Henry C. Kelly. "Weapons of Mass Disruption." *Scientific American*, vol. 287, November 2002, pp. 76–81. Gives a vivid account of the problems that a dirty bomb or other radiation dispersal device could cause. Includes protective measures for the government to take and what individuals can do if attacked.

Litman, Leah. "Cleaning House." *Harvard International Review*, vol. 25, spring 2003, pp. 32ff. Discusses the inadequacy of the Nuclear Non-Proliferation Treaty to control dirty bombs and other radiological weapons. Litman suggests alternative strategies for their control.

McGeary, Johanna, et al. "An Invitation to Terrorists?" *Time*, vol. 162, August 25, 2003, pp. 38ff. States that it is unclear whether or not terrorists have the skills to bring down the U.S. electricity grid by means of computer hacking. However, an attempt by computer is more likely than an attack on a power station itself.

"Nuclear Regulatory Commission (NRC) Review of 'Reducing the Hazards from Stored Spent Power-Reactor Fuel in the United States.'" *Science and Global Security*, vol. 11, May 2003, pp. 203–211. Presents the argument that the article in question does not realistically address the possibility of an accident in an irradiated fuel pool and does not make the case for storing irradiated fuel older than five years in aboveground casks.

Palmore, Julian. "'Dirty Bombs': An Analysis of Radiological Weapons." *Defense and Security Analysis*, vol. 19, March 2003, pp. 69ff. Outlines how dirty bombs can be created and what they can do. Palmore discusses the possibility that transportation of radioactive materials will allow terrorists to seize materials for dirty bombs.

Ripley, Amanda. "The Case of the Dirty Bomber: How a Chicago Street Gangster Allegedly Became a Soldier for Osama Bin Laden." *Time*, June 24, 2002, pp. 28ff. The story of Jose Padilla (Abdulah al-Muhajir), held by the federal government as an "enemy combatant" because he allegedly participated in a plot to use a dirty bomb against the United States.

Stone, Richard. "Radioactive Sources Move from a Concern to a Crisis." *Science*, vol. 302, December 5, 2003, pp. 1644ff. Presents the growing awareness that the many unsecured radioactive sources that have been discarded by companies and medical establishments may become material for dirty bombs.

Weikel, Dan. "Terror Risk to Nuclear Plants Is Debated." *Los Angeles Times*, September 16, 2004, p. B1ff. Describes the debate over whether nuclear power plants are vulnerable to attack and, if so, whether steps should be taken to make them safe.

CHAPTER 8

ORGANIZATIONS AND AGENCIES

Below are examples of the numerous organizations and agencies working on aspects of weapons of mass destruction. First are presented intergovernmental organizations, then U.S. government agencies, academic institutions, and public interest organizations from outside and inside the United States. All of the public interest organizations that are listed are international or national in scope. Space is lacking to present examples of the many worthy regional and local organizations working on nuclear, chemical, biological, and radiological weapons.

UNITED NATIONS AND OTHER INTERGOVERNMENTAL ORGANIZATIONS

Chemical and Biological Working Group
World Health Organization (WHO)
URL: http://www.who.int/csr/delibepidemics/preparedness/cbw/en
E-mail: deliberate@who.int
Phone: (41) (0)22 791 2111
Avenue Appia 20
1211 Geneva 27
Switzerland
A working group established by WHO, the United Nations agency for health, to promote collaboration among various sections of WHO in regard to the public health response to any accidental or deliberate release of biological, chemical, or radioactive agents.

International Atomic Energy Agency (IAEA)
URL: http://www.iaea.org
E-mail: Official.Mail@iaea.org
Phone: (431) 2600-0
P.O. Box 100
Wagramer Strasse 5
A-1400 Vienna
Austria
An "independent intergovernmental, science and technology-based organization, in the United Nations family" with the double purpose of promoting the peaceful use of nuclear energy and ensuring that the assistance provided

is not used to further any military purpose. Through its inspection system it verifies that states comply with their commitments under the Non-Proliferation Treaty and other nonproliferation agreements.

Organisation for the Prohibition of Chemical Weapons (OPCW)
URL: http://www.opcw.org
E-mail: inquiries@opcw.org
Phone: (31) 70 416 3300
Johan de Wittlaan 32
2517 JR The Hague
The Netherlands
An organization mandated by the Chemical Weapons Convention, which went into force in 1997. Its purpose is the elimination of chemical weapons worldwide and the fostering of cooperation in chemistry for peaceful purposes. Its activities include monitoring the inactivation and destruction or conversion of declared weapons-production facilities and the destruction of declared chemical weapons.

United Nations Department for Disarmament Affairs
URL: http://disarmament2.un.org/cab
E-mail: ddaweb@un.org
United Nations Headquarters
Room S-3170
First Avenue at 46th Street
New York, NY 10017
Works to promote the goal of nuclear disarmament and nonproliferation and to strengthen disarmament regimes in regard to chemical, biological, and conventional weapons. The department includes a weapons of mass destruction branch, which supports the activities of the United Nations, provides information, and participates in multilateral efforts. The department also supports the Conference on Disarmament at Geneva, a multilateral disarmament negotiating forum, which is affiliated with the United Nations but is autonomous.

United Nations Institute for Disarmament Research (UNIDIR)
URL: http://www.unidir.org
E-mail: unidir@unog.ch
Phone: (41) (0)22 917 3186
Palais des Nations
1211 Geneva 10
Switzerland
A research institute that proposes new ideas for security by bringing together the subjects of disarmament, security, and development. In its work it aims to put people first.

U.S. GOVERNMENT AGENCIES AND OTHER FEDERAL ENTITIES

Board on Radiation Effects Research (BRER)
National Academy of Sciences
URL: http://www7.nationalacademies.org/brer
E-mail: nrsb@nas.edu
Phone: (202) 334-2232
Keck Center of the National Academies, Keck 627
500 Fifth Street, NW
Washington, DC 20001
A board of the National Academy of Sciences concerned with the biologic effects of all types of radiation. Of particular interest among its projects

is its periodic assessments of the risks posed by low-level radiation.

Centers for Disease Control and Prevention (CDC)
URL: http://www.cdc.gov
E-mail: click on www.cdc.gov/netinfo.htm
Phone: (404) 639-3534 (for public inquiries)
1600 Clifton Road
Atlanta, GA 30333
The lead federal agency for protecting the health and safety of people at home and abroad. It gathers and provides information to improve decision making relating to health and promotes health through partnerships with other organizations.

Chemical and Biological Defense Information Analysis Center (CBIAC)
URL: http://www.cbiac.apgea.army.mil
E-mail: cbiac@battelle.org
Phone: (410) 676-9030
Aberdeen Proving Ground—Edgewood Area
P.O. Box 196
Gunpowder, MD 21010-0196
A Department of Defense Information Analysis Center operated by Battelle Memorial Institute. It is the Department of Defense's focal "point for information relating to chemical and biological defense technology." Service to parties other than governmental groups and their contractors is limited to publicly accessible portions of the center's web site.

Defense Threat Reduction Agency
URL: http://www.dtra.mil
E-mail: dtra.publicaffairs@dtra.mil
Phone: (703) 767-5870
8725 John J. Kingman Road
MSC 6201
Fort Belvoir, VA 22060-6201
A joint-service, Department of Defense agency responsible for safeguarding the United States and its friends from weapons of mass destruction. The agency works to prevent the spread of these weapons, to make available to our soldiers the necessary offensive and defensive tools, and to prepare for a future under the threat of terrorism.

National Institute of Allergy and Infectious Diseases (NIAID)
URL: http://www.niaid.nih.gov
6610 Rockledge Drive
MSC 6612
Bethesda, MD 20892-26612
Conducts and supports basic and applied research on infectious, immunologic, and allergic diseases. NIAID is the lead agency at the National Institutes of Health for infectious diseases and immunology research and for the implementation of Project Bioshield.

National Institutes of Health (NIH)
URL: http://www.nih.gov
E-mail: NIHInfo@nih.gov
Phone: (301) 496-4000
9000 Rockville Pike
Bethesda, MD 20892
A branch of the U.S. Department of Health and Human Services, which characterizes it as "the nation's premier biomedical research institution."

United States Army Chemical Materials Agency (CMA)
URL: http://www.cma.army.mil
E-mail: public_affairs@cma.army.mil

Phone: (800) 488-0648
Public Affairs
AMSCM-SSP
5183 Blackhawk Road
APG-EA, MD 21010-5424
Agency in charge of destroying U.S. stockpiles of nerve gas. The agency also stores and protects the nerve agents until they are destroyed and works on chemical and biological defense.

United States Army Medical Research Institute of Chemical Defense (USAMRICD)
URL: http://ccc.apgea.army.mil
E-mail: MRICD.PAO@apg.amedd.army.mil (for public affairs office)
Phone: (410) 436-2230 (commercial)
ATTN: MCMR-UV-ZM
3100 Ricketts Point Road
Aberdeen Proving Ground, MD 21010-5400
An agency with the mission of educating medical professionals and first responders in the management of chemical casualties and providing consultation to military and civilian authorities.

United States Army Medical Research Institute of Infectious Diseases (USAMRIID)
URL: http://www.usamriid.army.mil
E-mail: USAMRIIDweb@amedd.army.mil
1425 Porter Street
Frederick, MD 21702-5011
An agency with the mission of conducting basic and applied research on biological threats for the purpose of protecting members of the military. USAMRIID also plays a key role in preparing the nation to meet the threat of biological terrorism and biological warfare.

United States Department of Defense
URL: http://www.defenselink.mil
E-mail: click on www.defenselink.mil/faq/comment.html
Phone: (703) 692-7100 (general); (703) 428-0711 (information number)
1000 Defense Pentagon Room #3E880
Washington, DC 20301-1000
Civilian office that develops national security policies and has overall responsibility for administering national defense; responds to inquiries from the public on national defense matters. Its agencies include the Missile Defense Agency, created in January 2002 from the former Ballistic Missile Defense Organization.

United States Department of Energy (DOE)
URL: http://www.doe.gov
Phone: (202) 342-5363
1000 Independence Avenue, SW
Washington, DC 20585
Agency with the mission of protecting national, energy, and economic security with advanced science and technology and ensuring environmental cleanup. Through its semiautonomous National Nuclear Security Administration, it is responsible for nuclear weapons research, development, and engineering.

United States Department of Homeland Security (DHS)
URL: http://www.dhs.gov

Phone: (202) 282-8000
E-mail: [through the web site]
Washington, DC 20528
Established in 2002 to serve as the unifying core for the national network of organizations and institutions working to make the United States secure. Among its many initiatives is the creation of a National Biodefense Analysis and Countermeasure Center.

United States Department of State
URL: http://www.state.gov
Phone: (202) 647-4000
Harry S Truman Building
2201 C Street, NW
Washington, DC 20520
Includes various offices relating to weapons of mass destruction, among them the Bureau of Arms Control, the Bureau of Verification and Compliance, the Nuclear Risk Reduction Center, and the Bureau of Nonproliferation. The latter leads the U.S. effort to curb the proliferation of weapons of mass destruction and their delivery systems, to secure the nuclear materials in the former Soviet Union, and to promote nuclear safety and the responsible transfer of conventional arms and technology.

United States Food and Drug Administration (FDA)
URL: http://www.fda.gov
E-mail: [send questions and comments through the web site]
Phone: (888) 463-6332
5600 Fishers Lane
Rockville, MD 20857
Agency responsible for protecting the public health by assuring the safety of the nation's human and veterinary drugs, food supply, and products that emit radiation, among other areas. The agency helps the public to obtain the information they need to use medicines and food to improve their health.

United States Institute of Peace (USIP)
URL: http://www.usip.org
E-mail: usip_requests@usip.org
Phone: (202) 457-1700
1200 17th Street, NW
Washington, DC 20036
An independent, nonpartisan federal institution created by Congress to promote the prevention, management, and peaceful resolution of international conflicts. The Board of Directors is appointed by the president of the United States and confirmed by the Senate. Its programs include research grants, conferences, library services, and publications.

ACADEMIC INSTITUTIONS

INSTITUTIONS BASED OUTSIDE THE UNITED STATES

Department of Peace Studies
University of Bradford
URL: http://www.brad.ac.uk/acad/sbtwc
E-mail: generalconfres@bradford.ac.uk
Phone: (44) (0)1274 235 240
Pemberton Building
West Yorkshire BD7 1DP
United Kingdom

An internationally known university center for peace research, the Department of Peace Studies maintains a database on the subject: Preventing Biological Warfare: Strengthening the Biological and Toxin Weapons Convention.

Harvard Sussex Program (HSP)
URL: http://www.sussex.ac.uk/spru/hsp
Phone: (44) (0)1273 678 172
SPRU-Science and Technology Policy Research
University of Sussex
Freeman Centre
Brighton, East Sussex BN1 9QE
United Kingdom
A program linking research groups at Harvard University and the University of Sussex that seek the global elimination of chemical and biological weapons and the strengthening of constraints against hostile use of biotechnologies. The program aims to increase the influence of scholarship on the formation of public policy.

Institutions Based within the United States

Belfer Center for Science and International Affairs
John F. Kennedy School of Government
Harvard University
URL: http://bcsia.ksg.harvard.edu
E-mail: bcsia_ksg@harvard.edu
Phone: (617) 495-1400
79 JFK Street
Cambridge, MA 02138
Integrates insights of social scientists, natural scientists, technologists, and practitioners in regard to challenges of international security and other critical issues. The center is composed of a resident research community of 150 scholars and, each year, a new group of interdisciplinary research fellows. Managing the Atom is one of its projects.

Center for International Security and Cooperation (CISAC)
Stanford University
URL: http://cisac.stanford.edu
Phone: (650) 723-6925
616 Serra Street
Room E200
Stanford, CA 94305-6055
A teaching and research center that works on protection of fissile materials and response to biological weapons threats, among other topics.

Center for Peace and Security Studies (CPASS)
Edmund A. Walsh School of Foreign Service
Georgetown University
URL: http://cpass.georgetown.edu
E-mail: cpass@georgetown.edu
Phone: (202) 687-8590
111 Intercultural Center
Box 571029
Washington, DC 20057-1029
A center for teaching and research that is committed to examining the range of factors that impact peace and security issues. Arms and arms control, and terrorism and counterterrorism are two foci of current research projects.

Peace Studies Program
Cornell University
URL: http://www.einaudi.cornell.edu/PeaceProgram
E-mail: psp@is.cornell.edu

Phone: (607) 255-6484
Tower Road
130 Uris Hall
Ithaca, NY 14853-7601
Conducts research and teaching on arms control and disarmament, among other subjects. The program has received a MacArthur Foundation grant for a full-time faculty position to carry out research on new dimensions of weapons proliferation.

Security Studies Program
Massachusetts Institute of Technology
URL: http://web.mit.edu/ssp
E-mail: mrieb@mit.edu
Phone: (617) 258-7608
Building E38
6th Floor
Cambridge, MA 02139
A graduate-level research and educational program. Its Technical Working Group of independent academic technical analysts works on a range of technology-related international security problems, including nuclear arms reduction, fissile materials, and the future uses of space.

PUBLIC INTEREST ORGANIZATIONS

ORGANIZATIONS BASED OUTSIDE THE UNITED STATES

BioWeapons Protection Project (BWPP)
URL: http://www.bwpp.org
E-mail: bwpp@bwpp.org
Phone: (41) (0)22 908 5834
Avenue de Sécheron 12
CH-1202 Geneva
Switzerland
A "global civil society" that works to strengthen the norm against using disease as a weapon. It monitors implementation of treaties, tracks initiatives to reduce the bioweapons threat, and reports its findings, principally in its periodical *BioWeapons Monitor.* Partner organizations worldwide contribute to the collection and analysis of data.

Citizens Nuclear Information Center (CNIC)
URL: http://cnic.jp/english
E-mail: cnic-jp@po.iijnet.or.jp
38 Kotobuki Building
1-58-15
Higashi-nakan9, Nakano-ku
Tokyo 154-003
Japan
A nonprofit research, education, and policy organization advocating alternatives to nuclear power and nuclear weapons development.

Greenpeace International
URL: http://www.greenpeace.org
E-mail: supporter.services@int.greenpeace.org
Phone: (31) 20 5148150
Ottho Heldringstraat 5
1066 AZ Amsterdam
The Netherlands
An environmental organization known for its media events to draw attention to issues. It also commissions and publishes research reports. Stopping the nuclear threat is among its main concerns. The U.S. office can be reached at greenpeace.usa@wdc.greenpeace.org.

International Committee of the Red Cross (ICRC)
Biotechnology, Weapons and Humanity Initiative

URL: http://www.icrc.org/eng/bwh
E-mail: cid.gva@icrc.org (for library)
Phone: (41) (0)22 734 6001
19 Avenue de la Paix
CH-1202 Geneva
Switzerland
A humanitarian organization "mandated by the international community to be the guardian of international humanitarian law." The biotechnology, weapons and humanity initiative aims to promote serious reflection on the risks, rules, and responsibilities related to advances in biotechnology.

Stockholm International Peace Research Institute (SIPRI)
URL: http://www.sipri.se
E-mail: sipri@sipri.org
Phone: (46) 8 655 97 00
Signalistgatan 9
SE-169 70 Solna
Sweden
An independent peace research institute, SIPRI's publications and in particular the *SIPRI Yearbook* are known around the world as authoritative resources.

The Verification Research, Training and Information Centre (VERTIC)
URL: http://www.vertic.org
E-mail: info@vertic.org
Phone: (44) (0)20 7440 6960
Baird House
15-17 St. Cross Street
London EC1N 8UW
United Kingdom
An independent nonprofit organization with the mission of promoting effective verification as a means of ensuring confidence in international agreements. VERTIC's work includes research, training, disseminating information, and interacting with the relevant political, diplomatic, technical, scientific, and governmental communities.

National U.S. Organizations

Alliance for Nuclear Accountability (ANA)
URL: http://www.ananuclear.org
E-mail: ananuclear@earthlink.net
Phone: (206) 547-3175
1914 34th Street
Suite 407
Seattle, WA 98103
A network of organizations working on health, cleanup, and weapons issues. Most are located near sites in the nuclear weapons-production complex.

Arms Control Association (ACA)
URL: http://www.armscontrol.org
E-mail: aca@armscontrol.org
Phone: (202) 463-8270
1150 Connecticut Avenue, NW
Suite 620
Washington, DC 20036
A national nonpartisan membership organization dedicated to promoting public understanding of and support for effective arms control policies. Its major tools are its public education and media programs and its magazine *Arms Control Today*.

British American Security Information Council (BASIC)
URL: http://www.basicint.org
E-mail: basicus@basicint.org
Phone: (202) 546-8055
110 Maryland Avenue, NE
Suite 205
Washington, DC 20002

An independent research organization that analyzes government policies and promotes public awareness of defense, disarmament, military strategy, and nuclear policies in order to nurture informed debate.

Carnegie Endowment for International Peace (CEIP)
URL: http://www.carnegieendowment.org
E-mail: info@ceip.org
Phone: (202) 483-7600
1779 Massachusetts Avenue, NW
Washington, DC 20036-2103
A nonprofit organization, founded in 1910, that is dedicated to advancing cooperation between nations and promoting active international engagement by the United States. Its work is nonpartisan and dedicated to achieving practical results.

Cato Institute
URL: http://www.cato.org
Phone: (202) 842-0200
1000 Massachusetts Avenue, NW
Washington, DC 20001-5403
A nonprofit public policy research foundation that upholds the "traditional American principles" of individual liberty, limited government, free markets, and peace. It works to increase the involvement of the public in public policy debate. Issues on which the institute is working include bioterrorism, defense, and responses to terrorism.

Center for Arms Control and Non-Proliferation
URL: http://www.armscontrolcenter.org
E-mail: cacnp@armscontrolcenter.org
Phone: (202) 546-0795
322 4th Street, NE
Washington, DC 20002
A nonprofit research and education organization working to enhance international peace and security and to protect the American people from the threat of weapons of mass destruction.

Center for Defense Information (CDI)
URL: http://www.cdi.org
E-mail: info@cdi.org
Phone: (202) 332-0600
1779 Massachusetts Avenue, NW
Washington, DC 20036-2109
A center founded in 1972 by recently retired, senior U.S. military officers. It seeks to contribute alternative views on security to promote wide-ranging discourse and debate.

Center for Nonproliferation Studies (CNS)
Monterey Institute of International Studies
URL: http://cns.miis.edu
E-mail: cns@miis.edu
Phone: (831) 647-4154
460 Pierce Street
Monterey, CA 93940
The largest U.S. nongovernmental organization engaged in research and teaching exclusively on nonproliferation issues. It concerns itself with biological, chemical, and nuclear weapons.

Chemical and Biological Arms Control Institute (CBACI)
URL: http://www.cbaci.org
E-mail: cbaci@cbaci.org
Phone: (202) 296-3550
1747 Pennsylvania Avenue, NW

7th Floor
Washington, DC 20026
A private, nonprofit policy-research organization with a special, but not exclusive, focus on the elimination of chemical and biological weapons. It works in the areas of research, analysis, technical support, training, and education.

Council for Responsible Genetics (CRG)
URL: http://www.gene-watch.org
E-mail: crg@gene-watch.org
Phone: (617) 868-0870
5 Upland Road
Suite 3
Cambridge, MA 02140
A nonprofit organization that fosters public debate about the social, ethical, and environmental implications of genetic technologies. It distributes accurate information through individuals and through the media and represents the public interest on emerging issues in biotechnology. Its magazine, *GeneWatch*, monitors biotechnology's social, ethical, and environmental consequences.

Federation of American Scientists (FAS)
URL: http://www.fas.org
E-mail: webmaster@fas.org
Phone: (202) 546-3300
1717 K Street, NW
Suite 209
Washington, DC 20036
Founded in 1945 by members of the Manhattan Project, the federation is dedicated to ending the worldwide arms race and avoiding the use of nuclear weapons. The organization works on a variety of issues related to weapons of mass destruction.

The Henry L. Stimson Center
URL: http://www.stimson.org
E-mail: info@stimson.org
Phone: (202) 223-5956
11 Dupont Circle
Suite 900
Washington, DC 20036
A nonprofit, nonpartisan institution devoted to enhancing international peace and security through a combination of rigorous analysis and outreach.

Institute for Science and International Security (ISIS)
URL: http://www.isis-online.org
E-mail: isis@isis-online.org
Phone: (202) 547-3633
236 Massachusetts Avenue, NE
Suite 500
Washington, DC 20002
A nonprofit institution dedicated to informing the public about science and policy issuesv affecting international security. Its two main projects are the Nuclear Nonproliferation Project and the Nuclear Weapons Production Project.

National Association of Radiation Survivors (NARS)
URL: http://www.radiationsurvivors.org
E-mail: nars@radiationsurvivors.org
Phone: (800) 798-5102
P.O. Box 1587
Marysville, CA 95901-1587
A national nonprofit organization, most of whose members are citizens who have been exposed to ionizing radiation from the development, production, testing, use, or storage of nuclear weapons and nuclear waste. It works to obtain compensation for those exposed and for an end to the

development and testing of nuclear weapons.

National Institute for Public Policy (NIPP)
URL: http://www.nipp.org
Phone: (703) 696-0563
3031 Javier Road
Suite 300
Fairfax, VA 22031
Assesses U.S. foreign and defense policy in the post–cold war environment. The institute educates decision makers and the public about evolving issues.

National Security Archives
URL: http://www.gwu.edu/~nsarchiv
Phone: (202) 994-7000
George Washington University
Gelman Library
Suite 701
2130 H Street, NW
Washington, DC 20037
A nonprofit research institute that works to locate, secure the declassification of, organize, and index government documents on key areas of U.S. policy. The archive has collected extensive primary materials on nuclear history.

Natural Resources Defense Council (NRDC)
URL: http://www.nrdc.org
E-mail: nrdcinfo@nrdc.org
Phone: (212) 727-2700
40 West 20th Street
New York, NY 10011
A national, nonprofit organization of scientists, lawyers, and environmental specialists dedicated to protecting public health and the environment. The NRDC is a great source of statistics and other basic information on nuclear weapons production and stockpiles worldwide. Their current nuclear-related project is on nuclear weapons and waste.

NGO Committee on Disarmament, Peace and Security
URL: http://www.igc.org/disarm
E-mail: disarmtimes@igc.org
Phone: (212) 687-5340
777 United Nations Plaza
Suite 3B
New York, NY 10017
A nonprofit organization that for 25 years has provided services and facilities to hundreds of citizens' groups concerned with the peace and disarmament activities of the United Nations.

Nonproliferation Policy Education Center (NPEC)
URL: http://www.npec-web.org
E-mail: npec@npec-web.org
Phone: (202) 466-4406
1718 M Street, NW
Suite 244
Washington, DC 20036
A project of the Institute for International Studies that promotes understanding of nuclear- and missile-proliferation issues.

Nuclear Age Peace Foundation
URL: http://www.wagingpeace.org and http://www.nuclearfiles.org
E-mail: [send from web site]
Phone: (805) 965-3443
1187 Coast Village Road, Suite 1
PMB 121
Santa Barbara, CA 93108-2794
A nonprofit education and advocacy organization that advances initiatives

to eliminate nuclear weapons, foster the international rule of law, and build a legacy of peace.

Nuclear Policy Research Institute (NPRI)
URL: http://www.nuclearpolicy.org
E-mail: info@nuclearpolicy.org
Phone: (202) 822-9800
1925 K Street, NW
Suite 210
Washington, DC 20006
A nonprofit organization founded to educate Americans through the mass media about the nuclear threat. As of 2005, it was led by Helen Caldicott and Charles Sheehan-Miles.

Nuclear Threat Initiative (NTI)
URL: http://www.nti.org
E-mail: contact@nti.org
Phone: (202) 296-4810
1747 Pennsylvania Avenue, NW
7th Floor
Washington, DC 20006
A nonprofit organization founded by media mogul Ted Turner and former senator Sam Nunn to strengthen global security by reducing the risk of use and preventing the spread of nuclear, biological, and chemical weapons. NTI seeks to raise public awareness, serve as a catalyst for new thinking, and take direct action to reduce the threats.

Physicians for Social Responsibility (PSR)
URL: http://www.psr.org
E-mail: psrnatl@psr.org
Phone: (202) 667-4260
1875 Connecticut Avenue, NW
Suite 1012
Washington, DC 20009
A public policy organization composed of members of the medical and public health professions and other concerned citizens working for nuclear disarmament, a healthful environment, and an end to the epidemic of gun violence.

Pugwash Conferences on Science and World Affairs
URL: http://www.pugwash.org
E-mail: pugwashdc@aol.com
Phone: (202) 478-3440
11 Dupont Circle, NW
Suite 900
Washington, DC 20036
Sets up a series of international meetings and projects that bring together scientists, scholars, and individuals experienced in government diplomacy and the military to focus on problems lying at the intersection of science and world affairs. It promotes the resulting ideas and proposals through such means as publications and press conferences. The main aim of Pugwash is to eliminate weapons of mass destruction. Pugwash has offices in Frankfort, Germany; Geneva, Switzerland; and Rome, Italy, as well as in Washington, D.C.

Rand Corporation
URL: http://www.rand.org
Phone: (310) 393-0411
1700 Main Street
P.O. Box 2138
Santa Monica, CA 90407-2138
A nonprofit research institution that works with decision makers in the public and private sectors to find solutions to challenges facing the nation and world, including a wide range of national security issues.

Stanley Foundation
URL: http://www.stanleyfoundation.org
E-mail: stanley@stanleyfoundation.org
Phone: (563) 264-1500
209 Iowa Avenue
Muscatine, IA 5276
A nonprofit organization focusing on educational and communications approaches to effecting multinational approaches to resolving international conflicts.

The Sunshine Project
URL: http://www.sunshine-project.org
E-mail: tsp@sunshine-project.org
Phone: (512) 494-0545
101 West 6th Street
Suite 607
Austin, TX 78701
An international nonprofit organization, with offices in Hamburg, Germany, and Austin, Texas. It works against the hostile use of biotechnology. Research and publication are its main methods.

Union of Concerned Scientists (UCS)
URL: http://www.ucsusa.org/security/weapons.html
E-mail: ucs@ucsusa.org
Phone: (617) 547-5552
2 Brattle Square
Cambridge, MA 02238
An alliance of scientists and concerned citizens involved in scientific analysis, policy development, and citizen advocacy. UCS works toward deep cuts in nuclear forces and reduction of the alert status of nuclear weapons, among other subjects.

PART III

APPENDICES

APPENDIX A

TREATY BANNING NUCLEAR WEAPON TESTS IN THE ATMOSPHERE, IN OUTER SPACE AND UNDER WATER (1963)

Signed at Moscow August 5, 1963
Entered into force October 10, 1963

The Governments of the United States of America, the United Kingdom of Great Britain and Northern Ireland, and the Union of Soviet Socialist Republics, hereinafter referred to as the "Original Parties,"

Proclaiming as their principal aim the speediest possible achievement of an agreement on general and complete disarmament under strict international control in accordance with the objectives of the United Nations which would put an end to the armaments race and eliminate the incentive to the production and testing of all kinds of weapons, including nuclear weapons,

Seeking to achieve the discontinuance of all test explosions of nuclear weapons for all time, determined to continue negotiations to this end, and desiring to put an end to the contamination of mans environment by radioactive substances,

Have agreed as follows:

ARTICLE I

(1) Each of the Parties to this Treaty undertakes to prohibit, to prevent, and not to carry out any nuclear weapon test explosion, or any other nuclear explosion, at any place under its jurisdiction or control:

(a) in the atmosphere; beyond its limits, including outer space; or under water, including territorial waters or high seas; or
(b) in any other environment if such explosion causes radioactive debris to be present outside the territorial limits of the State under whose jurisdiction or control such explosion is conducted. It is understood in this connection that the provisions of this subparagraph are without prejudice to the conclusion of a Treaty resulting in the permanent banning of all nuclear test explosions, including all such explosions underground, the conclusion of which, as the Parties have stated in the Preamble to this Treaty, they seek to achieve.

(2) Each of the Parties to this Treaty undertakes furthermore to refrain from causing, encouraging, or in any way participating in, the carrying out of any nuclear weapon test explosion, or any other nuclear explosion, anywhere which would take place in any of the environments described, or have the effect referred to, in paragraph 1 of this Article.

ARTICLE II

(1) Any Party may propose amendments to this Treaty. The text of any proposed amendment shall be submitted to the Depositary Governments which shall circulate it to all Parties to this Treaty. Thereafter, if requested to do so by one-third or more of the Parties, the Depositary Governments shall convene a conference, to which they shall invite all the Parties, to consider such amendment.
(2) Any amendment to this Treaty must be approved by a majority of the votes of all the Parties to this Treaty, including the votes of all of the Original Parties. The amendment shall enter into force for all Parties upon the deposit of instruments of ratification by a majority of all the Parties, including the instruments of ratification of all of the Original Parties.

ARTICLE III

(1) This Treaty shall be open to all States for signature. Any State which does not sign this Treaty before its entry into force in accordance with paragraph 3 of this Article may accede to it at any time.
(2) This Treaty shall be subject to ratification by signatory States. Instruments of ratification and instruments of accession shall be deposited with the Governments of the Original Parties—the United States of America, the United Kingdom of Great Britain and Northern Ireland, and the Union of Soviet Socialist Republics—which are hereby designated the Depositary Governments.

(3) This Treaty shall enter into force after its ratification by all the Original Parties and the deposit of their instruments of ratification.

(4) For States whose instruments of ratification or accession are deposited subsequent to the entry into force of this Treaty, it shall enter into force on the date of the deposit of their instruments of ratification or accession.

(5) The Depositary Governments shall promptly inform all signatory and acceding States of the date of each signature, the date of deposit of each instrument of ratification of and accession to this Treaty, the date of its entry into force, and the date of receipt of any requests for conferences or other notices.

(6) This Treaty shall be registered by the Depositary Governments pursuant to Article 102 of the Charter of the United Nations.

ARTICLE IV

This Treaty shall be of unlimited duration.

Each Party shall in exercising its national sovereignty have the right to withdraw from the Treaty if it decides that extraordinary events, related to the subject matter of this Treaty, have jeopardized the supreme interests of its country. It shall give notice of such withdrawal to all other Parties to the Treaty three months in advance.

ARTICLE V

This Treaty, of which the English and Russian texts are equally authentic, shall be deposited in the archives of the Depositary Governments. Duly certified copies of this Treaty shall be transmitted by the Depositary Governments to the Governments of the signatory and acceding States.

IN WITNESS WHEREOF the undersigned, duly authorized, have signed this Treaty.

DONE in triplicate at the city of Moscow the fifth day of August, one thousand nine hundred and sixty-three.

APPENDIX B

TREATY ON THE NON-PROLIFERATION OF NUCLEAR WEAPONS (1970)

Signed at Washington, London, and Moscow July 1, 1968
Entered into force March 5, 1970

The States concluding this Treaty, hereinafter referred to as the "Parties to the Treaty",

Considering the devastation that would be visited upon all mankind by a nuclear war and the consequent need to make every effort to avert the danger of such a war and to take measures to safeguard the security of peoples,

Believing that the proliferation of nuclear weapons would seriously enhance the danger of nuclear war,

In conformity with resolutions of the United Nations General Assembly calling for the conclusion of an agreement on the prevention of wider dissemination of nuclear weapons,

Undertaking to cooperate in facilitating the application of International Atomic Energy Agency safeguards on peaceful nuclear activities,

Expressing their support for research, development and other efforts to further the application, within the framework of the International Atomic Energy Agency safeguards system, of the principle of safeguarding effectively the flow of source and special fissionable materials by use of instruments and other techniques at certain strategic points,

Affirming the principle that the benefits of peaceful applications of nuclear technology, including any technological by-products which may be derived by nuclear-weapon States from the development of nuclear explosive devices, should be available for peaceful purposes to all Parties of the Treaty, whether nuclear-weapon or non-nuclear weapon States,

Convinced that, in furtherance of this principle, all Parties to the Treaty are entitled to participate in the fullest possible exchange of scientific information for, and to contribute alone or in cooperation with other States to, the further development of the applications of atomic energy for peaceful purposes,

Declaring their intention to achieve at the earliest possible date the cessation of the nuclear arms race and to undertake effective measures in the direction of nuclear disarmament,

Urging the cooperation of all States in the attainment of this objective,

Recalling the determination expressed by the Parties to the 1963 Treaty banning nuclear weapon tests in the atmosphere, in outer space and under water in its Preamble to seek to achieve the discontinuance of all test explosions of nuclear weapons for all time and to continue negotiations to this end,

Desiring to further the easing of international tension and the strengthening of trust between States in order to facilitate the cessation of the manufacture of nuclear weapons, the liquidation of all their existing stockpiles, and the elimination from national arsenals of nuclear weapons and the means of their delivery pursuant to a Treaty on general and complete disarmament under strict and effective international control,

Recalling that, in accordance with the Charter of the United Nations, States must refrain in their international relations from the threat or use of force against the territorial integrity or political independence of any State, or in any other manner inconsistent with the Purposes of the United Nations, and that the establishment and maintenance of international peace and security are to be promoted with the least diversion for armaments of the worlds human and economic resources,

Have agreed as follows:

ARTICLE I

Each nuclear-weapon State Party to the Treaty undertakes not to transfer to any recipient whatsoever nuclear weapons or other nuclear explosive devices or control over such weapons or explosive devices directly, or indirectly; and not in any way to assist, encourage, or induce any non-nuclear weapon State to manufacture or otherwise acquire nuclear weapons or other nuclear explosive devices, or control over such weapons or explosive devices.

ARTICLE II

Each non-nuclear-weapon State Party to the Treaty undertakes not to receive the transfer from any transferor whatsoever of nuclear weapons or other nuclear explosive devices or of control over such weapons or explosive devices directly, or indirectly; not to manufacture or otherwise acquire nuclear weapons or other nuclear explosive devices; and not to seek or receive any assistance in the manufacture of nuclear weapons or other nuclear explosive devices.

ARTICLE III

1. Each non-nuclear-weapon State Party to the Treaty undertakes to accept safeguards, as set forth in an agreement to be negotiated and concluded with the International Atomic Energy Agency in accordance with the Statute of the International Atomic Energy Agency and the Agencys safeguards system, for the exclusive purpose of verification of the fulfillment of its obligations assumed under this Treaty with a view to preventing diversion of nuclear energy from peaceful uses to nuclear weapons or other nuclear explosive devices. Procedures for the safeguards required by this article shall be followed with respect to source or special fissionable material whether it is being produced, processed or used in any principal nuclear facility or is outside any such facility. The safeguards required by this article shall be applied to all source or special fissionable material in all peaceful nuclear activities within the territory of such State, under its jurisdiction, or carried out under its control anywhere.

2. Each State Party to the Treaty undertakes not to provide: (a) source or special fissionable material, or (b) equipment or material especially designed or prepared for the processing, use or production of special fissionable material, to any non-nuclear-weapon State for peaceful purposes, unless the source or special fissionable material shall be subject to the safeguards required by this article.

3. The safeguards required by this article shall be implemented in a manner designed to comply with article IV of this Treaty, and to avoid hampering the economic or technological development of the Parties or international cooperation in the field of peaceful nuclear activities, including the international exchange of nuclear material and equipment for the processing, use or production of nuclear material for peaceful purposes in accordance with the provisions of this article and the principle of safeguarding set forth in the Preamble of the Treaty.

4. Non-nuclear-weapon States Party to the Treaty shall conclude agreements with the International Atomic Energy Agency to meet the requirements of this article either individually or together with other States in accordance with the Statute of the International Atomic Energy Agency. Negotiation of such agreements shall commence within 180 days from the original entry into force of this Treaty. For States depositing their instruments of ratification or accession after the 180-day period, negotiation of such agreements shall commence not later than the date of such deposit. Such agreements shall enter into force not later than eighteen months after the date of initiation of negotiations.

ARTICLE IV

1. Nothing in this Treaty shall be interpreted as affecting the inalienable right of all the Parties to the Treaty to develop research, production and use of nuclear energy for peaceful purposes without discrimination and in conformity with articles I and II of this Treaty.

2. All the Parties to the Treaty undertake to facilitate, and have the right to participate in, the fullest possible exchange of equipment, materials and scientific and technological information for the peaceful uses of nuclear energy. Parties to the Treaty in a position to do so shall also cooperate in contributing alone or together with other States or international organizations to the further development of the applications of nuclear energy for peaceful purposes, especially in the territories of non-nuclear-weapon States Party to the Treaty, with due consideration for the needs of the developing areas of the world.

ARTICLE V

Each party to the Treaty undertakes to take appropriate measures to ensure that, in accordance with this Treaty, under appropriate international observation and through appropriate international procedures, potential benefits from any peaceful applications of nuclear explosions will be made available to non-nuclear-weapon States Party to the Treaty on a nondiscriminatory basis and that the charge to such Parties for the explosive devices used will be as low as possible and exclude any charge for research and development. Non-nuclear-weapon States Party to the Treaty shall be able to obtain such benefits, pursuant to a special international agreement or agreements, through an appropriate international body with adequate representation of non-nuclear-weapon States. Negotiations on this subject shall commence as soon as possible after the Treaty enters into force. Non-nuclear-weapon States Party to the Treaty so desiring may also obtain such benefits pursuant to bilateral agreements.

ARTICLE VI

Each of the Parties to the Treaty undertakes to pursue negotiations in good faith on effective measures relating to cessation of the nuclear arms race at an early date and to nuclear disarmament, and on a Treaty on general and complete disarmament under strict and effective international control.

ARTICLE VII

Nothing in this Treaty affects the right of any group of States to conclude regional treaties in order to assure the total absence of nuclear weapons in their respective territories.

ARTICLE VIII

1. Any Party to the Treaty may propose amendments to this Treaty. The text of any proposed amendment shall be submitted to the Depositary Governments which shall circulate it to all Parties to the Treaty. Thereupon, if requested to do so by one-third or more of the Parties to the Treaty, the Depositary Governments shall convene a conference, to which they shall invite all the Parties to the Treaty, to consider such an amendment.

2. Any amendment to this Treaty must be approved by a majority of the votes of all the Parties to the Treaty, including the votes of all nuclear-weapon States Party to the Treaty and all other Parties which, on the date the amendment is circulated, are members of the Board of Governors of the International Atomic Energy Agency. The amendment shall enter into force for each Party that deposits its instrument of ratification of the amendment upon the deposit of such instruments of ratification by a majority of all the Parties, including the instruments of ratification of all nuclear-weapon States Party to the Treaty and all other Parties which, on the date the amendment is circulated, are members of the Board of Governors of the International Atomic Energy Agency. Thereafter, it shall enter into force for any other Party upon the deposit of its instrument of ratification of the amendment.

3. Five years after the entry into force of this Treaty, a conference of Parties to the Treaty shall be held in Geneva, Switzerland, in order to review the operation of this Treaty with a view to assuring that the purposes of the Preamble and the provisions of the Treaty are being realized. At intervals of five years thereafter, a majority of the Parties to the Treaty may obtain, by submitting a proposal to this effect to the Depositary Governments, the convening of further conferences with the same objective of reviewing the operation of the Treaty.

ARTICLE IX

1. This Treaty shall be open to all States for signature. Any State which does not sign the Treaty before its entry into force in accordance with paragraph 3 of this article may accede to it at any time.

2. This Treaty shall be subject to ratification by signatory States. Instruments of ratification and instruments of accession shall be deposited with the Governments of the United States of America, the United Kingdom of Great Britain and Northern Ireland and the Union of Soviet Socialist Republics, which are hereby designated the Depositary Governments.

3. This Treaty shall enter into force after its ratification by the States, the Governments of which are designated Depositaries of the Treaty, and forty other States signatory to this Treaty and the deposit of their instruments of ratifica-

tion. For the purposes of this Treaty, a nuclear-weapon State is one which has manufactured and exploded a nuclear weapon or other nuclear explosive device prior to January 1, 1967.

4. For States whose instruments of ratification or accession are deposited subsequent to the entry into force of this Treaty, it shall enter into force on the date of the deposit of their instruments of ratification or accession.

5. The Depositary Governments shall promptly inform all signatory and acceding States of the date of each signature, the date of deposit of each instrument of ratification or of accession, the date of the entry into force of this Treaty, and the date of receipt of any requests for convening a conference or other notices.

6. This Treaty shall be registered by the Depositary Governments pursuant to article 102 of the Charter of the United Nations.

ARTICLE X

1. Each Party shall in exercising its national sovereignty have the right to withdraw from the Treaty if it decides that extraordinary events, related to the subject matter of this Treaty, have jeopardized the supreme interests of its country. It shall give notice of such withdrawal to all other Parties to the Treaty and to the United Nations Security Council three months in advance. Such notice shall include a statement of the extraordinary events it regards as having jeopardized its supreme interests.

2. Twenty-five years after the entry into force of the Treaty, a conference shall be convened to decide whether the Treaty shall continue in force indefinitely, or shall be extended for an additional fixed period or periods. This decision shall be taken by a majority of the Parties to the Treaty.

ARTICLE XI

This Treaty, the English, Russian, French, Spanish and Chinese texts of which are equally authentic, shall be deposited in the archives of the Depositary Governments. Duly certified copies of this Treaty shall be transmitted by the Depositary Governments to the Governments of the signatory and acceding States.

IN WITNESS WHEREOF the undersigned, duly authorized, have signed this Treaty.

DONE in triplicate, at the cities of Washington, London and Moscow, this first day of July one thousand nine hundred sixty-eight.

APPENDIX C

Convention on the Prohibition of the Development, Production, and Stockpiling of Bacteriological (Biological) and Toxin Weapons and on Their Destruction (1975)

Signed at Washington, London, and Moscow April 10, 1972

Entered into force March 26, 1975

The States Parties to this Convention,

Determined to act with a view to achieving effective progress towards general and complete disarmament, including the prohibition and elimination of all types of weapons of mass destruction, and convinced that the prohibition of the development, production and stockpiling of chemical and bacteriological (biological) weapons and their elimination, through effective measures, will facilitate the achievement of general and complete disarmament under strict and effective international control,

Recognizing the important significance of the Protocol for the Prohibition of the Use in War of Asphyxiating, Poisonous or Other Gases, and of Bacteriological Methods of Warfare, signed at Geneva on June 17, 1925, and conscious also of the contribution which the said Protocol has already made, and continues to make, to mitigating the horrors of war,

Reaffirming their adherence to the principles and objectives of that Protocol and calling upon all States to comply strictly with them,

Recalling that the General Assembly of the United Nations has repeatedly condemned all actions contrary to the principles and objectives of the Geneva Protocol of June 17, 1925,

Desiring to contribute to the strengthening of confidence between peoples and the general improvement of the international atmosphere,

Desiring also to contribute to the realization of the purposes and principles of the Charter of the United Nations,

Convinced of the importance and urgency of eliminating from the arsenals of States, through effective measures, such dangerous weapons of mass destruction as those using chemical or bacteriological (biological) agents,

Recognizing that an agreement on the prohibition of bacteriological (biological) and toxin weapons represents a first possible step towards the achievement of agreement on effective measures also for the prohibition of the development, production and stockpiling of chemical weapons, and determined to continue negotiations to that end,

Determined, for the sake of all mankind, to exclude completely the possibility of bacteriological (biological) agents and toxins being used as weapons,

Convinced that such use would be repugnant to the conscience of mankind and that no effort should be spared to minimize this risk,

Have agreed as follows:

ARTICLE I

Each State Party to this Convention undertakes never in any circumstances to develop, produce, stockpile or otherwise acquire or retain:

(1) Microbial or other biological agents, or toxins whatever their origin or method of production, of types and in quantities that have no justification for prophylactic, protective or other peaceful purposes;

(2) Weapons, equipment or means of delivery designed to use such agents or toxins for hostile purposes or in armed conflict.

ARTICLE II

Each State Party to this Convention undertakes to destroy, or to divert to peaceful purposes, as soon as possible but not later than nine months after the entry into force of the Convention, all agents, toxins, weapons, equipment and means of delivery specified in article I of the Convention, which are in its possession or under its jurisdiction or control. In implementing the provisions of this article all necessary safety precautions shall be observed to protect populations and the environment.

ARTICLE III

Each State Party to this Convention undertakes not to transfer to any recipient whatsoever, directly or indirectly, and not in any way to assist, encourage, or induce any State, group of States or international organizations to manufacture or otherwise acquire any of the agents, toxins, weapons, equipment or means of delivery specified in article I of the Convention.

ARTICLE IV

Each State Party to this Convention shall, in accordance with its constitutional processes, take any necessary measures to prohibit and prevent the development, production, stockpiling, acquisition, or retention of the agents, toxins, weapons, equipment and means of delivery specified in article I of the Convention, within the territory of such State, under its jurisdiction or under its control anywhere.

ARTICLE V

The States Parties to this Convention undertake to consult one another and to cooperate in solving any problems which may arise in relation to the objective of, or in the application of the provisions of, the Convention. Consultation and cooperation pursuant to this article may also be undertaken through appropriate international procedures within the framework of the United Nations and in accordance with its Charter.

ARTICLE VI

(1) Any State Party to this Convention which finds that any other State Party is acting in breach of obligations deriving from the provisions of the Convention may lodge a complaint with the Security Council of the United Nations. Such a complaint should include all possible evidence confirming its validity, as well as a request for its consideration by the Security Council.

(2) Each State Party to this Convention undertakes to cooperate in carrying out any investigation which the Security Council may initiate, in accordance with the provisions of the Charter of the United Nations, on the basis of the complaint received by the Council. The Security Council shall inform the States Parties to the Convention of the results of the investigation.

ARTICLE VII

Each State Party to this Convention undertakes to provide or support assistance, in accordance with the United Nations Charter, to any Party to the Convention which so requests, if the Security Council decides that such Party has been exposed to danger as a result of violation of the Convention.

ARTICLE VIII

Nothing in this Convention shall be interpreted as in any way limiting or detracting from the obligations assumed by any State under the Protocol for the Prohibition of the Use in War of Asphyxiating, Poisonous or Other Gases, and of Bacteriological Methods of Warfare, signed at Geneva on June 17, 1925.

ARTICLE IX

Each State Party to this Convention affirms the recognized objective of effective prohibition of chemical weapons and, to this end, undertakes to continue negotiations in good faith with a view to reaching early agreement on effective measures for the prohibition of their development, production and stockpiling and for their destruction, and on appropriate measures concerning equipment and means of delivery specifically designed for the production or use of chemical agents for weapons purposes.

ARTICLE X

(1) The States Parties to this Convention undertake to facilitate, and have the right to participate in, the fullest possible exchange of equipment, materials and scientific and technological information for the use of bacteriological (biological) agents and toxins for peaceful purposes. Parties to the Convention in a position to do so shall also cooperate in contributing individually or together with other States or international organizations to the further development and application of scientific discoveries in the field of bacteriology (biology) for prevention of disease, or for other peaceful purposes.

(2) This Convention shall be implemented in a manner designed to avoid hampering the economic or technological development of States Parties to the

Convention or international cooperation in the field of peaceful bacteriological (biological) activities, including the international exchange of bacteriological (biological) agents and toxins and equipment for the processing, use or production of bacteriological (biological) agents and toxins for peaceful purposes in accordance with the provisions of the Convention.

ARTICLE XI

Any State Party may propose amendments to this Convention. Amendments shall enter into force for each State Party accepting the amendments upon their acceptance by a majority of the States Parties to the Convention and thereafter for each remaining State Party on the date of acceptance by it.

ARTICLE XII

Five years after the entry into force of this Convention, or earlier if it is requested by a majority of Parties to the Convention by submitting a proposal to this effect to the Depositary Governments, a conference of States Parties to the Convention shall be held at Geneva, Switzerland, to review the operation of the Convention, with a view to assuring that the purposes of the preamble and the provisions of the Convention, including the provisions concerning negotiations on chemical weapons, are being realized. Such review shall take into account any new scientific and technological developments relevant to the Convention.

ARTICLE XIII

(1) This Convention shall be of unlimited duration.

(2) Each State Party to this Convention shall in exercising its national sovereignty have the right to withdraw from the Convention if it decides that extraordinary events, related to the subject matter of the Convention, have jeopardized the supreme interests of its country. It shall give notice of such withdrawal to all other States Parties to the Convention and to the United Nations Security Council three months in advance. Such notice shall include a statement of the extraordinary events it regards as having jeopardized its supreme interests.

ARTICLE XIV

(1) This Convention shall be open to all States for signature. Any State which does not sign the Convention before its entry into force in accordance with paragraph (3) of this Article may accede to it at any time.

(2) This Convention shall be subject to ratification by signatory States. Instruments of ratification and instruments of accession shall be deposited with the Governments of the United States of America, the United Kingdom of Great Britain and Northern Ireland and the Union of Soviet Socialist Republics, which are hereby designated the Depositary Governments.

(3) This Convention shall enter into force after the deposit of instruments of ratification by twenty-two Governments, including the Governments designated as Depositaries of the Convention.

(4) For States whose instruments of ratification or accession are deposited subsequent to the entry into force of this Convention, it shall enter into force on the date of the deposit of their instruments of ratification or accession.

(5) The Depositary Governments shall promptly inform all signatory and acceding States of the date of each signature, the date of deposit of each instrument of ratification or of accession and the date of the entry into force of this Convention, and of the receipt of other notices.

(6) This Convention shall be registered by the Depositary Governments pursuant to Article 102 of the Charter of the United Nations.

ARTICLE XV

This Convention, the English, Russian, French, Spanish and Chinese texts of which are equally authentic, shall be deposited in the archives of the Depositary Governments. Duly certified copies of the Convention shall be transmitted by the Depositary Governments to the Governments of the signatory and acceding states.

IN WITNESS WHEREOF the undersigned, duly authorized, have signed this Convention.

DONE in triplicate, at the cities of Washington, London and Moscow, this tenth day of April, one thousand nine hundred and seventy-two.

APPENDIX D

COMPREHENSIVE TEST BAN TREATY (1996): A SUMMARY

The Comprehensive Test Ban Treaty (CTBT) was opened for signature September 24, 1996. President Clinton signed the treaty, but the United States has not ratified it. The treaty is not yet in force.

The Comprehensive Test Ban Treaty (CTBT) will prohibit all nuclear weapon test explosions or other nuclear explosions anywhere in the world. In order to verify compliance with its provisions, the treaty establishes a global network of monitoring facilities and allows for on-site inspections of suspicious events. The overall accord contains a preamble, 17 treaty articles, two treaty annexes, and a protocol with two annexes detailing verification procedures.

PREAMBLE

The preamble, which lists disarmament principles and objectives, sets the overall political context of the treaty. In particular, it stresses the need for the continued reduction of nuclear weapons worldwide with the ultimate goal of their elimination. Also of significance, the preamble recognizes that a CTB will constitute an effective measure of nuclear disarmament and non-proliferation by "constraining the development and qualitative improvement of nuclear weapons and ending the development of advanced new types of nuclear weapons." It further recognizes that a test ban will constitute "a meaningful step in the realization of a systematic process to achieve nuclear disarmament."

SCOPE

Article I establishes that all states-parties are prohibited from conducting "any nuclear weapon test explosion or any other nuclear explosion" on the basis of the negotiating record this is understood to include all nuclear explosions with yields greater than zero, in accordance with President Bill Clinton's August 1995 proposal.

Appendix D

IMPLEMENTING ORGANIZATION

Article II establishes the Comprehensive Nuclear Test Ban Treaty Organization, which will ensure treaty implementation and provide states-parties with a forum for consultation and cooperation. The organization will consist of a Conference of the States Parties, an Executive Council, and a Technical Secretariat. The organization—to be located in Vienna—will be structurally independent from, but operating in collaboration with, the International Atomic Energy Agency (IAEA). The Conference of the States Parties—the overall governing body of the organization—will handle treaty-related policy issues and oversee the treaty's implementation, including the activities of the Executive Council and the Technical Secretariat. The conference will meet once a year, unless otherwise decided. The Executive Council, which will meet regularly and act as the treaty's principal decision-making body, will consist of 51 members. In an attempt to distribute membership evenly throughout the world, the Executive Council will comprise 10 states-parties from Africa; seven from Eastern Europe; nine from Latin America and the Caribbean; seven from the Middle East and South Asia; 10 from North America and Western Europe; and eight from Southeast Asia, the Pacific and the Far East. The states in each of these geographical regions are listed in Annex 1 to the treaty.

The members of the council will be elected by the conference. In order to ensure that [signatories] are adequately represented in the council, at least one-third of the seats allotted to each region will be filled by states-parties on the basis of their nuclear capabilities applicable to the treaty such as the number of monitoring facilities they contribute to the **International Monitoring System (IMS).** One seat allocated to each region will be designated on an alphabetical basis and the remaining seats will be determined by rotation or elections. Thus, each state-party will eventually have the right to serve on the council. The Technical Secretariat will be the primary body responsible for implementing the treaty's verification procedures. In this capacity it will supervise the operation of the IMS and receive, process, analyze and report on the system's data. It will also manage the **International Data Center (IDC)** and perform a series of procedural tasks related to conducting on-site inspections. Article III requires each state-party, in accordance with its constitutional process, to take any necessary measures to implement its treaty obligations.

VERIFICATION AND COMPLIANCE

Article IV and the verification protocol establish the treaty's verification regime which will consist of four basic elements: the IMS, consultation and clarification, on-site inspections and confidence building measures. The verification regime will not be completely operational until the treaty enters into force. For instance, on-site inspections cannot be authorized until the treaty formally comes into effect.

The purpose of the IMS is to detect and identify nuclear explosions prohibited under Article I. The monitoring system will comprise a network of 50 primary and 120 auxiliary seismological monitoring stations designed to detect seismic activity and distinguish between natural events, such as earthquakes, and nuclear explosions. In addition, the system will incorporate 80 radionuclide stations and 16 radionuclide laboratories that seek to identify radioactive particles released during a nuclear explosion. The IMS will also include 60 infrasound (acoustic) and 11 hydroacoustic stations designed to pick up the sound of a nuclear explosion conducted in the atmosphere or under water, respectively. The host state and location of each facility is listed in Annex 1 to the protocol.

Information collected by the IMS will then be transmitted to the IDC—an essential part of the Technical Secretariat responsible for data storage and processing. Because the IMS will generate an enormous amount of raw data, the IDC will regularly provide states-parties with a number of services designed to help them monitor compliance with the treaty's provisions. In this regard, the data center will produce integrated lists of all signals picked up by the IMS, as well as standard event lists and bulletins. In accordance with the parameters outlined in Annex 2 to the protocol, the center will also generate standard screened event bulletins that filter out those events that appear to be of a non-nuclear nature. However, notwithstanding this analysis role, the IDC must make both the raw and processed information available to all states-parties.

The consultation and clarification component of the verification regime encourages states-parties to attempt to resolve, either among themselves or through the organization, possible instances of non-compliance before requesting an on-site inspection. A state-party must provide clarification of an ambiguous event within 48 hours of receiving such a request from another state-party or the Executive Council.

If a suspicious occurrence cannot be resolved through consultation and clarification, each state-party has the right to request an on-site inspection in the territory of the party in question. The inspection request must be based on information collected by the IMS; data obtained through national technical means (NTM) of verification, such as satellites, in a manner consistent with international law (for example, not based on espionage); or a combination of IMS and NTM information. The request must contain the approximate geographical coordinates and the estimated depth of the ambiguous event, the proposed boundaries of the area to be inspected (not to exceed 1,000 square kilometers), the state- party or parties to be inspected, the probable environment and estimated time of the event, all evidence upon which the request is based, the identity of the proposed observer (if available) and the results of the consultation and clarification process.

The Executive Council will make a decision on the on-site inspection request within 96 hours of its receipt from the requesting state-party. The inspection will be authorized to proceed if it has been approved by at least 30 of the council's 51 members, the so called "green light" procedure.

An inspection team will arrive at the point of entry within six days of the council's receipt of the inspection request. During the course of the inspection, the inspection team may submit a proposal to begin drilling, which must be approved by 26 council members. The duration of the inspection must not exceed 60 days, but may be extended by a maximum of 70 additional days (subject to council approval) if the inspection team determines that more time is needed to fulfill its mandate.

If the Executive Council rejects an on-site inspection request (or terminates an inspection already underway) because it is of a frivolous or abusive nature, the council may impose punitive measures on the requesting state-party. In this regard, it may require the requesting state-party to provide financial compensation for preparations made by the Technical Secretariat and may suspend that party's right to request an inspection and serve on the council for an unspecified period of time.

The verification regime also incorporates confidence building measures intended to promote treaty compliance. In order to reduce the likelihood that verification data may be misconstrued, each state-party will voluntarily provide the Technical Secretariat with notification of any chemical explosion involving a magnitude of 300 tons or more of TNT-equivalent on its territory. Each state-party may also assist the Technical Secretariat in the calibration of IMS stations.

In order to ensure compliance with the treaty's provisions, Article V empowers the conference to revoke a state-party's rights under the treaty, recommend to the states-parties punitive measures such as sanctions, or bring the case to the attention of the United Nations. Article VI describes the mechanisms by which disputes pertaining to the application or interpretation of the treaty may be settled.

AMENDMENT PROCESS

Under Article VII, each state-party has the right to propose amendments to the treaty after its entry into force. The proposed amendment requires the approval of a simple majority of states-parties at an amendment conference with no party casting a negative vote.

PEACEFUL NUCLEAR EXPLOSIONS

Under Article VIII, a conference will be held 10 years after the treaty's EIF to review the implementation of its provisions, including the preamble. At this review conference, any state-party may request that the issue of so called "peaceful nuclear explosions" (PNE) be put on the agenda. However, the presumption is that PNEs remain prohibited unless certain virtually insurmountable obstacles are overcome. First, the review conference must decide without objection that PNEs may be permitted, then an amendment to the treaty must also be approved without objection at a separate amendment conference, as explained above. This "double hurdle" makes it extremely unlikely that peaceful nuclear explosions will ever be permitted under the treaty.

DURATION AND WITHDRAWAL

Under Article IX, the CTBT will be of unlimited duration. In addition, each state-party has the right to withdraw from the treaty if it decides that "extraordinary events related to the subject matter of this Treaty have jeopardized its supreme interests." Notice of intent to withdraw must be given at least six months in advance.

MISCELLANEOUS PROVISIONS

Article X specifies that the treaty's annexes, protocol and annexes to the protocol are a formal part of the treaty. Article XI declares that the treaty is open to all states for signature prior to its entry into force. Article XII maintains that each signatory state will ratify the treaty according to its own constitutional procedures. Under Article XIII, any state that has not signed the treaty prior to its entry into force may accede to it any time thereafter.

ENTRY INTO FORCE

Under Article XIV, the treaty will not enter into force until it has been signed and ratified by 44 states—including the five nuclear-weapon states (United States, Russia, Britain, France and China) and the three "threshold states" (India, Israel and Pakistan)—listed by name in Annex 2 to the treaty. (Actual EIF will occur 180 days after all 44 states deposit their instruments of ratification with the UN secretary-general.) The 44 states, all of which are participating members of the recently expanded Conference on Disarmament, possess nuclear power and research reactors as determined by the IAEA.

If the treaty has not come into effect "three years after the date of the anniversary of its opening for signature," then a conference may be held for those states that have already deposited their instruments of ratification to "decide by consensus what measures consistent with international law may be undertaken to accelerate the ratification process". However, this conference—to be repeated annually until the treaty's entry into force—will not have the authority to waive the original provision requiring ratification by the 44 states.

OTHER PROVISIONS

Article XV stipulates that the treaty's provisions will not be subject to reservations.

Article XVI establishes the UN secretary-general as the depository of the treaty. Under Article XVII, the treaty will be authentic in six languages.

Source: This summary appeared in the August 1996 issue of *Arms Control Today*.

APPENDIX E

THE CHEMICAL WEAPONS CONVENTION (1997): A SYNOPSIS OF THE TEXT

The Chemical Weapons Convention was signed by 130 countries January 12, 1993. It went into force April 29, 1997

The Preamble states the intent of the States Parties to prohibit and eliminate all types of weapons of mass destruction. It recalls the 1925 Geneva Protocol (prohibiting the use of chemical and biological weapons in war) and the 1972 Biological and Toxin Weapons Convention (outlawing biological and toxin weapons and requiring their destruction), both of which are multilateral instruments pertinent to the Convention. The Preamble also recognizes the prohibition, embodied in agreements and relevant principles of international law, of the use of herbicides as a method of warfare, and expresses the desire of States Parties to enhance their economic and technological development for peaceful purposes.

THE ARTICLES

Article I (General Obligations) prohibits the development, production, acquisition, retention, stockpiling, transfer and use of chemical weapons. It requires each State Party to destroy chemical weapons and chemical weapons production facilities (CWPFs) under its jurisdiction or control, as well as any chemical weapons it abandoned on the territory of other States Parties. All States Parties are prohibited from engaging in military preparations to use chemical weapons, from assisting or encouraging other states to engage in activities prohibited by the Chemical Weapons Convention (CWC) and from using riot control agents such as tear gas "as a method of warfare."

Article II (Definitions and Criteria) defines terms critical to the CWC. "Chemical weapons," defined in three parts, are identified first as all toxic chemicals and their precursors, except those intended for purposes allowed by the

CWC. Such purposes include peaceful uses, protection against toxic chemicals, military purposes not related to the use of toxic chemicals as a method of warfare, and law enforcement. Second, the definition includes munitions and devices specially designed to release these toxic chemicals. Third, it refers to any equipment specifically designed for use with such munitions or devices. "Toxic chemicals" are defined as chemicals which through chemical action on life processes cause death, temporary incapacitation or permanent harm to humans or animals. "Old chemical weapons" are those chemical weapons produced before 1925 or those produced between 1925 and 1946 that have deteriorated to the extent that they are unusable. "Abandoned chemical weapons" are those left by one State Party on the territory of another State Party without its consent at any time after 1 January 1925. "Chemical weapons production facility" covers, with three exceptions, all buildings or equipment designed, constructed or used since 1 January 1946 to produce or fill chemical weapons. Riot control agents are chemicals not listed in the Convention's Annex on Chemicals that rapidly produce in humans sensory irritation or disabling effects which disappear shortly after exposure.

Under Article III (Declarations) each State Party shall, not later than 30 days after the Convention enters into force for it, submit to the OPCW detailed declarations with respect to chemical weapons (including old and abandoned chemical weapons) and CWPFs, providing a general plan for their destruction. States Parties are also required to declare facilities used in the past for CW development, and chemicals held for riot control purposes.

Article IV (Chemical Weapons) and Article V (Chemical Weapons Production Facilities), together with the Annex on Implementation and Verification (or Verification Annex), contain detailed provisions regarding the destruction of chemical weapons and CWPFs and the verification of such destruction. Weapons and facilities must be completely destroyed within 10 years of the entry into force of the Convention, i.e. by 29 April 2007. Under extraordinary circumstances, the final deadline for the destruction of chemical weapons may be extended up to five additional years, if approved by the States Parties. In exceptional cases, CWPFs may be converted for peaceful purposes, with the approval of the OPCW. Each State Party must also pay for OPCW verification of destruction of its own chemical weapons and CWPFs.

Article VI (Activities Not Prohibited under the Convention), along with the Verification Annex, describes the comprehensive regime for routine monitoring of chemical industry through declarations and on-site inspections. Due to the possible commercial application of many toxic chemicals and precursors, the CWC categorises them into three Schedules. The declaration and inspection requirements for each Schedule vary depending on the risk its chemicals pose to the object and purpose of the Convention. Inspections of facilities which produce unscheduled discrete organic chemicals began in May 2000. Declaration and inspection requirements apply to chemical industry facilities if the amounts of chemicals handled by them exceed the relevant thresholds specified in the Convention.

Appendix E

Article VII (National Implementation Measures) deals with measures and legislation that States Parties must enact in order to ensure national implementation of the CWC and the establishment or designation of National Authorities to serve as contact points for the OPCW.

Article VIII (The Organisation) provides for the establishment of the OPCW with its headquarters in The Hague. Each State Party is automatically a member of the OPCW and cannot be deprived of membership. The OPCW consists of three principal organs. The Conference of the States Parties is its highest decision-making body, with one regular session convened annually, and special sessions when necessary. The Executive Council, composed of representatives of 41 States Parties from five regional groups, supervises the activities of the Secretariat and is responsible to the Conference. The Secretariat carries out the practical work of the Organisation. The largest portion of the Secretariat's resources is devoted to verification activities. The Director-General is appointed by the Conference and is responsible to it and the Council, inter alia, for the work of the Secretariat.

Article IX (Consultations, Cooperation and Fact-Finding), together with the Verification Annex, provides for short-notice challenge inspections by the OPCW upon request from a State Party of any facility or location on the territory, or anywhere under the jurisdiction, of any other State Party, to clarify and resolve questions regarding possible noncompliance. A State Party cannot refuse a challenge inspection, but may provide "managed access," using measures to protect sensitive installations and information unrelated to chemical weapons. Article IX also provides for consultation and clarification if concerns about possible noncompliance arise.

Article X (Assistance and Protection against Chemical Weapons) permits States Parties to conduct research into protection against chemical weapons. States Parties commit to the fullest possible exchange of equipment, material and information concerning protection. In addition, each State Party is to make resources available to the OPCW for use in assisting States Parties attacked or threatened by attack with chemical weapons. This may be done in at least one of three ways: by contributing to the Voluntary Fund for Assistance, by concluding an agreement with the OPCW concerning the procurement of assistance, or by declaring the kind of assistance it might provide. Article X mandates that the OPCW maintain a data bank of open-source information on protection against chemical weapons. Along with the Verification Annex, it also outlines the procedures for investigations of alleged use. States Parties (and only States Parties) can trigger investigations of alleged use of chemical weapons by requesting assistance under Article X, just as they can by requesting a challenge inspection under Article IX.

Article XI (Economic and Technological Development) encourages the fullest possible exchange of chemicals, equipment and scientific and technological information relating to the development and application of chemistry for peaceful purposes. States Parties must review their existing national regulations on trade in chemicals to ensure they are consistent with the object and purpose of the Convention.

Article XII (Measures of Redress to Ensure Compliance, Including Sanctions) states that the Conference may impose, in a manner consistent with information provided to it by the Executive Council, measures of redress or penalties against a State Party that fails to uphold its treaty obligations. The conference may, upon the Council's recommendation, invoke sanctions or restrict or suspend a State Party's rights and privileges. The Conference shall bring cases of particular gravity to the attention of the United Nations General Assembly and the Security Council.

Article XIII (Relation to Other International Agreements) states that the CWC does not limit or detract from any State's obligations under the 1925 Geneva Protocol or the Biological and Toxin Weapons Convention.

Article XIV (Settlement of Disputes) allows for the settlement of disputes concerning the application or interpretation of the CWC. When a dispute arises between States Parties, or between any State Party and the OPCW, the parties involved commit to consult together to resolve differences quickly and peacefully. The parties may enlist the aid of the Executive Council, the Conference or the International Court of Justice.

Article XV (Amendments) states that the articles and annexes of the Convention can be amended by an Amendment Conference. Such a conference shall be convened if at least one-third of all States Parties notify the Director-General within 30 days of a proposed amendment's circulation that they wish to give it further consideration.

Article XVI (Duration and Withdrawal) declares that the CWC is of unlimited duration. A State Party can withdraw from the CWC only if it decides its supreme interests have been jeopardized by extraordinary events. A withdrawing state must provide advance notice of 90 days to the OPCW, the UN Secretary-General and Security Council, explaining how the said events have jeopardised these interests.

Article XVII (Status of the Annexes) stipulates that the annexes are an integral part of the CWC.

Article XVIII (Signature) states that the CWC is open for signature before its entry into force.

Article XIX (Ratification) notes that signatories to the Convention shall ratify it according to their respective constitutional processes.

Article XX (Accession) allows States that did not sign the CWC before its entry into force to accede to it at any time thereafter.

Article XXI (Entry into Force) declares that the CWC will enter into force 180 days after the deposit of the 65th instrument of ratification. For States which deposit their instrument of ratification or accession after entry into force, the Convention enters into force 30 days after their instrument is deposited.

Article XXII (Reservations) states that the articles shall not be subject to reservations and that the annexes shall not be subject to reservations incompatible with the CWC's object and purpose.

Article XXIII (Depositary) designates the UN Secretary-General as the person who receives all instruments of ratification or accession.

Appendix E

Article XXIV (Authentic Texts) stipulates that the Arabic, Chinese, English, French, Russian and Spanish texts of the CWC are equally authentic.

THE ANNEXES

The Annex on Chemicals contains three Schedules, or lists, of toxic chemicals and their precursors. The chemicals listed in each of the Schedules are subject to different levels of verification activity. Guidelines for amending the Schedules are also provided.

The Annex on Implementation and Verification (the Verification Annex) contains eleven parts pertaining to the destruction of chemical weapons and CWPFs, and verification procedures for chemical weapons, CWPFs and chemical industry facilities. It also includes measures for challenge inspections and investigations of alleged use and restrictions on trade in scheduled chemicals with States not party to the CWC.

The Annex on Protection of Confidential Information (the Confidentiality Annex) articulates the principles for the handling of confidential information and for the employment and conduct of OPCW staff members. It also describes procedures and measures to ensure the confidentiality of sensitive information and installations in the course of inspections and outlines procedures to be followed in the event of a breach of confidentiality.

Source: The synopsis here has been published in Fact Sheet 2 of the Organization for the Prohibition of Chemical Weapons. It was produced by the External Relations Division of the Organization for the Prohibition of Chemical Weapons in collaboration with the Monterey Institute of International Studies Center for Nonproliferation Studies and the Harvard Sussex Program on CBW Armament and Arms Limitation.

APPENDIX F

A LIST OF BIOTERRORISM AGENTS/DISEASES, 2005

Category A (definition below):
- Anthrax *(Bacillus anthracis)*
- Botulism *(Clostridium botulinum toxin)*
- Plague *(Yersinia pestis)*
- Smallpox (variola major)
- Tularemia *(Francisella tularensis)*
- Viral hemorrhagic fevers (filoviruses [e.g., Ebola, Marburg] and arenaviruses [e.g., Lassa, Machupo])

Category B (definition below):
- Brucellosis *(Brucella species)*
- Epsilon toxin of *Clostridium perfringens*
- Food safety threats (e.g., *Salmonella* species, *Escherichia coli* O157:H7, *Shigella*)
- Glanders *(Burkholderia mallei)*
- Melioidosis *(Burkholderia pseudomallei)*
- Psittacosis *(Chlamydia psittaci)*
- Q fever *(Coxiella burnetii)*
- Ricin toxin from *Ricinus communis* (castor beans)
- Staphylococcal enterotoxin B
- Typhus fever *(Rickettsia prowazekii)*
- Viral encephalitis (alphaviruses [e.g., Venezuelan equine encephalitis, eastern equine encephalitis, western equine encephalitis])
- Water safety threats (e.g., *Vibrio cholerae, Cryptosporidium parvum*)

Category C (definition below):
- Emerging infectious diseases such as Nipah virus and hantavirus

CATEGORY DEFINITIONS

Category A Diseases/Agents: The U.S. public health system and primary health-care providers must be prepared to address various biological agents, including pathogens that are rarely seen in the United States. High-priority agents include organisms that pose a risk to national security because they can be easily disseminated or transmitted from person to person; result in high mortality rates and have the potential for major public health impact; might cause public panic and social disruption; and require special action for public health preparedness.

Category B Diseases/Agents: Second-highest priority agents include those that are moderately easy to disseminate; result in moderate morbidity rates and low mortality rates; and require specific enhancements of the CDC's diagnostic capacity and enhanced disease surveillance.

Category C Diseases/Agents: Third-highest priority agents include emerging pathogens that could be engineered for mass dissemination in the future because of availability; ease of production and dissemination; and potential for high morbidity and mortality rates and major health impact.

Source: Bioterrorism Agents/Diseases posted by the Centers for Disease Control and prevention, under Emergency Preparedness and Response, at URL http://www.bt.cdc.gov/agent/agentlist-category.asp (updated November 19, 2004).

APPENDIX G

CHEMICAL AGENTS, 2005

The agents listed in this appendix are substances that have been used or have the potential to be used in warfare or acts of terrorism to kill, seriously injure, or incapacitate people.

Biotoxins
Poisons that come from plants or animals:
- Abrin
- Brevetoxin
- Colchicine
- Digitalis
- Nicotine
- Ricin
- Saxitoxin
- Strychnine
- Tetrodotoxin
- Trichothecene

Blister Agents/Vesicants
Chemicals that severely blister the eyes, respiratory tract, and skin on contact:
- Mustards
  - Distilled mustard (HD)
  - Mustard gas (H) (sulfur mustard, also called Yperite)
  - Mustard/lewisite (HL)
  - Mustard/T
  - Nitrogen Mustard (HN-1, HN-2, HN-3)
  - Sesqui mustard
- Lewisites/chloroarsine agents
  - Lewisite (L, L-1, L-2, L-3)
  - Mustard/lewisite (HL)
- Phosgene oxime (CX)

Blood Agents
Poisons that affect the body by being absorbed into the blood:
- Arsine (SA)

Carbon Monoxide
Cyanide
- Cyanogen chloride (CK)
- Hydrogen cyanide (AC, used by the Germans under the name Zyklon B)
- Potassium cyanide (KCN)
- Sodium cyanide (NaCN)

Sodium monofluoroacetate (compound 1080)

Caustics (Acids)

Chemicals that burn or corrode people's skin, eyes, and mucus membranes (lining of the nose, mouth, throat, and lungs) on contact:
- Hydrofluoric acid (hydrogen fluoride)

Choking/Lung/Pulmonary Agents

Chemicals that cause severe irritation or swelling of the respiratory tract (lining of the nose and throat, lungs):
- Ammonia
- Bromine (CA)
- Chlorine (CL)
- Hydrogen chloride
- Methyl bromide
- Methyl isocyanate
- Osmium tetroxide
- Phosgene
  - Diphosgene (DP)
  - Phosgene (CG)
- Phosphine
- Phosphorus, elemental, white or yellow
- Sulfuryl fluoride

Incapacitating Agents

Drugs that make people unable to think clearly or that cause an altered state of consciousness (possibly unconsciousness):
- BZ
- Fentanyls and other opioids

Long-Acting Anticoagulants

Poisons that prevent blood from clotting properly, which can lead to uncontrolled bleeding:
- Super warfarin

Metals

Agents that consist of metallic poisons:
- Arsenic
- Barium
- Mercury
- Thallium

Nerve Agents

Highly poisonous chemicals that work by preventing the nervous system from working properly:

- G agents
  - Sarin (GB)
  - Soman (GD)
  - Tabun (GA)
- V agents
  - VX

Organic Solvents

Agents that damage the tissues of living things by dissolving fats and oils:

- Benzene

Riot-control Agents/Tear Gas

Highly irritating agents normally used by law enforcement for crowd control or by individuals for protection (for example, mace):

- Various agents and combinations of agents
  - Bromobenzylcyanide (CA)
  - Chloroacetophenone (CN)
  - Chlorobenzylidenemalononitrile (CS)
  - Chloropicrin (PS)
  - Dibenzoxazepine (CR)

Toxic Alcohols

Poisonous alcohols that can damage the heart, kidneys, and nervous system:

- Ethylene glycol

Vomiting Agents

Chemicals that cause nausea and vomiting:
Adamsite (DM)

Source: The list is adapted from the list of "Chemical Agents," posted by the Centers for Disease Control and Prevention, under Emergency Preparedness and Response, at URL: http://www.bt.cdc.gov/agent/agentlistchem-category.asp (updated March 17, 2005).

APPENDIX H

THE STATE OF PROLIFERATION OF WEAPONS OF MASS DESTRUCTION, 2005

The following table indicates which countries are capable or may be capable of using nuclear, biological, or chemical weapons in an attack. It also indicates whether each nation that is or may be capable of using these weapons possesses missiles that can deliver the weapons. (It does not list nations that possess missiles but that do not have nuclear, biological, or chemical capability.) A nation is a more serious threat to international stability if it possesses both weapons capability and missiles than if it has only one or the other. Cruise missiles, which can be carried, concealed, on ships to the coastal waters of a target nation, pose as much of a danger in terms of weapons of mass destruction as ballistic missiles.

Country	Nuclear Weapons Capability	Biological Weapons Capability	Chemical Weapons Capability	Ballistic Missiles (Longest)	Cruise Missiles
Algeria	...	research?	suspected	SRBM	Anti-ship
China	NWS	likely	has had	ICBM	Produce Anti-ship
Cuba	...	reported	...	...	Anti-ship
Egypt	...	known R&D	likely	SRBM	Anti-ship
France	NWS	ended	ended	SLBM	Produce Variety
India	Stockpile	...	has had	MRBM	Produce Variety
Indonesia	...	...	sought	...	Anti-ship
Iran	Seeking	likely	has had	MRBM	Produce Anti-ship
Iraq	Ended	ended	ended	SRBM	Produce Variety?
Israel	Stockpile	likely R&D	likely	MRBM	Produce Variety
Kazakhstan	Ended (Soviet)	...	suspected	SRBM	...
Libya	Ended	...	ended	MRBM	Anti-ship
Myanmar	...	...	suspected	...	...

Country	Nuclear Weapons Capability	Biological Weapons Capability	Chemical Weapons Capability	Ballistic Missiles (Longest)	Cruise Missiles
North Korea	Claims to have	likely	known	IRBM	Produce Anti-ship
Pakistan	Stockpile	...	likely	MRBM	Anti-ship
Russia	NWS	Suspected	known	ICBM	Produce Variety
Saudi Arabia	...	...	suspected	MRBM	Anti-ship
Serbia	...	...	known	...	...
South Africa	Ended	ended	suspected	Ended	Produce Anti-ship
South Korea	Ended	...	suspected	SRBM	Anti-ship
Sudan	...	...	suspected	...	...
Syria	...	Seeking	known	SRBM	Anti-ship
Taiwan	Ended	...	likely	SRBM	Produce Variety
United Kingdom	NWS	ended	ended	SLBM	Variety
United States	NWS	ended	known	ICBM	Produce Variety
Vietnam	...	...	likely	SRBM	Anti-ship

Abbreviations: NWS=declared nuclear-weapon state; R&D=research and development; SRBM=short-range ballistic missile (less than 1,000 km range); MRBM=medium-range ballistic missile (1,001–3,000 km); IRBM=intermediate-range ballistic missile (3,001–5,500 km range); ICBM=intercontinental ballistic missile (greater than 5,500 km range); SLBM=submarine-launched ballistic missile

Source: Adapted from Sharon A. Squassoni. *Nuclear, Biological, and Chemical Weapons and Missiles: Status and Trends.* CRS Report to Congress, Order Code RL30699. Washington, D.C.: Congressional Research Service, Library of Congress, January 14, 2005, Table 1, p. CRS-12. The original includes extensive notes that are omitted here. The report is available online and can be downloaded at http://www.fas.org/spp/starwars/crs/RL30699.pdf.

APPENDIX I

MAPS AND GRAPHS

Chemical weapons have been characterized as the developing nations' answer to nuclear weapons. Certainly, chemical weapons are less costly and technically easier to develop than nuclear weapons. Two of the following maps show the distribution of each type of weapon by country. They indicate that more countries have or are suspected of having chemical weapons than are known to possess nuclear weapons. They also reflect the fact that, with the exception of North Korea (which has stated that it possesses nuclear weapons but may not actually have them), there is little uncertainty about whether a given nation is a nuclear-weapon state but that there is considerable uncertainty about which nations possess chemical capabilities.

Two additional maps present the distribution of declared stocks of chemical weapons inside Russia and the United States. The stocks are slated for destruction, but neither country is expected to finish destroying them by the deadline imposed by the Chemical Weapons Convention. The United States is closer to meeting the goal than is Russia. However, the destruction facilities in Kentucky and Colorado, shown on the U.S. map, are in the planning stage rather than in existence. The pie charts beside the maps indicate the distribution by location and type of weapon at the time the stocks were declared.

The map of U.S. nuclear weapons facilities shows relatively few sites and includes a nuclear power plant. The U.S. Department of Energy and its predecessors operated additional facilities in the past; during the 1940s more than 100 privately owned facilities worked with nuclear materials for the government. The Watts Bar power plant is on the map because it has been irradiating lithium rods to make tritium for weapons since 2003.

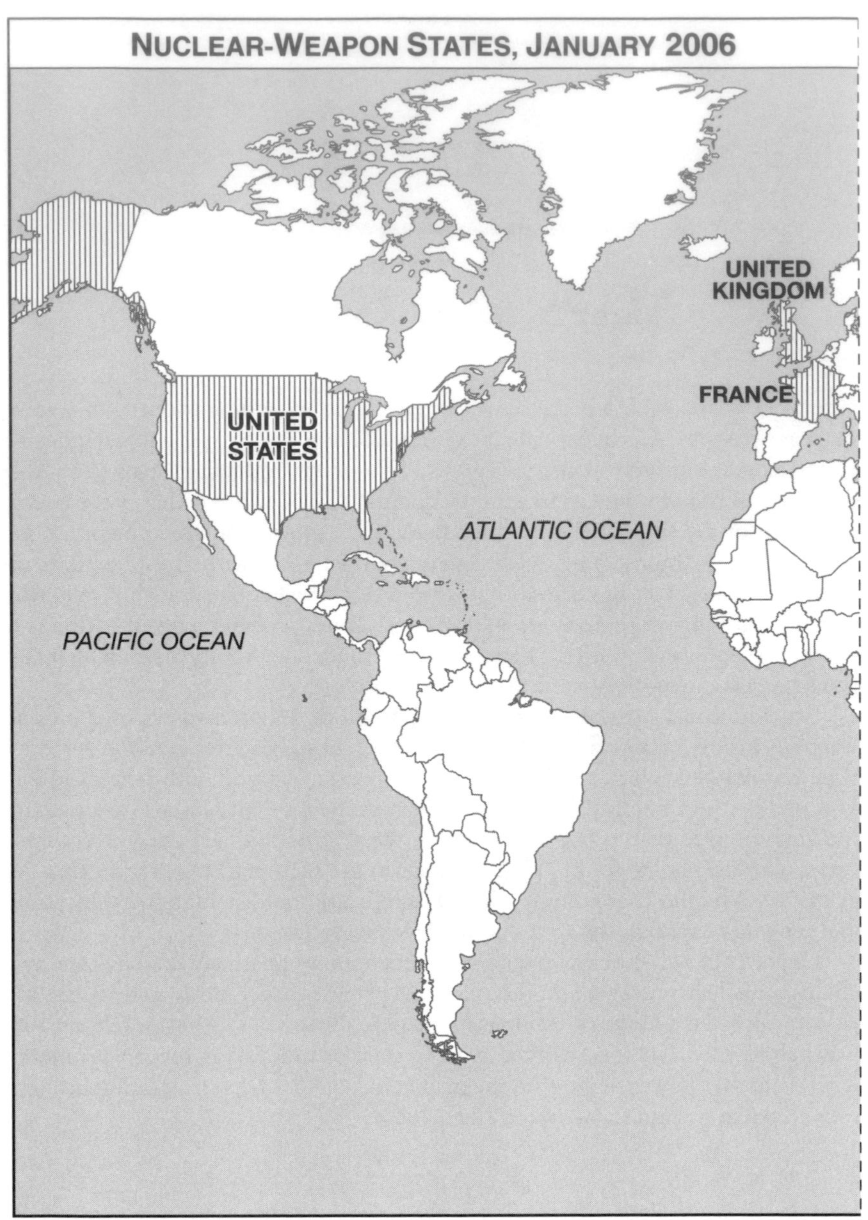
NUCLEAR-WEAPON STATES, JANUARY 2006
UNITED KINGDOM
FRANCE
UNITED STATES
ATLANTIC OCEAN
PACIFIC OCEAN

Appendix I

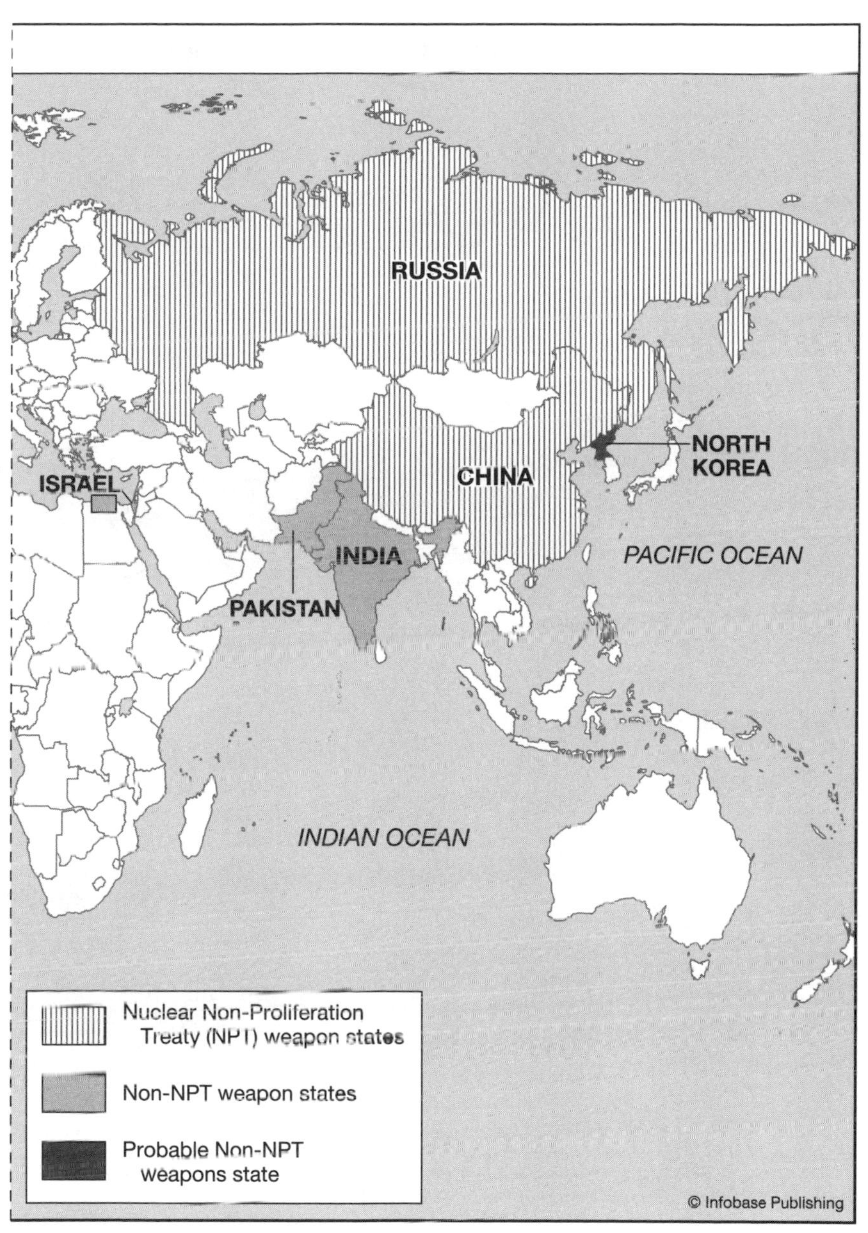
RUSSIA
CHINA
NORTH KOREA
ISRAEL
INDIA
PAKISTAN
PACIFIC OCEAN
INDIAN OCEAN
Nuclear Non-Proliferation Treaty (NPT) weapon states
Non-NPT weapon states
Probable Non-NPT weapons state
© Infobase Publishing

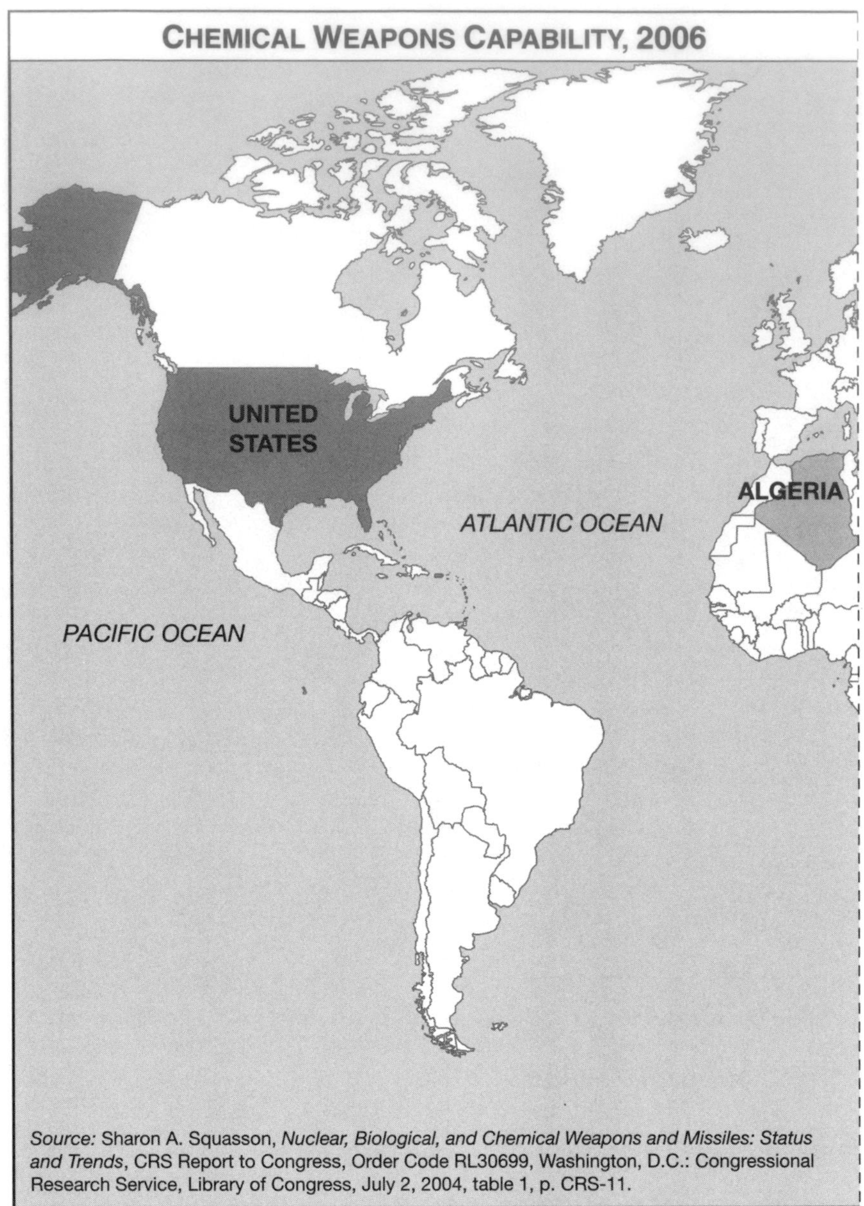

CHEMICAL WEAPONS CAPABILITY, 2006

Source: Sharon A. Squasson, *Nuclear, Biological, and Chemical Weapons and Missiles: Status and Trends*, CRS Report to Congress, Order Code RL30699, Washington, D.C.: Congressional Research Service, Library of Congress, July 2, 2004, table 1, p. CRS-11.

Appendix I

RUSSIA
SERBIA
KAZAKHSTAN
SYRIA
ISRAEL
CHINA
NORTH KOREA
SOUTH KOREA
EGYPT
SAUDI ARABIA
TAIWAN
VIETNAM
SUDAN
PAKISTAN
MYANMAR
PACIFIC OCEAN
INDIAN OCEAN
SOUTH AFRICA
States known to have chemical weapons
States suspected of having chemical weapons
States likely to have chemical weapons
© Infobase Publishing

U.S.-DECLARED CHEMICAL WEAPONS STOCKPILES, 2005

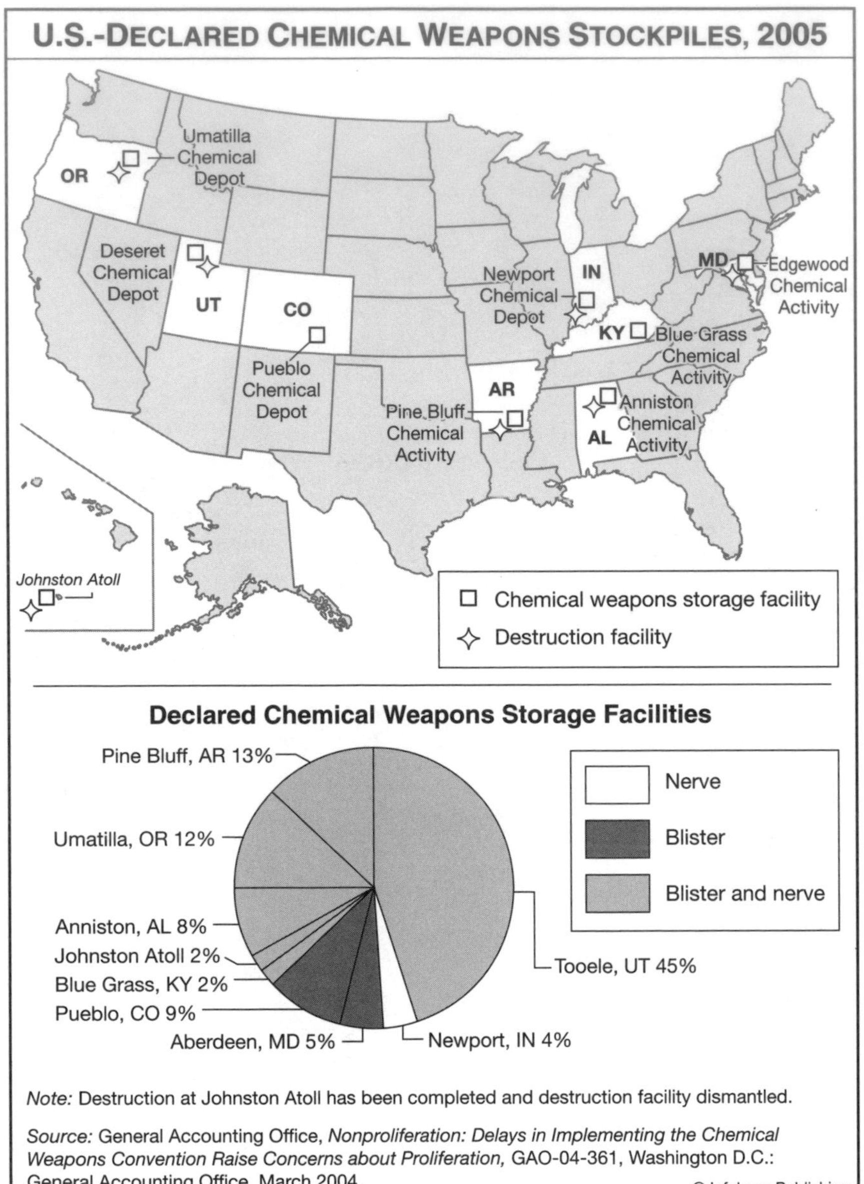

Note: Destruction at Johnston Atoll has been completed and destruction facility dismantled.

Source: General Accounting Office, *Nonproliferation: Delays in Implementing the Chemical Weapons Convention Raise Concerns about Proliferation,* GAO-04-361, Washington D.C.: General Accounting Office, March 2004.

© Infobase Publishing

Appendix I

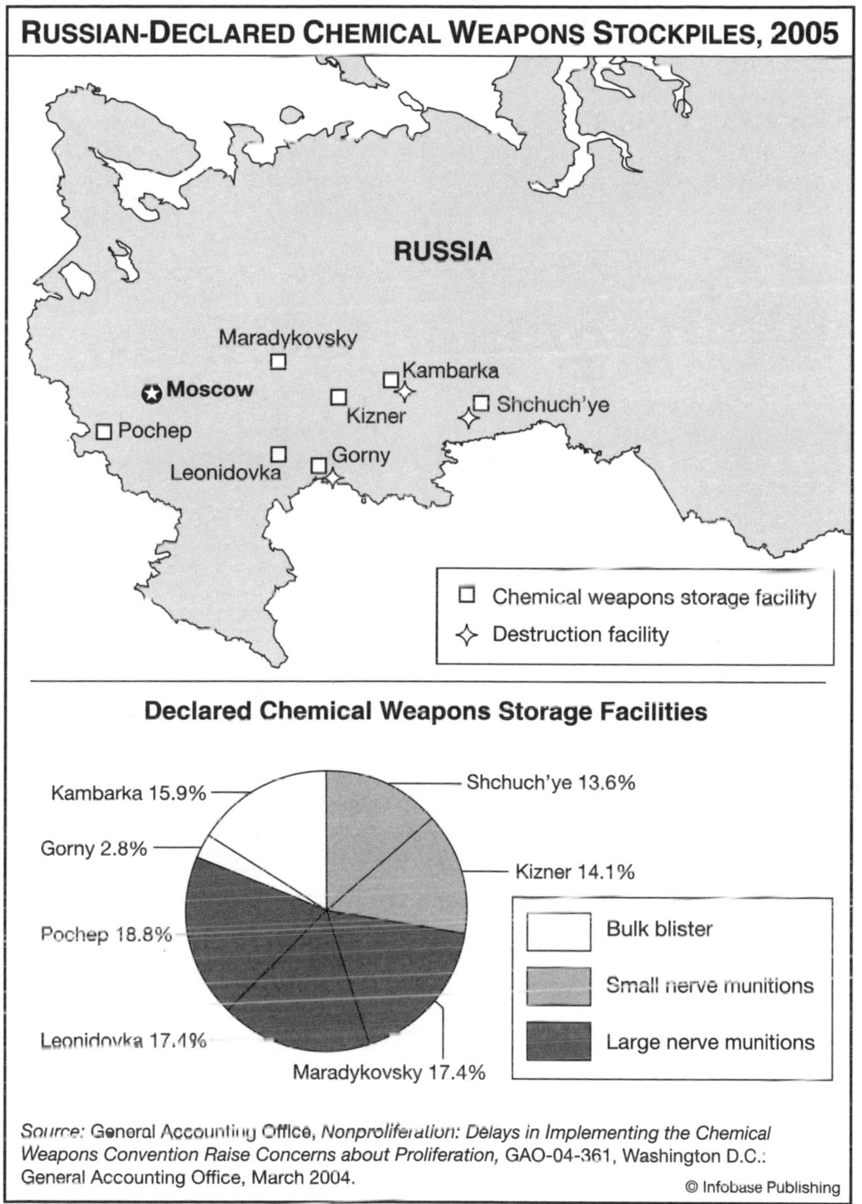

Source: General Accounting Office, *Nonproliferation: Delays in Implementing the Chemical Weapons Convention Raise Concerns about Proliferation,* GAO-04-361, Washington D.C.: General Accounting Office, March 2004.

© Infobase Publishing

Source: Adapted from Congress of the United States. Office of Technology Assessment. *Complex Cleanup: The Environmental Legacy of Nuclear Weapons Production.* OTA-0-484. Washington D.C.: U.S. Government Printing Office, February 1994.

© Infobase Publishing

INDEX

Locators in **boldface** indicate main topics. Locators followed by *c* indicate chronology entries. Locators followed by *b* indicate biographical entries. Locators followed by *g* indicate glossary entries.

Index

C

Index

Index

Index

Index

Index

Index

T

Index

Index

CABARRUS COUNTY PUBLIC LIBRARY
CONCORD LIBRARY
CONCORD, NORTH CAROLINA 28025